TRUTH COMMISSIONS AND INTERNATIONAL LAW

This book examines how truth commissions construct authoritative accounts of conflict, and how they account for the plurality of accounts across affected communities. Vázquez Guevara examines three of the earliest and most influential truth commissions: Argentina (1983–1984), Chile (1990–1991), and El Salvador (1992–1993), and examines how relevant cultural objects support or counter the official account for each. In doing so, she argues that these truth commissions drew on international law to authorize their accounts of violent conflict, and that this had the consequence of privileging an internationally authorized truth over other truths, whilst simultaneously strengthening the authority of international law over the post-conflict state. By demonstrating how truth commissions turn to international law for authority, the book shows how this produces an official account of past violence and promises of future community, which fundamentally affects how communities live together in the aftermath of violent conflict.

Valeria Vázquez Guevara is Assistant Professor at the Faculty of Law, University of Hong Kong. She is a member of the Executive Committee of the Law, Literature and Humanities Association of Australasia, and co-convener of the European Society of International Law's (ESIL) Critical Approaches to International Law Interest Group. Her doctoral thesis won The University of Melbourne Chancellor's Prize for Excellence and Melbourne Law School's Harold Luntz Thesis Prize.

LAW IN CONTEXT

Since 1970, the Law in Context series has been at the forefront of a movement to broaden the study of law. The series is a vehicle for the publication of innovative monographs and texts that treat law and legal phenomena critically in their cultural, social, political, technological, environmental and economic contexts. A contextual approach involves treating legal subjects broadly, using materials from other humanities and social sciences, and from any other discipline that helps to explain the operation in practice of the particular legal field or legal phenomena under investigation. It is intended that this orientation is at once more stimulating and more revealing than the bare exposition of legal rules. The series includes original research monographs, coursebooks and textbooks that foreground contextual approaches and methods. The series includes and welcomes books on the study of law in all its contexts, including domestic legal systems, European and international law, transnational and global legal processes, and comparative law.

Books in the Series

Acosta: The National versus the Foreigner in South America: 200 Years of Migration and Citizenship Law
Alaattinoğlu: Grievance Formation, Rights and Remedies
Ali: Modern Challenges to Islamic Law
Alyagon Darr: Plausible Crime Stories: The Legal History of Sexual Offences in Mandate Palestine
Anderson, Schum & Twining: Analysis of Evidence, 2nd Edition
Ashworth: Sentencing and Criminal Justice, 6th Edition
Barton & Douglas: Law and Parenthood
Baxi, McCrudden & Paliwala: Law's Ethical, Global and Theoretical Contexts: Essays in Honour of William Twining

Beecher-Monas: Evaluating Scientific Evidence: An Interdisciplinary Framework for Intellectual Due Process
Bell: French Legal Cultures
Bercusson: European Labour Law, 2nd Edition
Birkinshaw: European Public Law
Birkinshaw: Freedom of Information: The Law, the Practice and the Ideal, 4th Edition
Blick: Electrified Democracy: The Internet and the United Kingdom Parliament in History
Broderick & Ferri: International and European Disability Law and Policy: Text, Cases and Materials
Brownsword & Goodwin: Law and the Technologies of the Twenty-First Century: Text and Materials
Cakal: Law and Torture: Widening the Apertures, from the Doctrinal to the Critical
Cane & Goudkamp: Atiyah's Accidents, Compensation and the Law, 9th Edition
Clarke: Principles of Property Law
Clarke & Kohler: Property Law: Commentary and Materials
Collins: The Law of Contract, 4th Edition
Collins, Ewing & McColgan: Labour Law, 3rd Edition
Corrias, Law and Inhumanity: Dehumanization, Silent Claims and Atrocity Crimes
Cowan: Housing Law and Policy
Cranston: Making Commercial Law Through Practice 1830–1970
Cranston: Legal Foundations of the Welfare State
Darian-Smith: Laws and Societies in Global Contexts: Contemporary Approaches
Dauvergne: Making People Illegal: What Globalisation Means for Immigration and Law
David: Kinship, Law and Politics: An Anatomy of Belonging
Davies: Perspectives on Labour Law, 2nd Edition
Dembour: Who Believes in Human Rights?: Reflections on the European Convention
de Sousa Santos: Toward a New Legal Common Sense: Law, Globalization, and Emancipation
Diduck: Law's Families
Douglas-Scott: Brexit, Union, and Disunion: The Evolution of British Constitutional Unsettlement
Dowdle: Transnational Law: A Framework for Analysis
Dupret: Positive Law from the Muslim World: Jurisprudence, History, Practices
Dutta: A Jurisprudence of Conversations: Law, Life and Feminism in Post-colonial India

Emon: Jurisdictional Exceptionalisms: Islamic Law, International Law, and Parental Child Abduction
Estella: Legal Foundations of EU Economic Governance
Fortin: Children's Rights and the Developing Law, 3rd Edition
Garnsey: The Justice of Visual Art: Creative State-Building in Times of Political Transition
Garton, Probert & Bean: Moffat's Trusts Law: Text and Materials, 7th Edition
Ghai & Woodman: Practising Self-Government: A Comparative Study of Autonomous Regions
Glover-Thomas: Reconstructing Mental Health Law and Policy
Gobert & Punch: Rethinking Corporate Crime
Goldman: Globalisation and the Western Legal Tradition: Recurring Patterns of Law and Authority
Goodrich, Kimmel & Meyler: Performing Law: Actors, Affects, Spaces
Graber: The Technosystem of Free Speech: Enriching Fundamental Rights in a Digital Society
Haack: Evidence Matters: Science, Proof, and Truth in the Law
Harlow & Rawlings: Law and Administration, 4th Edition
Harris: An Introduction to Law, 8th Edition
Harris, Campbell & Halson: Remedies in Contract and Tort, 2nd Edition
Harvey: Seeking Asylum in the UK: Problems and Prospects
Herring: Law and the Relational Self
Hervey & McHale: European Union Health Law: Themes and Implications
Hervey & McHale: Health Law and the European Union
Holder & Lee: Environmental Protection, Law and Policy: Text and Materials, 2nd Edition
Hommes: The Convention and the Kingdom: How the Netherlands Received the European Convention on Human Rights
Jackson & Summers: The Internationalisation of Criminal Evidence: Beyond the Common Law and Civil Law Traditions
Jeutner: The Reasonable Person: A Legal Biography
Katila: Imagining Transitional Justice: The Construction of Meaning in the Arts and Law
Kennedy: Inducing Intimacy: Deception, Consent and the Law
Kostakopoulou: The Future Governance of Citizenship
Kreiczer-Levy: Destabilized Property: Property Law in the Sharing Economy
Kubal: Immigration and Refugee Law in Russia: Socio-Legal Perspectives
Lewis: Choice and the Legal Order: Rising above Politics
Likosky: Law, Infrastructure and Human Rights
Likosky: Transnational Legal Processes: Globalisation and Power Disparities
Lixinski: Legalized Identities: Cultural Heritage Law and the Shaping of Transitional Justice
Loughnan: Self, Others and the State: Relations of Criminal Responsibility

Lunney: A History of Australian Tort Law 1901–1945: England's Obedient Servant?
Maughan & Webb: Lawyering Skills and the Legal Process, 2nd Edition
McGaughey: Principles of Enterprise Law
McGlynn: Families and the European Union: Law, Politics and Pluralism
Mertens: A Philosophical Introduction to Human Rights
Miller: An Introduction to German Law and Legal Culture: Text and Materials
Moffat: Trusts Law: Text and Materials
Monti: EC Competition Law
Morgan: Contract Law Minimalism: A Formalist Restatement of Commercial Contract Law
Morgan & Yeung: An Introduction to Law and Regulation: Text and Materials
Nash: British Islam and English Law: A Classical Pluralist Perspective
Ng: Political Censorship in British Hong Kong: Freedom of Expression and the Law (1842–1997)
Nicola & Davies: EU Law Stories: Contextual and Critical Histories of European Jurisprudence
Norrie: Crime, Reason and History: A Critical Introduction to Criminal Law, 3rd Edition
Norrie: Rethinking Criminal Justice: Punishment, Abolition And Moral Psychology
O'Dair: Legal Ethics: Text and Materials
Oliver: Common Values and the Public–Private Divide
Oliver & Drewry: The Law and Parliament
Palmer & Roberts: Dispute Processes: ADR and the Primary Forms of Decision-Making, 1st Edition
Palmer & Roberts: Dispute Processes: ADR and the Primary Forms of Decision-Making, 3rd Edition
Petersen: Practices of Restitution: Law and Aesthetics in Modern Germany
Picciotto: International Business Taxation
Pieraccini: Regulating the Sea: A Socio-Legal Analysis of English Marine Protected Areas
Probert: The Changing Legal Regulation of Cohabitation, 1600–2010: From Fornicators to Family, 1600–2010
Qiao: The Authoritarian Commons: Neighborhood Democratization in Urban China
Radi: Rules and Practices of International Investment Law and Arbitration
Reed: Internet Law: Text and Materials
Richardson: Law, Process and Custody

Roberts & Palmer: Dispute Processes: ADR and the Primary Forms of Decision-Making, 2nd Edition
Rowbottom: Democracy Distorted: Wealth, Influence and Democratic Politics
Sauter: Public Services in EU Law
Scott & Black: Cranston's Consumers and the Law
Seneviratne: Ombudsmen: Public Services and Administrative Justice
Seppänen: Ideological Conflict and the Rule of Law in Contemporary China: Useful Paradoxes
Siems: Comparative Law, 3rd Edition
Stapleton: Product Liability
Stewart: Gender, Law and Justice in a Global Market
Tamanaha: Law as a Means to an End: Threat to the Rule of Law
Taylor: Fortin's Children's Rights and the Developing Law, 4th Edition
Trundle: Injurious Law: Nuclear Exposure and the Harms of Redress
Tuori: Properties of Law: Modern Law and After
Turpin & Tomkins: British Government and the Constitution: Text and Materials, 7th Edition
Twining: General Jurisprudence: Understanding Law from a Global Perspective
Twining: Globalisation and Legal Theory
Twining: Human Rights, Southern Voices: Francis Deng, Abdullahi An-Na'im, Yash Ghai and Upendra Baxi
Twining: Jurist in Context: A Memoir
Twining: Karl Llewellyn and the Realist Movement, 2nd Edition
Twining: Rethinking Evidence: Exploratory Essays, 2nd Edition
Twining & Miers: How to Do Things with Rules, 5th Edition
Varney: Disability, Human Rights and Contract Law
Wan: Film and Constitutional Controversy: Visualizing Hong Kong Identity in the Age of 'One Country, Two Systems'
Ward: A Critical Introduction to European Law, 3rd Edition
Ward: Law, Text, Terror
Ward: Shakespeare and Legal Imagination
Watt: The Making Sense of Politics, Media, and Law: Rhetorical Performance as Invention, Creation, Production
Wells & Quick: Lacey, Wells and Quick: Reconstructing Criminal Law: Text and Materials, 4th Edition
Woodhead: Caring for Cultural Heritage: An Integrated Approach to Legal and Ethical Initiatives in the United Kingdom
Yeung and Ranchordás: An Introduction to Law and Regulation: Text and Materials, 2nd Edition
Young: Turpin and Tomkins' British Government and the Constitution: Text and Materials, 8th Edition

Zander: Cases and Materials on the English Legal System, 10th Edition
Zander: The Law-Making Process, 6th Edition

International Journal of Law in Context: A Global Forum for Interdisciplinary Legal Studies

The *International Journal of Law in Context* is the companion journal to the Law in Context book series and provides a forum for interdisciplinary legal studies and offers intellectual space for ground-breaking critical research. It publishes contextual work about law and its relationship with other disciplines including but not limited to science, literature, humanities, philosophy, sociology, psychology, ethics, history and geography. More information about the journal and how to submit an article can be found at http://journals.cambridge.org/ijc

TRUTH COMMISSIONS AND INTERNATIONAL LAW

Jurisdiction, Representation, Authority

Valeria Vázquez Guevara

The University of Hong Kong

CAMBRIDGE
UNIVERSITY PRESS

CAMBRIDGE
UNIVERSITY PRESS

Shaftesbury Road, Cambridge CB2 8EA, United Kingdom

One Liberty Plaza, 20th Floor, New York, NY 10006, USA

477 Williamstown Road, Port Melbourne, VIC 3207, Australia

314–321, 3rd Floor, Plot 3, Splendor Forum, Jasola District Centre,
New Delhi – 110025, India

Cambridge University Press is part of Cambridge University Press & Assessment,
a department of the University of Cambridge.

We share the University's mission to contribute to society through the pursuit of
education, learning and research at the highest international levels of excellence.

www.cambridge.org
Information on this title: www.cambridge.org/9781009679978

DOI: 10.1017/9781009679961

When citing this work, please include a reference to the DOI 10.1017/9781009679961

First published 2026

Cover image: Girls learning traditional embroidery in the Colomoncagua Salvadoran
refugee camp in Honduras. Photograph by Steve Cagan

A catalogue record for this publication is available from the British Library

Library of Congress Cataloging-in-Publication Data
Names: Vázquez Guevara, Valeria author
Title: Truth commissions and international law : jurisdiction, representation,
authority / Valeria Vázquez Guevara.
Description: Cambridge, United Kingdom ; New York, NY : Cambridge University Press,
2026. | Series: Law in context (lic) | Includes bibliographical references and index.
Identifiers: LCCN 2025052178 | ISBN 9781009679978 hardback | ISBN
9781009679992 paperback | ISBN 9781009679961 ebook
Subjects: LCSH: Truth commissions | Reparation (Criminal justice) | Jurisdiction
(International law) | Transitional justice | Restitution | Human rights | Conflict
management
Classification: LCC K970 .V39 2026
LC record available at https://lccn.loc.gov/2025052178

ISBN 978-1-009-67997-8 Hardback

a mamá, Claudia
a papá, Raúl
a mi hermano, Abraham
por la profundidad de su amor

Contents

List of Figures — *page* xiv
Preface — xv
Acknowledgments — xxii
Note on the Text — xxviii

1 Truth Commissions and International Law: Jurisdiction, Representation, Authority . . . 1
2 Invoking the Promises of International Law . . . 41
3 Using the Language of Human Rights . . . 87
4 Linking the 'Local' to the 'International' . . . 128
5 Receiving Truth Commissions through International Law . . . 191
6 Conclusion: Truth Commissions and the Authority of International Law . . . 223

Select Bibliography — 226
Index — 246

Figures

2.1 Fence surrounding the Casa Rosada with banners protesting against the IMF (FMI in Spanish) during the Madres de Plaza de Mayo's weekly demonstration in Buenos Aires (Argentina). The banner says: "Out IMF." Photograph by Valeria Vázquez Guevara (2018). . . . . *page* 82
2.2 Banner protesting against the IMF (FMI in Spanish) hanging from the street fence of the Park of Memory and Human Rights in Buenos Aires (Argentina). Banner says: "Yes to national sovereignty. No to the agreement with the IMF." Photograph by Valeria Vázquez Guevara (2018). 83
3.1 Esplanade or Memory Square at the Museum of Memory and Human Rights in Santiago (Chile). Photograph by Valeria Vázquez Guevara (2018). 105
3.2 UDHR in Braille (left) and Camnitzer's "The Museum is a School" (right) at the Museum of Memory and Human Rights in Santiago (Chile). Photograph by Valeria Vázquez Guevara (2018). . . . 108
3.3 UDHR (right) and "Asylum-Exile" staircase (center) at Memory Square at the Museum of Memory and Human Rights in Santiago (Chile). Photograph by Valeria Vázquez Guevara (2018). . . . 111
4.1 Author Unknown. "Esta es la Historia." Undated – 1980s. Museo de la Palabra y la Imagen in San Salvador (El Salvador). Reproduced with permission of the museum. 155
4.2 "Learning *manualidad* – embroidery" at the Colomoncagua Salvadoran refugee camp in Honduras. Photograph by Steve Cagan (www.stevecagan.com) (1988). Reproduced with permission of the photographer. 162

Preface

Since the 1990s, Truth Commissions have expanded the scope of their investigations and increased their presence around the world.[1] Truth Commissions are now being established to investigate not only state violence during a dictatorship or armed conflict, but also the legacies of colonialism and slavery, and other forms of violence against society. In the United States, in the wake of the 2020 killing of George Floyd, there have been calls to establish a nationwide "Truth, Racial Healing, and Transformation Commission."[2] Across the Atlantic, in January 2021, a report commissioned by French president Emmanuel Macron recommended "the creation of a mixed French-Algerian 'truth and memory commission'" to address "issues of memories" during Algeria's independence war against French rule.[3] In Australia, in the same year, the State of Victoria authorized the Yoorrook Justice Commission,[4] a "truth-telling process" to inquire into "contemporary and historical injustices committed against Aboriginal Victorians since colonization."[5] In the Philippines,

[1] I explain this in greater detail in Chapter 1. For an overview of Truth Commissions, see generally, Jeremy Sarkin, "Introduction," in *The Global Impact and Legacy of Truth Commissions*, Jeremy Sarkin (ed) (Intersentia, 2019).

[2] United States Congress, Rep. Lee, Barbara [D-CA-13], *H.Con.Res.19 – Urging the Establishment of a United States Commission on Truth, Racial Healing, and Transformation* (25 February 2021).

[3] Benjamin Stora, *Les Questions Mémorielles Portant sur la Colonisation et la Guerre d'Algérie* (Présidence de la République, 2021).

[4] Victoria State Government, *Letters Patent for the Royal Commission to be known as Yoo-rrook Justice Commission, Register of Patents Book No 47 Page 174* (12 May 2021).

[5] Victoria State Government, Premier of Victoria, "Media Release: Historic Truth-Telling Commissioners Appointed" (14 May 2021). www.premier.vic.gov.au/historic-truth-telling-commissioners-appointed.

in the wake of the International Criminal Court's arrest of former president Rodrigo Duterte for his purported war on drugs,[6] politicians and groups of victims are advocating for a Truth Commission to "expose why it happened, who enabled it, and how we make sure it never happens again."[7] In Bangladesh, following the 2024 social uprising that brought down Prime Minister Sheikh Hasina, the Yunus interim government announced that it would create a Truth and Reconciliation Commission to "build national unity" to address a long history of state violence.[8] In Syria, in 2025, interim president Ahmed al-Sharaa announced the establishment of a National Transitional Justice Commission to "expos[e] the truth about the grave violations committed" during Bashar al-Assad's presidency.[9] Meanwhile, with the Israeli government's ongoing systematic violence against Palestinians, especially

[6] International Criminal Court, "Press Release: Situation in the Philippines: Rodrigo Roa Duterte in ICC Custody" (12 March 2025). www.icc-cpi.int/news/situation-philippines-rodrigo-roa-duterte-icc-custody.

[7] Thanks to Alex Dela Cruz for bringing this to my attention. Carlo Caoile, "'Truth Commission' needed following Rodrigo Duterte's ICC arrest – Kristina Conti," *Bilyonaryo News Channel* (12 April 2025). https://bnc.ph/truth-commission-needed-following-rodrigo-dutertes-icc-arrest-kristina-conti/news/; Delon Porcalla, "With Time Running Out, Truth Commission on EJKs Proposed," *The Philippine Star* (23 January 2025). www.philstar.com/headlines/2025/01/23/2416221/time-running-out-truth-commission-ejks-proposed.

[8] Mubashar Hasan, "Yunus Should Prioritize Probe into Enforced Disappearances Under Hasina's Rule," *The Diplomat* (24 August 2024). https://thediplomat.com/2024/08/yunus-should-prioritize-probe-into-enforced-disappearances-under-hasinas-rule/. The new government headed by Yunus did establish a commission of inquiry. See Julhas Alam, "Bangladesh's Government led by Yunus signs UN Convention Involving Enforced Disappearance," *AP* (29 August 2024). https://apnews.com/article/hasina-yunus-bangladesh-enforced-disappearance-convention-418b7048c649bc541e64d33869876c84; Staff Correspondent, "Truth and Reconciliation Commission to Be Formed: Asif Nazrul," *Prothom Alo* (10 May 2025). https://en.prothomalo.com/bangladesh/politics/uojx4w46tp.

[9] Two commissions were announced, a National Transitional Justice Commission and a Commission for Missing Persons. The former works as a Truth Commission. Reuters, "Syria Forms Transitional Justice, Missing Persons Commissions," *Reuters* (18 May 2025). www.reuters.com/world/middle-east/syria-forms-transitional-justice-missing-persons-commissions-2025-05-18/; AFP Damascus, "Syria Announces Commissions for Missing Persons, Transitional Justice," *France24* (17 May 2025). www.france24.com/en/live-news/20250517-syria-announces-commissions-for-missing-persons-transitional-justice.

since October 2023 under Benjamin Netanyahu, the possibility of a Truth Commission is being raised again.[10]

Truth Commissions, it would seem, have never been more popular. Perhaps that is because, in their endeavor to deliver truth as justice, Truth Commissions present themselves as grounded in, and responsive to, national constituencies. And yet 'the international' continues to loom large. Soon after Syria announced its plan to establish a Truth Commission in 2025, prominent international human rights and transitional justice organizations – Amnesty International, the International Center for Transitional Justice, Human Rights Watch – reacted by issuing their own statements.[11] While they welcomed Syria's announcement, their concern was to emphasize the international standards that had to be observed in any truth-telling process.[12] In its press release, the

[10] For a recent discussion see as example, Ahmed Moor, "The Palestine-Israel Nightmare Won't End Until We Accept These Basic Truths," *The Guardian* (8 July 2024). www.theguardian.com/world/article/2024/jul/08/palestine-israel-gaza-war-end. For a recent initiative featuring Ruti Teitel (the most renowned transitional justice scholar) and Pablo de Greiff (inaugural UN Special Rapporteur on the Promotion of Truth, Justice, Reparation and Guarantees of Non-Recurrence), see Minerva Center for the Rule of Law under Extreme Conditions at the University of Haifa and the Clinical Legal Education Center (CLEC) at the Hebrew University of Jerusalem, "International Webinar: Transitional Justice for Israel-Palestine in Comparative Perspective" (5 June 2025). www.allmep.org/all-events/transitional-justice-for-israel-palestine-in-comparative-perspective-june-5-2025-international-webinar-the-minerva-center-for-the-rule-of-law-under-extreme-conditions-at-the-univ/. For older pieces see, Zinaida Miller, "Settling with History: A Hybrid Commission of Inquiry for Israel/Palestine," *Harvard Human Rights Journal*, vol 20 (2007); Adrien Katherine Wing, "A Truth and Reconciliation Commission for Palestine/Israel: Healing Spirit Injuries?" *Transnational Law & Contemporary Problems* vol 17, no 1 (2008).

[11] Amnesty International, "Press Release. Syria: New Government Must Prioritize Justice and Truth Measures to Prevent Further Abuse" (16 May 2025). www.amnesty.org/en/latest/news/2025/05/syria-new-government-must-prioritize-justice-and-truth-measures-to-prevent-further-abuse/; Alice Autin/Human Rights Watch, "Syria's Transitional Justice Commission: A Missed Opportunity for Victim-Led Justice" (19 May 2025). www.hrw.org/news/2025/05/19/syrias-transitional-justice-commission-missed-opportunity-victim-led-justice; International Center for Transitional Justice, "Press Release: ICTJ Welcomes Establishment of Syria's New National Commissions for Transitional Justice and the Missing" (22 May 2025). www.ictj.org/latest-news/ictj-welcomes-establishment-syria's-new-national-commissions-transitional-justice-and.

[12] Amnesty International, "Press Release"; Alice Autin/Human Rights Watch, "Syria's Transitional Justice Commission"; International Center for Transitional Justice, "Press Release."

International Center for Transitional Justice made sure to highlight its role in the Syrian initiative (having "worked closely with Syrian partners to lay the groundwork for a national justice and reconciliation process");[13] while Human Rights Watch stressed the importance of working with international organizations (urging Syria to "build on successful examples of collaboration between UN mechanisms and victims' groups").[14] That Syria's truth-telling initiative would have an international dimension is not exceptional. Historically, international law and its institutions has provided a means to make visible different forms of violence and to mobilize solidarity against it.[15] But international law and its institutions has also had the effect of mobilizing and privileging certain understandings of what 'truth-telling' involves, including how it should be conducted and the kinds of truths that should be privileged. These are typically packaged in the institutional form of the 'Truth Commission'.

The influence of the international can be seen in the Yoorrook Justice Commission, at work on the country of the Wurundjeri Peoples of the Kulin Nations, in Australia, my home for most of the writing of this book.[16] The Yoorrook Justice Commission was established as part of the

[13] International Center for Transitional Justice, "Press Release: ICTJ Welcomes Establishment."

[14] Autin, "Syria's Transitional Justice Commission."

[15] See as examples the events discussed in Mohammed Bedjaoui, *Towards a New International Economic Order* (Holmes & Meier, 1979); Jochen von Bernstorff and Philipp Dann (eds) *The Battle for International Law: South-North Perspectives on the Decolonization Era* (Oxford University Press, 2019); Nicolás Perrone, "Solidarity & the Charter of Economic Rights and Duties of States," *Progressive International* (29 March 2023). https://progressive.international/blueprint/0e48f7d6-6897-46c8-9e7e-05b26b027cbf-perrone-past-and-future-new-international-economic-orders-is-solidarity-their-keystone/en; Claerwen O'Hara and Valeria Vázquez Guevara, "Salvador Allende, Populism and an International Law of Solidarity," *NUS Centre for International Law Dialogues* (19 December 2023). https://cil.nus.edu.sg/blogs/salvador-allende-populism-and-an-international-law-of-solidarity/. Most recently, South Africa's genocide case against Israel at the International Court of Justice (2023, ongoing), International Court of Justice, "Latest Developments: Application of the Convention on the Prevention and Punishment of the Crime of Genocide in the Gaza Strip (South Africa v. Israel)." www.icj-cij.org/case/192.

[16] This place is called Naarm, which is one place in the country of the Wurundjeri Peoples of the Kulin Nations. Its settler-colonial name is City of Melbourne.

Victorian Government's response to the First Peoples' Assembly of Victoria's call "for a truth and justice process."[17] Along with substantial involvement of the First Peoples' Assembly of Victoria,[18] there has also been close engagement with international Truth Commission models. This has provoked different reactions. Some have celebrated the establishment of the Commission by drawing comparisons with other 'successful' Truth Commissions, notably South Africa's Truth and Reconciliation Commission (1995–2003), and Canada's Truth and Reconciliation Commission (2008–2015).[19] Others, however, have raised concerns about international influence over the Yoorrook Justice Commission process. One especially influential voice has been First Nations' leader, Cobble Cobble woman and professor of law, Megan Davis.[20] For Davis, the recent global push for, and celebration of, Indigenous truth-telling processes in the form of Truth Commissions has not led to meaningful justice outcomes.[21] She cautions against modelling these processes after

[17] Yoorrook Justice Commission. yoorrookjusticecommission.org.au.

[18] Victoria State Government, Premier of Victoria, "Media Release: Historic Truth-Telling Commissioners Appointed."

[19] See for example, Lorena Allam, "Victoria to Set Up Australia's First Truth and Justice Commission to Recognise Wrongs Against Aboriginal People," *The Guardian* (11 July 2020). www.theguardian.com/australia-news/2020/jul/11/victoria-to-se…tralias-first-truth-telling-commission-led-by-first-peoples-assembly; Harry Hobbs, "Drawing History into the Present: Victoria Takes Up the Challenge of Truth-Telling," *Inside Story* (16 March 2021). insidestory.org.au/drawing-history-into-the-present/; Michael Fowler and Ashleigh McMillan, "'Deep Sadness, Deep Joy': Victoria's Truth-Telling Commissioners Announced," *The Age* (14 May 2021). www.theage.com.au/national/victoria/deep-sadness-deep-joy-victoria-s-truth-telling-commissioners-announced-20210514-p57rvw.html.

[20] Professor Megan Davis is a constitutional lawyer, and one of the designers and drafters of the *Uluru Statement from the Heart*. The *Uluru Statement* is a constitutional dialogue and reform process coming from, and led by, First Nations peoples from across the Australian continent. It seeks to achieve meaningful voice in political institutions, treaty-making with the Australian state (Makarrata), and truth-telling as a deeply First Nations-centered process, not as something "that has to be done by a truth and reconciliation commission." See Contact Magazine, "Voice, Treaty, Truth: Q&A with Professor Megan Davis," *Contact Magazine* (2020). https://stories.uq.edu.au/contact-magazine/2020/voice-treaty-truth/; Megan Davis and George Williams, *Everything You Need to Know about the Uluru Statement from the Heart* (NewSouth Publishing, 2021).

[21] Megan Davis, "The Truth about Truth-Telling," *The Monthly* (2 December 2021). www.themonthly.com.au/issue/2021/december/1638277200/megan-davis/truth-about-

other internationally acclaimed Truth Commissions, endorsed and promoted by transitional justice actors.[22]

In the case of the Yoorrook Justice Commission, two additional actors were involved in its design (alongside the First Peoples' Assembly of Victoria and the Victorian Government). These were the New York-based International Center for Transitional Justice, and the Washington-based George Mason University Mary Hoch Centre for Reconciliation.[23] As the Victorian Government explained, the formation of the Yoorrook Justice Commission had "incorporated advice from [these] international experts on best-practice in truth telling."[24] In particular, the International Center for Transitional Justice was directly involved in short-listing and nominating the Yoorrook Commissioners,[25] using a selection process that "aligned with international best practice in truth-telling."[26] Not much else has been said, officially, about the participation of these transitional justice actors, and it is too early to know the extent of their influence, or the influence of their Truth Commission models, over the Yoorrook Justice Commission and its resulting account of the truth. Despite this – or perhaps because of this – Davis' words remain hard to ignore: "Beware the ally spruiking truth."[27]

The purpose of this book is to take the warning seriously. It does so by asking how Truth Commissions produce an authoritative account of past violence and promises of future community; and it asks this as a question of law. This is all the more important when it appears that law is absent from the work of a Truth Commission. This question, and the answer that

truth-telling. Davis specifically discussed critiques to the Canadian Truth Commission which focused on the violence suffered by First Nations children at the Indian Residential Schools program.

22 Ibid.

23 Victoria State Government, First Peoples-State Relations, "Outcomes: Establishing a Truth and Justice Process" (1 November 2021). www.firstpeoplesrelations.vic.gov.au/advancing-victorian-treaty-process-annual-report-2020–21/outcomes-establishing-truth-and-justice.

24 Ibid.

25 Victoria State Government, Premier of Victoria, "Media Release: Historic Truth-Telling Commissioners Appointed."

26 Victoria State Government, First Peoples-State Relations, "Outcomes: Establishing a Truth and Justice Process."

27 Davis, "The Truth about Truth-Telling."

the book offers – an answer that finds (international) law to be central to the work of Truth Commissions – is not just an intellectual concern for me. It is also deeply personal. The Salvadoran post-conflict state, where I spent my childhood, was profoundly shaped by the post-Cold War expansion of international law and its institutions across the Global South. I was born in San Salvador on November 22, 1989, during the final days of the Salvadoran civil war. Eleven days before, the Farabundo Martí National Liberation Front (FMLN) guerrillas had successfully launched their final offensive to seize the capital city of San Salvador. This precipitated a process that led to the signing of the Chapultepec Peace Agreement, which established the UN-led Truth Commission. It is in the shadow of this Truth Commission that I studied law and undertook the graduate research that has culminated in this book, which is why it cannot be entirely separated from my heritage in El Salvador or experiences growing up in Spain and living and working in Australia.

Acknowledgments

Beyond the intellectual and professional training involved in writing one's first monograph, the process has also been personally formative. Through the more than five years that it took to research and write this book, I discovered something that the Irish poet Seamus Heaney once observed: "getting started, keeping going, getting started again – in art and in life, it seems . . . is the essential rhythm not only of achievement but of survival." Undertaking a major research project like this can certainly be experienced as an exercise in "getting started, keeping going," again and again and again. Yet, I received the gift of not going through this alone, but accompanied by a community who made it a real pleasure.

This book first took the form of a PhD thesis at Melbourne Law School (MLS). At MLS I found a wonderfully collegial and supportive academic environment. Sundhya Pahuja and Shaun McVeigh played a crucial role in making MLS an intellectual community. So many great things can be said about the joint supervision of Sundhya and Shaun, but I would just like to thank them for their sustained intellectual care, the laughs during supervision, the freedom to explore and ask questions, and their generous but necessarily tough feedback. I thank Sundhya for her characteristic human touch, genuine spirit of service to others, and for paving the way for her students and mentees. As a supervisor and mentor, Sundhya has shown me that one can be a brilliant scholar while remaining kind and generous. I thank Shaun for listening with such care and wisdom. As a supervisor, and through his scholarship, Shaun has shown me that slow and discrete scholarship can be an intellectually and personally enriching lifelong journey worth embarking on. My gratitude also goes to my thesis examiners, Vasuki Nesiah and Sarah Ramshaw, whose careful and generous feedback provided the boost that I needed to keep believing that the thesis could be a book. At Cambridge University Press, I am grateful to the Law in Context series editors, especially Maks del Mar for his kindness and for seeing the potential in this book; to Toby Ginsburg and Gemma Smith for their guidance and patience throughout the publication process; and to the two anonymous readers for their supportive and helpful feedback.

At MLS I also want to thank Peter Rush, who served as my academic assessor. I thank Peter not only for his scholarship, from which I have learnt so much, but also for his constant support and generous engagement with my work, and for helping me to take my first steps as a teacher in his course. I am also grateful to Margaret Young for offering the support I needed when the weight of the PhD, and life, became unbearably heavy. At MLS, I have been fortunate to be part of the Institute for International Law and the Humanities (IILAH). IILAH and its members quickly became a welcoming community, and a source of lifelong friendships, especially the 'IILAH gang.' To Claerwen O'Hara, Tim Lindgren, Caitlin Murphy, Nina Araneta-Alana, André Dao, Danish Sheik, Jo Commins, Alex Dela Cruz, Sanam Amin, and Haris Jamil – thank you for your friendship, the parties, agreeing to eat all those French fries (or is it chips?), and for the conversations about 'jurisdiction' in the journey to finding our 'law question.' Special thanks to Claerwen: I could have not wished for a more generous, genuine, and super fun 'PhD sibling' with whom to share the PhD years, and life beyond them. Also thanks to Caitlin for the gift of her friendship over the years. And to the 'elders' of the gang – Robi Rado, Andrea Leiter, and Laura Petersen – thank you for providing the sort of wise advice that emerges from experience. Thank you for your friendship, for listening, and for offering encouragement when I needed it – about life and law – in order to keep going. I am also grateful to the broader PhD community at MLS. I could not have wished for a better PhD community with whom to share the doctoral studies, life, and many coffees at Seven Seeds. Thank you to Anna Dziedzic, Dewi Apsari, Arturo Villagrán, Will Phillips, Sebastián Rioseco, Liz Sheargold, Neha Mishra, Odette Mazel, Luís Bogliolo, Marnie Lloyd, Balawyn Jones, Anjalee de Silva, Sayomi Ariyawansa, Tess Whitton, Sebastián Machado, Liam Elphick, Philippa Duell-Pining, Darshan Datar, Toerin van Wyc, and Anna Saunders. Across IILAH, MLS, and other institutions, I also want to thank Kathleen Birrell, James Parker, Maria Elander, Cait Storr, Adil Hassan Khan, Ann Genovese, Hilary Charlesworth, Anne Orford, Julia Dehm, Di Otto, Olivia Barr, Fabia Veçoso, Emma Nyhan, Alice Palmer, Tim D. Peters, Kathryn Greenman, Linda Steele, and Rachel Killean. I am also indebted to the Office for Research at MLS: thanks to Bec Croser, Ade Suharto, and Steph Johnson for their support in helping me to navigate all the administrative responsibilities of my candidature. I also want to give special thanks to Connor Foley, who was a crucial teacher and collaborator in organizing academic events. The research for this book would have been impossible without the outstanding support of the librarians of the University of Melbourne. Thank you for providing all the scholarly and archival materials I needed to pursue this research – even when we were going through the different COVID-19 lockdowns. It is also with deep gratitude that I thank Australians for financially supporting my research through the publicly funded PhD scholarship program (University of Melbourne Research Scholarship [2017–2020] and the Australian Government Research Training Program Scholarship [2020–2022]). In a world in which education is increasingly privatized, having well-funded public research universities is more important than ever – not least to help us to imagine and create better ways of living in this world.

I completed this book at the Faculty of Law of the University of Hong Kong (HKU). I am grateful for all the support and encouragement I have received from many colleagues and mentors since joining HKU in 2023. Jed Kroncke has been a generous and supportive mentor; Scott Veitch and Marco Wan have been welcoming beyond imagination, as well as personally and intellectually generous since day one; John Murphy read portions of the manuscript and became a supportive mentor. Sida Liu, Cora Chan, Simon N. M. Young, and Michael Ng helped me to find my feet at my new institution; and, either over coffee or spontaneously in the hallways of Cheng Yu Tung Tower, Hui Jing, Massimo Lando, Jiahui Duan, and Steffano Osella have offered memorable chitchats. Finally, I also thank the Faculty's leadership, especially Dean Fu, and professional staff, Agnes Ip and Victoria Kwok, for their ongoing support and assistance.

An important part of this research project involved visiting Argentina, Chile, and El Salvador. While it is likely that the arguments in this book do not reflect their views, I am forever grateful to the following people and institutions for their time and for generously sharing their insights. In Argentina I thank Juan Pablo Scarfi (University of San Andrés, now at Pontifical Catholic University of Chile), Roberto Gargarella (Torcuato Di Tella University), the staff at the National Archives of Memory, and Mothers of Plaza de Mayo. In Chile, I am grateful to Cristián Correa (International Center for Transitional Justice), María Luisa Sepúlveda (Museum of Memory and Human Rights), Juan René Maureira (José Domingo Cañas Memory House), José Manuel Rodríguez (Museum of Memory and Human Rights), Tomás Vial (Diego Portales University), and Joaquín Castillo (Instituto de Estudios de la Sociedad). In El Salvador, sincere gratitude goes to Carlos 'Santiago' Henríquez Consalvi (Museum of the Word and the Image), Manuel Escalante (Human Rights Institute of the Central American University), Nelson Rauda Zablah (*El Faro*), and Óscar Martínez Peñate.

Many parts of this book were written during writing retreats with special friends. Writing retreats with Shane Chalmers, Tim Lindgren, and Caitlin Murphy on the Great Ocean Road were a reminder that one must persevere (when they went surfing and left me writing), but more importantly, that deep and honest conversations among friends are something to be cherished. The original magical Walkerville writing retreats with Shane and Christoph Sperfeldt were crucial reminders that friends are the family that we choose – especially when they cook for you! I also want to thank those friends who kept sharing life with me one way or the other despite my absences and often long silences: Eva Arjona, Ainhoa Martínez, Mariola Guijarro, Miriam Mejías, Mayra Tirira, Quique Martínez, Nelson Melgar, Iván Meléndez, Becca Williams, Kata Fodor, Fran and Gabby Cáceres, Rebe Martí and Felipe Zelaya, and my cousin Samuel Guevara.

I have been very fortunate to grow up surrounded by my extended family's love and support – even across time and place. I thank my maternal grandfather Samuel Guevara for being there for my mom, and for us. On my dad's side, I thank everyone in the Vásquez García family for bringing us together through an admirable spirit of loving generosity and unconditional support. To Lindy and Jim Chalmers, thank you for lovingly welcoming me into your family, and for all those wonderful evenings at the blue bench. To Petr and Ben Chalmers, thank you for all the good times and adventures, and for your world-class barista coffees.

To my parents, Claudia and Raúl, and to my brother, Abraham, thank you for the depth of your love. To *Mamá*: for your inspiring creative spirit, and for teaching me that the most important thing in life is to learn to love unconditionally because God loved us first. To *Papá*: for your inspiring optimism, and for teaching me that there is beauty and blessing in remaining a student because we all inherit, and will leave, a spiritual legacy. To Abraham, thank you for being my friend, and for exemplifying what a life of honesty, kindness, and perseverance means (and that a dose of stubbornness does not hurt!).

To my husband Shane thank you for being the most exceptionally loving and selfless *compañero*. More important than your intellectual brilliance, it is your humbleness and your ability to listen (and ask questions) with an open heart that remains a source of inspiration in my life and academic work. That I get to share this life with you is the greatest blessing I have received.

***

Earlier and shorter versions of Chapter 2 and Chapter 3 are published in "Prologue to Truth: Argentina's National Commission on the Disappeared and the Authority of International Law," *Leiden Journal of International Law*, vol 35, no 1 (2022); "Crafting the Lawful Truth: Chile's 1990 Truth Commission, International Human Rights and the Museum of Memory," *London Review of International Law*, vol 7, no 2 (2019); and "Living Together after Violent Conflict: Museum-Making as Lawful Truth-Making," in *Routledge Handbook of International Law and the Humanities*, Shane Chalmers and Sundhya Pahuja (eds) (Routledge, 2021). These publications use the material to advance a different argument to the one developed in this book.

EXPLANATORY NOTE ON THE COVER

The cover image is a photograph by Steve Cagan, who has generously granted permission to reproduce it. Steve and Beth Cagan documented the lives of Salvadorans in the UNHCR refugee camps in Honduras during the civil war in the 1980s. The cover image portrays a group of Salvadoran girls learning the artisan tradition of embroidery while living at the camps. Steve and Beth's ethnographic work is one of the few records bearing witness to the everyday lives, and courage to live life against all odds, of the Salvadoran refugees during the war. This work can be found in their books, *El Salvador: La Tierra Prometida* (Ediciones Arcoiris, 1993) and *This Promised Land, El Salvador* (Rutgers University Press, 1991). For Steve's photographic work, see: www.stevecagan.com and https://stevecagan.smugmug.com/El-Salvador.

Note on the Text

All translations from Spanish into English are mine unless otherwise stated. I provide the original text and its source in each footnote. In the case of proper names I provide, where necessary, a translation in brackets alongside the original.

As a native Spanish speaker I have also consulted the original texts in Spanish of some key texts translated into English, which have not been translated by myself. I have indicated in the respective footnote whenever my interpretation of the original text in Spanish differs from the English translation.

CHAPTER 1

Truth Commissions and International Law

Jurisdiction, Representation, Authority

1.1 INTRODUCTION

In the late 1980s, toward the end of the Cold War, a growing number of states began to establish a new kind of institution, directed toward investigating and publicly presenting an official account of past violent events. By the late 1990s, this institution had been given the name of a 'Truth Commission.'[1] Since the 1980s there have been about fifty Truth Commissions.[2] The vast majority of these institutions have operated so

1 There are different ways to describe or define Truth Commissions. However, Priscilla Hayner's definitions can be considered the most influential ones. In 1994 (article) and 2001 (book) Hayner published the first comprehensive studies on Truth Commissions, in which she put forward a general definition of a 'Truth Commission.' In 2011 Hayner revised and expanded the original 1994/2001 definitions. In part, this was to reflect the innovations in the design and implementation of the 'new' Truth Commissions, but also a response to different critiques (notably, Mark Freeman). See Priscilla B. Hayner, "Fifteen Truth Commissions – 1974 to 1994: A Comparative Study," *Human Rights Quarterly*, vol 16, no 4 (1994): 603–604; 607–611; 655; Priscilla B. Hayner, *Unspeakable Truths: Transitional Justice and the Challenge of Truth Commissions* (Routledge, 2001; 2011), 10–18; Mark Freeman, *Truth Commissions and Procedural Fairness* (Cambridge University Press, 2006), 12–22. For a recent overview about the varying definitions/descriptions and conceptual debates, see Jeremy Sarkin, "Introduction," in *The Global Impact and Legacy of Truth Commissions*, Jeremy Sarkin (ed) (Intersentia, 2019).

2 The exact number of Truth Commissions varies depending on their definition. Putting aside conceptual debates, what it is interesting is how since the 1990s Truth Commissions have kept growing in number. In this sense, it is less important if only forty of those fifty are 'proper' Truth Commissions according to a particular author (e.g., Mark Freeman). My point is mostly to emphasize that Truth Commissions have become highly popular post-conflict institutions, and that their global presence is telling of the significant social power and appeal that Truth Commissions wield. For a helpful list see Hayner, *Unspeakable Truths*, xi–xii; 256–262. For updated lists see The Auschwitz Institute for the Prevention of Genocide and Mass Atrocities, "Truth

far in states in the Global South.[3] More recently, Truth Commissions have also been created in the Global North.[4] This includes increasing calls to create Truth Commissions to address the legacies of colonialism for contemporary state-society relations.[5]

Commissions and Their Contributions to Atrocity Prevention" (2020), 29–30. www.auschwitzinstitute.org/wp-content/uploads/2020/05/AIPG-TruthCommissionsReport.pdf; Harvard Kennedy School, Harvard T. H. Chan School of Public Health, and University of Toronto, "Transitional Justice Evaluation Tools" (2025). https://transitionaljusticedata.org/en/; McMaster University, "Truth Commission Reports" (2025). https://truthcommissions.humanities.mcmaster.ca/truth-commission-reports/.

3 I use 'Global South' and 'Third World' interchangeably. By these terms I mean the political place(s) where the quality of life and state-society relations has been historically, and still is, conditioned in unequal ways by different international legal actors and institutions. An early articulation of this is attributed to Sauvy in Alfred Sauvy, "Document: Trois Mondes, Une Planète," *Vingtième Siècle. Revue d'histoire,* no 12 (1986). For an historical overview see Christoph Kalter, *The Discovery of the Third World: Decolonization and the Rise of the New Left in France, c. 1950–1976* (Cambridge University Press, 2016). For similar uses in the field of international law, see Antony Anghie and B. S. Chimni, "Third World Approaches to International Law and Individual Responsibility in Internal Conflicts," *Chinese Journal of International Law,* vol 2, no 1 (2003): 78; Sundhya Pahuja, *Decolonising International Law: Development, Economic Growth, and the Politics of Universality* (Cambridge University Press, 2011), 261–262; Luis Eslava, *Local Space, Global Life: The Everyday Operation of International Law and Development* (Cambridge University Press, 2015), xiv at 1.

4 See for example, Truth and Reconciliation Commission of Canada, *Honoring the Truth, Reconciling for the Future: Summary of the Final Report of the Truth and Reconciliation Commission of Canada* (2015); Victoria State Government, *Letters Patent for the Royal Commission to be known as Yoo-rrook Justice Commission, Register of Patents Book No 47 Page 174* (12 May 2021). In 1997 the Australian government tasked its Human Rights and Equal Opportunity Commission to investigate the state's practice of "separat[ing] Aboriginal and Torres Strait Islander children from their families." See Commonwealth of Australia, Human Rights and Equal Opportunity Commission, *Report of the National Inquiry into the Separation of Aboriginal and Torres Strait Islander Children from Their Families* (1997).

5 At the United Nations (UN), there is a push to use transitional justice institutions to address breaches of international law "in colonial contexts"; see in UN Doc A/76/180 (19 July 2021), *Report of the Special Rapporteur on the Promotion of Truth, Justice, Reparation and Guarantees of Non-recurrence, Fabián Salvioli.* In 2021, in the United States (US), legislation was introduced in Congress to establish a Truth Commission to address issues concerning the historical and ongoing contemporary legacies of slavery. See United States Congress, Rep. Lee, Barbara [D-CA-13], *H.Con.Res.19 – Urging the establishment of a United States Commission on Truth, Racial Healing, and Transformation* (25 February 2021). In the US there have been two local Truth Commission experiences; see The Greensboro Truth and Reconciliation Commission, https://greensborotrc.org; The Maryland Lynching Truth and

Internationally, different actors – including states, international institutions, and nongovernmental organizations, as well as activist and solidarity networks – have shaped and promoted a recognizable public role for Truth Commissions in post-conflict states.[6] That role is to investigate

Reconciliation Commission, https://msa.maryland.gov/lynching-truth-reconciliation/. In January 2021 a report, commissioned by French president Emmanuel Macron, recommended "the creation of a mixed French-Algerian 'truth and memory commission'" to address some of the legacies of the Algerian independence war. See Benjamin Stora, *Les Questions Mémorielles Portant sur la Colonisation et la Guerre d'Algérie* (Présidence de la République, 2021).

[6] On how, during and after the Cold War, international networks mobilized Truth Commissions and other transitional justice institutions and concepts, and institutions such as human rights and democracy, see The Aspen Institute, *State Crimes: Punishment or Pardon: Papers and Report of the Conference* (The Aspen Institute, 1988); Yves Dezalay and Bryant G. Garth, *The Internationalization of Palace Wars: Lawyers, Economists, and the Contest to Transform Latin American States* (University of Chicago Press, 2002); Nicolas Guilhot, *The Democracy Makers: Human Rights and International Order* (Columbia University Press, 2005); Paige Arthur, "How 'Transitions' Reshaped Human Rights: A Conceptual History of Transitional Justice," *Human Rights Quarterly*, vol 31, no 2 (2009); Jamie Rowen, *Searching for Truth in the Transitional Justice Movement* (Cambridge University Press, 2017); Sara Dezalay, "The Role of International NGOs in the Emergence of Transitional Justice: A Case Study of the International Center for Transitional Justice," in *Research Handbook on Transitional Justice*, Cheryl Lawther, Luke Moffett, and Dov Jacobs (eds) (Edward Elgar Publishing, 2017). Over the last fifteen years at the UN there has been increasing support for promoting transitional justice institutions, including Truth Commissions. See for example, UN Doc S/2014/616 (23 August 2004), *The Rule of Law and Transitional Justice in Conflict and Post-conflict Societies*; UN Doc E/CN.4/2005/102 (18 February 2005), *Impunity: Report of the Independent Expert to Update the Set of Principles to Combat Impunity, Diane Orentlicher*, 7–10; UN Doc E/CN.4/2005/102/Add.1 (8 February 2005), *Impunity: Report of the Independent Expert to Update the Set of Principles to Combat Impunity, Diane Orentlicher: Addendum*, 8–11; Office of the United Nations High Commissioner for Human Rights, *Rule-of-Law Tools for Post-conflict States: Truth Commissions* (2006); UN Doc ST/SG(09)/A652 (March 2010), *Guidance Note of the Secretary-General: United Nations Approach to Transitional Justice*; UN Doc A/HRC/24/42 (28 August 2013), *Report of the Special Rapporteur on the Promotion of Truth, Justice, Reparation and Guarantees of Non-recurrence, Pablo de Greiff*; UN Doc S/RES/2282 (27 April 2016), *Security Council Resolution 2282 (2016) [on post-conflict peacebuilding]*; UN Doc A/HRC/37/65 (6 June 2018), *Joint Study on the Contribution of Transitional Justice*; UN Department of Public Information SC/14109 (13 February 2020), *To Rebuild Lives, Suffering Must Be Acknowledged, 'Justice Done', Human Rights High Commissioner Says, as Security Council Takes Up Transitional Justice*, www.un.org/press/en/2020/sc14109.doc.htm; UN Doc A/HRC/48/60 (9 July 2021), *Accountability: Prosecuting and Punishing Gross Violations of Human Rights and Serious Violations of International Humanitarian Law in the Context of Transitional Justice Processes. Report of the Special Rapporteur on the Promotion of Truth, Justice, Reparation and Guarantees of Non-recurrence, Fabián Salvioli.*

violent events that occurred in a specific place, during a particular time.[7] The purpose of the investigation is to deliver a public, official, yet independent account of those violent events (the 'truth'),[8] which takes the form of a Final Report. For those who support the creation of a Truth Commission, the overarching expectation is generally that the Truth Commission's account of the truth will have the potential to help make post-conflict state-society relations more peaceful, more just, and more law-abiding.[9] In conducting the investigation and delivering the Final Report, a Truth Commission's account is usually understood to be a crucial element in supporting the transformation of state-society relations and in preventing a return to violent conflict.[10] Yet, as both supporters and critics of Truth Commissions point out, there are many factors that condition the potentially transformative power of Truth

[7] Hayner, *Unspeakable Truths*, 11–12; Cheryl Lawther, "Transitional Justice and Truth Commissions," in *Research Handbook on Transitional Justice*, Cheryl Lawther, Luke Moffett, and Dov Jacobs (eds) (Edward Elgar Publishing, 2017), 343.

[8] Hayner, *Unspeakable Truths*, 20; Robert I. Rotberg, "Truth Commissions and the Provision of Truth, Justice, and Reconciliation," in *Truth v. Justice: The Morality of Truth Commissions*, Robert I. Rotberg and Dennis F. Thompson (eds) (Princeton University Press, 2000), 4; Paul van Zyl and Mark Freeman, "The Legacy of Abuse: Conference Report," in *The Legacy of Abuse: Confronting the Past, Facing the Future*, Alice H. Henkin (ed) (The Aspen Institute, 2002), 4–5; Freeman, *Truth Commissions*, 11; 18; Anita Ferrara, *Assessing the Long-Term Impact of Truth Commissions: The Chilean Truth and Reconciliation Commission in Historical Perspective* (Routledge, 2015), 4; Sarkin, "Introduction," 16; Filipa Raimundo and Joana Rebelo Morais, "Is Anyone Listening? A Review of the Research on Attitudes Towards Truth Commissions," in *The Global Impact and Legacy of Truth Commissions*, Jeremy Sarkin (ed) (Intersentia, 2019), 45.

[9] See generally, Hayner, *Unspeakable Truths*, 20–23; Eric Wiebelhaus-Brahm, *Truth Commissions and Transitional Societies: The Impact on Human Rights and Democracy* (Routledge, 2010); Ferrara, *Assessing the Long-Term Impact of Truth Commissions*; Cath Collins, Jemima Garcia-Godos, and Elin Skaar, *Transitional Justice in Latin America: The Uneven Road from Impunity Towards Accountability* (Routledge, 2016); Guillermo Trejo, Juan Albarracín, and Lucía Tiscornia, "Breaking State Impunity in Post-authoritarian Regimes: Why Transitional Justice Processes Deter Criminal Violence in New Democracies," *Journal of Peace Research*, vol 55, no 6 (2018). See also, UN Doc A/HRC/37/65 (6 June 2018), *Joint Study on the Contribution of Transitional Justice.*

[10] Hayner, *Unspeakable Truths*; Wiebelhaus-Brahm, *Truth Commissions*; Ferrara, *Assessing the Long-Term Impact of Truth Commissions*; Collens, Garcia-Godos, and Skaar, *Transitional Justice in Latin America*; Trejo, Albarracin, and Tiscornia, "Breaking State Impunity in Post-authoritarian Regimes." See also, UN Doc A/HRC/37/65.

Commissions and their accounts of the truth.[11] This book examines one of those factors: how Truth Commissions gain *authority* for their investigatory activities and for their resulting truths.

Scholars and practitioners who study and work on Truth Commissions understand their authority to be central to the establishment and operation of the institution.[12] For a significant group in this field, this authority has two primary sources.[13] One is the state that legislatively creates the

[11] See for example, Audrey R. Chapman and Patrick Ball, "The Truth of Truth Commissions: Comparative Lessons from Haiti, South Africa, and Guatemala," *Human Rights Quarterly*, vol 23, no 1 (2001); Greg Grandin, "The Instruction of Great Catastrophe: Truth Commissions, National History, and State Formation in Argentina, Chile, and Guatemala," *The American Historical Review*, vol 110, no 1 (2005); Onur Bakiner, "Truth Commission Impact: An Assessment of How Commissions Influence Politics and Society," *International Journal of Transitional Justice*, vol 8, no 1 (2014); Jennifer Balint, Julie Evans, and Nesam McMillan, "Justice Claims in Colonial Contexts: Commissions of Inquiry in Historical Perspective," *Australian Feminist Law Journal*, vol 42, no 1 (2016); Renee Jeffrey, "Truth Commissions and Democratic Transitions: Neither Truth and Reconciliation nor Democratization in Nepal," *Journal of Human Rights* vol 20, no 3 (2021). See also, UN Doc A/HRC/24/42 (28 August 2013), *Report of the Special Rapporteur, Pablo de Greiff*, 6–9.

[12] For some of the most important contributions see Hayner, "Fifteen Truth Commissions," 604; Margaret Popkin and Naomi Roht-Arriaza, "Truth as Justice: Investigatory Commissions in Latin America," *Law & Social Inquiry*, vol 20, no 1 (1995): 93–99; Ruti G. Teitel, *Transitional Justice* (Oxford University Press, 2000), 83–88; Hayner, *Unspeakable Truths*, 11–12; 210–215; Freeman, *Truth Commissions*, 27–28; 133–134; 138–140; Wiebelhaus-Brahm, *Truth Commissions and Transitional Societies*, 3–4; Onur Bakiner, "One Truth Among Others? Truth Commissions' Struggle for Truth and Memory," *Memory Studies*, vol 8, no 3 (2015); Jeremy Sarkin, "Redesigning the Definition a Truth Commission, but Also Designing a Forward-Looking Non-Prescriptive Definition to Make Them Potentially More Successful," *Human Rights Review*, vol 19, no 3 (2018): 354–356. See also, International Center for Transitional Justice, "Drafting a Truth Commission Mandate: A Practical Tool" (2013), 3; UN Doc A/HRC/24/42 (28 August 2013), *Report of the Special Rapporteur, Pablo de Greiff*, 15–16; 25; Auschwitz Institute, "Truth Commissions and Their Contributions to Atrocity Prevention," 5.

[13] For some of the most important contributions see Hayner, "Fifteen Truth Commissions," 604; Popkin and Roht-Arriaza, "Truth as Justice"; Teitel, *Transitional Justice*, 83–88; Hayner, *Unspeakable Truths*, 11–12; 210–215; Freeman, *Truth Commissions*, 27–28; 133–134; 138–140; Wiebelhaus-Brahm, *Truth Commissions and Transitional Societies*, 3–4; Bakiner, "One Truth Among Others?"; Jeremy Sarkin, "Redesigning the Definition." See also, International Center for Transitional Justice, "Drafting a Truth Commission Mandate: A Practical Tool"; UN Doc A/HRC/24/42; Auschwitz Institute, "Truth Commissions and Their Contributions to Atrocity Prevention," 5.

Truth Commission and its activities.[14] In these accounts, it is usually the state that provides the Truth Commission with a legal-institutional form of authority, although the UN, in prior agreement with a state or the parties in conflict, can also authorize the establishment of a Truth Commission.[15] The second source of a Truth Commission's authority is usually said to be personal, in the sense that it is based on the moral and political reputation of the individuals who have been appointed as truth-commissioners.[16] As Pablo de Greiff, UN Special Rapporteur on the

[14] See Hayner, "Fifteen Truth Commissions," 604; Popkin and Roht-Arriaza, "Truth as Justice"; Teitel, *Transitional Justice*, 83–88; Hayner, *Unspeakable Truths*, 11–12; 210–215; Freeman, *Truth Commissions*, 27–28; 133–134; 138–140; Wiebelhaus-Brahm, *Truth Commissions and Transitional Societies*, 3–4; Bakiner, "One Truth Among Others?"; Jeremy Sarkin, "Redesigning the Definition." See also, International Center for Transitional Justice, "Drafting a Truth Commission Mandate: A Practical Tool"; UN Doc A/HRC/24/42; Auschwitz Institute, "Truth Commissions and Their Contributions to Atrocity Prevention," 5.

[15] El Salvador's 1990 Truth Commission was the first one of its kind to be designed, fully funded, and operated by the UN. I analyze this Truth Commission in Chapter 4. Other examples of significant UN involvement in Truth Commissions include Guatemala (1997–1999), Timor-Leste (2002–2005), Sierra Leone (2002–2004), and Liberia (2006–2009). See UN Doc A/46/553 – S/23130 (9 October 1991), *Letter dated 8 October 1991 from the Permanent Representative of El Salvador to the United Nations addressed to the Secretary-General* (*Mexico Agreements*, 27 April 1991), 5; 16–18; UN Doc S/1994/751 (1 July 1994), *Letter Dated 28 July 1994 from the Secretary-General to the President of the General Assembly and to the President of the Security Council (Agreement on the Establishment of the Commission to Clarify Past Human Rights Violations and Acts of Violence that have caused the Guatemalan Population to Suffer)*, 13–16; UN Doc UNTAET/REG/2001/10 (13 July 2001), *Regulation No. 2001/10 – On the Establishment of a Commission for Reception, Truth And Reconciliation in East Timor*; UN Doc S/1999/777 (12 July 1999), *Letter dated 8 July 1999 from the Chargé d'affaires a.i. of the Permanent Mission of Togo to the United Nations addressed to the Secretary-General (contains, Peace Agreement between the Government of Sierra Leone and the Revolutionary United Front of Sierra Leone)*, 25; UN Doc S/2003/850 (29 August 2003) *Letter Dated 29 August 2003 from the Permanent Representative of Ghana (contains, Peace Agreement between the Government of Liberia, the Liberians United for Reconciliation and Democracy, the Movement for Democracy in Liberia and the Political Parties*), 12. On the role of the UN in funding, managing and promoting transitional justice institutions, including Truth Commissions, see generally, Leena Grover, "Transitional Justice, International Law and the United Nations," *Nordic Journal of International Law*, vol 88, no 3 (2019).

[16] On this see for example, UN Doc A/HRC/24/42 (28 August 2013), *Report of the Special Rapporteur on the Promotion of Truth, Justice, Reparation and Guarantees of Non-recurrence, Pablo de Greiff*, 7; Popkin and Roht-Arriaza, "Truth as Justice," 93–95; Teitel, *Transitional Justice*, 81–83; Hayner, *Unspeakable Truths*, 211–213; 233; Freeman, Truth

Promotion of Truth,[17] emphasized in his 2013 report: "the authority and legitimacy of truth commissions depends heavily on the qualities and standing of commissioners."[18] In short, in these accounts, if a Truth Commission does not have both legal-institutional and personal-reputational authority, it risks delivering an account of the truth that will have little or no power to transform state-society relations.

The contexts in which Truth Commissions must gain authority for their investigatory activities and for their accounts of the truth are especially challenging, with highly sensitive social, political, legal, and economic conditions. These conditions include a plurality of accounts of the events that led to, and occurred during, the conflict. These accounts may not only differ in detail, but can also be in rivalrous relation with each other. This plurality of accounts poses a challenge for a Truth Commission's mandated goal of determining 'the truth' in the form of a single, coherent account of what happened. And yet, achieving this outcome – determining *the* truth

Commissions, 133–134; 138–140; Wiebelhaus-Brahm, *Truth Commissions* and Transitional Societies, 30; Onur Bakiner, *Truth Commissions: Memory, Power, and Legitimacy* (University of Pennsylvania Press, 2015), 51–53; 57–60; Sarkin, "Redesigning the Definition a Truth Commission," 359–360; 366; Office of the United Nations High Commissioner for Human Rights, *Rule-of-Law Tools for Post-conflict States: Truth Commissions*, 13–14. More broadly, on the fundamental role of personal reputation in professional practice and institution-building, see Yves Dezalay and Bryant G. Garth, *Dealing in Virtue: International Commercial Arbitration and the Construction of a Transnational Legal Order* (University of Chicago Press, 1996).

17 Pablo de Greiff served as the inaugural UN Special Rapporteur between 2012 and 2018. The full title of this position is: Special Rapporteur on the Promotion of Truth, Justice, Reparation and Guarantees of Non-Recurrence. See UN Doc A/HRC/RES/18/7 (13 October 2011), *Special Rapporteur on the Promotion of Truth, Justice, Reparation and Guarantees of Non-Recurrence: Resolution adopted by the Human Rights Council.*

18 UN Doc A/HRC/24/42 (28 August 2013), *Report of the Special Rapporteur, Pablo de Greiff*, 27. On the UN's emphasis on having "credible commissioners" see UN Doc S/2014/616 (23 August 2014), *The Rule of Law and Transitional Justice*, 17. For instance, the Liberian Truth Commission is said to have 'failed' because all the commissioners were 'tainted' by the civil war see Carla De Ycaza, "A Search for Truth: A Critical Analysis of the Liberian Truth and Reconciliation Commission," *Human Rights Review*, vol 14, no 3 (2013): 196–197. I discuss in Chapter 4 how El Salvador's UN Truth Commission was deliberately comprised only by non-Salvadorans under the claim that there were no 'apolitical' Salvadoran public figures capable of delivering an 'objective' account of the truth. On this see Mark Ensalaco, "Truth Commissions for Chile and El Salvador: A Report and Assessment," *Human Rights Quarterly*, vol 16, no 4 (1994): 661.

from among the plurality of accounts – is understood to be integral to the potential transformative work of a Truth Commission.[19] What this book examines is how Truth Commissions produce their shared, public accounts or 'truths' in the face of this plurality. The understanding of 'truth' that this book is concerned with could also be called "factual or forensic truth."[20] My concern is how Truth Commissions have privileged this type of truth in public life over other coexisting truths, which might not entirely 'fit' with its design to establish a shared, official account of the past.

The more that I investigated the way Truth Commissions create an authoritative account of violent conflicts, how they deal with the plurality of accounts – and what they do to rival accounts – the more I noticed that Truth Commissions were drawing authority for those accounts from another source: international law. If this book's driving question is how Truth Commissions have established their accounts of the truth, then this relationship between the work of Truth Commissions and international law is a crucial part of the answer, which has not yet been adequately understood.

Distinct from the authority that the Truth Commission relies on in its establishment as an institution, there is something else at work in the production of the account of the truth itself. My argument is that Truth Commissions have drawn on international law to authorize their claim to address the truthfulness of their accounts of violent conflict. This can be seen in three of the most important Truth Commissions of the twentieth century:[21] Argentina's National Commission on the Disappeared (1983–

[19] See notes 9 and 12 above, see especially Teitel's discussion of establishing 'the truth' in the face of coexisting "truth regimes" in Teitel, *Transitional Justice*, 70–73; 81–92; Bakiner, "One Truth Among Others? Truth Commissions' Struggle for Truth and Memory."

[20] I thank Vasuki Nesiah for pointing this out. The "factual or forensic truth" is one of "the four notions of truth" that the South African Truth Commission (1996–2003) put forward and worked with. See in Truth and Reconciliation Commission of South Africa, "Truth and Reconciliation Commission of South Africa Report. Volume 1" (1998), 110–114.

[21] On the influence of these three Truth Commissions on other Truth Commissions, including on South Africa's Truth and Reconciliation Commission, see, for example, Ensalaco, "Truth Commissions," 656–657; Priscilla B. Hayner, "Commissioning the Truth: Further Research Questions," *Third World Quarterly*, vol 17, no 1 (1996): 20; Neil J. Kritz, "Where We Are and How We Got Here: An Overview of Developments in the Search for Justice and Reconciliation," in *The Legacy of Abuse: Confronting the Past,*

1984);[22] Chile's National Commission on Truth and Reconciliation (1990–1991);[23] and El Salvador's UN Commission on the Truth (1992–1993).[24] It can also be seen in what human rights and transitional justice experts retrospectively described in the 1990s to be the inaugural Truth Commission, the 1974 Commission of Inquiry into the Disappearances of People in Uganda.[25] Through in-depth studies of these Truth Commissions, the book shows how they draw on international law in four main ways: by invoking its promises of democracy and peace (Argentina in Chapter 2); by using international human rights language (Chile in Chapter 3); by linking the Truth Commission to the identity and status of the UN (El Salvador in Chapter 4); and by retrospectively redescribing the historical connection of Truth Commissions to international human rights (the 1974 Commission of Inquiry in Chapter 5). At the same time, it is not only the Truth Commissions that benefit from this relationship with international law. As I show in each of the studies,

Facing the Future, Alice H. Henkin (ed) (The Aspen Institute, 2002), 22–23; Elin Skaar, "Transitional Justice for Human Rights: The Legacy and Future of Truth and Reconciliation Commissions," in *International Human Rights Institutions, Tribunals, and Courts*, Gerd Oberleitner (ed) (Springer, 2018), 402; Marcos Zunino, *Justice Framed: A Genealogy of Transitional Justice* (Cambridge University Press, 2019), 67; 76; 107; Alejandro Chehtman, "Latin America as a Laboratory of Transitional Justice," in *Latin American International Law in the Twenty-First Century*, Alejandro Chehtman, Alexandra Huneeus, and Sergio Puig (eds) (Oxford University Press, 2025), 420–421.

22 Comisión Nacional sobre la Desaparición de Personas (CONADEP), *Nunca Más: The Report of the Argentine National Commission on the Disappeared* (Farrar, Straus, Giroux, 1986).

23 Comisión Nacional de Verdad y Reconciliación, *Report of the Chilean National Commission on Truth and Reconciliation*, trans by Phillip Berryman (University of Notre Dame Press, 1993; United States Institute of Peace, 2002).

24 UN Doc S/25500 (1 April 1993), *From Madness to Hope.*

25 Commission of Inquiry into the Disappearances of People in Uganda since the 25th of January 1971, *Final Report of the Commission of Inquiry into the Disappearances of People in Uganda since the 25th of January 1971* (1974), www.usip.org/publications/1974/06/truth-commission-uganda-74. In Chapter 5 I show how this Commission of Inquiry became the inaugural Truth Commission. For exemplary literature that considers this Commission of Inquiry as the inaugural Truth Commission, see for example, Hayner, "Fifteen Truth Commissions," 611–613; Joanna R. Quinn, *The Politics of Acknowledgement: Truth Commissions in Uganda and Haiti* (UBC Press, 2010), 40; Alicia C. Decker, "'Sometime You May Leave Your Husband in Karuma Falls or in the Forest There': A Gendered History of Disappearance in Idi Amin's Uganda, 1971–79," *Journal of Eastern African Studies*, vol 7, no 1 (2013).

the authority of international law, too, is strengthened by the way that Truth Commissions hold international law as central to the work of shaping post-conflict state-society relations.

This offers a novel way of understanding Truth Commissions as post-conflict institutions that both rely upon and advance the authority of international law. As each of the studies show, one consequence of the relationship between Truth Commissions and international law is that it privileges in public life a form of truth that tends to conform with the values and worldviews of international law. In Argentina (Chapter 2), the Truth Commission silenced interpretations and meanings of the dictatorship's socioeconomic state violence in its privileging of an internationally authorized account of the truth about the violent events. Similarly in Chile (Chapter 3), by placing an internationally authorized truth about its dictatorship in a 'major' position in public life, the Truth Commission displaced to a 'minor' position the truths of communities – especially Indigenous peoples and women – who are pushed to the margins of public life.[26] In El Salvador (Chapter 4), too, the consequence of linking the truth produced by the Truth Commission to the UN was to silence truths that rivaled the UN's (emerging) post-Cold War worldview for the Global South. Finally, in the case of the 1974 Commission of Inquiry (Chapter 5), the consequence of its 1994 retrospective redescription as the inaugural Truth Commission using the language of human rights, is that it displaced the legal language that had given authority to the original 1974 Commission's account.

There is an extensive literature examining questions of authority in international law and its institutions.[27] In this literature, international

[26] In Chapter 3 I explain in greater detail what I mean by 'major' and 'minor' truths, drawing on Goodrich's conceptualization of "minor jurisprudences" in Peter Goodrich, *Law in the Courts of Love: Literature and Other Minor Jurisprudences* (Routledge, 1996), 2.

[27] See as examples, Antony Anghie, *Imperialism, Sovereignty and the Making of International Law* (Cambridge University Press, 2005); Armin von Bogdandy et al., "Special Issue: The Exercise of Public Authority by International Institutions," *German Law Journal*, vol 9, no 11 (2008); Samantha Besson, "The Authority of International Law: Lifting the State Veil," *Sydney Law Review*, vol 31, no 3 (2009); Anne Orford, *International Authority and the Responsibility to Protect* (Cambridge University Press, 2011); Nicole Roughan, *Authorities: Conflicts, Cooperation, and Transnational Legal Theory*

'authority' takes many different forms, with a wide range of international actors drawing on and asserting it through their practices.[28] In this book, I focus on authority in terms of a power to

(Oxford University Press, 2013); Başak Cali, *The Authority of International Law: Obedience, Respect, and Rebuttal* (Oxford University Press, 2015); Samantha Besson and Jean d'Aspremont (eds), *The Oxford Handbook of the Sources of International Law* (Oxford University Press, 2017); Armin von Bogdandy, Matthias Goldmann, and Ingo Venzke, "From Public International to International Public Law: Translating World Public Opinion into International Public Authority," *European Journal of International Law*, vol 28, no 1 (2017); Nico Krisch, "Symposium: Liquid Authority in Global Governance," *International Theory*, vol 9, no 2 (2017); Cait Storr, *International Status in the Shadow of Empire: Nauru and the Histories of International Law* (Cambridge University Press, 2020).

[28] For instance, to briefly unpack the previous footnote, Anghie's legal-historical analysis approaches the question of authority as 'sovereign authority,' and pays attention to the influential sixteenth-century jurist Francisco de Vitoria's role in crafting novel (international) legal arrangements that would authorize the lawfulness of the Spanish kingdom's exercise of power to colonize, and rule over, certain geographical places and their peoples; see Anghie, *Imperialism, Sovereignty and the Making of International Law.* Bodgandy et al. conceptualize, from a liberal tradition, authority as 'public authority,' and are particularly concerned with the consequences of 'domestic' decision-making and policies of how international institutions (broadly understood) might "unilaterally" exercise that authority on matters of 'public' concern (understood ultimately as a matter of constraining individual freedom); see in, von Bogdandy et al., "Special Issue – The Exercise of Public Authority by International Institutions"; Armin von Bogdandy et al. (eds), *The Exercise of Public Authority by International Institutions: Advancing International Institutional Law* (Springer, 2010); von Bogdandy, Goldmann, and Venzke, "From Public International to International Public Law." Besson develops an understanding of authority as 'legitimacy' by drawing on European moral philosophy; see in, Besson, "The Authority of International Law." In Orford's analysis, international authority takes a novel form in the 2000s through the practice of the UN's 'executive' authority, as the exercise of the international concept of the 'responsibility to protect'; see in Orford, *International Authority.* While Roughan's analysis of authority is mostly concerned with transnational law rather than with international law, their analysis places legal plurality at the heart of theoretical questions about the practice of 'public authority' in contexts of legal plurality. Cali examines how authority as a concept is shaped through certain 'domestic' legal-political debates that concern 'international' legal issues in, Cali, *The Authority of International Law.* As editors Besson and d'Aspremont note, questions of international authority remain central in the studies and debates about 'the' sources of international law, see in, Besson and d'Aspremont, *The Oxford Handbook of the Sources of International Law.* As Krisch notes, a number of recent contributions to a Symposium on authority also complicate dominant legal imaginaries about international/global authority as a static and solid authority by pushing for an understanding of authority in more "dynamic" and "liquid" terms; see in Krisch, "Symposium – Liquid Authority

decide upon, and establish, the 'true' history of the violent events of a society, which is also a matter of who has the power to "author,"[29] or 'speak,' the truth about a society's past. The emphasis here is less on authority as a fixed quality ('an' authority), and more on a power and a practice ('authorizing'). As I explain in Section 1.2, below, this draws on a tradition of thinking about authority as a matter of "jurisdiction" (literally, 'speaking the law').[30]

This jurisprudential tradition of 'jurisdictional thought' also offers a way of examining *how* Truth Commissions have authorized their accounts of violent events as the truth by drawing on different dimensions of international law – in this case, on its promises, its language, the identity and status of its international institutions, as well as its doctrine (international human rights). As I also explain in Section 1.2, below, one of the crucial 'techniques' that enables Truth Commissions to authorize their accounts is *representation*.[31] The argument here is that the power of international law to authorize the work of a Truth Commission is contingent on how the truth is represented to publics both domestically and internationally. Truth Commissions are institutions which are directed toward publicly presenting an official account of past violent events. As I show through the book, that public presentation of the Truth

in Global Governance." In Storr's analysis, international authority takes the form of administrative practice, in which by virtue of an international arrangement, a state becomes the administrative authority over another state, see in Storr, *International Status.*

29 Shaunnagh Dorsett and Shaun McVeigh, *Jurisdiction* (Routledge, 2012), 13.

30 See generally, Peter Rush, "An Altered Jurisdiction: Corporeal Traces of Law," *Griffith Law Review*, vol 6 (1997); Dorsett and McVeigh, *Jurisdiction*, 23; Sundhya Pahuja, "Laws of Encounter: A Jurisdictional Account of International Law," *London Review of International Law*, vol 1, no 1 (2013).

31 On representations and their work of law and authority, see generally Louis Marin, *Portrait of the King* (Springer, 1988); Dorsett and McVeigh, *Jurisdiction*, 12–14; Timothy D. Peters and Karen Crawley (eds), *Envisioning Legality: Law, Culture and Representation* (Routledge, 2017); Marco Wan, *Masculinity and the Trials of Modern Fiction* (Routledge, 2017); Desmond Manderson (ed), *Law and the Visual: Representations, Technologies, and Critique* (University of Toronto Press, 2018); Maria Elander, *Figuring Victims in International Criminal Justice: The Case of the Khmer Rouge Tribunal* (Routledge, 2018); Peter Rush and Maria Elander, "Working through the Cinematography of International Criminal Justice: Procedures of Law and Images of Atrocity," *London Review of International Law*, vol 6, no 1 (2018).

Commission's investigation involves an act of representing the truth, and is a crucial technique through which 'authority' is also transmitted and becomes socially effective as an authorizing force.[32]

The book develops this argument, primarily through the three core studies that form the basis of Chapters 2, 3, and 4 (although Chapter 5 contributes to this argument, albeit in a different way, as explained further). The core studies focus on three of the earliest and most internationally influential Truth Commissions, in Argentina, Chile, and El Salvador. In studying the work of these Truth Commissions, I have focused on how truths are represented, or contested, through three 'cultural objects': a literary prologue (for Argentina), a museum of memory (for Chile), and a tapestry (for El Salvador). On the one hand, the analysis shows how the prologue's textual representation (Argentina), and the museum of memory's spatial representation (Chile), continue to give public life to their respective Truth Commission's internationally authorized truth. On the other hand, the analysis shows how, in the case of El Salvador, the tapestry's visual representation of a local truth works to contest the UN Truth Commission's account. Analyzing these textual, spatial, and visual representations of the truth makes 'sensible' the ways in which these institutions have drawn on international law to authorize their accounts,[33] as well as the implications for rival truths and for the states after conflict. The argument is that, through the study of representations, we can gain a deeper understanding of the subtle yet powerful ways in which Truth Commissions have worked with international law, as well as the consequences. These are the ways in which the internationally authorized truth of the Truth

[32] Or perhaps 'affective.' On how the workings of international justice institutions mobilize and deploy affective techniques and practices in a way that contributes to socially legitimizing their particular ideas of justice, see Kamari Maxine Clarke, *Affective Justice: The International Criminal Court and the Pan-Africanist Pushback* (Duke University Press, 2019). For an analysis that shares a similar concern with international justice institutions' affective social power (in this case, understood as a "striking impression") deployed through the creation and promotion of particular images of victimhood see Christine Schwöbel-Patel, "Spectacle in International Criminal Law: The Fundraising Image of Victimhood," *London Review of International Law*, vol 4, no 2 (2016).

[33] Dorsett and McVeigh, *Jurisdiction*, 12.

Commission works to deauthorize other truths and rival ways of imagining and shaping post-conflict state-society relations.

In the final substantive chapter (Chapter 5) I examine how, in the mid-1990s after the international success of the Truth Commissions in Argentina, Chile, and El Salvador, international human rights experts and activists gave Truth Commissions institutional coherency through an 'origins story'. I show how this happened through two influential texts in particular, which in the 1990s redescribed the 1974 Commission of Inquiry not only as an institution advancing international human rights, but also as the 'inaugural' Truth Commission.[34]

The rest of this introductory chapter is divided into three parts. In Section 1.2, I explain the book's theoretical orientation and methodology. In Section 1.3, I address the book's specific contributions. And in Section 1.4, I provide a chapter-by-chapter outline.

1.2 A JURISDICTIONAL APPROACH TO REPRESENTATIONS OF TRUTH AND AUTHORITY

The following discussion of the book's methodology is divided into two sections. In Section 1.2.1, I explain why the book engages with the jurisprudential tradition of 'jurisdictional thought' in its analysis of Truth Commissions. I also explain how thinking about the work of Truth Commissions jurisdictionally has enabled me to draw out their relationship with international law. In Section 1.2.2, I then explain how I have focused on representations of truth and authority in my analysis of the Argentinian, Chilean, and Salvadoran Truth Commissions. I also explain why and how I have selected the specific cultural objects in relation to each Truth Commission (the literary prologue for Argentina, the museum of memory for Chile, and the handmade tapestry for El Salvador). Chapter 5 is slightly different. It was conceived as an 'exit' chapter that re-considers how Truth Commissions have been

[34] I explain this in greater detail in Part 4 of this Introduction (the chapter outlines), and in Chapter 5 of the book. The two texts referred to here are Richard Carver, "Called to Account: How African Governments Investigate Human Rights Violations," *African Affairs*, vol 89, no 356 (1990); Hayner, "Fifteen Truth Commissions."

received. For this reason, it is also methodologically different to the three core chapters, in that it does not focus on a cultural object, although its analysis remains grounded in the same jurisprudential tradition of 'jurisdictional thought'.

1.2.1 JURISDICTIONAL THOUGHT. The book's analysis is informed by scholarship in the tradition of 'jurisdictional thought'.[35] As a jurisprudential approach, jurisdictional thought directs attention to law's "site or space of enunciation."[36] In Dorsett and McVeigh's terms, jurisdiction is a "mod[e] of thinking about law"[37] that is concerned with "the inauguration or creation of law and its articulation."[38] In this mode,

[35] Of this scholarship, Shaunnagh Dorsett and Shaun McVeigh's book *Jurisdiction*, and Sundhya Pahuja's jurisdictional analysis of international law, have been especially influential. See Dorsett and McVeigh, *Jurisdiction*; Shaun McVeigh and Sundhya Pahuja, "Rival Jurisdictions: The Promise and Loss of Sovereignty," in *After Sovereignty: On the Question of Political Beginnings*, Charles Barbour and George Pavlich (eds) (Routledge, 2010); Pahuja, "Laws of Encounter"; Shaun McVeigh, "Critical Approaches to Jurisdiction and International Law," in *The Oxford Handbook of Jurisdiction in International Law*, Stephen Allen et al. (eds) (Oxford University Press, 2019). More generally, however, I have learnt to think with jurisdiction through my engagement with a community of scholars associated with the Melbourne Law School's Institute for International Law and the Humanities, who have each contributed in their own ways to this school of thought. For a collection of exemplary work of Institute for International Law and the Humanities (IILAH) and its broader intellectual community, see Shane Chalmers and Sundhya Pahuja (eds), *Routledge Handbook of International Law and the Humanities* (Routledge, 2021). For other contributions see James E. K. Parker, *Acoustic Jurisprudence: Listening to the Trial of Simon Bikindi* (Oxford University Press, 2015); Ann Genovese, Shaun McVeigh, and Peter Rush, "Lives Lived with Law: An Introduction," *Law Text Culture*, vol 20, no 1 (2016); Olivia Barr, *A Jurisprudence of Movement: Common Law, Walking, Unsettling Place* (Routledge, 2016); Jake Goldenfein and Andrea Leiter, "Legal Engineering on the Blockchain: 'Smart Contracts' as Legal Conduct," *Law & Critique*, vol 29, no 2 (2018); Maïa Pal, *Jurisdictional Accumulation: An Early Modern History of Law, Empires, and Capital* (Cambridge University Press, 2020); Storr, *International Status*; Shane Chalmers, "The Festival as Constitutional Event and as Jurisdictional Encounter: Colonial Victoria and the Independent Order of Black Fellows," *Griffith Law Review*, vol 30, no 4 (2021). For a recent example of the growing interest in a jurisdictional approach to the study of international law see Sué González Huack and Julian A. Hettihewa, "Symposium: Who Speaks International Law? Introducing the Symposium on the 2021 AjV-DGIR Conference," *Völkerrechtsblog* (30 August 2021).

[36] Rush, "An Altered Jurisdiction," 150. [37] Dorsett and McVeigh, *Jurisdiction*, 6.

[38] Ibid, 10.

jurisdiction is not "just a descriptive concept"[39] about where "the practice of pronouncing the law" takes place;[40] instead it is a matter of who has "the power and authority to speak in the name of law," and of how they exercise that power.[41] As Dorsett and McVeigh write, "jurisdictional thought and practice"[42] takes the form of "practical questions" about who "bring[s] law into existence," and how they do it;[43] about who has "the authority to speak in the name of the law," and how they acquire that authority;[44] and about "what belongs to law, or becomes the subject of law."[45] By extension, thinking jurisdictionally focuses attention on how historical and contemporary institutions – whether legal, sociocultural, political, or economic – "actively wor[k] to produce something" through their operations.[46] Put another way, asking questions jurisdictionally invites us to focus not only on how institutions have "the power and authority to speak in the name of law,"[47] but also how they give a particular "legal form to life," and thus to "our existence" in community.[48]

In this book, thinking about Truth Commissions jurisdictionally has enabled me to think about how these institutions relate to international law. Truth Commissions are generally perceived and presented as not doing any meaningful *legal* work in post-conflict state-society relations.[49] Approaching Truth Commissions jurisdictionally has enabled an analysis that does not take for granted the absence, or insignificance, of a relationship between Truth Commissions and (international) law. The widespread view of Truth Commissions is that neither international law nor any other form of law plays a substantive role in the operation of

39 Ibid, 5. 40 Ibid, 4. 41 Rush, "An Altered Jurisdiction," 150.

42 McVeigh, "Critical Approaches to Jurisdiction and International Law," 183.

43 Dorsett and McVeigh, *Jurisdiction*, 4.

44 Shaunnagh Dorsett and Shaun McVeigh, "Questions of Jurisdiction," in *Jurisprudence of Jurisdiction*, Shaun McVeigh (ed) (Routledge, 2007), 4.

45 Dorsett and McVeigh, *Jurisdiction*, 16. 46 Ibid, 5.

47 Rush, "An Altered Jurisdiction," 150. 48 Dorsett and McVeigh, *Jurisdiction*, 1.

49 See the following descriptions as examples: Teitel, *Transitional Justice*, 81; Hayner, *Unspeakable Truths*, 13–14; 91–104; Freeman, *Truth Commissions*, 69–72; Bakiner, *Truth Commissions*, 9; Wiebelhaus-Brahm, *Truth Commissions and Transitional Societies*, 5; Alison Bisset, *Truth Commissions and Criminal Courts* (Cambridge University Press, 2012); Sarkin, "Redesigning the Definition a Truth Commission," 364.

Truth Commissions and the accounts of the truth they produce.[50] To the extent that researchers and practitioners address the relationship between Truth Commissions and (international) law, the tendency is to frame it as a question of how the work of Truth Commissions might "complement" the work of judicial institutions,[51] for example by providing the 'true' facts for future criminal prosecutions.[52] Even then, however, the aims and scope of a Truth Commission and its truth for post-conflict state-society relations are understood to exceed a relationship with law. For instance, Priscilla Hayner, author of several early and highly influential studies of Truth Commissions,[53] argues that while "truth commissions cover many events that could also be subject to trials ... they should be seen as quite separate and independent" institutions.[54] For Hayner and others who share this view,[55] "what is

[50] Ibid. On the importance of Truth Commissions' regulatory function or policy recommendations see for example, International Center for Transitional Justice, "Challenging the Conventional: Can Truth Commissions Strengthen Peace Processes?" (2014), 20–21; UN Doc A/HRC/45/45 (9 July 2020), *Memorialization Processes in the Context of Serious Violations of Human Rights and International Humanitarian Law: The Fifth Pillar of Transitional Justice*, 12.

[51] See for example, Teitel, *Transitional Justice*, 88–92; William A. Schabas, "The Relationship between Truth Commissions and International Courts: The Case of Sierra Leone," *Human Rights Quarterly*, vol 25, no 4 (2003); Bisset, *Truth Commissions and Criminal Courts*; Office of the United Nations High Commissioner for Human Rights, *Rule-of-Law Tools for Post-conflict States: Truth Commissions*; Amnesty International, "Truth, Justice and Reparation: Establishing an Effective Truth Commission" (2007).

[52] Ferrara, *Assessing the Long-Term Impact of Truth Commissions*, 133.

[53] Hayner, "Fifteen Truth Commissions"; Hayner, "Commissioning the Truth"; Hayner, *Unspeakable Truths*. In Chapter 5 I discuss in more detail the influential role of Hayner. For a general reference on Hayner's prominent role see Rowen, *Searching for Truth*, 23; 28.

[54] Hayner, *Unspeakable Truths*, 13.

[55] Ibid, 11. For a similar view see for example, Teitel, *Transitional Justice*, 81–88; Félix Reátegui, "The Victims Remember. Notes on the Social Practice of Memory," in *Transitional Justice: Handbook for Latin America*, Félix Reátegui (ed) (Brazilian Amnesty Commission, Ministry of Justice; International Center for Transitional Justice, 2011); Eduardo González and Howard Varney (eds), "Truth Seeking: Elements of Creating an Effective Truth Commission" (International Center for Transitional Justice, 2013), 47–53; Cath Collins, "The Many Faces of Truth: Does the Truth Commission Have a Future?" *Peace in Progress/ Por la Paz* (2017). www.icip-perlapau.cat/numero31/articles_centrals/article_central_1/.

special about truth commissions is their intention of affecting the social understanding and acceptance of the country's past, not just to resolve specific facts."[56] This is understood as standing in productive contrast to judicial institutions, and related investigatory institutions such as commissions of inquiry.

This view of the relationship between Truth Commissions and (international) law is also shared in practice. In 2020, when Father Francisco de Roux, president of the Colombian Truth Commission, spoke before the UN Security Council, he characterized the Truth Commission's account as a "moral, historical and social truth ... that is not built but, instead, uncovered."[57] He specifically distinguished that truth from a "legal truth," which he defined as a determination of "those who are guilty under the law."[58] For de Roux, making such a determination (of the 'legal truth') in Colombia is the role of the Special Jurisdiction for Peace, a court created for that purpose. That was in 2020. Nearly forty years earlier, the truths of three of the earliest and most influential Truth Commissions – Argentina (1983–1984), Chile (1990–1991), and El Salvador (1992–1993) – were also explicitly presented, and later institutionally memorialized, as fundamentally separate from any form of law, including international law.[59]

This book does not contest the view that Truth Commissions are different in nature to domestic judicial institutions, nor to international criminal justice institutions such as the International Criminal Court.[60]

[56] On this see generally, Freeman, *Truth Commissions*, 14; 22–24; 57–58; Balint, Evans, and McMillan, "Justice Claims in Colonial Contexts: Commissions of Inquiry in Historical Perspective"; Zoë Laidlaw, "Investigating Empire: Humanitarians, Reform and the Commission of Eastern Inquiry," *Journal of Imperial & Commonwealth History*, vol 40, no 5 (2012).

[57] UN Doc S/PV.8723 (13 February 2020), *Security Council, 75th year: 8723rd Meeting*, 5.

[58] Ibid.

[59] I show this in detail in Chapters 2, 3, and 4. Note how in the legal-institutional documents authorizing these Truth Commissions they are not tasked to do legal work, but to 'find' and establish 'the truth.' For Argentina see Gobierno de la Argentina, *Decreto 187/83 Comisión Nacional sobre la Desaparición de Personas – Constitución – Integración y Funciones* (15 December 1983). For Chile see Gobierno de Chile, *Decreto Supremo No. 355 Crea Comisión de Verdad y Reconciliación* (25 April 1990). For El Salvador see UN Doc A/46/553 – S/23130 (9 October 1991), *Mexico Agreements*, 5; 16–18.

[60] See notes 50 and 51 above.

Nor does it contest the view that Truth Commissions' accounts of violent conflict have different aims to that of a court's judgment.[61] However, there is a growing body of scholarship – which this book draws on and contributes to – which shows that law, including international law, plays a more significant role in the operation of Truth Commissions than is commonly thought.[62] One thing that this emerging literature shows is that the extent to which we can identify a significant relationship between Truth Commissions and (international) law depends on how we think about law, or the kinds of 'law' questions that we ask.

In thinking jurisdictionally, the first set of questions to ask is "whether law exists at all" in one's object of study, and if so, "which law"?[63] In studying the work of Truth Commissions for the book, this meant

61 Ibid.

62 Some of this literature includes, Vasuki Nesiah, "Discussion Lines on Gender and Transitional Justice: An Introductory Essay Reflecting on the ICTJ Bellagio Workshop on Gender and Transitional Justice," *Columbia Journal of Gender and Law*, vol 15, no 3 (2006): 141; Anne Orford, "Commissioning the Truth," *Columbia Journal of Gender and Law*, vol 15, no 3 (2006); Claire Moon, "Narrating Political Reconciliation: Truth and Reconciliation in South Africa," *Social and Legal Studies*, vol 15, no 2 (2006); Mark Sanders, *Ambiguities of Witnessing: Law and Literature in the Time of a Truth Commission* (Stanford University Press, 2007); Elizabeth S. Anker, *Fictions of Dignity: Embodying Human Rights in World Literature* (Cornell University Press, 2012); Carrol Clarkson, *Drawing the Line: Toward an Aesthetics of Transitional Justice* (Fordham University Press, 2013); Peter Rush, "Dirty War Crimes: Jurisdictions of Memory and International Criminal Law," in *The Hidden Histories of War Crimes Trials*, Gerry Simpson and Kevin John Heller (eds) (Oxford University Press, 2013); Adam Sitze, *The Impossible Machine: A Genealogy of South Africa's Truth and Reconciliation Commission* (University of Michigan Press, 2013); Vasuki Nesiah, "The Trials of History: Losing Justice in the Monstrous and the Banal," in *Law in Transition: Human Rights, Development and Transitional Justice*, Ruth Buchanan and Peer Zumbansen (eds) (Bloomsbury, 2014); Eliana Cusato, "International Law, the Paradox of Plenty and the Making of Resource-Driven Conflict," *Leiden Journal of International Law*, vol 33, no 3 (2020); Valeria Vázquez Guevara, "Crafting the Lawful Truth: Chile's 1990 Truth Commission, International Human Rights and the Museum of Memory," *London Review of International Law*, vol 7, no 2 (2019); Vasuki Nesiah, "The Ambitions and Traumas of Transitional Governance: Expelling Colonialism, Replicating Colonialism," in *International Law and Transitional Governance: Critical Perspectives*, Emmanuel H. D. De Groof and Micha Wiebusch (eds) (Routledge, 2020); Valeria Vázquez Guevara, "Prologue to Truth: Argentina's National Commission on the Disappeared and the Authority of International Law," *Leiden Journal of International Law*, vol 35, no 1 (2022).

63 Dorsett and McVeigh, *Jurisdiction*, 6.

searching for the traces or presence of law, and identifying what that law is, within the two most important texts of any Truth Commission: (1) the legal-institutional document authorizing the creation of the institution (which also defines its aims and scope); and (2) the Final Report containing the resulting account of the truth (that is, the outcome of a Truth Commission's investigation).[64]

As I show through the studies in Chapter 2 (Argentina), Chapter 3 (Chile), and Chapter 4 (El Salvador), my analysis reveals the presence of a number of different international legal forms within key sections of the texts. In Chapter 3, for example, I show how from the outset the Chilean state established its Truth Commission (1990–1991) to "clarify the truth about the grave violations of human rights" that occurred during Pinochet's 1973–1990 dictatorship.[65] This is the opening sentence of the decree with which the Chilean state established its Truth Commission,[66] and as it makes clear, the work of the Truth Commission was framed from the outset in relation to international human rights law. This can also be seen in the Final Report, which explicitly established international human rights law as the legal framework of the investigation.[67] In following this thread, the chapter shows how, in a subtle yet powerful way, the Chilean state anchored both the *raison d'être* of the Truth Commission and the object of its investigation in international human rights law. This not only authorized the work of the Truth Commission, but also supported international human rights law by narrating Chilean history as part of the triumphal global history of universal human rights. In a similar way, my analysis in Chapters 2 and 4 shows how the Truth Commissions either invoked international law's promises of peace and democracy (in Argentina), or was linked to the identity and status of the UN as an international institution (in El Salvador). In turn, I show how the work

[64] Teitel, *Transitional Justice*, 81–92; González and Varney (eds), "Truth Seeking," 9–11; 23; 27.

[65] ("esclarecimiento de la verdad sobre las graves violaciones a los derechos humanos"). Gobierno de Chile, *Decreto Supremo No. 355*, Art. 1.

[66] Ibid.

[67] In the Final Report international human rights law was also established as the legal framework see in, Comisión Nacional de Verdad y Reconciliación, *Report of the Chilean National Commission on Truth and Reconciliation*, 15–19.

of these three Truth Commissions elevated international law in authorizing their accounts of the truth.

By asking the initial jurisdictional questions of "whether law exists at all" and if so, "which law,"[68] the book shows that Truth Commissions have a significant relationship with international law (at least in the three that I have studied in-depth). The next questions to ask were how that relationship worked, and what were the implications for post-conflict state-society relations. In thinking about these two questions, I have drawn on Sundhya Pahuja's jurisdictional analysis of international law, as well as on the work of other scholars of international law whose research engages with, and contributes to, jurisdictional thought.[69] This body of work has been crucial to understanding the role of international law and its institutions in organizing lawful relations between the state and society after conflict.

Pahuja (herself building on Rush, Dorsett, and McVeigh's work) notes that "jurisdictional thinking alters the usual way of thinking about [international] law" and its relationship with the state.[70] The "usual way," as Pahuja describes it, is to think that "sovereignty is an attribute of the state," and that "jurisdiction" is the outcome of the state's "exercise of sovereignty."[71] On this view, "both territory and population are givens."[72] In other words, the sovereign state is presumed to have jurisdiction, or "the power and authority to speak in the name of law,"[73] to organize relationships within a specific territorial location.[74] Understood in this way, it is the 'sovereign state,' together with other 'equally sovereign states,' that participates in the collective creation of international law and its institutions.[75]

68 Dorsett and McVeigh, *Jurisdiction*, 6.

69 See note 35, above, and generally, McVeigh and Pahuja, "Rival Jurisdictions: The Promise and Loss of Sovereignty"; Pahuja, "Laws of Encounter"; McVeigh, "Critical Approaches to Jurisdiction and International Law"; Storr, *International Status*; Pal, *Jurisdictional Accumulation.*

70 Pahuja, "Laws of Encounter," 69. 71 Ibid. 72 Ibid, 70.

73 Rush, "An Altered Jurisdiction," 150.

74 On the complex relationship between international law, decolonization, and the creation of the postcolonial state see Vasuki Nesiah, "Placing International Law: White Spaces on a Map," *Leiden Journal of International Law*, vol 16, no 1 (2003).

75 See for example, Malcolm N. Shaw, *International Law*, 9th ed. (Cambridge University Press, 2021), 176–196. For a critical analysis of this dominant view see Richard Joyce, "Westphalia: Event, Memory, Myth," in *Events: The Force of International Law*, Fleur Johns, Richard Joyce, and Sundhya Pahuja (eds) (Routledge, 2010);

By extension, the authority of international law and its institutions to establish a 'shared' legal order directly stems from the collective authority of the sovereign states.

This understanding of states, as equal sovereign authorities that create international law, can also be seen in how international law and its institutions are designed for, and deployed in, post-conflict states.[76] The "broader assumption" in these contexts, as Orford argues, is "that local institutions, actors, or cultures pose the major threats to democracy and human rights, while international institutions and laws act primarily in the interests of human rights, democracy, and the people."[77] Framed in this way, "international law and international lawyers bear no special responsibility other than to help to resolve [conflict] according to 'law'."[78] In other words, deploying international law and its institutions in a post-conflict state is imperative to 'save' that state from "lawlessness" and to give it the "modern law" which can "secur[e] and unif[y] society through its rule."[79]

Luis Eslava and Sundhya Pahuja, "The State and International Law: A Reading from the Global South," *Humanity*, vol 11, no 1 (2020).

76 See for example, Jane Stromseth, David Wippman, and Rosa Brooks, *Can Might Make Rights? Building the Rule of Law after Military Interventions* (Cambridge University Press, 2006); Thomas Carothers, "The Rule-of-Law Revival," in *In Promoting the Rule of Law Abroad: In Search of Knowledge*, Thomas Carothers (ed) (Carnegie Endowment for International Peace, 2006); Brett Bowden, Hilary Charlesworth, and Jeremy Matam Farrall (eds), *The Role of International Law in Rebuilding Societies after Conflict: Great Expectations* (Cambridge University Press, 2009); Stephen Humphreys, *Theatre of the Rule of Law: Transnational Legal Intervention in Theory and Practice* (Cambridge University Press, 2012); Laura Grenfell, *Promoting the Rule of Law in Post-Conflict States* (Cambridge University Press, 2013).

77 Anne Orford, "Locating the International: Military and Monetary Interventions after the Cold War," *Harvard International Law Journal*, vol 38, no 2 (1997): 444. For a similar point see also Naomi Klein, *The Shock Doctrine* (Penguin Books, 2008); Usha Natarajan, "Creating and Recreating Iraq: Legacies of the Mandate System in Contemporary Understandings of Third World Sovereignty," *Leiden Journal of International Law*, vol 24, no 4 (2011); Joseph R. Slaughter, "Hijacking Human Rights: Neoliberalism, the New Historiography, and the End of the Third World," *Human Rights Quarterly*, vol 40, no 4 (2018); Ntina Tzouvala, *Capitalism as Civilisation: A History of International Law* (Cambridge University Press, 2020), 167–211.

78 Pahuja, "Laws of Encounter," 64.

79 Shane Chalmers, "The Mythology of International Rule-of-Law Promotion," *Law & Social Inquiry*, vol 44, no 4 (2019): 6.

This way of seeing the relationship between international law and the post-conflict state and society, gained strength at the end of the Cold War,[80] but it is not new. The creation and deployment of (international) post-conflict state-building institutions after the end of the Cold War,[81] needs to be understood within the broader history of international law and its institutions, especially in the Global South.[82] In his groundbreaking international legal history, Anghie showed that "the colonial encounter" between the European Empires and the peoples and laws beyond the European continent "shaped the very foundations of international law."[83] In turn, as Anghie points out, since the fifteenth century, international law became crucial to advancing and authorizing European colonial projects across the world,[84] often through an international legal framing of 'terra nullius.'[85] A key contribution of Anghie's work, has

80 See generally, Guilhot, *The Democracy Makers*; Odd Arne Westad, *The Global Cold War: Third World Interventions and the Making of Our Times* (Cambridge University Press, 2007); Mark Mazower, *No Enchanted Palace: The End of Empire and the Ideological Origins of the United Nations* (Princeton University Press, 2009).

81 See note 80 above. See also for example, Anne Orford, *Reading Humanitarian Intervention: Human Rights and the Use of Force in International Law* (Cambridge University Press, 2003); Pahuja, *Decolonising International Law*; Guy Fiti Sinclair, *To Reform the World: The Legal Powers of International Organizations* (Oxford University Press, 2017); Nesiah, "The Ambitions and Traumas of Transitional Governance," 140–141.

82 See for example, Anghie, *Imperialism, Sovereignty and the Making of International Law*; Samuel Moyn, *The Last Utopia: Human Rights in History* (Harvard University Press, 2010); B. S. Chimni, "A Just World under Law: A View from the South," *American University International Law Review*, vol 22, no 2 (2007); Michael Fakhri, *Sugar and the Making of International Trade Law* (Cambridge University Press, 2014); Matthew Craven, "Between Law and History: the Berlin Conference of 1884–1885 and the Logic of Free Trade," *London Review of International Law*, vol 3, no 1 (2015); Rose Parfitt, *The Process of International Legal Reproduction: Inequality, Historiography, Resistance* (Cambridge University Press, 2019); Luis Eslava, "The Developmental State: Independence, Dependency, and the History of the South," in *The Battle for International Law: South-North Perspectives on the Decolonization Era*, Jochen von Bernstorff and Philipp Dann (eds) (Oxford University Press, 2019).

83 Anghie, *Imperialism, Sovereignty and the Making of International Law*, 8.

84 See generally, ibid.

85 On this see, for example, Brenna Bhandar, *Colonial Lives of Property: Law, Land, and Racial Regimes of Ownership* (Duke University Press, 2018). See also Nesiah's discussion of 'terra nullius' in the context of the Western Sahara in, Nesiah, "Placing International Law."

been to show "how these [colonial] origins create[d] a set of structures that continually repeat themselves at various stages in the history of international law."[86] Building on Anghie's work, many scholars of international law have shown how, over time, international law has continued to relate to its 'non-European/Anglo-Saxon others' under multiple (changing) names, while being deployed across the Global South through different international legal forms and institutions.[87] During the 'Age of Empire,'[88] adjectives such as 'barbaric' or 'uncivilized' were frequently used to categorize peoples and places across the non-European South.[89] After the end of World War II and formal decolonization, these categories were replaced by others, such as 'underdeveloped' or 'developing.'[90] These categories set Global South states

[86] Anghie, *Imperialism, Sovereignty and the Making of International Law*, 3. See also Storr, *International Status*.

[87] See for example this selected literature, Pahuja, *Decolonising International Law*; Natarajan, "Creating and Recreating Iraq: Legacies of the Mandate System in Contemporary Understandings of Third World Sovereignty"; Eslava, *Local Space, Global Life*; Luis Eslava, Michael Fakhri, and Vasuki Nesiah (eds), *Bandung, Global History, and International Law: Critical Pasts and Pending Futures* (Cambridge University Press, 2017); Parfitt, *The Process of International Legal Reproduction*; Storr, *International Status*; Tzouvala, *Capitalism as Civilisation*; Juan Pablo Scarfi, "Francisco de Vitoria and the (Geo)politics of Canonization in Spain/America," *Leiden Journal of International Law*, vol 35, no 3 (2022); Sujith Xavier, "Locating and Situating Justice Pal: TWAIL, International Criminal Tribunals, and Judicial Powers," *Asian Journal of International Law* (2022).

[88] Anghie borrows from Hobsbawm's conceptualization of 'Age of Empire' in Anghie, *Imperialism, Sovereignty and the Making of International Law*, 32.

[89] On the use of those categories see Liliana Obregón, "The Civilized and the Uncivilized," in *The Oxford Handbook of the History of International Law*, Bardo Fassbender and Anne Peters (eds) (Oxford University Press, 2012). Peter Fitzpatrick also examined how these racial binaries were (and still are) fundamental in constituting the normativity of modern law and advancing European colonial projects; see in, Peter Fitzpatrick, *The Mythology of Modern Law* (Routledge, 1992).

[90] On the relationship between international law and its institutions, and the deployment of the development project see generally, Balakrishnan Rajagopal, *International Law from Below: Development, Social Movements and Third World Resistance* (Cambridge University Press, 2003); Jennifer Beard, *The Political Economy of Desire: International Law, Development and the Nation State* (Routledge, 2007); Pahuja, *Decolonising International Law*; Eslava, *Local Space, Global Life*; Eslava, "The Developmental State." For politico-historical accounts about the development see Arturo Escobar, *Encountering Development: The Making and Unmaking of the Third World* (Princeton University Press, 2012); Gilbert Rist, *The History of Development from Western Origins to*

in a constitutive opposition to the putatively 'developed' European and North American states. Importantly, this was also a moment when international human rights law began to be mobilized by the United States and other Western states as well as by the UN, as a shared 'universal legal standard' against which the quality of state-governance was measured, especially in the 'developing' states of the Global South.[91]

As noted above, this history is relevant for this book because a similar rationality organized the relationship between international law and its institutions and post-conflict states at the end of the Cold War, in the late 1980s and early 1990s, the period in which the Truth Commissions in Argentina, Chile, and El Salvador were established (and in which the Ugandan Commission of Inquiry was redescribed as a Truth Commission). In this book, thinking with jurisdiction enables us to see how this rationality is also at work in the ways in which these Truth Commissions sought to establish an authoritative account about the violent events, which led to the conflict. As Cait Storr argues, thinking jurisdictionally "emphasises aspects of law as a socio-political phenomenon that are often relegated within the discipline."[92] It does this by focusing attention on "the ritualised behaviours, the forms of words and the symbolic vocabularies that mark out the legal from other registers of socio-political conduct," and by inviting us to "pa[y] attention to conflict at the thresholds across which the political becomes legal, and to the material forms those thresholds take."[93] Taking this approach enables us to examine the creation and role of Truth Commissions in light of the changes in international law and politics that occurred during the late and post-Cold War period of the 1980s and 1990s.

Global Faith (Zed Books, 2014); Joseph Morgan Hodge, "Writing the History of Development (Part 1: The First Wave)," *Humanity*, vol 6, no 3 (2016); Joseph Morgan Hodge, "Writing the History of Development (Part 2: Longer, Deeper, Wider)," *Humanity*, vol 7, no 1 (2017).

91 On this see generally, Orlando Letelier, "Economic 'Freedom's' Awful Toll: The 'Chicago Boys' in Chile," *Review of Radical Political Economics*, vol 8, no 3 (1976); Klein, *The Shock Doctrine*; Vasuki Nesiah, "Theories of Transitional Justice: Cashing in the Blue Chips," in *The Oxford Handbook of The Theory of International Law*, Anne Orford and Florian Hoffmann (eds) (Oxford University Press, 2016); Slaughter, "Hijacking Human Rights"; Jessica Whyte, *The Morals of the Market: Human Rights and the Rise of Neoliberalism* (Verso, 2019).

92 Storr, *International Status*, 16.

93 Ibid.

Considering this Cold War context in the analysis of Truth Commissions also draws attention to the ways in which different Global South post-conflict states, and later the UN (in the 1990s), decided to create Truth Commissions to settle the struggles between plural and rival accounts of the conflicts in these states.

My jurisdictional analysis of the relationship between Truth Commissions and international law also reveals the complexities that Argentina, Chile, and El Salvador faced in creating post-conflict institutions that were not authorized internationally. As this book highlights, for these states (and for others in the Global South), going against, or proposing alternatives to, the Western-influenced international legal rationality and post-Cold War geopolitics was not a viable option. That was (and still is) especially the case when international law and its institutions continued to portray the violent events in these states as another unfortunate consequence (and proof) of them being 'uncivilized' and 'lawless,' in need of being 'fixed' and 'developed.' In this context, as a way for post-conflict states such as Argentina, Chile, and El Salvador to demonstrate that they were able to be different – to be 'peaceful' and 'lawful,' 'civilized' and 'developed.' But for the Truth Commissions to successfully signal to the world that the state had 'transitioned' according to this international rationality, they needed the authority of international law.

In the next section I outline the methods – especially, the technique of representation, archival research and in-country visits – I have used to show how the Truth Commissions in Argentina, Chile, and El Salvador have sought to authorize in public life their accounts of the respective conflicts as 'the truth' through international law.

1.2.2 REPRESENTATIONS OF TRUTH AND AUTHORITY. Representation is a powerful way of exercising authority, and is therefore a resource for analyzing it.[94] Both sides of this doubling can be seen in the work of Truth Commissions. Truth Commissions are institutions that must present publicly the results of their investigations in order to achieve their objectives of establishing *the* truthful account of past violent events. The

94 On this see generally, Marin, *Portrait of the King*; Alain Cantillon and Nigel Saint, "Louis Marin: An Introduction," *Early Modern French Studies*, vol 38, no 1 (2016).

activities of Truth Commissions involve transmitting 'the truth' in a way that is both socially effective and authoritative. This is important because, as Desmond Manderson writes, "[t]here could be no world and no subject without images; no public, no imagined community, no state or nation or law or sovereign without the representations that bring them into existence."[95] In this sense, focusing on representations in the activities or practices of the Truth Commissions allows us to study their truths, not so much as the "end product" of their investigations, but as a "process," as Sara Ramshaw reminds us.[96] In a post-conflict context where a plurality of (rival) truths about past violent events coexist, representation is a jurisdictional technique[97] that enables Truth Commissions to influence which past violent events are remembered, and how they are remembered. In other words, it is through the practice of representation that a Truth Commission exercises it power to establish its account of the truth as the authoritative one, while silencing or displacing other rival truths.

While representation is central to the exercise of authority by public institutions,[98] it is especially important for the work of Truth Commissions. Truth Commissions are explicitly designed as temporary investigatory institutions.[99] Once their investigation concludes with the delivery of the

95 Desmond Manderson, *Danse Macabre: Temporalities of Law in the Visual Arts* (Cambridge University Press, 2019), 16. While representations can work in this way, as Ramshaw and Stapleton point out, paying attention to representations also affords us the possibility of learning, and thus imagining, alternative ways to live together after conflict; see generally in Sara Ramshaw and Paul Stapleton, "From Prepeace to Postconflict: The Ethics of (Non)Listening and Cocreation in a Divided Society," in *Playing for Keeps: Improvisation in the Aftermath*, Daniel Fischlin and Eric Porter (eds) (Duke University Press, 2021).

96 Sara Ramshaw, "Law and Humanities: A Field Without a Canon," *Law, Culture and the Humanities* (2019): 11. In earlier work, Ramshaw makes a similar point about the importance of examining the relationship between law and justice from 'within,' and what we can discover about it in doing so; see in, Sara Ramshaw, *Justice as Improvisation: The Law of the Extempore* (Routledge, 2013).

97 Dorsett and McVeigh, *Jurisdiction*, 12–14; 49–50; Chalmers, "The Festival as Constitutional Event"; Desmond Manderson, "Indigenous People and the Law," *Australian Financial Review* (2008).

98 Dorsett and McVeigh, *Jurisdiction*, 12–14; 49–50; Chalmers, "The Festival as Constitutional Event"; Manderson, "Indigenous People and the Law."

99 Anita Ferrara, "Assessing the Long-Term Impact and Legacy of Truth Commissions," in *The Global Impact and Legacy of Truth Commissions*, Jeremy Sarkin (ed) (Intersentia, 2019), 75.

Final Report, Truth Commissions cease to have a visible material presence in public life. This is especially clear in the Truth Commissions of Argentina (1983–1984), Chile (1990–1991), and El Salvador (1992–1993). These Truth Commissions concluded their official work over two decades ago, and they have long ceased to have an official presence. Nevertheless, they live on – or their work lives on – through their representations. As with most Truth Commissions, the expectation is that the Final Report of these Truth Commissions, as well as subsequent memorialization policies and/or practices, will preserve and make their account publicly accessible for generations to come.[100]

In response to these temporal and material qualities of Truth Commissions, over the last two decades many post-conflict states, civil society organizations, communities and individuals have created new, or repurposed old, public and private cultural institutions and objects in order to represent and memorialize a Truth Commission's account of the past. Cultural institutions and objects have become an especially important material means for preserving publicly, and giving ongoing social relevance to, the Truth Commission. As Lucas Lixinski notes, in the aftermath of violent conflict new cultural institutions or objects and "cultural heritage can be used to create, resurrect, and preserve certain narratives about the past that significantly impact national cultural identity and the overall possible directions" of state-society relations.[101] Examples include dedicated national archives for the Truth Commission;[102] museums of memory or memorialization spaces;[103] national

[100] On this see for example, UN Doc A/HRC/45/45 (9 July 2020), *Memorialization Processes*; Erin Daly, "Truth Skepticism: An Inquiry into the Value of Truth in Times of Transition," *International Journal of Transitional Justice*, vol 2, no 1 (2008): 38.

[101] Lucas Lixinski, *Legalized Identities: Cultural Heritage Law and the Shaping of Transitional Justice* (Cambridge University Press, 2021), 1.

[102] For an overview on the practices of creating archives for Truth Commissions see Trudy Huskamp Peterson, *Final Acts: A Guide to Preserving the Records of Truth Commissions* (Woodrow Wilson Center Press; Johns Hopkins University Press, 2005). See for example Argentina's National Archive of Memory in, Archivo Nacional de la Memoria. www.argentina.gob.ar/derechoshumanos/ANM.

[103] I examine an example of this in Chapter 3, which focuses on Chile's Museum of Memory and Human Rights. For a discussion of museums of memory and similar memorializing institutions see Silke Arnold-de Simine, *Mediating Memory in the Museum: Trauma, Empathy, Nostalgia* (Palgrave Macmillan, 2013).

remembrance days;[104] reclaimed sites where violent episodes occurred;[105] ongoing publication of the Final Report,[106] as well as other secondary literature on the Report;[107] along with the creation of a wide range of artworks, including plays, movies, songs, murals, documentaries, books, and photography.[108]

In recent years, scholars in the field of transitional justice,[109] and to a lesser extent in international law,[110] have paid increasing attention to

104 See for example South Africa's National Reconciliation Day on 16 December in, Mandela.Gov.Za, "Message by President Nelson Mandela on National Reconciliation Day." www.mandela.gov.za/mandela_speeches/1995/reconciliation.

105 For example, in Chile a former clandestine torture house is now known as 'Londres 38.' See Londres 38 – Espacio de Memorias. www.londres38.cl/1937/w3-channel.html. For a discussion of similar spaces in Chile and Argentina see for example, Nelly Richard, *Eruptions of Memory: The Critique of Memory in Chile, 1990–2015*, trans by Julia Sanches (Polity Press, 2019); Vikki Bell, *The Art of Post-dictatorship: Ethics and Aesthetics in Transitional Argentina* (Routledge, 2014).

106 For example, Argentina's Truth Commission Report, which has been in publication since 1984, is also available as an electronic-book (Amazon's Kindle); see Comisión Nacional sobre la Desaparición de Personas (CONADEP), *Nunca Más: Informe de la Comisión Nacional sobre la Desaparición de Personas* (Eudeba; Kindle edition, 1985; 2011).

107 After Timor-Leste's Truth Commission, there have been children's books focusing on themes addressed in the Final Report. See for example, Galuh Wandita et al., *Chega! Book 1: What Happened and How to Stop It Happening Again*, trans Mayra Walsh (AJAR, STP-CAVR, INSISTPress, 2010; 2015).

108 See some examples in, Peter Rush and Olivera Simić, *The Arts of Transitional Justice: Culture, Activism, and Memory After Atrocity* (Springer, 2014).

109 For a discussion of the relationship between transitional justice and artistic expressions see for example, Clara Ramírez-Barat (ed), *Transitional Justice, Culture, and Society: Beyond Outreach* (International Center for Transitional Justice; Social Science Research Council, 2014); Bell, *The Art of Post-dictatorship*; Rush and Simić, *The Arts of Transitional Justice: Culture, Activism, and Memory After Atrocity*; Sherin Shefik, "Reimagining Transitional Justice through Participatory Art," *International Journal of Transitional Justice*, vol 12, no 2 (2018); Eliza Garnsey, *The Justice of Visual Art: Creative State-Building in Times of Political Transition* (Cambridge University Press, 2019); Véronique Tadjo (ed), *The Culture of Dissenting Memory: Truth Commissions in the Global South* (Routledge, 2019); Arnaud K. Kurze and Christopher Lamont (eds), *New Critical Spaces in Transitional Justice: Gender, Art, and Memory* (Indiana University Press, 2019); Marina Aksenova et al., "AJIL Unbound by Symposium: Art, Aesthetics, and International Justice," *AJIL Unbound*, vol 114 (2020); Lixinski, *Legalized Identities*; Cynthia E. Cohen et al., "Special Issue: Creative Approaches to Transitional Justice: Contributions of Arts and Culture," *International Journal of Transitional Justice*, vol 14, no 1 (2020).

110 See for example, Parker, *Acoustic Jurisprudence: Listening to the Trial of Simon Bikindi*; Daniel Joyce and Gabrielle Simm, "Zero Dark Thirty: International Law, Film and

cultural institutions and objects that offer representations of the violent past. Many researchers, policy-makers, international and nongovernmental organizations, have also encouraged the creation of cultural institutions and objects as a way of achieving the justice outcomes sought by transitional justice processes.[111] In part this is a conscious effort to move away from an exclusively "institutional perspective,"[112] by paying attention to 'local' or social representations of a violent conflict.[113] An example of this is the 2020 Report of the UN Special Rapporteur on the Promotion of Truth.[114] In this Report, the Special Rapporteur approached post-conflict "[m]emory as a battlefield," with the battle taking place in "a broader cultural framework in which

Representation," *London Review of International Law*, vol 3, no 2 (2015); Helene Kazan, "The Architecture of Slow, Structural, and Spectacular Violence and the Poetic Testimony of War," *Australian Feminist Law Journal*, vol 44, no 1 (2018); Luis Eslava, "The Moving Location of Empire: Indirect Rule, International Law, and the Bantu Educational Kinema Experiment," *Leiden Journal of International Law*, vol 31, no 3 (2018); Jessie Hohmann and Daniel Joyce (eds), *International Law's Objects* (Oxford University Press, 2018); Maria Elander, "Images of Victims: The ECCC and the Cambodian Genocide Museum," in *Law and the Visual: Representations, Technologies, and Critique*, Desmond Manderson (ed) (University of Toronto Press, 2018); Vasuki Nesiah, "Freedom at Sea," *London Review of International Law*, vol 7, no 2 (2019); Kate Grady, "For Whom the Bell Tolls: London's Iraq and Afghanistan Memorial 1990–2015," *London Review of International Law*, vol 7, no 3 (2019); Vázquez Guevara, "Crafting the Lawful Truth"; Miriam Bak McKenna, "Designing for International Law: The Architecture of International Organizations 1922–1952," *Leiden Journal of International Law*, vol 34, no 1 (2020); Kate Miles, "Visuality of a Treaty: Reflection on Versailles," *London Review of International Law*, vol 8, no 1 (2020); Chalmers and Pahuja, *Handbook of International Law and the Humanities*; Vázquez Guevara, "Prologue to Truth."

111 See note 109 above, especially Ramírez-Barat, *Transitional Justice, Culture, and Society*; Shefik, "Reimagining Transitional Justice through Participatory Art."

112 Ramírez-Barat, *Transitional Justice, Culture, and Society*, 27. For an earlier and influential proposal to rethink transitional justice institutions through 'the local' voices see Kieran McEvoy, "Beyond Legalism: Towards a Thicker Understanding of Transitional Justice," *Journal of Law and Society*, vol 34, no 4 (2007); Kieran McEvoy and Lorna McGregor (eds), *Transitional Justice from Below: Grassroots Activism and the Struggle for Change* (Hart Publishing, 2008).

113 For a powerful critique of the instrumentalization of 'local' voices see Tshepo Madlingozi, "On Transitional Justice Entrepreneurs and the Production of Victims," *Journal of Human Rights Practice*, vol 2, no 2 (2010); Nesiah, "The Ambitions and Traumas of Transitional Governance," 143–144.

114 UN Doc A/HRC/45/45 (9 July 2020), *Memorialization Processes*.

different visions, values and narratives come together."[115] What is interesting for this book is that the Special Rapporteur emphasized the sociocultural importance of disseminating a Truth Commission's internationally authorized truth through different sociocultural outreach initiatives or by supporting artistic work.[116] Doing so both during and after a Truth Commission process concludes, the Special Rapporteur argues, will ensure there are no "gaps in the narratives of the past that can be exploited by political actors who are oblivious to the suffering of victims and the requirements of a peaceful society."[117] Importantly, for the Special Rapporteur, the "narrative of the past" can only be a "good practice" of memorialization if "the authorities in charge of the public space … properly represent the views of the victims and" those narratives "are established in collaboration with civil society, especially human rights organizations."[118]

This raises a jurisdictional question about which accounts, and whose accounts, of violent conflicts are being authorized as representations of the truth and memorialized as such within the post-conflict states' public spaces. The answer that I develop through this book is that only those cultural institutions and objects whose representations of the conflict transmit the Truth Commission's internationally authorized truth are given a prominent and privileged place in a post-conflict state's public life. As we can see in the analysis of the Truth Commissions in Argentina, Chile, and El Salvador, this has resulted in the deauthorizing of other truths – the representations of which are silenced or displaced in public life.

Examining the representational work of a Truth Commission helps us to understand the place, time, and circumstances in which these representations were created, and the historical truths that they establish. It also enables us to draw out the cultural forms that give them authority, including that of law, and to see how this can work to bind the post-conflict state, and its peoples and their histories of the violent conflict, to that law. My argument here is that the textual, spatial, and visual representations that I have analyzed for this book show two things. One is how international law, by being represented "in the

[115] Ibid, 6. [116] Ibid. [117] Ibid, 12. [118] Ibid, 10.

very detail of [the] composition" of the truth,[119] works to authorize the Truth Commissions' account as the truth. And two, this shows the contest of truth that runs alongside it.

1.2.3 VISITING THE SITES OF THE TRUTH COMMISSIONS. As I explain in detail in the chapter outline (Section 1.4), the analysis presented here focuses on three cultural objects: a literary prologue (for Argentina), a museum of memory (for Chile), and a handmade tapestry (for El Salvador). Each of these objects offers a representation of truth and authority through a different medium: textually (in Argentina), spatially (in Chile), and visually (in El Salvador). By focusing on these representations it is possible to study, and better understand, how the Truth Commissions drew on international law in ways that worked to authorize their truths. For example, Argentina's prologue and Chile's museum of memory can be seen to give temporal and material continuity in public life to the Truth Commissions' internationally authorized accounts of the truth. In contrast, the Salvadoran tapestry works to contest the Truth Commission's internationally authorized account of the truth, throwing it into sharper relief.

I selected the three cultural objects after visiting the places where the Truth Commissions were largely run: Buenos Aires (Argentina) and Santiago (Chile) in September 2018, San Salvador (El Salvador) in February–March 2020, with a brief visit to New York City (United States) in February 2020.[120] I visited these cities with a broad yet very specific curiosity: would I be able to 'see' law in the representations of the Truth Commissions' truth, and if so, what law, or whose law, would it be? To answer those questions, I consulted archives, including Argentina's

119 Edward Said and Raymond Williams, "Appendix. Media, Margins and Modernity," in *Raymond Williams, Politics of Modernism: Against the New Conformists* (Verso, 2007), 185.

120 El Salvador's UN Truth Commission began its investigation in San Salvador, and later moved to New York for security reasons. See Thomas Buergenthal, "The United Nations Truth Commission for El Salvador," *Vanderbilt Journal of Transnational Law*, vol 27, no 3 (1994): 504–505.

National Archive of Memory in Buenos Aires.[121] I dwelled in numerous sites of memorialization, including the Monument for the Disappeared in Chile's General Cemetery in Santiago. I experienced remembrance days, including Pinochet's 1972 coup against President Salvador Allende in Santiago. I walked in and around places where violent events occurred and continue to represent sites of collective social trauma, such as the house in El Salvador's Central American University where the six Jesuit academics were killed in 1989 by the Salvadoran armed forces. I also went to the Madres de Plaza de Mayo's ongoing weekly demonstrations in Buenos Aires (Argentina); Salvador Allende's tomb/memorial in the General Cemetery in Santiago (Chile); and Monsignor Romero's crypt in the Metropolitan Cathedral of San Salvador (El Salvador).

Dwelling in these sites helped to give unexpected yet vital context-specific nuance to the research. It drew my attention to how people in these post-conflict states live at present with their truths about the 'past.' For instance, in September 2018, during a cold but sunny winter morning in Santiago, after spending a couple of hours at Chile's Monument for the Disappeared in the General Cemetery, I noticed someone discretely approaching the memorial. The person took out a small brush from their bag and began cleaning one of the plaques with the name of someone who disappeared during the dictatorship. The caring and careful way in which the person patiently cleaned every corner of the plaque was telling of the personal meaning it held for them. In a way, in witnessing that moment, I was being invited to pay attention to the nuances of how Chileans continue to honor, in intimate yet public ways, their own truths about life, love, grief, loss, and survival. And how they continue to do so, not necessarily through the language of international law, but through their everyday, mundane activities: in this case, an act of carefully cleaning the plaque with the name of a loved one.

Before starting the research for this book, I understood that these truths about 'the past' were too telling to ignore. I learnt this through my childhood in post-conflict El Salvador, as well as through my professional experience in post-apartheid South Africa, and as a research assistant for a UN Development Program project on post-conflict reconciliation in Iraq. These

[121] Argentina's National Archive of Memory.

experiences stayed with me through the research leading to this book. They reminded me that there are dissonances between how people might express and understand their truths about a conflict, and how a literature on Truth Commissions might celebrate and promote the legacies of Truth Commissions. Bearing that in mind, I came to understand that if the aim of my research was to understand how Truth Commissions established their accounts as truth, and the implications for state-society relations, then it was important to visit Argentina, Chile, and El Salvador.

It was through these visits that I encountered the three cultural objects that are the focus of the book – the literary prologue (Argentina), the museum of memory (Chile), and the tapestry (El Salvador). I use the word 'encounter' to emphasize that my decision to work with these objects came through an unplanned meeting. While I had planned to visit several sites in Buenos Aires, Santiago, and San Salvador, I had decided that I was not going to search for images or read about the specific sites of memorialization, or sites related to their Truth Commissions. I wanted to experience these sites, as much as possible, in ways that were not mediated by existing frames (whether scholarly or journalistic). In doing so, I hoped to be surprised by how the Truth Commissions of Argentina, Chile, and El Salvador continued to represent over time, their accounts of the truth, and the role of international law through them.

The result was a highly emotional experience of encounter.[122] Encountering the archives of Argentina's Truth Commission at the National Archive of Memory was an especially traumatic experience. I consulted those archives every day for about two weeks. Every night I had nightmares; I would wake up in the middle of the night feeling nauseous at the thought of going to the Archives the following morning. The Archives are located in a former clandestine detention and torture center, the ex-Escuela de Mecánica de la Armada or Higher School of Mechanics of the Navy. The site was repurposed and renamed Memory Space and Human Rights.[123] What haunted me in the middle of the night

[122] I briefly reflected on my experience at Argentina's National Archive of Memory in, Vázquez Guevara, "Prologue to Truth," 124–125 and in Chapter 2 of this book.

[123] Espacio Memoria y Derechos Humanos, "Sobre el Lugar." www.espaciomemoria.ar/lugar.

were the poster-size portraits of the people who were disappeared during the dictatorship.[124] Many of the walls of the ex-ESMA were covered with them, in bigger than life size. Every day upon entering the site and after consulting the archives, I felt that those who disappeared were watching me. Their gaze felt like a reminder that whatever was kept in those archives, and whatever documents I gathered, were about them, about their lives, about their truths. And yet, in this book, I am not relaying an unmediated relation, or set of relations, between truth and justice, or between the dead, justice, and truth.

The disruptive power of the portraits of the disappeared came not so much from being at a place renamed as 'Memory Space and Human Rights,' but from the histories of the lives of those who were killed by the dictatorship's state violence. Yet, as I show in Chapter 2 of the book, when I encountered and read closely the prologue to the Argentinian Truth Commission's Final Report, its account of the truth seemed to draw its authority not from people's lives and truths, but from another source. The prologue to the Final Report shows how Argentina's Truth Commission authorized its account as the truth by drawing on the promises being made by international law experts through their narratives about what life will be like, after conflict is over.

I went through similar experiences when I encountered the spatial representation of truth and authority at the Chilean museum of memory in Santiago, and in San Salvador, when I encountered the tapestry's rival representation of truth and authority. These are discussed in Chapters 3 and 4. More broadly, however, visiting these places also gave me the opportunity to understand each of the Truth Commissions through informal conversations with Argentineans, Chileans, and Salvadorans. These informal conversations in Spanish, my mother-tongue, challenged and broadened my understanding of the Truth Commissions, pointed me in the direction of sites of memorialization, and pushed me to engage with a wide range of local accounts and scholarship about the violent conflicts and their aftermath. The conversations also helped me to be

[124] This was an artistic initiative titled "Presentes." See Espacio Memoria y Derechos Humanos, "Intervención 'Presentes' en la ex ESMA." www.youtube.com/watch?v=MOX-jPC4Tc8.

more attentive to the significant role that the Cold War's geopolitics, and the United States' foreign policy in Latin America, had on the regional and national politics during the time when the Truth Commissions were created and operated.

1.3 THE CONTRIBUTION OF THE BOOK

This book is an invitation to scholars and practitioners in the fields of international law and transitional justice to reflect on the relationship between Truth Commissions and international law. The book seeks to shift, and deepen, our understanding of this relationship, by showing how Truth Commissions both draw upon and strengthen international law's world-making power. In showing this, the book makes two main contributions. One is a methodological contribution, which the book makes through the development of an innovative approach or methodology to the study of Truth Commissions and international law. And second, by taking this approach, the book is able to contribute new knowledge about the international legal work of Truth Commissions. I will expand on both of these contributions in turn.

One of the contributions of the book is its focus on cultural objects to examine the relationship between Truth Commissions and international law. By taking this approach, the book seeks to draw out the ways in which international law's world-making power and authority over the post-conflict state is exercised and actualized. I try to show how international law diffuses through the work of Truth Commissions, their cultural representations and the rival representations that travel alongside them. In this, the book offers a way of examining how 'non-legal' institutions might engage in (international) legal work.

By taking this approach, the book offers a new way of understanding Truth Commissions as post-conflict institutions that draw upon and advance international law's world-making power. As this book shows, by paying attention to how Truth Commissions engage with international law in their representations of the truth, we can see how they draw on international law to authorize their accounts as truthful. This is an important finding in itself. Yet, what makes it especially significant is that, in the process, Truth Commissions can be seen to privilege and reproduce a homogenizing, 'global' international legal history and developmental narrative about the Global South's post-conflict states and their peoples. As I show through the in-depth studies of Argentina, Chile, and El Salvador, the effect is to silence voices in these countries, and to displace rival truths. More broadly, in making this argument, the book also contributes to three main areas of scholarship: to international law and transitional justice, by showing that law has a significant role in the operation of Truth Commissions;[125] to thinking with jurisdiction in the study of international law and institutions;[126] and to law and humanities scholarship by examining the relationships between international law, culture, and society.[127]

1.4 BOOK OUTLINE

In Chapter 2, "Invoking the Promises of International Law," the book focuses on Argentina's 1983–1984 Truth Commission. This chapter analyzes how the Argentinian Truth Commission accounted for the dictatorship's state violence, and how international law is involved in the making of this account as truth. My argument is that the Truth Commission draws on international law's promises of peace and democracy to authorize its account as truth. In turn, the Truth Commission deauthorizes, and thereby silences, accounts of the dictatorship's state violence that do not conform with the official version embedded in, and mobilized by, the promises of international law of the late-Cold War. To show this, I read the Prologue to the Truth Commission's Final Report as a literary text that not only works to establish the truth that is set out in the Final Report, but that also authorizes that truth by connecting it to international law. This reading of the Prologue to the Final Report draws on scholarship in the field of law and literature,[128] especially the work of Joseph Slaughter on the

[125] See note 62 above. [126] See note 35 above. [127] See notes 31 and 110 above.

[128] For an overview of the field see Maria Aristodemou, *Law and Literature: Journeys from Her to Eternity* (Oxford University Press, 2000); Julie Stone Peters, "Law, Literature, and the Vanishing Real: On the Future of an Interdisciplinary Illusion," *PMLA*, vol 120, no 2 (2005); Desmond Manderson, *Kangaroo Courts and the Rule of Law: The Legacy of Modernism* (Routledge, 2012), 9; 20; Greta Olson, "De-Americanizing Law and Literature Narratives: Opening Up the Story," *Law and Literature*, vol 22, no 2

relationship between international human rights law and literature.[129] The analysis in this chapter shows how, through the Prologue, the Final Report enabled the Truth Commission to establish the unlawfulness of the dictatorship's state violence, in part because of the Prologue's literary form, or genre, as a *prologue*, and in part because of the language it used. This language drew on the 'promises' of international law to describe and categorize events that occurred during the dictatorship.[130] The chapter shows how in turn, the Prologue uses international law's promises to authorize the Truth Commission's resulting truth in a way that silences the truths about the dictatorship's socioeconomic violence.[131]

In Chapter 3, "Using the Language of International Law," I examine the relationship between Chile's 1990–1991 National Commission on Truth and Reconciliation and international human rights law, and the way this relationship continues to shape state-society in the aftermath of Pinochet's dictatorship (1973–1990). The argument in this chapter is twofold. First, I argue that the Truth Commission draws on the language of international human rights law to authorize its account as the 'major' truth. Second, in doing so, the Truth Commission displaces from public life 'minor' truths, specifically the experiences of state violence by Indigenous communities (here, the Mapuche people) and women (in this case, the Arpilleristas). The argument is based on an analysis of the representation of truth and authority embodied in Chile's Museo de la

(2010); Elizabeth S. Anker and Bernadette Meyler (eds), *New Directions in Law and Literature* (Oxford University Press, 2017). See Manderson's critique of using literature to redeem law in Manderson, *Kangaroo Courts*, 12–15. See generally, Peter Goodrich, *Law in the Courts of Love: Literature and Other Minor Jurisprudences* (Routledge, 1996); Adam Gearey, *Law and Aesthetics* (Hart Publishing, 2001); Kathleen Birrell, *Indigeneity: Before and Beyond the Law* (Routledge, 2016); Wan, *Masculinity and the Trials of Modern Fiction.*

129 Joseph R. Slaughter, "Enabling Fictions and Novel Subjects: The 'Bildungsroman' and International Human Rights Law," *PMLA*, vol 121, no 4 (2006): 1407.

130 On legal categories as technologies of jurisdiction see Dorsett and McVeigh, *Jurisdiction*, 71–76.

131 On how international law's promises were mobilized in Latin America in the late-Cold War see Dezalay and Garth, *The Internationalization of Palace Wars*, 61–72; 127–140. See also Vasuki Nesiah, "The Specter of Violence That Haunts the UDHR: The Turn to Ethics and Expertise," *Maryland Journal of International Law*, vol 24, no 1 (2009).

Memoria y los Derechos Humanos (Museum of Memory and Human Rights). I show how the Museo gives temporal continuity to the work of the Truth Commission by giving it a material (spatial and experiential) form. While the Truth Commission and the Museo remain two distinct institutions, in visiting the Museo/Truth Commission it becomes apparent how international human rights law is working to authorize the account of the Truth Commission, and, importantly, how the Museo gives continuity in public life to the Truth Commission's account and its displacement of the truths of the Mapuche and the Arpilleristas.

In Chapter 4, "Linking the 'Local' to the 'International'," I examine the role of international law and its institutions in El Salvador's UN Truth Commission (1992–1993). This Truth Commission was the first one to be established and fully operated by the UN,[132] after the end of the Cold War. The argument that I develop through the chapter is that this Truth Commission drew on the identity and status of the UN as an international institution to authorize its account about the unlawfulness of the violence of the civil war. In doing so, the Truth Commission's truth displaced 'other' coexisting and context-specific truths (in this case those of peasant and Indigenous communities) which rivalled international law's authorized understanding of the violence that had occurred. Excluding these truths about the socioeconomic circumstances that led to, and sustained, the civil war, allowed the UN Truth Commission to claim that it had contributed to making El Salvador a peacebuilding 'model' for post-conflict states. To show this, I examine the account of the truth produced by the Truth Commission alongside a rival account, which I encountered embroidered in a tapestry. The tapestry was handmade in the 1980s by a Salvadoran woman while she was living in a refugee camp run by the UNHCR in the neighboring country of Honduras, on El Salvador's northern border.[133] The tapestry represents the Masacre del Río Sumpul (Sumpul River Massacre),[134] which was investigated thirteen

[132] See note 15 above.

[133] Beth Cagan and Steve Cagan, *This Promised Land, El Salvador: The Refugee Community and Their Return to Morazán* (Rutgers University Press, 1991).

[134] Also called 'Masacre de Las Aradas.' See Asociación de Sobrevivientes de la Masacre del Sumpul, *Memorias del Sumpul: Testimonios del Genocidio contra Población Campesina Organizada en Las Aradas, Chalatenango, Mayo de 1980* (Equipo Maíz, 2019), 7.

years later by the country's Truth Commission and recorded in its Final Report.[135] Both the Truth Commission's Report and the tapestry record the same event, but they do it in different ways. By juxtaposing the tapestry's account with the Truth Commission's, I show how the tapestry exposes the socioeconomic roots leading to, and sustaining, the civil war – a truth that the Truth Commission's account displaces and renders irrelevant for post-conflict state-society relations.

Chapter 5, "Receiving Truth Commissions through International Law," is the book's 'exit' chapter. It examines how, in the 1990s, following the success of the Truth Commissions in Argentina, Chile, and El Salvador, this institution was given an 'origins story.' My argument is that this occurred through the retrospective redescription of Uganda's 1974 Commission of Inquiry as the 'inaugural' Truth Commission. The 1974 Commission of Inquiry was established as part of Idi Amin's response to growing international pressure from human rights groups, in particular the International Commission of Jurists' Report on state violence perpetrated by Idi Amin's government. In this chapter I discuss how the redescription of the 1974 Commission of Inquiry began after the Cold War, in 1990, with the publication of an article by Richard Carver,[136] and in 1994, with an article by Priscilla Hayner, who would go on to write the first book on Truth Commissions.[137] The central point in the redescription of the 1974 Commission of Inquiry as a 'Truth Commission' turns on the extent to which it is considered an institution that advanced human rights. By critically examining the redescription, it is possible to see how, from the very 'beginning,' the authority of Truth Commissions has depended on their connection to international law, especially human rights. Overall, the aim of the chapter is to conclude the book with an invitation: to consider how the authority of international was, and continues to be, central to the reception of Truth Commissions today.

[135] UN Doc S/25500 (1 April 1993), *From Madness to Hope*, 121–124.

[136] Carver was at that time the director of Africa Watch, a predecessor of Human Rights Watch. See Carver, "Called to Account," 391. See also, Aryeh Neier, *The International Human Rights Movement: A History* (Princeton University Press, 2012), 204–232.

[137] Hayner, "Fifteen Truth Commissions." See also, Hayner, *Unspeakable Truths.*

CHAPTER 2

Invoking the Promises of International Law

2.1 INTRODUCTION

I WALKED OUT OF THE BUILDING IN SEARCH of an open space where I could sit and have lunch. The building's backdoor led to a paved *caminito* (small narrow path) surrounded by modest garden beds and small trees. It was August 2018, late winter in Buenos Aires. I looked at the sky. It might rain, I thought. The trees had barely any leaves left but the buds on their branches announced that spring was around the corner. I did not want to get lost – not at the Escuela Superior de Mecánica de la Armada (Higher School of Mechanics of the Navy), now known as ex-ESMA.[1] So I stayed on the *caminito*. Would it be appropriate to do an ordinary and mundane activity – such as having lunch – at this place? I had been told that sometimes the relatives of the *desaparecidos* (disappeared people) would walk across the grounds of ex-ESMA. This was not just any public space, I kept reminding myself while silently walking. During Argentina's 1976–1983 military dictatorship, ex-ESMA was officially a training school for navy officers. But it also worked as one of the dictatorship's largest clandestine detention, torture, and extermination centers in Argentina.[2] The silence of the place, the austerity characterizing the site's architectural design, and the crumpling exterior walls of the building complex made it hard to ignore that ex-ESMA still held so much of the unimaginable pain and violence endured by the *desaparecidos* and their families.

1 Espacio Memoria y Derechos Humanos, "Historia." www.espaciomemoria.ar/historia/.
2 Espacio Memoria y Derechos Humanos, "Historia."

At the far end of the *caminito*, on the wall behind the trees, three black and white poster-size portraits stood in-between the tree trunks.[3] Because the trees were covering most of the portraits all I could see were eyes or half faces. The uneasiness I had been feeling since I walked into ex-ESMA that morning only increased. I did not dare to get closer to the portraits. What if someone was looking at me from inside the buildings? The more I walked around ex-ESMA, the more posters I encountered on the walls of its buildings. It then became clear that these were portraits of the *desaparecidos*.[4] Rationally, I knew that because of its history ex-ESMA would not be an easy place to visit. Yet, there was something deeply unsettling about the portraits.

Being before the portraits felt as if the *desparecidos* were there, in person, observing those coming and going – like me – and witnessing how everyday life unfolded on the grounds of ex-ESMA. It felt as if the *desaparecidos* were, here and now, guarding not only ex-ESMA's representation of the life they lived, but also why and how it ended. Overwhelmed, I looked at the sky once again. Instead of finding relief in the clearing skies, my eyes turned to the words *Memoria, Verdad, Justicia* (Memory, Truth, Justice). The words seemed thoughtfully placed on top of a water-tank tower overlooking ex-ESMA.[5] Neither memory nor justice had taken me all the way from Australia to Argentina. Truth had. Forty-one years ago, Argentina's Truth Commission, the Comisión Nacional sobre la Desaparición de Personas (National Commission on the Disappeared, or CONADEP),[6] concluded its investigation with the delivery of its Final

[3] Espacio Memoria y Derechos Humanos, "Presentes." www.espaciomemoria.ar/proyectos/presentes/.

[4] Ibid.

[5] A virtual audio tour is available in different languages here: Espacio Memoria y Derechos Humanos, "Visítanos." www.espaciomemoria.ar/visitanos/.

[6] I use CONADEP's name in English as it appears in the official translation of the Final Report in, Comisión Nacional sobre la Desaparición de Personas (CONADEP), *Nunca Más: The Report of the Argentine National Commission on the Disappeared* (Farrar, Straus, Giroux, 1986). CONADEP is considered the "first successful truth commission" (Zunino) and the earliest one that "receive[d] widespread international attention" (Hayner). See Marcos Zunino, *Justice Framed: A Genealogy of Transitional Justice* (Cambridge University Press, 2019), 72; Priscilla B. Hayner, "Fifteen Truth Commissions – 1974 to 1994: A Comparative Study," *Human Rights Quarterly*, vol 16, no 4 (1994), 614. See also, Carlos Santiago Nino, *Radical Evil on Trial* (Yale University

Report.[7] For the next weeks almost every day I returned to ex-ESMA, where the archives of Argentina's Truth Commission are held at the Archivo Nacional de la Memoria (National Archive of Memory).[8] In consulting the Archives, my purpose was to examine whether international law informed the way that the Truth Commission established its account of the truth.

Within Argentina, one of the achievements attributed to CONADEP is that the vast majority of Argentinians do not contest the fact of the dictatorship's forced disappearance of 30,000 people.[9] For the first democratic government after the dictatorship, the Final Report was important because it not only explained CONADEP's investigation (about the dictatorship's violence, understood as the country's 'past'), but also created an archival record that would ensure the dictatorship continued to be remembered in a particular way.[10] To that end, the government published the Final Report as a publicly accessible book, titled *Nunca Más: The Report of the Argentine National Commission on the Disappeared*, which became popularly known in Argentina as "*el Nunca Más*" (Never Again).[11] The *Nunca Más* reproduced the Final Report almost in its entirety, and can still be found in ordinary bookshops throughout the country.[12]

Press, 1996), 146; Ruti G. Teitel, *Transitional Justice* (Oxford University Press, 2000), 78–79; Cath Collins, Jemima Garcia-Godos, and Elin Skaar, *Transitional Justice in Latin America: The Uneven Road from Impunity Towards Accountability* (Routledge, 2016), 6.

7 See generally, CONADEP, *Nunca Más.*

8 Gobierno de la Argentina, Ministerio de Justicia, Secretaría de Derechos Humanos, "Archivo Nacional de la Memoria." www.argentina.gob.ar/derechoshumanos/ANM.

9 In Argentina, those who disappeared during the dictatorship are referred as the 'disappeared' ('*desaparecidos*'). In Chile, they are called the 'detained-disappeared' ('*detenidos-desaparecidos*'). According to Abuelas de Plaza de Mayo there were at least 30,000 *desaparecidos.* See Abuelas de Plaza de Mayo, "Historia." www.abuelas.org.ar/abuelas/historia-9.

10 Gobierno de la Argentina, *Decreto 187/83 Comisión Nacional sobre la Desaparición de Personas – Constitución – Integración y Funciones* (15 December 1983).

11 CONADEP, *Nunca Más.*

12 CONADEP, *Nunca Más: Informe de la Comisión Nacional sobre la Desaparición de Personas* (Eudeba; Kindle edition, 1985; 2011). The Final Report's list and technical information about each *desaparecido* was later updated and published. Comisión Nacional sobre la Desaparición de Personas (CONADEP), *Anexo del Nunca Más (2 Tomos)* (Eudeba, 2006).

Since the publication of the Final Report/*Nunca Más*, CONADEP and the other institutions established to shape the Argentinian state's transition from dictatorship to democracy between 1983 and 1989,[13] captured the imagination of scholars, practitioners, international organizations, and foreign governments around the world.[14] In particular, one of the legacies attributed to CONADEP is that of "initiat[ing] the cascade of truth commissions" across the world.[15] CONADEP is considered to have chartered a new and sophisticated nationally led institutional "model" through which post-conflict states could officially acknowledge the extent to which violent events caused past and ongoing suffering to individuals,

13 Although it is impossible to determine the precise moment of when a state 'begins' and 'concludes' a so-called political transition, for practical purposes my analysis focuses on the period between 1983 and 1989. In 1983 the Argentinian state formally changed – with general elections – from a dictatorial form of government to a democratic one, and established a set of public institutions to consolidate that change. The most well-known of those institutions are the CONADEP (1983–1984), the Junta Trials (1985–1986), and the 1986 and 1987 amnesty laws. See Nino, *Radical Evil*, 67–104; Zunino, *Justice Framed*, 62–67.

14 See for example, Hayner, "Fifteen Truth Commissions," 614; Neil J. Kritz (ed), *Transitional Justice: How Emerging Democracies Reckon with Former Regimes* (United States Institute of Peace Press, 1995); Nino, *Radical Evil*, 146; Teitel, *Transitional Justice*; Kathryn Sikkink and Carrie Walling Booth, "Argentina's Contribution to Global Trends in Transitional Justice," in *Transitional Justice in the Twenty-First Century: Beyond Truth versus Justice*, Naomi Roht-Arriaza and Javier Mariezcurrena (eds), (Cambridge University Press, 2006); Emilio A. Crenzel, "Argentina's National Commission on the Disappearance of Persons: Contributions to Transitional Justice," *International Journal of Transitional Justice*, vol 2, no 2 (2008); Paige Arthur, "How "Transitions" Reshaped Human Rights: A Conceptual History of Transitional Justice," *Human Rights Quarterly*, vol 31, no 2 (2009); Kathryn Sikkink, *The Justice Cascade: How Human Rights Prosecutions Are Changing World Politics* (W. W. Norton & Company, 2011); Lorena Balardini, "Argentina. Regional Protagonist of Transitional Justice," in *Transitional Justice in Latin America: The Uneven Road from Impunity Towards Accountability*, Cath Collins, Jemima Garcia-Godos, and Elin Skaar (eds), (Routledge, 2016); Zunino, *Justice Framed*, 72; Neha Jain and Sarah M. H. Nouwen, "North-South Skirmishes over Transitional Justice: 1975–2000," Jochen von Bernstorff, Philipp Dann, and Surabhi Ranganathan (eds), *The Battle for International Law II* (Oxford University Press, forthcoming); Alejandro Chehtman, "Latin America as a Laboratory of Transitional Justice," in *Latin American International Law in the Twenty- First Century*, Alejandro Chehtman, Alexandra Huneeus, and Sergio Puig (eds), (Oxford University Press, 2025), 420–421.

15 Sikkink and Walling Booth, "Argentina's Contribution to Global Trends in Transitional Justice," 306.

families, communities, and society at large.[16] It is then unsurprising that there is towering literature analyzing the global influence, overarching success, and limitations of CONADEP, as well as its contribution to pioneering,[17] from the Global South, an institution that has become a core case study in the research and practice of international human rights law and transitional justice.[18]

The Final Report/*Nunca Más* remains central in Argentina's public debates over exactly what happened, and the meanings attached to this history. At the heart of this debate is the state's truth about why the disappearances occurred, an account that is represented in the Prologue to the Final Report/*Nunca Más.* The contestation over the state's truth played out, once again, at the start of the twenty-first century. In 2006 the government of the day decided to rewrite the Prologue for a re-edition of the Final Report/*Nunca Más.*[19] In 2016, that rewrite was removed and replaced with the original 1984 Prologue by a new oppositional government (Mauricio Macri's conservative government). Then, at the end of 2023, the presidency of Javier Milei began to empower the narratives of groups who are sympathetic to the military's role during the dictatorship, and are active *negacionistas* [denialists] of the facts and narrative about the dictatorship's disappearances that CONADEP and its Prologue established.[20] These groups include members of parliament of Milei's party, as well as Milei's administration.[21] The *negacionistas* argue that they are committed to memory, truth, and justice but want to "tell the full history," as the government's spokesperson said in a press conference in 2025.[22]

[16] Ibid, 305–306. [17] Ibid, 305. [18] See note 14 above.

[19] Oliver Galak, "Controversia por el Prólogo agregado al Informe 'Nunca más'," *La Nación* (19 May 2006). www.lanacion.com.ar/politica/controversia-por-el-prologo-agregado-al-informe-nunca-mas-nid807208.

[20] La Nación, "Seis diputados de La Libertad Avanza visitaron a Astiz y a otros represores en la cárcel de Ezeiza y desataron una crisis en el bloque," *La Nación* (17 July 2024). www.lanacion.com.ar/politica/seis-diputados-de-la-libertad-avanza-visitaron-a-represores-condenados-en-la-carcel-de-ezeiza-y-nid17072024/.

[21] Rosa D'Alesio, "A 41 años. La Creación de la CONADEP: La Teoría de los Dos Demonios y el Impacto del Informe 'Nunca Más'," *La Izquierda Diario* (13 December 2024). www.laizquierdadiario.com/La-creacion-de-la-Conadep-la-teoria-de-los-dos-demonios-y-el-impacto-del-Informe-Nunca-Mas.

[22] ("contar la historia completa"). Gobierno de la Argentina, Subsecretaría de Vocería y Comunicación de Gobierno, "Anuncio del Vocero Presidencial – Día de la Memoria

The contemporary struggle over control of the Prologue points to the ongoing influence on Argentina's public life of CONADEP's authorized truth about the dictatorship. My argument in this chapter is that, through the Prologue of the Report/*Nunca* Más, CONADEP drew on international law's promises in a way that authorizes its account of the truth. In turn, CONADEP's truth establishes the unlawfulness of the dictatorship's state violence by interpreting and explaining that violence through a Eurocentric/Anglo-American lens embedded in a particular kind of international law circulating in the late-Cold War.[23] As I show throughout this chapter, the problem is that this made CONADEP's account of the dictatorship too vulnerable to the normativity of international law and the politics surrounding its mobilization, particularly in the Global South.

To develop this argument, I read the Prologue as a literary text that is doing international legal work. I show how the Prologue does that work even though CONADEP had a narrow mandate, to conduct a public investigation and not to develop an account of lawfulness about the dictatorship.[24] As mentioned in Chapter 1, this way of reading the Prologue, as a work of both

Completa" (24 March 2025). www.argentina.gob.ar/noticias/el-gobierno-del-presidente-milei-tiene-un-compromiso-inclaudicable-con-los-derechos-humanos.

[23] See Yves Dezalay and Bryant G. Garth, *The Internationalization of Palace Wars: Lawyers, Economists, and the Contest to Transform Latin American States* (University of Chicago Press, 2002). On the centrality of European empires' colonial project in the making of international law see Antony Anghie, *Imperialism, Sovereignty and the Making of International Law* (Cambridge University Press, 2005). On how international law suppresses its 'others' through its different technologies and institutions see Sundhya Pahuja, "Laws of Encounter: A Jurisdictional Account of International Law," *London Review of International Law,* vol 1, no 1 (2013); Shane Chalmers and Sundhya Pahuja, "(Economic) Development and the Rule of Law," in *The Cambridge Companion to the Rule of Law,* Martin Loughin and Jens Meierhenrich (eds), (Cambridge University Press, 2021); Shane Chalmers, *Liberia and the Dialectic of Law: Critical Theory, Pluralism, and the Rule of Law* (Routledge, 2018). For an ethnographic study about the consequences of mobilizing international law as 'standard' to measure local truth-telling processes, see Phil Clark, *The Gacaca Courts, Post-Genocide Justice and Reconciliation in Rwanda: Justice without Lawyers* (Cambridge University Press, 2010). On Global South jurists resisting international law, and fighting for a meeting of international laws, see Luis Eslava, Michael Fakhri, and Vasuki Nesiah (eds), *Bandung, Global History, and International Law: Critical Pasts and Pending Futures* (Cambridge University Press, 2017).

[24] Gobierno de la Argentina, *Decreto 187/83 Comisión Nacional sobre la Desaparición de Personas.*

literature and law, draws on scholarship in the field of 'law and literature.'[25] One of the contributions of this scholarship has been to show how international law "cooperates," or operates together, with literary works to create, reinforce, and deploy legal subjectivities according to particular normative worldviews.[26] My reading of the Prologue is informed in particular by Joseph

[25] For an overview of the field see Maria Aristodemou, *Law and Literature: Journeys from Her to Eternity* (Oxford University Press, 2000); Julie Stone Peters, "Law, Literature, and the Vanishing Real: On the Future of an Interdisciplinary Illusion," *PMLA*, vol 120, no 2 (2005); Desmond Manderson, *Kangaroo Courts and the Rule of Law: The Legacy of Modernism* (Routledge, 2012), 9; 20; Greta Olson, "De-Americanizing Law and Literature Narratives: Opening Up the Story," *Law & Literature*, vol 22, no 2 (2010); Elizabeth S. Anker and Bernadette Meyler (eds), *New Directions in Law and Literature* (Oxford University Press, 2017); Benjamin Goh, "Planetary Gifts of Law and Literature," *Law & Literature* (online first, March 2024); Shane Chalmers and Desmond Manderson, "Vortext," *Law & Literature*, vol 36, no 2 (2024). See Manderson's critique of using literature to redeem law in, Manderson, *Kangaroo Courts*, 12–15. See generally, Peter Goodrich, *Law in the Courts of Love: Literature and Other Minor Jurisprudences* (Routledge, 1996); Adam Gearey, *Law and Aesthetics* (Hart Publishing, 2001); Kathleen Birrell, *Indigeneity: Before and Beyond the Law* (Routledge, 2016); Marco Wan, *Masculinity and the Trials of Modern Fiction* (Routledge, 2017); Christopher Gevers, "International Law, Literature and Worldmaking," in *Routledge Handbook of International Law and the Humanities*, Shane Chalmers and Sundhya Pahuja (eds), (Routledge, 2021).

[26] Joseph R. Slaughter, *Human Rights, Inc.: The World Novel, Narrative Form, and International Law* (Fordham University Press, 2007), 4. Other scholars have also examined how literature and modern law, including international law, cooperate through Truth Commissions to create and deploy legal subjectivities, see generally, Vasuki Nesiah, "Discussion Lines on Gender and Transitional Justice: An Introductory Essay Reflecting on the ICTJ Bellagio Workshop on Gender and Transitional Justice," *Columbia Journal of Gender and Law*, vol 15, no 3 (2006); Anne Orford, "Commissioning the Truth," *Columbia Journal of Gender and Law*, vol 15, no 3 (2006); Claire Moon, "Narrating Political Reconciliation: Truth and Reconciliation in South Africa," *Social and Legal Studies*, vol 15, no 2 (2006); Mark Sanders, *Ambiguities of Witnessing: Law and Literature in the Time of a Truth Commission* (Stanford University Press, 2007); Elizabeth S. Anker, *Fictions of Dignity: Embodying Human Rights in World Literature* (Cornell University Press, 2012), 149–185; Adam Sitze, *The Impossible Machine: A Genealogy of South Africa's Truth and Reconciliation Commission* (University of Michigan Press, 2013); Carrol Clarkson, *Drawing the Line: Toward an Aesthetics of Transitional Justice* (Fordham University Press, 2013); Vasuki Nesiah, "The Trials of History: Losing Justice in the Monstrous and the Banal," in *Law in Transition: Human Rights, Development and Transitional Justice*, Ruth Buchanan and Peer Zumbansen (eds), (Bloomsbury, 2014); Valeria Vázquez Guevara, "Crafting the Lawful Truth: Chile's 1990 Truth Commission, International Human Rights and the Museum of Memory," *London Review of International Law*, vol 7,

Slaughter's work on the cooperative and "mutually enabling" relationship between international human rights law and literature.[27] For Slaughter this relationship is not so much about "a narratological alliance" between human rights and literary texts; rather, the relationship is fundamentally one of "complicity."[28] That is, literature does not occupy a domain separate from (international) law, but is complicit in "disseminating and naturalizing the norms of human rights" by "making them both legible and common-sensical" for society.[29] This is what is important for this book's argument: how the Prologue's engagement with international law generated a "mutually enabling" relationship,[30] which gave the Final Report/*Nunca Más* account both narrative coherency and authorized it for Argentinians, as well as internationally.

Specifically, my analysis shows how the Final Report/*Nunca Más* enabled CONADEP to authorize the unlawfulness of the dictatorship's state violence, in part because of the Prologue's literary form, or genre, as a *prologue*, and in part because of the language it used, which invoked the promises of international law, to describe and categorize events that occurred during the dictatorship.[31] In doing that, the Prologue creates a coherent, singular account of the violent conduct of the state under dictatorship, out of the disparate, plural accounts of the dictatorship's violence. At the same time, the Prologue uses international law's promises to authorize CONADEP's (and thus the state's) narrow account of the dictatorship's state violence as a coherent truth. These promises were carried by many international lawyers and human rights activists, and their narratives about how the establishment of a democracy under the rule of (international) law will put an end to all forms of state violence against society.[32] As I show in Section 2.3, a consequence of drawing on

no 2 (2019); Eliana Cusato, "International law, the Paradox of Plenty and the Making of Resource-Driven Conflict," *Leiden Journal of International Law*, vol 33, no 3 (2020).

27 See generally, Joseph R. Slaughter, "Enabling Fictions and Novel Subjects: The 'Bildungsroman' and International Human Rights Law," *PMLA*, vol 121, no 4 (2006). See also, Slaughter, *Human Rights, Inc.*

28 Slaughter, "Enabling Fictions," 1408. 29 Ibid. 30 Ibid, 1407.

31 On legal categories as technologies of jurisdiction see Shaunnagh Dorsett and Shaun McVeigh, *Jurisdiction* (Routledge, 2012), 71–76.

32 On mobilizing international law's promises in Latin America during the late-Cold War see Dezalay and Garth, *The Internationalization of Palace Wars*, 61–72; 127–140. See

those promises of international law has been the separation of the dictatorship's economic violence from the political violence in CONADEP's resulting account. This separation, and silencing of the economic aspect, is important because many of the *desaparecidos* were labor union or socioeconomic activists, and because of that, they (and their families) were subject to the dictatorship's state violence.

I begin in Section 3.2 of this chapter by focusing on the literary work that the Prologue does as a 'prologue' to the *Nunca Más*/Final Report, rather than as an 'introduction' or 'executive summary.' The analysis draws on records of CONADEP's sessions, which I obtained during a visit in 2018 to Argentina's Archivo Nacional de la Memoria (National Archive of Memory). The analysis shows how CONADEP's commissioners carefully designed the bi-partite structure of the Final Report/*Nunca Más*, to provide a normative account of the dictatorship. In Section 2.3, I then turn to the content (rather than the form) of the 1984 Prologue, to examine the language that it uses. To do this, I reread the Prologue in light of the major events and debates surrounding the creation of CONADEP in 1983, and the delivery of its Final Report in 1984, within the international context of the late-Cold War. The analysis shows how the Prologue, using international law's promises, authorizes 'the' meaning and interpretation of the dictatorship's unlawfulness according to a Eurocentric/Anglo-American worldview.[33] Finally, in Section 2.4, I show how CONADEP's account, as represented through the 1984

also, Vasuki Nesiah, "The Specter of Violence that Haunts the UDHR: The Turn to Ethics and Expertis," *Maryland Journal of International Law*, vol 24, no 1 (2009).

[33] There is a complex debate (beyond the scope of this book) as to whether Latin America is 'Western/Occidental.' In my view, it is important to highlight that categorizing Latin America as 'Western/Occidental' is underpinned by (to name a few): the racism of the Spanish colonial project in the Americas; the ongoing denial and extermination of the indigenous peoples and their laws; binary worldviews (e.g., civilized/savage; modern/traditional; developed/backward). For a critique of a Western/Occidental identity in Argentina see Ignacio Aguiló, *The Darkening Nation: Race, Neoliberalism and Crisis in Argentina* (University of Wales Press, 2018). On identity, race and international law in Colombia (also helpful to consider other Latin America countries) see Luis Eslava, "Trigueño International Law: On (Most of the World) being (Always, Somehow) Out of Place," in *Out of Place: Power, Person and Difference in Socio-Legal Research*, Lynette Chua and Mark Massoud (eds), (Cambridge University Press, 2024).

Prologue, continues to shape the meanings and interpretations of Argentina's 'past.' I do this by discussing the public debates sparked in 2006 by the Kirchner government's insertion of a new Prologue in the re-edition of the 1984 *Nunca Más*/Final Report, and how in 2016 the Macri government removed the 2006 Prologue and reinserted the original 1984 Prologue. The analysis shows how the literary form of the prologue, and the promises of international law, continue to shape Argentina's public life according to the internationally authorized truth of the day.

2.2 WRITING THE PROLOGUE, WRITING THE FINAL REPORT/ *NUNCA MÁS*

2.2.1 A FINAL REPORT "TO ENLIGHTEN". The minutes recording CONADEP's sessions reflect the care the commissioners took to ensure the Report/*Nunca Más* communicated to Argentinians, and the international community, a coherent truth about the dictatorship's state violence.[34] This sense of care was driven not only by the responsibility and complexity of having to produce a document on which the authorized truth about the dictatorship's state violence would rest, but also by the sociopolitical circumstances in which CONADEP was created and operated.[35]

As I explain in detail in Section 2.3 of this chapter, although the creation of CONADEP in 1983 was one of the first decisions taken by president Raúl Alfonsín,[36] it was not part of his government's original plan.[37] Alfonsín, from the political party Unión Cívica Radical,

[34] Minute No. 20-27, 80–109; Minute No. 37, 151–152, *Libro de Actas*, Fondo CONADEP, 1983–1984 (Archivo Nacional de la Memoria); Emilio A. Crenzel, *The Memory of the Argentina Disappearances: The Political History of Nunca Más*, trans by Laura Pérez Carrara (Routledge, 2012), 32–75.

[35] Ibid.

[36] Gobierno de la Argentina, *Decreto 187/83 Comisión Nacional sobre la Desaparición de Personas.*

[37] Diego Galante, *El Juicio a las Juntas: Discursos entre Política y Justicia en la Transición Argentina* (Universidad Nacional de General Sarmiento; Universidad Nacional de La Plata; Universidad Nacional de Misiones, 2019), 33; Nino, *Radical Evil*, 62–63; 73; Jaime Malamud-Goti, *Game Without End: State Terror and the Politics of Justice* (University of Oklahoma Press, 1996), 4; Crenzel, *The Memory of the Argentina Disappearances*, 38–39.

unexpectedly won the 1983 elections,[38] which were called by the military Junta after Argentina lost the 1982 Malvinas/Falklands War against the United Kingdom.[39] By then, it was impossible to deny publicly the fact that thousands of people disappeared during the dictatorship. It was impossible to deny, not only because the Junta itself confirmed the disappearances,[40] but more fundamentally, because of the years of struggle by relatives of the *desaparecidos* to expose the disappearances. In Argentina, in addition to the Madres and Abuelas de Plaza de Mayo's ongoing public demonstrations in front of the Casa Rosada (the executive government's offices), relatives of the *desaparecidos* legally registered the disappearances before a judge with the legal form of *habeas corpus*.[41] Internationally, many human rights organizations also published reports documenting the disappearances.[42] And yet, while the fact of the disappearances was no longer contested, what remained unanswered was *why* and *how* the disappearances occurred, and the whereabouts of the *desaparecidos*.

[38] Gobierno de la Argentina, Dirección Nacional Electoral, "Elecciones 1983" (30 October 1983).

[39] Horacio Verbitsky, *Malvinas: La Última Batalla de la Tercera Guerra Mundial* (Editorial Sudamericana, 2002).

[40] The Junta declared the *desaparecidos* dead in the "Documento Final," with which it aimed to stop public pressure. Radio y Televisión Argentina, "Cadena Nacional: Documento Final de la Junta Militar" (Archivo Histórico RTA, 1983). www.archivorta.com.ar/asset/cadena-nacional-documento-final-de-la-junta-militar/; Gobierno de la Argentina, Ministerio de Defensa, "Documento Final de la Junta Militar sobre la Guerra contra la Subversión y el Terrorismo (1983)," in "Actas de la Dictadura: Documentos de la Junta Militar Encontrados en el Edificio Cóndor (Tomo 6)," (2014). www.argentina.gob.ar/sites/default/files/actas_tomo6.pdf.

[41] Abuelas de Plaza de Mayo, "El Papel del Sistema de Justicia frente a las Violaciones Masivas de Derechos Humanos: Problemáticas Actuales" (2008), 20. On the international influence of Argentina's *desaparecidos* judicial process see Ariel E Dulitzky, "Argentina, Desapariciones Forzadas y el Sistema Interamericano de Derechos Humanos: A Propósito del Caso Julien-Grisonas," *Revista de Pensamiento Penal* (2020).

[42] Amnesty International, "Report of an Amnesty International Mission to Argentina, 6–15 November 1976" (1977); Inter-American Commission on Human Rights, Organization of the American States, "Report on the Situation of Human Rights in Argentina" (1980); Marina Franco, "El 'Documento Final' y las Demandas en torno a los Desaparecidos en la Última Etapa de la Dictadura Militar Argentina," *Antítesis*, vol 11, no 11 (2018).

In this context, Alfonsín committed himself and his government to provide an official answer about the *desaparecidos*, and to do so by putting the military on trial in a civilian court.[43] To do that, the government persuaded the congress to approve *Decreto 158/83*, to revoke the Junta's self-amnesty law.[44] Yet, even with *Decreto 158/83*, relatives of the *desaparecidos* and human rights organizations were skeptical that a trial would ever take place.[45] For that reason, they proposed to the government the creation of a parliamentary investigatory commission, comprising members of congress from all political parties, with a mandate to find the *desaparecidos* and the circumstances in which they went missing.[46] Against this, the government considered that the political circumstances would make it impossible for political parties to work together.[47] Instead, the government proposed the creation of a "special commission of notables" or of "citizens,"[48] comprising activists or members of prominent human rights organizations, well-known and respected in "public life" for their "commitment to the defense of democracy and human rights."[49] In this way, the moral and political reputation of the individuals appointed as commissioners would be a source of authority for CONADEP before Argentinian society, and internationally.

43 Raúl Alfonsín, "No es Palabra Final: Respuesta del candidato Alfonsín al 'Documento Final'" (2 May 1983). www.desaparecidos.org/arg/doc/secretos/candi.html.

44 Raúl Alfonsín, *Memoria Política: Transición a la Democracia y Derechos Humanos; con prólogo de Juan Carlos Portantiero* (Fondo de Cultura Económica, 2009), 37. See also, Presidencia de la Nación Argentina, *Ley 22.924 de Pacificación Nacional* (22 September 1983). Gobierno de la Argentina, *Decreto 158/83* (13 December 1983).

45 Alfonsin, Memoria Política; Presidencia de la Nación Argentina, *Ley 22.924*; Gobierno de la Argentina, *Decreto 158/83*; Emilio Mignone, *Derechos Humanos y Sociedad: El Caso Argentino* (Centro de Estudios Legales y Sociales; Ediciones del Pensamiento Social, 1991), 156–157.

46 Nino, *Radical Evil*, 72; Alfonsín, *Memoria Política*, 39; Mignone, *Derechos Humanos y Sociedad*, 158; Crenzel, *The Memory of the Argentina Disappearances*, 37.

47 Alfonsín, *Memoria Política*, 39.

48 Crenzel, *The Memory of the Argentina Disappearances*, 37–38 ("ciudadanos"). Raúl Alfonsín, "Prólogo," in *Juicio Al Mal Absoluto: ¿Hasta Dónde Debe Llegar la Justicia Retroactiva en Casos de Violaciones Masivas de los Derechos Humanos?*, Carlos Santiago Nino, trans by Martín Böhmer (Siglo Veintiuno Editores, 2015), 22.

49 ("vida pública"); ("compromiso con la defensa de la democracia y los derechos humanos"). Alfonsín, *Memoria Política*, 40.

Following a similar institutional design to commissions of inquiry used in common law countries (especially the United States),[50] CONADEP was created with presidential decree *Decreto 187/83* (*Decreto*), just a few days after Alfonsín's inaugural address.[51] The *Decreto* authorized CONADEP to "clarify the facts related to the disappearance of people in the country."[52] The *Decreto* also stated that CONADEP's investigation was an "issue" that "transcend[ed] public powers,"[53] because the "facts" that it was charged with investigating concerned "grave violations of human rights."[54] Furthermore, the *Decreto* declared that the investigation was a response to "the legitimate interest[s]" of both Argentinian "civil society" and the "international community."[55] In light of that, the *Decreto* established that the investigation's outcome would be recorded in the form of a "report," which would "offer a detailed explanation of the facts investigated" in order to "enlighten national and international public opinion" about the "tragic episodes in which thousands of people disappeared" in Argentina.[56]

The commissioners began work in December 1983 in Buenos Aires. Nine months later, CONADEP formally delivered the Final Report/*Nunca Más* to Alfonsín in a televised ceremony at the Casa Rosada.[57] During the

50 Crenzel, *The Memory of the Argentina Disappearances*, 37–38; 159 at 18. According to Crenzel CONADEP "was modeled on special civil society commissions set up by the United States Congress to deal with specific issues," see in Emilio A. Crenzel, "Argentina's National Commission on the Disappearance of Persons: Contributions to Transitional Justice," *International Journal of Transitional Justice*, vol 2, no 2 (2008), 177. On the similarities between Truth Commissions and commissions of inquiry see Jennifer Balint, Julie Evans, and Nesam McMillan, "Justice Claims in Colonial Contexts: Commissions of Inquiry in Historical Perspective," *Australian Feminist Law Journal*, vol 42, no 1 (2016).

51 Gobierno de la Argentina, *Decreto 187/83 Comisión Nacional sobre la Desaparición de Personas.*

52 ("esclarecer los hechos relacionados con la desaparición de personas ocurridos en el país"). Ibid.

53 ("la cuestión de los derechos humanos trasciende a los poderes públicos"). Ibid.

54 ("los hechos"); ("gravísimas violaciones a los derechos humanos"). Ibid.

55 ("el interés legítimo"); ("sociedad civil"); ("comunidad internacional"). Ibid.

56 ("informe"); ("que ofrezca una explicación detallada de los hechos investigados, que sirva para ilustrar a la opinión pública nacional e internacional"); ("los trágicos episodios en los que desaparecieron miles de personas"). Ibid.

57 Radio y Televisión Argentina, "Entrega del Informe de la CONADEP" (Archivo Histórico RTA, 1984). www.archivorta.com.ar/asset/entrega-del-informe-de-la-conadep-20-09-1984/.

ceremony, CONADEP's president, internationally renowned Argentinian writer Ernesto Sábato, handed over the Final Report/*Nunca Más*, and gave a speech. The words that Sábato read were excerpts of the Prologue.[58] Alfonsín then expressed his gratitude to the commissioners for their service to the nation.[59] Regarding the Final Report/*Nunca Más*, Alfonsín proclaimed "the country . . . needed to know *the truth* about what happened because on the basis of a lie or of darkness we cannot build national unity."[60] With this ceremony, the Final Report/*Nunca Más* began to fulfill the purpose that the state had envisioned for it: "to enlighten" Argentinian society, and the international community, with its account.[61]

And yet, for CONADEP's truth to have such "enlighten[ing]" power,[62] the commissioners knew it was necessary to do more than merely report in writing the findings of the investigation. They knew not only that the Report/*Nunca Más* had to communicate publicly a coherent answer about how and why the disappearances had occurred, but also that its content – its truth – had to carry a clear ethical judgment about the state's wrongdoing.

2.2.2 WRITING THE PROLOGUE. The idea of a bipartite structure for the Final Report/*Nunca Más*, and the choice of the Prologue as its introductory text, emerged from three concerns: the Final Report/*Nunca Más* had to present a coherent narrative about the victims' experiences of state violence; it had to be compelling and intelligible, primarily to Argentinians but also to the international community; and it had to have very broad social reach.[63]

To address these concerns, from the early stages of the drafting process the commissioners worked on giving the Final Report/*Nunca Más* an accessible structure and language.[64] To achieve that, the

58 Ibid. 59 Ibid.

60 ("el país . . . necesita saber *la verdad* acerca de lo que pasó porque sobre la base de la mentira o de la oscuridad no podemos construir la unión nacional"). Ibid. Italics mine.

61 ("para ilustrar"). Gobierno de la Argentina, *Decreto 187/83 Comisión Nacional sobre la Desaparición de Personas.*

62 Ibid.

63 Minute No. 27, 108; Minute No. 28, 109; Minute No. 30, 115–116; Minute No. 37, 154; Minute No. 39, 158, *Libro de Actas*, Fondo CONADEP.

64 Ibid.

commissioners created a Drafting Commission,[65] which they decided should be assisted by "a trustworthy journalist."[66] This would ensure that all of the theme-specific "essays" written by CONADEP's investigatory committees would be coherently integrated in the report.[67] Additionally, the commissioners considered the writing of a prologue as the Final Report/*Nunca Más*'s opening text.[68]

A draft of the Prologue was ready a little over a month before the Final Report/*Nunca Más* was due in late September 1984. It was Sábato who introduced it as "a project of a prologue" to the commissioners.[69] While the minutes of the sessions do not record whose idea it was to choose that specific literary genre to open the Final Report/*Nunca Más*, what is recorded is that the Prologue was deemed important because it "would contain the essential points of the Report."[70] Even though the commissioners carefully thought through the relationship between the Prologue and the body of the Final Report/*Nunca Más*, as a literary genre the Prologue carried with it a particular function. From a literary point of view, a prologue is understood to "provide a directional framework for the reader" prior to reading (or viewing, in the case of performances) the main body of the literary work.[71] Although the specific "directional" function of the prologue depends on the literary genre of the text that

65 Drafting Commission members: Graciela Fernández Meijide (teacher; CONADEP Secretary of Depositions; her son Pablo is among the *desaparecidos*), Alberto Mansur (lawyer; CONADEP-Secretary of Legal Affairs), Ernesto Sábato (writer; CONADEP president), Eduardo Rabossi (analytic legal philosopher), and Carlos Gattinoni (Protestant-Methodist pastor). Minute No. 27, 108, *Libro de Actas*, Fondo CONADEP.

66 ("periodista de confianza"). Minute No. 27, 108, *Libro de Actas*/Fondo CONADEP. The name of the journalist is only recorded as 'Gazola' in Minute No. 37, *Libro de Actas*, Fondo CONADEP.

67 In the final writing stage, they are called "essays" (Minutes No. 39, 158). At the beginning they are called "ideas" or "themes" (Minutes No. 24, 99–100), and later "ideas in writing" (Minutes No. 30, 116). *Libro de Actas*, Fondo CONADEP.

68 Minute No. 30, 116, *Libro de Actas*, Fondo CONADEP.

69 ("un proyecto de prólogo"). Minute No. 36, 149, *Libro de Actas*, Fondo CONADEP. See also, Crenzel, *The Memory of the Argentina Disappearances*, 67.

70 ("contendría los puntos esenciales del Informe"). Minute No. 30, 116, *Libro de Actas*, Fondo CONADEP.

71 Elizabeth Dearnley, *Translators and their Prologues in Medieval England* (Boydell and Brewer, D. S. Brewer, 2016), 2.

follows it (e.g., a novel, poem, play, etc.),[72] in general terms prologues "have introductory features *to something*."[73] Through a prologue, the audience gains "insights into the way in which a text was composed, and the attitudes which led to its creation, which are rarely found elsewhere."[74] With a prologue, the author aims to "compel" the reader "to take a position ... in relation to" a text's story.[75] In other words, despite being a 'minor' literary text that complements a 'major' one, through a prologue the author seeks to create a desired affective bond between the story narrated in the main text and its audience.[76]

Yet, as Slaughter reminds us, the use of preambles or prologues as compelling introductory texts is not exclusive to literature, nor have they only been used by writers or playwrights.[77] In the field of law, literary genres have a history of "cooperation in naturalizing" and deploying law's normative arrangements of how to live together.[78] Lawmakers frequently turn to prologues (typically called 'preambles' in law) as the literary device that offers a socially accessible explanation of a law's "origins and purposes," with the aim of making it normatively accepted.[79] Generally, through such prologues, legislators "place the law in its historical and political context,"[80] and provide "reasons to assist in understanding" the "object of the law."[81] Yet, despite being common across different legal fields, prologues are especially prominent in constitutions and international treaties.[82] In constitutions, lawmakers include a preambular section to "set

[72] On the varying role of a prologue, see Alberto Porqueras Mayo, *El Prólogo como Género Literario: Su Estudio en el Siglo de Oro Español* (Consejo Superior de Investigaciones Científicas, 1957).

[73] ("su carácter introductorio *a algo*"). Ibid, 100. Emphasis in original.

[74] Dearnley, *Translators and Their Prologues*, 2.

[75] Gérard Genette, *Paratexts: Thresholds of Interpretation*, trans by Jane E. Lewin (Cambridge University Press, 1997), 224.

[76] Ibid, 212.

[77] See especially chapter 1 of Slaughter, *Human Rights, Inc.* See also, Shane Chalmers, "The Beginning of Human Rights: The Ritual of the Preamble to Law," *Humanity*, vol 9, no 1 (2018).

[78] Slaughter, "Enabling Fictions," 1419.

[79] Wim Voermans, Maarten Stremler, and Paul Cliteur, *Constitutional Preambles: A Comparative Analysis* (Edward Elgar, 2017), 9.

[80] Ibid, 6. [81] Chalmers, "The Beginning of Human Rights," 109.

[82] See Marie Theres Fögen, "The Legislator's Monologue: Notes on the History of Preambles," *Chicago-Kent Law Review*, vol 70 (1995); Chalmers, "The Beginning of

the tone for the subsequent constitutional text," and, in many cases, to ensure that the constitution's articles are "read and interpreted" as a coherent text.[83] In international law, prologues are also frequently used to "defin[e] in general terms, the purposes and considerations that led the parties to conclude the treaty," and "may also incorporate the parties' motivations for concluding the treaty by describing the foundation of their past, present, and future relations."[84] Put differently, prologues allow lawmakers to narrate "a creation story" about the "need" for a new legal form to reorganize international or state-society relations.[85] Narrating such a need in an accessible and compelling form gives the law social reach, ensuring that its normative content is known and, importantly, accepted.

Similarly, in the circumstances in which the Final Report/*Nunca Más* was written, through its final structure the Prologue deployed a normative narrative that directs its audiences as to how to interpret the body of the Final Report/*Nunca Más.*[86] In doing so, CONADEP, and by extension the state, could shape not only how the past would be remembered, but also how a future life in a lawful democracy would be imagined. During the drafting process of the Final Report/*Nunca Más*, the commissioners looked for ways to transmit to its audience how unethical, and how unlawful, the state's violence was against Argentinian society, and ultimately, against "humanity."[87] Many commissioners felt an ethical responsibility to produce the Final Report/*Nunca Más*, regardless of the fact that they were required to do it by the *Decreto.*[88] One of them emphasized that it was not a "political" but "a spiritual necessity"[89] to give the report a "form and content" faithful to the gravity

Human Rights"; Makane Moïse Mbengue, "Preamble," in *Max Planck Encyclopedia of Public International Law*, Rüdiger Wolfrum (ed), (Oxford University Press, 2006).

83 Voermans, Stremler, and Cliteur, *Constitutional Preambles*, 90.

84 Mbengue, "Preamble."

85 Chalmers, "The Beginning of Human Rights," 111.

86 Caroline Levine, *Forms: Whole, Rhythm, Hierarchy, Network* (Princeton University Press, 2015), 5; Chalmers, "The Beginning of Human Rights," 1.

87 CONADEP, *Nunca Más*, 2.

88 Minutes No. 20, 86; and Minute No. 24, 99-100, *Libro de Actas*, Fondo CONADEP. See also, Crenzel, *The Memory of the Argentina Disappearances*, 32–75.

89 ("necesidad espiritual"); ("política"). Minute No. 20, 86, *Libro de Actas*, Fondo CONADEP. See also, Crenzel, *The Memory of the Argentina Disappearances*, 32–75.

of the evidence gathered throughout the investigation.[90] CONADEP's minutes show how the commissioners understood that part of their public responsibility was to ensure that the Final Report/*Nunca Más* would "mar[k] a limit" by "making an ethical decision" about what was wrong and right in state-society relations.[91] Drawing that ethical line was fundamental, because it would publicly represent a normative threshold in the social imaginary between two forms of organizing state-society relations: dictatorship and democracy.[92] Importantly, while the dictatorship would be represented as the unethical and unlawful 'past,' democracy would be the ethically lawful 'future.' CONADEP's truth would enable Argentinian state-society relations to transition from being wrongful and in a state of "darkness,"[93] to being rightful and enlightened. But to leave the dictatorship behind and bring about democracy, CONADEP's truth needed to be socially known and normatively accepted. As the deadline for the Final Report/*Nunca Más* approached, Sábato became especially concerned that these objectives would be met.

Aware of the risk that the Final Report/*Nunca Más* could be written in a highly technical language (even with the assistance of a journalist), Sábato emphasized to the commissioners that "a basically technical book will not be read widely, that is why it is important to make it dramatic, which can be achieved with the transcription of testimonies."[94] Commissioner Horacio Huarte agreed with Sábato, and proposed that it was "necessary" to structure the report in two clearly distinct parts.[95] One part would set out the "facts," which would give the report "force . . . through objective content."[96] The other part would impart "a message for the people"; it would be "a general part, which reaches all sectors" and has "a broad political content."[97] CONADEP's minutes show how, for the

90 ("forma y contenido"). Minute No. 23, 92–94, *Libro de Actas*, Fondo CONADEP.

91 Clarkson, *Drawing the Line*, 1. 92 Ibid, 18.

93 Radio y Televisión Argentina, "Entrega del Informe de la CONADEP."

94 ("un libro básicamente técnico no será leído masivamente, por lo que es importante cargarlo de dramaticidad lo cual se logra fundamentalmente con la transcripción de testimonios"). Minute No. 37, 152, *Libro de Actas*, Fondo CONADEP.

95 ("necesario"). Ibid.

96 ("hechos"); ("fuerza . . . a través del contenido objetivo"). Ibid.

97 ("un mensaje a la población; . . . una parte general, que llegue a todos los sectores"); ("un contenido político amplio"). Ibid.

commissioners, given the fragility of the situation, the priority was to make the normative meaning of CONADEP's truth accessible and intelligible.

Indeed, the seemingly simple structure of the Final Report/*Nunca Más* was not so simple.[98] The commissioners used the Prologue to communicate a coherent and unitary narrative about the dictatorship's state violence, while guiding its audiences on how to interpret the un/lawfulness of the events. To that end, Sábato commissioned Gerardo Taratuto (a lawyer, playwright, and screenwriter of the TV documentary on CONADEP's investigation, also titled *Nunca Más*) to "participate in the drafting."[99] The minutes record how, from that moment until the delivery of the Final Report/*Nunca Más,* Taratuto's role was fundamental in giving the Final Report/*Nunca Más* narrative coherency and dramatic appeal.[100] In the resulting final form of the Final Report/*Nunca Más*, the Prologue would "frame,"[101] in general political terms, the emergence of state violence and how the dictatorship practiced it, while the body of the Final Report/*Nunca Más* would reproduce the testimonies and facts. By communicating this narrative to public audiences (primarily Argentinian, but also internationally), the Prologue sought to establish a particular normative interpretation of the unlawfulness of state violence during the dictatorship.

It is that aim, of *authorizing* the new shared imaginary of lawful state-society relations, that points to the ways in which there is a "mutually enabling" relationship between international law and the Prologue as a literary genre.[102] I now turn to unpack the Prologue's text, and to

[98] On how literary "simple forms" manifest worldviews see André Jolles, *Simple Forms: Legend, Saga, Myth Riddle, Saying Case, Memorabile Fairytale, Joke* trans by Peter J. Schwartz (Verso, 2017).

[99] ("participe en su redacción"). Minute No. 38, 156; and Minute No. 29, 115, *Libro de Actas,* Fondo CONADEP. See also Crenzel, *The Memory of the Argentina Disappearances,* 57; 68–71.

[100] Minute No. 42, 173, Minute No. 38, 156, *Libro de Actas,* Fondo CONADEP. Taratuto's role raised doubts (even among commissioners) about the authorship of the Prologue, which is, in Argentina and elsewhere, attributed to Sábato. Taratuto denied it and said that "the prologue was 'all Sábato'," in Crenzel, *The Memory of the Argentina Disappearances,* 68; 70.

[101] Brian W. Schneider, *The Framing Text in Early Modern English Drama: 'Whining' Prologues and 'Armed' Epilogues* (Ashgate, 2011), 28.

[102] Slaughter, "Enabling Fictions," 1407.

discuss how the Prologue invokes the promises of international law to authorize as truthful the account about the dictatorship's unlawfulness.

2.3 READING THE PROLOGUE: INTERNATIONAL LAW'S PROMISES FOR ARGENTINA

The Prologue begins not only by broadly situating in time (the 1970s) and place (Argentina) the sociopolitical context in which the dictatorship's violence emerged, but also by describing it as being "torn by terror."[103] However, this 'terrorism' was not unique to Argentinian society. According to the Prologue, it was a general "phenomenon" that occurred in other states, such as Italy.[104] The Prologue presents the Italian state's response to "the heartless attacks of Fascist groups, the Red Brigades, and other similar organizations" as an example to follow.[105] The Prologue describes the conduct of the Italian state as one that "[n]ever at any time . . . abandon-[ed] the principles of law in its fight against . . . terrorists," and that "managed to resolve the problem through the normal courts of law."[106] The Prologue sets this in opposition to what the dictatorial Argentinian state had done.[107] The conduct of the Argentinian state, since the coup d'état on "24 March 1976," is presented as more like that of "an absolute state,"[108] which "misuse[s]" its "power" to "abduct, torture and kill thousands of human beings."[109] Furthermore, the Argentinian state's conduct in response to the "terrorist crimes" is described as "far worse than the one [terrorist groups] they were combating."[110]

In Argentina, one predominant way of interpreting the Prologue, particularly through its opening paragraph, is to focus on whether it institutionalizes the *teoría de los dos demonios* (theory of two demons).[111] The most common understanding of this theory is that it seeks "to explain the violence of the past" that occurred during the 1970s "as

[103] CONADEP, *Nunca Más*, 1. [104] Ibid. [105] Ibid. [106] Ibid. [107] Ibid, 1.
[108] Ibid. [109] Ibid. [110] Ibid.
[111] Marina Franco, "La 'Teoría de los Dos Demonios': Un Símbolo de la Posdictadura en la Argentina," *A Contra Corriente: A Journal on Social History and Literature in Latin American*, vol 11, no 2 (2014); Emilio A. Crenzel, "Dos Prólogos para un mismo Informe. El Nunca Más y la Memoria de las Desapariciones," *Prohistoria*, vol 9, no 11 (2007).

being the responsibility and outcome of *two opposing forms of violence*,"[112] one being the state, the other the guerrilla groups, such as Los Monteros and Ejército Revolucionario del Pueblo-Partido Revolucionario de los Trabajadores. According to Argentinian historian Marina Franco, the theory's meaning largely depends on who is using it and for what purpose.[113] For those who support this theory, it is understood to justify the dictatorship's state violence, as a legitimate means of protecting the state and society against the violence caused by "the guerrillas of the left."[114] In this view, "left-wing" political groups have "causal responsibility in starting the violence" before and during the dictatorship.[115] Those who oppose the theory consider that it aims to "equat[e] the violence" of both the state and guerrilla/left-wing groups, giving both sides "symmetry of strength and/or methods" in prosecuting the violence, and ultimately assigns "equa[l] historical responsibilities" for the conflict.[116]

For many, especially groups of relatives of the *desaparecidos*, such as the Madres de Plaza de Mayo, the Prologue signals the state's support for the theory of two demons.[117] In 2006, Hebe de Bonafini (then president of the Madres), in expressing her explicit disapproval of the 1984 Prologue and endorsing the Kirchner government's decision to write a new prologue for the re-edition of the Report/*Nunca Más*, said "our children were not demons: they were revolutionaries, wonderful and unique guerrilla members who defended the motherland."[118] As this suggests,

112 ("la explicación del pasado de violencia de los años setenta"); ("como responsabilidad y resultado de *dos violencias enfrentadas*"). Franco, "La 'Teoría de los Dos Demonios'," 26. Emphasis in original.

113 Ibid. 114 ("las guerrillas de izquierda"). Ibid, 25.

115 ("la responsabilidad causal de la izquierda en el inicio de la violencia"). Ibid, 24.

116 ("equiparación entre ambas violencias"); ("responsabilidades históricas"); ("simetría de fuerzas y/o de métodos"). Ibid.

117 Marguerite Guzmán Bouvard, *Revolutionizing Motherhood: The Mothers of the Plaza de Mayo* (Scholarly Resources Inc., 1994), 134–137; Berber Bevernage, *History, Memory, and State-Sponsored Violence: Time and Justice* (Routledge, 2011), 38–43.

118 ("Nuestros hijos no eran demonios: eran revolucionarios, guerrilleros maravillosos y únicos que defendieron a la patria"). As quoted in Greg Grandin, "Living in Revolutionary Time: Coming to Terms with the Violence of Latin America's Long Cold War," in *A Century of Revolution: Insurgent and Counterinsurgent Violence During Latin America's Long Cold War*, Greg Grandin and Gilbert M. Joseph (eds), (Duke University Press, 2010), 37 at note 35. Bonafini made similar remarks. See Asociación Madres de Plaza de Mayo, "Hebe De Bonafini: Las Madres Necesitamos que

what is at stake in the Prologue, and in particular its opening sentences, is the question of whether CONADEP, and thus the state, sought to equate the violence of guerrilla/left-wing groups *prior* to the dictatorship with the violence of the 1976–1983 dictatorship.

Interpreting the Prologue only through the theory of two demons, however, frames the Prologue's narrative as being just 'an Argentinian problem' that needed, and was given, 'an Argentinian solution' in the transition to democracy.[119] But if the opening paragraph is interpreted in a broader international context, not only in which the Prologue was written, but also in which the dictatorship occurred, then the 'problem' and 'solution' begin to take on a more global significance.

With the opening paragraph, the Prologue situates the 'Argentinian problem' in an international context that held great significance in Latin America: the Cold War.[120] The interventions of the Western Bloc, led by the United States, and the Eastern Bloc, led by the United Soviet Socialist Republic (USSR), in the public life of many Latin American states during this period, shaped social, political, economic and legal relations between, and within, them.[121] As the renowned Mexican writer Octavio Paz wrote, "the models of development that today are offered to us by the West and the East are compendiums of horrors: can we invent more human models that correspond to what we are?"[122] Paz's words were a critique of what seemed to be an impossible endeavor for many Latin American states: to

Reconozcan a Nuestros Hijos y a Nuestras Hijas como Revolucionarios que Dieron su Vida por esta Patria" (21 April 2022). https://madres.org/index.php/marcha-n-2297-de-las-madres-de-plaza-de-mayo/.

119 On this see Anne Orford, "Locating the International: Military and Monetary Interventions after the Cold War," *Harvard International Law Journal*, vol 38, no 2 (1997), 449–450; 481.

120 See generally, Greg Grandin, *The Last Colonial Massacre: Latin America in the Cold War* (University of Chicago Press, 2011); Odd Arne Westad, *The Global Cold War: Third World Interventions and the Making of Our Times* (Cambridge University Press, 2007); William Blum, *Killing Hope: US Military and CIA Interventions since World War II* (Common Courage Press, 1995).

121 Grandin, *The Last Colonial Massacre*; Westad, *The Global Cold War*; Blum, *Killing Hope*.

122 ("Los modelos de desarrollo que hoy nos ofrecen el Oeste y el Este son compendios de horrores: ¿podremos nosotros inventar modelos más humanos y que correspondan a lo que somos?"). Octavio Paz, "Nota," in *Postdata* (Fondo de Cultura Económica, 1970; 2004), 237.

create their own ways to live together within the state – and importantly, to do so outside the Cold War's ideological paradigms embedded in the models of United States liberalism and USSR communism. In this context, the internal socioeconomic and political struggles that many Latin American states were going through since before the Cold War did not cease, but rather took on an internationalized dimension. Struggles – or revolutions – to address socioeconomic inequalities were caught between what Paz called "the models of development,"[123] actively promoted on both sides of the Cold War as mutually exclusive solutions to all of Latin America's deep-rooted and longstanding socioeconomic problems.[124]

Reading the Prologue in light of the late-Cold War years anticipates the 'post-conflict state-building' (via 'peacebuilding') model which international law and its institutions would formally promote after the Cold War in the 1990s.[125] In particular, the Prologue deploys a subtle yet powerful account of how international law offers a 'state-building model' to lay 'civilizing' legal foundations for state-society relations in the aftermath of violent conflict. That model *promised* to deliver the kind of peace, justice, and economic prosperity enjoyed by the states in the Global North, through the embrace of democracy, the rule of law, and economic prescriptions for 'development,' so that states in the Global

123 Ibid.

124 Although it is beyond the scope of this chapter, it is worth noting how actors in the Global South resisted and actively challenged Western approaches to international law and development project. See for example, Walter D. Mignolo, *The Darker Side of Western Modernity: Global Futures, Decolonial Options* (Duke University Press, 2011); Arturo Escobar, *Encountering Development: The Making and Unmaking of the Third World* (Princeton University Press, 2012); Arnulf Becker Lorca, *Mestizo International Law: A Global Intellectual History 1842–1933* (Cambridge University Press, 2014); Eslava, Fakhri, and Nesiah, *Bandung, Global History, and International Law*; Jochen von Bernstorff and Philipp Dann (eds), *The Battle for International Law: South-North Perspectives on the Decolonization Era* (Oxford University Press, 2019); Jessica Whyte, *The Morals of the Market: Human Rights and the Rise of Neoliberalism* (Verso, 2019), 75–115.

125 Sundhya Pahuja, *Decolonising International Law: Development, Economic Growth, and the Politics of Universality* (Cambridge University Press, 2011), 172–253. Coined by Secretary-General Annan as "post-conflict peace-building," in UN Doc A/47/277–S/24111 (17 June 1992), *An Agenda for Peace: Preventive Diplomacy, Peacemaking and Peace-keeping: Report of the Secretary-General pursuant to the statement adopted by the Summit Meeting of the Security Council on 31 January 1992.*

South could finally be "free from either [Western or Eastern] pole," and thus become masters of their own destiny.[126]

2.3.1 REALIZING INTERNATIONAL LAW'S PROMISES: 'SAVING' ARGENTINA (AND THE SOUTH). The transition from dictatorship to democracy that Argentina officially began in 1983 seemed to be the moment to realize international law's promises.[127] After a longer history of predominantly US interventions in Latin America – not limited to the Cold War[128] – Alfonsín's government remained concerned with interventions in Argentina's post-dictatorial public life.[129] That concern was also coupled with the pressing need to establish credible legal grounds for democratic and nonviolent state-society relations in the post-dictatorship. Alfonsín's government attempted to address that concern through the creation of CONADEP (1983) and the Junta Trials (1985) – the transition's signature public institutions. While CONADEP was set up to establish 'the truth' about the dictatorship's state violence, the Junta Trials would bring about 'justice.'[130] In other words, both 'truth' and 'justice' would be authorized by the Argentinian state. For Carlos Nino – Alfonsín's closest adviser, and directly involved in designing CONADEP and the Junta Trials – the transition demonstrated that there was no need for the international community to push for "an international duty to punish human rights violations of a prior regime,"[131] notably in the form of

126 Matthew Craven, Sundhya Pahuja, and Gerry Simpson (eds), *International Law and the Cold War* (Cambridge University Press, 2019), 3.

127 See note 13 above.

128 On how the Junta adopted the US's 'national security doctrine,' see Fernando López, "The Feathers of Cóndor: Transnational State Terrorism, Exiles and Civilian Anticommunism in South America" (PhD Thesis, University of New South Wales, 2014). Scarfi develops two excellent historical accounts of how the operation of international law in Latin American states was determined by United States' imperialism, see Juan Pablo Scarfi, *The Hidden History of International Law in The Americas: Empire and Legal Networks* (Oxford University Press, 2017); Juan Pablo Scarfi, *El Imperio de la Ley: James Brown Scott y la Construcción de un Orden Jurídico Interamericano* (Fondo de Cultura Económica, 2014).

129 Nino, *Radical Evil*, 186–189; Alfonsín, *Memoria Política*, 33–39.

130 Malamud-Goti, *Game Without End*, 59–60; Nino, *Radical Evil*, 81; CONADEP, *Nunca Más*, 1–2; 6.

131 Nino, *Radical Evil*, 186–187.

a Nuremberg-style tribunal.[132] That was the case, Nino argued, because the Argentinian state was leading the refoundation of its own rule of law, and in doing that, setting its own institutional arrangements to peacefully coexist in democracy.[133]

While there was no international intervention in the way that Alfonsín and Nino feared, the Prologue's descriptions of the dictatorship's violence reveal how CONADEP was, subtly but powerfully, shaping the social, political, legal, and economic aspects of the transition according to the 'standards' mobilized by international law and its institutions. This becomes apparent not only by paying close attention to the Prologue's engagement with international law, but also in more subtle expressions of faith in the 'civilizing' and 'saving' possibilities of Western-based values and ideas.[134] For example, while the Prologue positions itself against the Junta's forceful imposition of "Western, Christian values,"[135] it makes the Junta explicitly "responsible for" tainting those values,[136] through kidnapping, torturing and forcing the disappearance of all those who dissented (called 'subversives' in the Junta's rhetoric),[137] or who worked in the areas of socioeconomic justice and labor rights. The Prologue's fierce disapproval of how the dictatorship's rhetoric used Western values to justify the practice of violence is not surprising. What is surprising, considering that Alfonsín's government was committed to escaping the Cold War's ideological paradigms and interventions, is the Prologue's

[132] Nino rejected international interventions for cases like Argentina. Nino proposed to create an "international forum" that would not "destabiliz[e] democratic governments" in Nino, *Radical Evil*, 186–189. See Nino's debate with Orentlicher in, Diane F. Orentlicher, "Settling Accounts: The Duty to Prosecute Human Rights Violations of a Prior Regime," *The Yale Law Journal*, vol 100, no 8 (1991); Carlos Nino, "The Duty to Punish Past Abuses of Human Rights Put into Context: The Case of Argentina," *The Yale Law Journal*, vol 100, no 8 (1991); Diane F. Orentlicher, "A Reply to Professor Nino," *The Yale Law Journal*, vol 100, no 8 (1991).

[133] Nino, *Radical Evil*, 186–187; Alfonsín, *Memoria Política*, 33–48.

[134] On the historical relationship between the concept of 'civilization' in international law see Liliana Obregón, "The Civilized and the Uncivilized," in *The Oxford Handbook of the History of International Law*, Bardo Fassbender and Anne Peters (eds), (Oxford University Press, 2012), 918–940.

[135] CONADEP, *Nunca Más*, 4. [136] Ibid, 5.

[137] On the Junta's rhetoric see Margarite Feitlowitz, *A Lexicon of Terror: Argentina and the Legacies of Torture* (Oxford University Press, 1998). Also mentioned in CONADEP, *Nunca Más*, 4.

defense of the virtue of Western values through democracy, which was presented as the "only" political model capable of delivering peace, justice, and economic prosperity.[138] This is remarkably explicit in the Prologue's concluding paragraph, which opens by affirming that "[g]reat catastrophes are always instructive."[139] Then it claims that although Argentina's dictatorship is the "most terrible" "tragedy" "ever suffered,"[140] the lesson is that "only democracy" is able to "save a people from horror on this scale," and "keep and safeguard the sacred, essential rights of man."[141] The Prologue concludes by affirming that "[o]nly with democracy will we be certain that NEVER AGAIN will events such as these, which have made Argentina so sadly infamous throughout the [civilized] world, be repeated in our nation."[142] Although the Prologue concludes with the promises that democracy will 'civilize' and 'save' Argentina, throughout the text the Prologue represents international law, in the form being advanced in the Cold War's final years, as necessary for its achievement.

2.3.2 DELEGITIMIZING THE DICTATORSHIP'S STATE VIOLENCE. The Prologue mobilizes the promises of 'salvation' and 'civilization,' not by describing in detail what life within the democratic state will look like, but by drawing on international law to delegitimize the violence of the Argentinian state under dictatorship. For instance, the Prologue's constant emphasis that the Final Report/*Nunca Más* is 'just' describing facts, and is not a legal judgment or equivalent to justice,[143] is contradicted by the Prologue's own references to the international legal forms that shape its description of the kinds of state conduct that are unlawful. Thus the Prologue describes how the dictatorship's state violence was "the greatest and most savage tragedy in the history of Argentina,"[144] and argues that it "went far beyond what might be considered criminal offences, and takes us into the shadowy realm of crimes against humanity."[145] According to the Prologue, what made that form of state violence a crime against humanity

[138] CONADEP, *Nunca Más*, 6. [139] Ibid. [140] Ibid. [141] Ibid.

[142] Capitalization in original. The word "*civilizado*" ("civilized") appears in the original in Spanish in, CONADEP, *Nunca Más: Informe*, 393.

[143] CONADEP, *Nunca Más*, 1; 7. [144] Ibid, 1. [145] Ibid, 2.

was that, "[t]hrough the technique of disappearance and its consequences, all the ethical principles which the great religions and the noblest philosophies have *evolved* through centuries of suffering and calamity have been trampled underfoot and barbarously ignored."[146] In other words, the violence of the state violated international law (by committing "crimes against humanity") as well as 'universal' religious and philosophical principles. According to the Prologue, those 'universal' principles informed the "sanctity of individual rights" and were, in the first instance, given legal form through "the French Revolution," and later through "the universal declarations of human rights,"[147] "the great encyclicals of this century," and "constitution[s]."[148] They were, and are, the symbols of "[e]very civilized nation."[149] Additionally, although the Prologue acknowledges that the Argentinian state had been one of those "civilized nation[s]," according to the universal principles and rights,[150] the Prologue explicitly declares that CONADEP's investigation reveals that "human rights were violated at all levels by the Argentinian state" during the dictatorship.[151]

By stating that the acts of violence of the dictatorial state are a crime according to international law, the Prologue "attach[es]" the definition of the Argentinian dictatorship's particular forms of violence "to a larger normative story" of progress and universality.[152] In this story a state 'evolves' from 'barbaric to civilized' through a process facilitated by state-authorized "closure mechanisms" (e.g., trials),[153] which would make anew the legal grounds for state-society relations in the aftermath of state violence in order to prevent a repetition of such violence. This story of progress and civilization was not only formally institutionalized as part of the operation of international law since the Nuremberg and Tokyo Trials,[154] but also

146 Ibid. Italics mine.

147 Ibid. Plural "declaration" as in "declarations" is in the original text. 148 Ibid.

149 Ibid. 150 Ibid. 151 Ibid, 2–3.

152 Peter Rush, "Dirty War Crimes: Jurisdictions of Memory and International Criminal Law," in *The Hidden Histories of War Crimes Trials*, Gerry Simpson and Kevin John Heller (eds) (Oxford University Press, 2013), 370.

153 Sara Kendall, "New Histories of the Present: Revisiting Post-WWII Juridical Forms (Review essay of Heller and Tanaka, et al.)," *Melbourne Journal of International Law*, vol 12, no 1 (2012), 349.

154 For example, at the influential 1988 Aspen Institute's State Crimes conference, which focused on transitions to democracy, the first agenda item was to discuss

universalized as 'the' internationally authorized way a state should hold accountable a previous government for acts categorized as 'violent,' and therefore unlawful, by international law.[155] In this way, the Prologue represents CONADEP as the Argentinian state's first institutional step in the process of becoming a 'civilized' state through the "reconstruction of the rule of [l]aw,"[156] just like the states in the Global North did after World War II.

As part of that 'universal' story of progress, the Prologue outlines what would be the second institutional step toward civilization and lawfulness: the Junta Trials, which would take place in 1985, a year after the delivery of CONADEP's Final Report/*Nunca Más*. The Prologue explains that CONADEP was authorized *not to judge* the dictatorship's "terrorism,"[157] "but to investigate the fate of the people who disappeared during those ill-omened years of our nation's life."[158] The Prologue specifies that the Final Report/*Nunca Más*, as the outcome of CONADEP's investigation, is a way of breaking with the dictatorship-imposed silence about the *desaparecidos*.[159] The Prologue emphasizes that the findings of the investigation, set out in the body of the report/book, are not "the final word" and cannot be considered to deliver "justice" for the *desaparecidos* and their relatives.[160] The "final word" had to be pronounced by "justice," that is, by Argentinian civilian courts.[161] With this, the Prologue outlines and establishes the relationship between CONADEP and the Junta Trials, by differentiating between the contributions of both institutions to the reestablishment of civil and lawful state-society relations in democracy. While the Prologue describes CONADEP as the investigatory institution that delivers an authorized facts-based truth of the dictatorship's state violence, it presents the Junta Trials as the legal institution that judges and declares what is unlawful based on CONADEP's authorized truth.

those trials. The Aspen Institute, *State Crimes: Punishment of Pardon: Papers and Report of the Conference* (The Aspen Institute, 1988), 1.

155 Gerry Simpson, *Law, War and Crime: War Crimes Trials and the Reinvention of International Law* (Polity, 2007). On the jurisdictional work of legal categories see Dorsett and McVeigh, *Jurisdiction*, 71–76.

156 ("reconstrucción del estado de [d]erecho"). Alfonsín, *Memoria Política*, 33.

157 CONADEP, *Nunca Más*, 1. 158 Ibid. 159 Ibid, 1–2. 160 Ibid, 1. 161 Ibid.

Although the Prologue describes as different yet complementary the work of both institutions, the creation of CONADEP and its role in the transition to democracy was more accidental than planned, unlike the Junta Trials. Alfonsín's personal endeavor was to prosecute the military through a civilian court (like the Prologue states), but the political circumstances forced him to adopt a position he later described as somewhere between "what is desirable and what is possible to pay off the debts of the past; without losing sight of the future."[162] According to Argentinian historian Marina Franco and sociologist Emilio Crenzel, most politicians – except for Alfonsín and a minority of his party (Partido Radical) and Partido Intransigente – rejected the idea of prosecuting the military, and were in favor of a "mantle of oblivion."[163] Firmly against this, during his inaugural presidential speech in 1983, Alfonsín affirmed that his government would not "ac[t] as if nothing happened here,"[164] and was "determined to clarify the situation of the disappeared people."[165] Moreover, Alfonsín promised that his government was going to "correct and eliminate forever" the consequences of the dictatorship's "irresponsible decisions,"[166] and "set the foundations for the free, grand, prosperous, fraternal and generous Argentina that we all want."[167] To achieve this, the government promoted the revocation of the Junta's self-amnesty law at congress.[168]

However, even without the self-amnesty law, relatives of the *desaparecidos* and Argentinian human rights organizations were skeptical about the likelihood of putting the Junta on trial in a civilian court. The reason was that, under those political circumstances, Alfonsín's government

162 ("lo deseable y lo posible para saldar las deudas del pasado; pero siempre teniendo en miras el futuro"). Alfonsín, *Memoria Política*, 37.

163 ("un manto de olvido"). Franco, "El 'Documento Final'," 247; Crenzel, *The Memory of the Argentina Disappearances*, 31–75.

164 ("como si aquí no hubiera ocurrido nada"). Raúl Alfonsín, "El Discurso de Asunción de Raúl Alfonsín ante la Asamblea Legislativa," *Parlamentario.com* ([10 December 1983] 10 December 2013). www.parlamentario.com/noticia-68393.html.

165 ("en esclarecer la situación de las personas desaparecidas"). Ibid.

166 ("corregirlos y eliminarlos para siempre"); ("decisiones irresponsables"). Ibid.

167 ("echar los cimientos de la Argentina libre, grande, próspera, fraterna y generosa que queremos"). Ibid.

168 Alfonsín, *Memoria Política*, 37.

negotiated for Junta members to be tried at first instance by a military court (Supreme Council of the Armed Forces) with the possibility of appealing the ruling in a civilian court.[169] Yet, for relatives of the *desaparecidos*, justice could only be delivered by the state's civilian institutions, not the military.[170] As I discussed in Section 2.2, that led Argentinian human rights organizations to propose the creation of an investigatory commission, comprised by members of congress representing all political parties. The aim of this commission would be to locate the *desaparecidos* and explain the circumstances in which they disappeared.[171] But in the government's view, such a commission would fail to deliver answers.[172] The government considered that the circumstances would make it impossible for political parties to collaborate, and it could ultimately generate social and political confusion with the outcome of the civilian trials – if they were ever to take place.[173] As an alternative, Alfonsín and his advisers proposed the creation of CONADEP.[174] Within days after Alfonsín's inaugural address, CONADEP was created as a response to the "the legitimate interest[s]" of both Argentinian "civil society" and the "international community."[175]

Considering this background, the way in which the Prologue differentiates between both institutions (CONADEP and Junta Trials) is telling of the subtle (international) legal groundwork taking place through CONADEP's authorized truth, so that the Junta Trials would be legally and politically feasible, and socially acceptable. Furthermore, the Prologue reveals how international law was embedded in CONADEP's truth-making process, and gave the *desaparecidos* legal subjectivity. In turn, there would be an identifiable victim for whom to deliver justice through the Junta Trials. The Prologue does that by representing the forced disappearance of people conducted by the state as a legal action

169 Nino, *Radical Evil*, 67–70. 170 Mignone, *Derechos Humanos y Sociedad*, 156–157.

171 Ibid, 158; Nino, *Radical Evil*, 72; Alison Brysk, *The Politics of Human Rights in Argentina: Protest, Change, and Democratization* (Stanford University Press, 1994), 68–70.

172 Alfonsín, *Memoria Política*, 39. 173 Ibid.

174 Crenzel, *The Memory of the Argentina Disappearances*, 37–38; Alfonsín, *Memoria Política*, 40.

175 ("el interés legítimo"); ("sociedad civil"); ("comunidad internacional"). Gobierno de la Argentina, *Decreto 187/83 Comisión Nacional sobre la Desaparición de Personas.*

that violently stripped human beings of "their rights," and in turn, transformed them into something similar to "mere objects."[176] The Prologue then states that the *desaparecidos* were "[s]eized against their will" and that they "no longer had civil presence [*presencia civil*],"[177] because "[f]rom the moment of their abduction, victims lost all rights."[178] To make the *desaparecidos* subjects of rights, the Prologue acknowledges that they "were not mere objects ... and still possessed all the human attributes ... They were people."[179] With this, the Prologue gives legal meaning to the *desaparecidos* through an international legal category of 'victim' – which was conceived, and since then developed, in the context of World War II's Nuremberg Trials.[180] This victim is typically considered as an "absent figure," to which international law "promises" legal "representation" through its institutions – that is, trials, but also, since CONADEP, through Truth Commissions.[181] By 1983–1984, when CONADEP operated and delivered its report/book, the situation of the *desaparecidos* – from Argentina and elsewhere – was beginning to take legal form under international law. In 1977 Amnesty International issued a report about the dictatorship's violence, which included a description of different forms of violence – torture, prisoners, and forced disappearances – and a list of *desaparecidos*.[182] In 1982, the UN Working Group on Enforced or Involuntary Disappearances defined the forced disappearances as "one of the cruelest forms of violation of the human rights of both the victims and their families" committed by the state.[183] The Prologue's recognition of the 'inherent' (human) rights of the *desaparecidos*, based on the 'fact' that they were human, began to

[176] CONADEP, *Nunca Más*, 4–5.

[177] The original text in Spanish captures better this point in, CONADEP, *Nunca Más: Informe*, 345. The text in English says: "no longer existed as citizens." CONADEP, *Nunca Más*, 3.

[178] CONADEP, *Nunca Más*, 4. [179] Ibid.

[180] Maria Elander, *Figuring Victims in International Criminal Justice: The Case of the Khmer Rouge Tribunal* (Routledge, 2018), 15–33.

[181] Ibid, 2; 15; Zunino, *Justice Framed*, 67–72.

[182] Amnesty International, "Report of an Amnesty International Mission to Argentina."

[183] UN Doc E/CN.4/1982/30 (1 February–12 March 1982), *United Nations Commission on Human Rights, Commission on Human Rights: Report on the 38th Session*, 48; 46–50.

give an identifiable international legal form to the *desaparecidos*. In turn it made the state directly responsible for violating international law.

2.3.3 AUTHORIZING DEMOCRACY'S SILENCES: 'POLITICAL' AND 'ECONOMIC' STATE VIOLENCE. The way in which the Prologue worked (and continues to work) in Argentina's public life shows how CONADEP went beyond its narrow mandate through its operation.[184] The Prologue's way of attributing international legal responsibility *only* to the Argentinian state, channeled the ways in which international law does not hold equally accountable all international actors and institutions.[185]

From the outset CONADEP focused solely on investigating the issue of the *desaparecidos* under the premise that it was the outcome of the Argentinian state's lack of Western-like civility, as opposed to the exemplary Global North's post–World War II state-society relations grounded on rule of law (and human rights) and democracy. The Prologue's description of the Argentinian state as 'barbaric' and underdeveloped also resonates with the (then) increasingly predominant theories of dependency and modernization, and later democratization, which were largely developed by academics educated in the US.[186] Argentinian academic Guillermo O'Donnell was particularly influential in the analyses that focused on the

[184] Gobierno de la Argentina, *Decreto 187/83 Comisión Nacional sobre la Desaparición de Personas.*

[185] Orford, "Locating the International," 444; 447–448.

[186] See generally, Nicolas Guilhot, *The Democracy Makers: Human Rights and International Order* (Columbia University Press, 2005); Dezalay and Garth, *The Internationalization of Palace Wars.* For influential theory of modernization proponents see David E. Apter, *The Politics of Modernization* (University of Chicago Press, 1965); Guillermo O'Donnell, *Modernization and Bureaucratic-Authoritarianism: Studies in South American Politics* (University of California Press, 1979); Guillermo O'Donnell, Philippe C. Schmitter, and Laurence Whitehead (eds), *Transitions from Authoritarian Rule* (Johns Hopkins University Press, 1986). In Latin America, O'Donnell, an Argentinian, was influential because of his particular focus on political arrangements in Argentina and Brazil. For an informative overview of O'Donnell's influences see Kees Biekart, "Guillermo O'Donnell's 'Thoughtful Wishing' about Democracy and Regime Change," *Development & Change*, vol 46, no 4 (2015). Nesiah also addresses the influential role of O'Donnell and Schmitter's project in, Vasuki Nesiah, "The Ambitions and Traumas of Transitional Governance: Expelling Colonialism, Replicating Colonialism," in *International Law and Transitional Governance: Critical Perspectives*, Emmanuel H. D. De Groof and Micha Wiebusch (eds) (Routledge, 2020).

emergence of South American dictatorships in the 1960s–1980s and their transition to democracy.[187] At the heart of O'Donnell's theory was this rationality: the more modernized (through industrialization) the 'underdeveloped' South American states were, the more authoritarian they would be.[188] Yet, in O'Donnell's thinking, democracy was "a more civilized form of social life,"[189] necessary to secure "human rights" and achieve a "much more equitable distribution of resources."[190] What is telling about the resonance of the Prologue's categorization of the Argentinian state as uncivilized with theories of modernization and democratization, especially with O'Donnell's, is that they deploy an uncritically redemptive representation of democracy. As the Prologue concludes, "only democracy . . . can save" Argentina from state violence, because "only democracy . . . can keep and safeguard the sacred, essential rights of humans."[191] This redemptive representation of democracy was also famously mobilized by President Alfonsín, who said during his inaugural address, "with democracy one not only votes, but one is also educated, fed and healed."[192]

The Prologue thus not only describes but also embraces international law's late-Cold War promises that 'becoming civilized' is possible "only with democracy" and the rule of law, which in turn will prevent a return of the violence.[193] This post-dictatorial state represented by the Prologue was, and still is, deeply informed by conceptions of democracy, the rule of law, and human rights, coupled with a market-based economic model. Importantly, this post-conflict state not only decouples the interrelated political and economic dimensions as two independent issues of a given conflict's background, but also places primary responsibility on the state for creating and sustaining them.[194] In turn, international law promotes its

[187] In the Postscript of the 1979 re-edition to the book's 1973 edition, O'Donnell compares the 1960s governments and asserts that the 1970s dictatorships are worse, see O'Donnell, *Modernization and Bureaucratic-Authoritarianism*, 203–209.

[188] Ibid, 198–201. [189] Ibid, 205.

[190] Ibid, 207. See also, Guilhot, *The Democracy Makers*, 143.

[191] CONADEP, *Nunca Más*, 6.

[192] ("con la democracia no sólo se vota, sino que también se come, se educa y se cura"). Alfonsín, "El Discurso de Asunción de Raúl Alfonsín ante la Asamblea Legislativa."

[193] CONADEP, *Nunca Más*, 6.

[194] Pahuja, *Decolonising International Law*, 10–43. See also, Orford, "Locating the International."

post-dictatorial (or 'post-conflict') state as the solution to 'correct' the state's 'wrongs' for the sake of development and civilization. The decoupling of the 'political' and 'economic' was, since the end of World War II, part of what Sundhya Pahuja calls "the constructed separation" between the 'political' institutions of international law – for example, international human rights and rule of law promotion – and the 'economic' ones – for example, the International Monetary Fund (IMF) and the World Bank.[195]

After Argentina's experience, especially following the end of the Cold War, this rationality became even more prominent in international development projects for post-conflict peace/state-building (as I discuss in Chapter 4 on El Salvador's 1992 Truth Commission).[196] As I show here, the Prologue's silence about the 'economic' dimension sustaining the dictatorship, reflects "the constructed separation" of the 'political' institutions and the 'economic' ones.[197] However, as Pahuja argues, decoupling the operation of international law is "in fact impossible because what is defined as economic or political is itself a political question."[198]

This political decoupling also manifests in the silence of the Final Report/*Nunca Más*'s authorized truth about the implication of international law and its institutions – notably, the IMF – as well as the silence of the US, in sustaining the state violence that led to the *desaparecidos.*[199] While the Prologue promised that democracy would 'save' public life and state-society relations, democracy was not 'saving' either the majority of Argentinians from sustained economic crises (aggravated with the public spending in the 1982 Malvinas/Falklands War),[200] or the state from

195 Pahuja, *Decolonising International Law*, 19–20.

196 See chapter 5 in Pahuja, *Decolonising International Law*; Shane Chalmers, "The Mythology of International Rule-of-Law Promotion," *Law & Social Inquiry*, vol 44, no 4 (2019); Guilhot, *The Democracy Makers.*

197 Pahuja, *Decolonising International Law*, 19–20.

198 Ibid, 20. See also, Ellen Meiksins Wood, "The Separation of the Economic and the Political in Capitalism," *New Left Review*, vol 127, no 1 (1981).

199 Orford, "Locating the International."

200 The impact of the sovereign debt on the socioeconomic situation of the majority of Argentinians was of great concerned for the Junta's opposition. See in Multipartidaria Nacional, *Propuesta de la Multipartidaria* (El Cid Editor/Libros para la Democracia, 1983).

inheriting the major foreign debt acquired by the dictatorship.[201] Tellingly, in September 1984, when the Final Report/*Nunca Más* was made public, the Argentinian state reached the first loan agreement of the post-dictatorship with the IMF.[202] The involvement of these international organizations was known by many who were leading the transition to democracy in 1983, among them President Alfonsín. But, as Argentinian historian Claudia Kedar's analysis shows, even though the loan contradicted Alfonsín's initial "anti-imperialist" discourse, he was "ambivalent and not as hostile toward the IMF" as it seemed.[203] Interestingly, writing about this twenty years later, in his memoir, Alfonsín said that during dictatorship the state was "far away from the notion of the rule of law . . . [b]ut paradoxically it was during that period that Argentina was lent more money, which demonstrates the enormous hypocrisy of international financial organizations back then."[204] Yet, for a majority of Argentinians, the *desaparecidos*, and the unceasing foreign debts and financial crises, both of which the democratic state inherited from the dictatorship, were two sides of the same coin.[205]

There is another very important silence that international legal narratives help to authorize in the Prologue. The Prologue also omits the

[201] Claudia Kedar, *The International Monetary Fund and Latin America: The Argentine Puzzle in Context* (Temple University Press, 2013), 155. See also, Claudia Kedar, "The Beginning of a Controversial Relationship: The IMF, the World Bank, and Argentina, 1943–1946," *Canadian Journal of Latin American & Caribbean Studies*, vol 35, no 69 (2010). For an analysis of Argentina's 2000s foreign debt caused socioeconomic crisis, Jerome E. Roos, *Why Not Default?: The Political Economy of Sovereign Debt* (Princeton University Press, 2019), 173–222.

[202] Agencia Télam, "Uno por uno: Los Acuerdos de Argentina con el FMI en 35 años de Democracia," *La Voz* (8 May 2018). www.lavoz.com.ar/politica/uno-por-uno-los-acuerdos-de-argentina-con-el-fmi-en-35-anos-de-democracia.

[203] Kedar, *The International Monetary Fund and Latin America*, 165.

[204] ("se estuvo más lejos de la noción de estado de [d]erecho . . . [p]ero paradójicamente es el período en que más dinero se le prestó a la Argentina, lo que demuestra la enorme hipocresía de los organismos internacionales de crédito en aquel entonces"). Alfonsín, *Memoria Política*, 33. On how relying on international law to redress state violence advances impunity and obscures the violence of capitalism in the roots of the conflict, see Tor Krever, "Ending Impunity? Eliding Political Economy in International Criminal Law," in *Research Handbook on Political Economy and Law*, John D. Haskell and Ugo Mattei (eds) (Edward Elgar, 2015).

[205] On this see generally, Naomi Klein, *The Shock Doctrine* (Penguin Books, 2008).

participation of foreign corporations, particularly US-owned ones such as the Ford Motor Company,[206] the support of the US Central Intelligence Agency (CIA) in Operation Cóndor, and the US Army's School of the Americas.[207] Operation Cóndor and the School of the Americas were initiatives in which the US became involved to support many of Latin America's dictatorships to 'counter' communism. At the School of the Americas, located in Panamá, the US Army "trained over sixty thousand soldiers in combat-related skills and counterinsurgency doctrine."[208] One of the Junta's dictators, Roberto Viola, was trained there.[209] Operation Cóndor was an international secret alliance created in 1975 between the intelligence services of Argentina, Uruguay, Chile, Paraguay, and Bolivia.[210] The CIA was the "secret partner and sponsor" of Operation Cóndor.[211] Under Operation Cóndor, dictatorships were able to collaborate to find and disappear citizens opposing the dictatorships as well as to smuggle their children to other countries.[212] Although the Final Report/ *Nunca Más* registers the fact that many witnesses before the CONADEP identified Ford Falcon cars as the vehicle in which *desaparecidos* were taken to clandestine torture centers, the involvement of Ford Motor Company in providing those cars was not addressed until 2008.[213] In 2008, under the

[206] On the role of Ford Motor Company and other foreign-owned corporations, such as Mercedes Benz, in the dictatorship, see Centro de Estudios Legales y Sociales, "Responsabilidad Empresarial en Delitos de Lesa Humanidad (Vol I and II)" (Editorial Ministerio de Justicia y Derechos Humanos de la Nación, 2015). www.cels.org.ar/especiales/empresas-y-dictadura/.

[207] On the Cóndor Plan see López, "The Feathers of Cóndor"; J. Patrice McSherry, *Predatory States: Operation Condor and Covert War in Latin America* (Rowman & Littlefield Publishers, 2005). On the School of the Americas see Lesley Gill, *The School of the Americas: Military Training and Political Violence in the Americas* (Duke University Press, 2004).

[208] Gill, *The School of the Americas*, 6. [209] Ibid.

[210] See generally, López, "The Feathers of Cóndor"; Francesca Lessa, *The Condor Trials: Transnational Repression and Human Rights in South America* (Yale University Press, 2022).

[211] McSherry, *Predatory States*, 1–34. [212] Lessa, *The Condor Trials*, 15–135.

[213] See Centro de Estudios Legales y Sociales, "Megacausa ESMA: El Juicio." www.cels.org.ar/especiales/megacausaesma/; Mar Centenera, "Juicio a Ford Argentina por convertirse en centro de detención de la dictadura," *El País* (19 December 2017). https://elpais.com/internacional/2017/12/19/argentina/1513717354_408056.html.

Kirchner government a court established that the collaboration of the Argentinian branch of Ford Motor Company was indispensable for the Junta to make the disappearances happen over time.[214] Interestingly, the legal responsibility was limited to 'Argentinian' actors, continuing to overlook the broader role of Ford Motor Company in sustaining the state violence of the Latin American dictatorships.[215] The Prologue, thus the Argentinian state, in representing the situation of the *desaparecidos* by drawing on international law's promises, continued to authorize this decoupling to be part of CONADEP's truth about the dictatorship's state violence.[216]

Importantly, in channeling (and thus giving continuity to) the rationality of separating these 'political' and 'economic' institutions, the Prologue deploys a totalizing representation of what state violence was (and is). This representation of how state violence touched *every* aspect of everyday life also clashes with the Prologue and the accounts of the two intellectual designers of the transition's signature institutions. In contrast with the totalizing representation that Argentinian state-society relations were like "hell" (as Ronald Dworkin famously described them),[217] both Nino and Malamud-Goti, senior presidential advisers to Alfonsín, shared in their respective political memoirs (both published in 1996), that Argentinian society was deeply divided about what many felt were 'positive' aspects of the dictatorship's early years – such as low delinquency and relative socioeconomic stability.[218] Similarly, the Prologue acknowledges that, while many Argentinians were not aware of the disappearances, others considered that there must have been 'a reason' for why some people were being held under arrest.[219]

214 Centro de Estudios Legales y Sociales, "Responsabilidad Empresarial en Delitos de Lesa Humanidad."

215 Klein, *The Shock Doctrine*, 107–109; 123–124. See also, Inderjeet Parmar, *Foundations of the American Century: The Ford, Carnegie, and Rockefeller Foundations in the Rise of American Power* (Columbia University Press, 2012).

216 Whyte, *The Morals of the Market*, 32. Italics in original. See also, Joseph R. Slaughter, "Hijacking Human Rights: Neoliberalism, the New Historiography, and the End of the Third World," *Human Rights Quarterly*, vol 40, no 4 (2018).

217 Ronald Dworkin, "Report from Hell," *The New York Review of Books* (1986).

218 Nino, *Radical Evil*; Malamud-Goti, *Game Without End*.

219 CONADEP, *Nunca Más*, 3–4.

In the Prologue's final remarks, the commissioners state that to achieve "true reconciliation" it is necessary that "the guilty repent" so that there can be "justice based on truth."[220] And yet, as I have shown, this "truth" could lead to "justice" because it was internationally authorized. The Prologue did that by drawing on international law's post-conflict promises to authorize CONADEP's account. However, what this did was to establish the unlawfulness of the dictatorship's state violence by subjecting its meaning and interpretation to a Eurocentric/Anglo-American lawfulness embedded in, and mobilized by, international law in the late-Cold War.[221] While it can be considered that the Prologue authorized an Argentinian truth (written by Argentinians working for an Argentinian institution), what the analysis here shows is how international law was fundamental, not only in giving CONADEP's account narrative coherency, but more importantly, authority.

2.4 REWRITING THE 1984 PROLOGUE: RIVAL PROLOGUES, RIVAL AUTHORITIES

The fundamental aim of the Final Report/*Nunca Más* was to establish its account as authoritative. Yet, forty years after its publication in 1984, the six pages of the Prologue continue to generate public debate.

In 2006, Argentina's Secretary of Human Rights, Eduardo Duhalde, under the presidency of Néstor Kirchner, announced that the latest edition of the Final Report/*Nunca Más* would include a new prologue.[222] The reason, the government said, was that "[t]he original Prologue did not reproduce the political philosophy that animates the State today in the prosecution of crimes against humanity."[223] Although the original 1984 Prologue was not removed from the 2006 edition of the Final Report/

220 Ibid, 5.

221 See Dezalay and Garth, *The Internationalization of Palace Wars*. On the centrality of the European colonial project in the craft and operation of international law see Anghie, *Imperialism, Sovereignty and the Making of International Law*.

222 Partido Justicialista (Kircher) is the most influential political party representing the *Peronismo*.

223 ("[e]l prólogo original no reproducía la filosofía política que hoy anima al Estado en la persecución de los crímenes de lesa humanidad"). Galak, "Controversia por el Prólogo."

Nunca Más, many public figures – including Alfonsín and former commissioner Magdalena Ruíz Guiñazú – considered that the new prologue was an attempt to "re-write history ... in the name of the present's political interest,"[224] "a dangerous tendency to reinvent history,"[225] and "an example of intolerance and disfigurement of reality."[226]

Ten years later, in 2016, Mauricio Macri's government announced its decision to remove the 2006 Prologue. Like in 2006, the Secretary of Human Rights, Claudio Avruj, was responsible for communicating the government's decision. At the new edition's official presentation, Avruj said that it "show[ed] the Report as it was, without additional ideology."[227] Avruj also emphasized that the removal of the 2006 Prologue was "a political debt we had from politics, from the State."[228] Even Sábato's son publicly welcomed the return to the original text.[229] At the time of this chapter's writing, the 1984 Prologue remains *the* Prologue to the Final Report/*Nunca Más*.[230] However, the writing (in 1984 and 2006) or removing (in 2016) of the prologues reveals the importance of who gets to be the author of 'the truth.' It also shows, on the one hand, how international law attempts to give normative coherency to accounts of the dictatorship's state violence which are inherently plural and nuanced. At the same time, that shows how the experiences of state violence that comprise an official account are dependent on political

224 ("en nombre del interés político del presente"). Luis Gregorich, "Opinión. El peligro de reescribir la historia," *La Nación* (17 July 2006). www.lanacion.com.ar/opinion/el-peligro-de-reescribir-la-historia-nid822374.

225 ("una peligrosa tendencia a reinventar la historia"). La Nación, "Dura réplica de Alfonsín," *La Nación* (22 May 2006). www.lanacion.com.ar/politica/dura-replica-de-alfonsin-nid808028.

226 ("ejemplo de intolerancia y de desfiguración de la realidad"). La Nación, "Editorial I. Cuando se Deforma la Verdad," *La Nación* (24 May 2006). www.lanacion.com.ar/editoriales/cuando-se-deforma-la-verdad-nid808438.

227 ("muestra al Informe tal cual fue, sin aditamento ideológico"). Clarín.com, "Circula un Petitorio que Será Presentado ante la Editorial Eudeba. Piden que el prólogo del "Nunca Más" lleve la firma de Sábato," *Clarín* (13 November 2012). www.clarin.com/sociedad/Piden-prologo-lleve-firma-Sabato_0_H1imQ3TivQe.html.

228 ("una deuda que teníamos desde la política, desde el Estado"). Ibid.

229 Clarín.com, "La Versión Original, de 1985. Editan el "Nunca más" sin los Agregados del Kirchnerismo: Hay Polémica," *Clarín* (18 June 2016). www.clarin.com/cultura/editan-agregados-kirchnerismo.

230 Crenzel, "Dos Prólogos."

interests which are also contingent on the lawfulness advanced by international law at that time.

During the left-wing oriented Kirchner governments (Néstor's 2003–2007 and Cristina's 2007–2015), the state developed substantive public policies focused on memorialization and remembrance of the dictatorship's violence as a form of state violence that encompassed socioeconomic inequality.[231] Part of the Kirchner governments' policies was to create sites of memorialization and remembrance, by transforming public buildings that had operated as clandestine detention and torture centers, or by putting plaques on sidewalks to mark the place where a person had been taken by the state's security forces.[232] Another major decision of the Kirchner governments (especially Néstor's) was to annul the amnesty laws passed during Alfonsín and Menem's presidencies. That led to new trials against Junta members.[233] Yet, these trials also showed that one can become a *desaparecido* even in democracy. In 2006, Jorge Julio López, a key witness in the contemporary trials, disappeared following their conclusion.[234] This was the second time that López went missing. The first was during the dictatorship. However this time he has not returned.

Apart from removing the 2006 Prologue, Macri's right-wing government did not work much on memorialization policies. Rather, the efforts of Macri's government were geared toward demonstrating that Argentina was a liberal Western-minded state. At the 2016 Clinton Global Foundation's annual meeting, after being introduced by former US President Clinton, Macri said that under his presidency Argentina was on the road to "being part of the world again."[235] Internationally, Macri's

[231] Balardini, "Argentina. Regional Protagonist," 52; 56–57. See also, Michelle Frances Carmody, *Human Rights, Transitional Justice, and the Reconstruction of Political Order in Latin America* (Palgrave Macmillan, 2018), 117–206; ikki Bell, *The Art of Post-dictatorship: Ethics and Aesthetics in Transitional Argentina* (Routledge, 2014), 1–15.

[232] Espacio Memoria y Derechos Humanos, "Baldosas por la Memoria." www.espaciomemoria.ar/baldosas-por-la-memoria/.

[233] Centro de Estudios Legales y Sociales, "Megacausa ESMA."

[234] Agencia Télam, "Se Cumplen 13 años de la Desaparición de Julio López," *La Voz* (18 September 2019). www.lavoz.com.ar/politica/se-cumplen-13-anos-de-desaparicion-de-julio-lopez.

[235] Casa Rosada, "Macri: 'Queremos volver a ser parte del mundo'" (19 September 2016). www.casarosada.gob.ar/slider-principal/37334-mauricio-macri-queremos-volver-a-ser-parte-del-mundo-y-cortar-con-el-aislacionismo.

government sought to demonstrate to Western states that Argentina was "again a reliable country" and ready to receive "global corporations."[236] With this, Macri aimed to undo the Kirchner administrations' foreign and economic policy, which had prioritized South-South alliances (e.g., MERCOSUR over FTAA/NAFTA).[237] For that reason, the Kirchner governments' foreign and economic policy was viewed with suspicion by Western states. To improve Argentina's reputation among Western states, during Macri's presidency Argentina hosted high-profile international events, including the G20 Summit.[238] Simultaneously, the Argentinian state was, once again, negotiating an IMF loan.[239] The success of the IMF negotiations was causing much social, political, and economic distress to Argentinians. That could be seen not only in the September 2018 national strike,[240] but also in banners hanging from the façade of many sites of memorialization as seen in Figure 2.2 – such as CONADEP's archives – or in posters made by the Madres de Plaza de Mayo as seen in Figure 2.1.

Macri was not alone in his desire to show that Argentina was addressing the increasing socioeconomic inequality, by becoming a liberal Western state and being internationally rule of law abiding. As I discussed in the previous section, back in 1984 Alfonsín was in a similar position. But nearly two decades later, Alfonsín admitted his bewilderment about the operation of international law in Argentina. As Alfonsín wrote:

> I do not know how this conflict will be resolved, between an international norm that is said to be imperative for all States and the right of peoples to

[236] ("para volver a ser un país confiable"); ("empresas globales"). Ibid.

[237] Eduardo Barcelona, "Los Presidentes Entierran el ALCA," *Página 12* (5 November 2015). www.pagina12.com.ar/diario/elpais/1-285456-2015-11-05.html.

[238] Daniel Pardo, "¿Por qué Argentina está en el G20 si tiene una de las economías más frágiles del mundo?," *BBC* (30 November 2018). www.bbc.com/mundo/noticias-america-latina-46390007.

[239] IMF Communications Department, "Press Release No. 18/362: IMF and Argentina Authorities Reach Staff-Level Agreement on First Review Under the Stand-By Arrangement" (26 September 2018). www.imf.org/en/News/Articles/2018/09/26/pr18362-argentina-imf-and-argentina-authorities-reach-staff-level-agreement.

[240] Clarín.com, "Martes de Protesta. Paro General: Todo lo que Hay que Saber," *Clarín* (24 September 2018). www.clarin.com/sociedad/paro-general-25-septiembre-saber_0_JwSvcFkq2.html.

2.1 Fence surrounding the Casa Rosada with banners protesting against the IMF (FMI in Spanish) during the Madres de Plaza de Mayo's weekly demonstration in Buenos Aires (Argentina). The banner says: "Out IMF." Photograph by Valeria Vázquez Guevara (2018).

"self-determination," to decide the best way to resolve their democratic transitions …

In some instances, even the United Nations has legitimated the sanction of amnesty laws … Are all those amnesties null? Are societies obligated to always punish even if it is at the expense of making democracy fail? Those are the questions for a debate that I think reaches the entire world.[241]

241 ("No sé cómo se va a resolver este conflicto entre una norma internacional que se dice imperativa para todos los Estados y el derecho de los pueblos a 'autodeterminarse,' a decidir el mejor modo de resolver sus transiciones democráticas … En algunas oportunidades, incluso las Naciones Unidas han legitimado la sanción de leyes de amnistía … ¿Son nulas todas esas amnistías? ¿Las sociedades están obligadas siempre a castigar aunque de esa manera fracase el establecimiento de la democracia? Estas son las preguntas de un debate que creo alcanza al mundo entero"). Alfonsín, *Memoria Política*, 244.

2.2 Banner protesting against the IMF (FMI in Spanish) hanging from the street fence of the Park of Memory and Human Rights in Buenos Aires (Argentina). Banner says: "Yes to national sovereignty. No to the agreement with the IMF." Photograph by Valeria Vázquez Guevara (2018).

Alfonsín wrote these words in 2003, in a letter addressed to members of his party at congress. In the letter, Alfonsín openly disagreed with president Kirchner's initiative to request the congress to annul the amnesty laws, which were passed in 1986 under Alfonsín's presidency.[242] Kirchner's government argued the laws were unconstitutional because they went against the UN Convention on the Non-Applicability of Statutory Limitations to War Crimes and Crimes Against Humanity – which Kirchner signed in 2003 right before the congress approved the laws' annulment.[243] Alfonsín's main point against Kirchner's argument was that, what was once lawful before international law in 1984, had become unlawful in 2003. Alfonsín's government believed that, by grounding the transition to democracy's institutions, such as CONADEP's account, in what was lawful under international law, Argentina would be seen as a civilized and lawful state by Western states. For Alfonsín, it was confusing that Kirchner's memorialization policies

[242] Ibid, 242–246.

[243] Eduardo Tagliaferro, "Crímenes Imprescriptibles," *Página 12* (7 August 2003). www.pagina12.com.ar/diario/elpais/subnotas/1-8848-2003-08-07.html; Carmody, *Human Rights, Transitional Justice*, 181–197.

were also grounded in an international law that still did not recognize Argentina as civilized unless it adopted the 'new' authorized lawfulness. This reveals how fundamental decisions taken during Alfonsín's presidency were ultimately subjected to the authority of international law and its institutions, while constraining the Argentinian state's authority.

These recent debates show how, on the one hand, the state's decision to either write or remove prologues is contingent on the particular interests of the government of the day. On the other hand, it also shows how both international law and the Truth Commission (through its Final Report/*Nunca Más*) continued to be useful to reimagine the lawfulness of the state's account about the dictatorship's state violence. Throughout, the 1984 and 2006 prologues of the Final Report/*Nunca Más* consistently deployed the promises of democracy and the rule of (international) law as the pillars of an Argentinian state that would deliver peace, justice, and prosperity. But in turn, the way in which the dictatorship's unlawful state violence is given meaning and understood is contingent on international law's authorized conception of lawfulness.

2.5 CONCLUSION

It is undeniable that the driving force of Argentina's transition was the courageous struggle and resistance of Argentinians against the dictatorship's state violence. This was coupled with the vision and commitment of Alfonsín's government to secure peaceful democratic coexistence. CONADEP's work was remarkable in tracing and recording the facts – names and circumstances – in which at least 30,000 people were forcefully disappeared. This also created the possibility for relatives of the *desaparecidos* (with citizenships from European states) to begin criminal processes in Europe against key people for their involvement in the mass disappearances.[244] As Francesca Lessa's research on the trials against the Operación Cóndor's forced disappearances shows, that also "directly

244 Lessa, *The Condor Trials*, 211; Eugenio Palopoli, "A 40 años de la CONADEP y la Presentación del Informe Nunca Más: El testimonio Irrefutable de la Dictadura Argentina," *El Observador* (21 September 2024). www.elobservador.com.uy/argentina/sociedad/a-40-anos-la-co... nca-mas-el-testimonio-irrefutable-la-dictadura-argentina-n5961958

contributed to reactivating local accountability efforts" in Argentina.[245] Yet, although many Argentinians do not dispute the facts, they do continue to disagree about the way in which the Prologue narrated the facts. In their view, the Prologue gives continuity to the dictatorship's theory of two demons.[246] Taking those debates into account, this chapter has analyzed the Prologue in light of the international context of the late-Cold War. I have sought to show how a Eurocentric/Anglo-American worldview, embedded in particular narratives of international law, played a fundamental role in authorizing the Prologue's, and hence CONADEP's, account as a coherent truth.

As I discussed throughout this chapter, the main aim of CONADEP's investigation was to give answers about the whereabouts of the *desaparecidos* and the circumstances in which they disappeared, primarily to their relatives, then to Argentinians and the international community. In doing so, CONADEP's account was meant to establish a shared normative understanding across Argentinian society about the ethical wrongfulness of the forced disappearances. One of the things that this chapter began to show is how, in the process of establishing their truth, not does a Truth Commission benefit from exercising the authority of international law, but so too does international law benefit. As I continue to show in the next chapters, Truth Commissions have also strengthened and advanced international law's world-making power by placing it at the heart of how 'the past' should be memorialized, and therefore of how post-conflict state-society relations are to be imagined. One consequence is that, by drawing on international law to establish an authoritative truth, the resulting truths are made vulnerable to both the politics of international law and to those of the different national governments. For instance, that vulnerability, as I discussed in this chapter's introduction, has become especially advantageous for Argentina's *negacionistas* (including, president Milei and members of the current government and congress), and other right-wing oriented groups who weaponize their critiques of the

245 Lessa, *The Condor Trials*, 211.

246 Emilio A. Crenzel, "El Prólogo del Nunca Más y La Teoría de los Dos Demonios. Reflexiones sobre una Representación de la Violencia Política en la Argentina," *Contenciosa*, vol 1, no 1 (2013).

international legal order and globalization, with the purpose of denying and erasing from public memory the brutal state violence that occurred.

In the following chapter, by turning to examine Chile's 1990 Truth Commission, I continue to show how Truth Commissions have drawn on international law to authorize the truthfulness of their accounts of violent conflict, and the consequences. Specifically, I show how Chile's Truth Commission authorized its account of the truth by drawing on a side of international law that dominated the post-Cold War international politics of the 1990s: international human rights law.

CHAPTER 3

Using the Language of Human Rights

3.1 INTRODUCTION

THIS CHAPTER THICKENS THE BOOK'S analysis of the relationship between Truth Commissions and international law. The focus here is on how the Chilean Truth Commission (1990–1991) drew on a dimension of international law that dominated post-Cold War international politics for post-conflict states in the early 1990s: international human rights law. There are two parts to my argument about this Truth Commission and its relationship with international human rights law. First, I argue that the Truth Commission used the language of international human rights law in a way that authorizes its account as the 'major' truth. And second, in doing that, the Truth Commission's truth can be seen to subordinate other 'minor' truths.

By 'major' truth I mean that international human rights law can be seen to provide an authoritative idiom for describing which manifestations of violence during the dictatorship are to be understood as unlawful (for being in violation of 'human rights'). In doing so, international human rights gives the Truth Commission a purportedly universal legal language with which to describe, and authorize, its account of violence. In a country in which many accounts about the dictatorship's state violence subsist simultaneously, 'the truth' of the Truth Commission assumes the highest authority as a 'major' truth through its relationship to international human rights law. Following on from this, the second part of the argument is that the ways in which the Truth Commission authorizes its account as truth subordinates other accounts, which are seen to rival international human rights law and its normative organization of post-conflict state-society relations. This not only renders as 'minor' the coexisting accounts, but also forecloses any possibility of living together after dictatorship that does not conform with the normative order of international human rights law.

In making this argument, the chapter shows how international human rights law not only provided the justification for the Chilean Truth Commission's initial enquiry, but has continued to provide an authoritative language through which the Truth Commission's findings are represented as the unquestionable truth. The chapter shows this through an analysis of the spatial representation of truth and authority deployed by Chile's Museo de la Memoria y los Derechos Humanos (Museum of Memory and Human Rights). The argument here is that the Museo is a continuation of the Chilean Truth Commission. As the state's official public place where the authorized truth about Chile's dictatorship is memorialized, the Museo has been designed and built with the intention of preserving and transmitting the truth delivered by the 1990 Truth Commission, as registered in its Final Report.[1] This is distinct from other museums built for the purpose of collective memorialization of past violent events, which do not tend to have a direct relationship with a Truth Commission.[2] The Museo, through visual and experiential technologies, mediates and transmits to visitors the state's truth established decades before, in 1990–1991.[3]

[1] The Chilean state implemented two Truth Commissions (1990 *Comisión Nacional de Verdad y Reconciliación* and 2004 *Comisión de Prisión Política y Tortura*) and two ad hoc presidential commissions (1996 *Corporación Nacional de Reparación y Reconciliación* and 2011 *Comisión Presidencial Asesora para la Calificación de Detenidos Desaparecidos, Ejecutados Políticos y Víctimas de Prisión Política*). The 1990 Truth Commission is considered the one that established the official account of the truth, and the other three commissions are considered to complement and update the account established in 1990–1991. For an historical overview of previous investigatory commissions in Chile see, Elizabeth Lira, *Historia, Política y Ética de la Verdad en Chile, 1891–2001: Reflexiones sobre la Paz Social y la Impunidad* (LOM Ediciones; Universidad Alberto Hurtado, 2001). See also, Priscilla B. Hayner, *Unspeakable Truths: Transitional Justice and the Challenge of Truth Commissions* (Routledge, 2011), 47–49; 60–62.

[2] Similar museums/spaces of memory: Espacio Memoria y Derechos Humanos, "Historia." www.espaciomemoria.ar/historia/; Apartheid Museum, "About the Museum-the Apartheid Museum's Genesis." www.apartheidmuseum.org/about-museum-0.

[3] On the relationship between international courts and museums (Elander) and between constitutions and museums (Douglas) see Maria Elander, "Images of

The relationship between the Museo and the 1990 Truth Commission, I argue, is best understood as a metonymic one. By metonymy I mean a discursive form that is present not only in literature but also in other media of communication or artistic expression.[4] A metonymic relationship emerges when one of two elements, which are somewhat associated or related, is used to refer to the other without losing its identity.[5] It is in this association, or "referential function," that metonymy occurs and works to "facilitate speedy communication" about "something that is more complex or abstract, or even sensitive," and therefore difficult to express or communicate on its own.[6] For instance, a metonymic relationship can be created and experienced through cultural artifacts that are used to represent the findings of the Truth Commission's investigation, and to keep it alive beyond the life of the investigation. While the Truth Commission's Final Report is one such cultural artifact, other more accessible and in some ways more effective artifacts include memory museums, songs, literature, memorials, and so on.[7] The metonymic relationship between the Museo and the Truth Commission emerges

Victims: The ECCC and the Cambodian Genocide Museum," in *Law and the Visual: Representations, Technologies, and Critique*, Desmond Manderson (ed) (University of Toronto Press, 2018); Stacy Douglas, *Curating Community: Museums, Constitutionalism, and the Taming of the Political* (University of Michigan Press, 2017).

4 Jeannette Littlemore, *Metonymy: Hidden Shortcuts in Language, Thought and Communication* (Cambridge University Press, 2015), 111–113.

5 Ibid, 1–2. 6 Ibid, 1; 4.

7 On the growing social and international importance of museums of memory and sites of consciousness, including museums of memory, monuments, and memorials, see for example, The Latin America and Caribbean Sites of Memory Network, "About Us." https://sitiosdememoria.org/en/about-us/; International Coalition of Sites of Consciousness. www.sitesofconscience.org. The Colombian Truth Commission is a recent excellent example of how a Truth Commission can use the influential role of audio-visual artifacts, including social media platforms like TikTok or Instagram to disseminate its account of the truth. See for example, Cuenta Oficial de la Comisión de la Verdad (@comisionverdadc), Instagram. www.instagram.com/comisionverdadc/; Cuenta Oficial de la Comisión de la Verdad (@comisionverdadc), TikTok. www.tiktok.com/@comisionverdadc. Colombia's Truth Commission also created, in the music platform Spotify, a podcast called "Nombrar lo Innombrable: Conversaciones sobre Arte y Verdad" (Naming the Unnameable: Conversations about Art and Truth), to discuss the role of art in dealing with the violent conflict. Comisión de la Verdad Colombia, "Nombrar lo Innombrable: Conversaciones sobre Arte y Verdad." https://open.spotify.com/show/0aVW44q7vdiindaJr6pEKf.

because the Museo simultaneously creates an experience that facilitates the transmission of the authorized truth of the dictatorship (as recorded in the Truth Commission Final Report). And in doing so, it gives temporal continuity to the work of the Truth Commission, by giving it a material (visual and experiential) form. While the Truth Commission and the Museo remain two distinct institutions, they also – by virtue of this metonymic relationship – are integrally connected: in visiting the Museo, it is as if one were visiting the Truth Commission.

In the account presented in this chapter I recreate my own experience of this, as a visitor to the Museo. Paying close attention to the Museo's architectural design and conceptualization, as well as its museological space, this account shows how the relationship between the Chilean Truth Commission and international human rights law manifests and works – that is, how international human rights law authorizes the Truth Commission's account as the truth. To do this, I focus on how the Museo gives material form and continuity to the Truth Commission's authorized truth. I show the ways in which the Museo communicates and reasserts how the Truth Commission draws on international human rights law to authorize its account of the dictatorship's state violence. As the Museo's museological space shows, drawing on international human rights law gives authority to the Truth Commission's truth while also hierarchically ordering coexisting truths. This ordering places the other truths under the Truth Commission's internationally authorized truth, while rendering them as 'minor,' and thus irrelevant for state-society relations. This reveals how international human rights law authorizes a society's relation to the past (or collective memory) after violent conflict, and thus life together in the present.

The chapter begins by recounting the circumstances in which the Chilean Truth Commission emerged and its relation to the Museo (Section 3.2). The chapter then turns to my experience as a visitor of the museum's 'outside' and 'inside' spaces. The visual structure of the 'outside/inside' is used to analyze how a visitor encounters the Museo both physically (Section 3.3) and thematically (Section 3.4), as she enters the museum's precinct and is slowly immersed in the stories memorialized there. I show throughout Sections 3.3 and 3.4 how the Museo simultaneously gives material form and continuity to the Truth

Commission and its relationship with international human rights law. I also show here how, through the Museo's museological space, international human rights law continues to authorize the account resulting from the Truth Commission's investigation. Through the analysis in Section 3.5, I show the consequences of the Truth Commission's/ Museo's truth on the Arpilleristas (women relatives of the detained-disappeared) and the Mapuche (the largest Indigenous group in Chile). I do this by focusing on how the Arpilleristas and the Mapuche describe their truth about the dictatorship's violence, and how their accounts have been cast as 'minor' truths. This, I argue, involves a continuation of the state violence that marked Chile's dictatorship.

3.2 AUTHORIZING 'MAJOR' TRUTHS: AT THE MUSEO, AT THE TRUTH COMMISSION

In August 2018, over 10,000 people attended an event organized by the Museo under the motto "Volver a Pasar por el Corazón" (Going Back through the Heart), and the Twitter hashtag #YoProtejoLaMemoria (I Protect the Memory).[8] This was a collective response, led by a group of influential Chilean artists, to the words of the then newly appointed Minister of Culture, Mauricio Rojas, who described the Museo as a "*montaje*" (montage).[9] For Rojas, the Museo is a project of the "left-wing" that "tell[s] a false version of the history of Chile."[10] The Chilean public's reaction and subsequent fierce defense of the Museo seemed to manifest something greater than the museum itself: protecting the Museo was to protect 'the memory.' Although the Twitter hashtag could be translated as "I Protect Memory," in a literal sense the hashtag

8 The Clinic, "Más de 15.000 personas se reunieron en el Museo de la Memoria bajo la consigna 'Volver a Pasar por el Corazón'," *The Clinic* (16 August 2018). www.theclinic.cl/2018/08/16/mas-de-15-000-personas-se-reunieron-en-el-museo-de-la-memoria-bajo-la-consigna-volver-a-pasar-por-el-corazon/.

9 CNN en Español, "La Entrevista en CNN donde Mauricio Rojas Afirmó que el Museo de la Memoria Cuenta una 'Versión Falsa de la Historia de Chile'," *CNN Chile* (11 August 2018). www.cnnchile.com/pais/la-entrevista-en-cnn-donde-mauricio-rojas-afirmo-que-el-museo-de-la-memoria-cuenta-una-version-falsa-de-la-historia-de-chile_20180811/.

10 ("izquierda ... para contar una versión falsa de la historia de Chile"). Ibid.

might suggest something deeper because it uses the Spanish linguistic determiner "*la*" (the).[11] This determiner is used to point to a well-known reference, in this case, *la memoria* – a *memoria* preserved in, and by, the Museo, and grounded on the truth authorized by the 1990 Truth Commission.

What makes the Museo the place associated with 'the memory as truth,' or 'truthful memory,' has to do with the museum's relationship with the 1990–1991 Truth Commission, officially named National Commission on Truth and Reconciliation.[12] The 1991 Final Report, titled the Report of the Chilean National Commission on Truth and Reconciliation,[13] was especially influential in determining not only the creation of the Museo, but also its scope.[14] The uniqueness of Chile's Museo is that, unlike museums of an otherwise similar nature, its conceptualization is informed by the account authorized in the reports of Chile's Truth Commissions.[15] Yet, it was with the 1990–1991 Truth Commission and its Final Report that universal human rights were formally – and most importantly, subtly – introduced into Chilean institutional life and discourses after the dictatorship.[16] This subtlety was considered necessary by Chile's recently elected government, led by Patricio Aylwin.

In 1989, Patricio Aylwin became the first democratically elected president after seventeen years of dictatorship. The election of Aylwin was made possible through the 1988 plebiscite and the highly effective political campaign of the Concertación de Partidos por la Democracia (Coalition of Parties for Democracy, also known as the Concertación), the dictatorship's political opposition. In Chile's Constitution, drafted in

11 "el, la", Diccionario de la Lengua Española; "the" Oxford English Dictionary.

12 Gobierno de Chile, *Decreto Supremo No. 355 Crea Comisión de Verdad y Reconciliación* (25 April 1990). In Chile this Truth Commission is also known as 'Rettig Commission.'

13 Comisión Nacional de Verdad y Reconciliación, *Report of the Chilean National Commission on Truth and Reconciliation*, trans by Phillip Berryman (University of Notre Dame Press, 1993; United States Institute of Peace, 2002).

14 Museo de la Memoria y Derechos Humanos, "About the Museum." https://ww3.museodelamemoria.cl/english-version/.

15 See note 2 above.

16 Fernando Atria, "The Time of Law: Human Rights between Law and Politics," *Law & Critique*, vol 16, no 2 (2005), 140–141. Atria's analysis is worth reading to understand the pragmatic difficulties that the government faced at the time, and the role of the Truth Commission played in helping to navigate them.

1980 by Pinochet's close adviser and jurist, Jaime Guzmán,[17] it was established that in 1988 a plebiscite would take place to ask Chileans if they wanted to continue under Pinochet's leadership. In the month leading up to the plebiscite, Pinochet allowed the Concertación to have television segments each day until before the plebiscite on October 5, 1988. The Concertación's television segment was popularly known as "Franja del No" (The 'No' Campaign), which aimed to mobilize the vote against continuing under dictatorship. With a catchy jingle, a clear argument, and persuasive narrative, this campaign for the Concertación was offering Chileans an alternative to dictatorship. The Concertación's jingle "Chile, la Alegría Ya Viene" (Chile, Happiness is Coming), was key in transmitting and illustrating the type of joyous future that voting 'no' in the 1988 referendum would create for Chileans: without dictatorship Chileans would gain back their freedom to think and speak together in peace, in a place where human life, dignity, and sociopolitical plurality would be respected.[18] Finally, on November 8, Chile's electoral tribunal declared that 54.71 percent of Chileans voted 'no' while 43.01 percent voted 'yes' to continue under Pinochet's dictatorship.[19] In light of that outcome, the electoral tribunal "decided to proclaim as approved, the option that obtained the largest number of votes."[20] Although this was the outcome that many dreamed of, and fought for, the Concertación had to work in the midst of complex circumstances.[21] The 1980

[17] Jaime Guzmán is regarded as the leading intellectual who designed the legal foundations of the dictatorship. Guzmán's murder after the publication of the Final Report shifted public attention from its publication to the ongoing divisions of Chilean society. See, Daniel Mansuy, *Nos Fuimos Quedando en Silencio: La Agonía del Chile de la Transición* (Instituto de Estudios de la Sociedad, 2016), 21–48.

[18] Brian Loveman and Elizabeth Lira, *Las Ardientes Cenizas del Olvido: Vía Chilena de Reconciliación Política 1932–1994* (LOM Ediciones; DIBAM, 2000), 402. P. Reyes, "La Olvidada Cantante Del Himno Del No: 'Sentí Que Habíamos Sido Incapaces De Cambiar Este País'," *La Tercera* (5 October 2018). www.latercera.com/la-tercera-pm/noticia/la-olvidada-cantante-del-himno-del-no-senti-habiamos-incapaces-cambiar-este-pais/343543/.

[19] Gobierno de Chile, Tribunal Calificador de Elecciones de Chile, "Sentencia Plebiscito 1988" (4 November 1988).

[20] ("decidió proclamar como aprobada, aquella opción que obtuvo el mayor número de votos"). Ibid.

[21] Lira, *Historia, Política*, 493–497.

Constitution provided that, in case the outcome of the 1988 plebiscite was unfavorable to Pinochet, democratic elections would be held the following year and the president-elect would assume office in 1990. At the same time, the Constitution provided that Pinochet would have a lifetime position in Chilean public institutions as Senator and Commander-in-Chief of the Armed Forces.[22]

The Concertación also faced socioeconomic challenges. During his dictatorship, Pinochet aimed to 'modernize' Chile's economy by adopting economic policies such as the privatization of natural resource exploitation, tax-cuts, and embracing free trade. To do this, Pinochet sought the advice of a group of Chilean economists, popularly called the Chicago Boys, who were trained in Milton Friedman's neoliberal model at the University of Chicago in the United States.[23] However, the neoliberal economic policies designed by the Chicago Boys drove Chileans into a deep socioeconomic crisis.[24] Those economic policies not only determined the Aylwin government's basic economic decisions, including renegotiating the external debt acquired by the regime, but also conditioned the government to preserve and transmit to future governments a state rooted in a market-based economy.[25] It was not going to be easy for president-elect Aylwin and the Concertación to deal with those inherited social, legal, political, and economic conditions.

In those circumstances Aylwin's government inaugurated the 1990 Truth Commission at the beginning of a period called La Transición (the

22 This was established in article 45 of the Chilean Constitution of 1980. See Junta de Gobierno de la República de Chile, *Constitución Política de la República de Chile* (21 October 1980). See also República de Chile, "Legitimidad de Asunción de Señor Augusto Pinochet Ugarte como Senador Vitalicio," *Diario de Sesiones del Senado*, no 35 (10 March 1997).

23 For detailed account see, Juan Gabriel Valdés, *Pinochet's Economists: The Chicago School in Chile* (Cambridge University Press, 1995); chapters 2–4 in Naomi Klein, *The Shock Doctrine* (Penguin Books, 2008); David Harvey, *A Brief History of Neoliberalism* (Oxford University Press, 2005), 8.

24 Valdés, *Pinochet's Economists*; chapters 2–4 in Klein, *The Shock Doctrine*; Harvey, *A Brief History*.

25 James F. Petras, Fernando Ignacio Leiva, and Henry Veltmeyer, *Democracy and Poverty in Chile: The Limits to Electoral Politics* (Westview Press, 1994), 99–139; Eduardo Silva, *The State and Capital in Chile: Business Elites, Technocrats, and Market Economics* (Westview Press, 1996), especially chapter 8.

Transition), which refers to Chile's transition from dictatorship to democratic government. The 1990 Truth Commission was inaugurated in April, a month after Aylwin assumed the presidency.[26] The Truth Commission was created as part of a process to smoothly deinstitutionalize the dictatorship's systematic practices of sociopolitical repression, and at the same time to institutionalize international human rights law as the safeguard to prevent a return of those practices.[27] Aylwin, in his inaugural presidential speech, assured Chileans and the representatives of foreign states that "the moral conscience of the Nation demands the clarification of the truth about the disappearances of people, about the horrible crimes and other gross human rights violations that occurred during the dictatorship."[28] Aylwin's inaugural address shows that one of the concerns of the new government was to transmit to Chileans (and the international community) its commitment to pursue national reconciliation and truth as justice, but not by any conventional means, such as criminal trials.[29] This pointed to one of the main challenges of the Aylwin government in the Transición: to strike a balance between fostering national reconciliation and addressing the dictatorship's human rights violations. The Truth Commission emerged as the institution that could help Aylwin's government to make a 'balanced' transition to democracy.[30] According to its advocates, this Truth Commission would allow the government to navigate the Transición's political-legal constraints and satisfy the demands for truth as justice of the Chilean groups of human rights activists and relatives of the disappeared, without threatening Pinochet and his supporters with the possibility of being

26 Gobierno de Chile, *Decreto Supremo No. 355 Crea Comisión de Verdad.*

27 Margaret Popkin and Naomi Roht-Arriaza, "Truth as Justice: Investigatory Commissions in Latin America," *Law & Social Inquiry*, vol 20, no 1 (1995).

28 ("la conciencia moral de la Nación exige que se esclarezca la verdad respecto de los desaparecimientos de personas, de los crímenes horrendos y de otras graves violaciones a los derechos humanos ocurridas durante la dictadura"). "El Discurso Con Que Patricio Aylwin Reinauguró La Democracia" ([12 March 1990] 20 April 2016). www.gob.cl/noticias/el-discurso-con-que-patricio-aylwin-reinauguro-la-democracia-1/.

29 Ibid.

30 Yves Dezalay and Bryant G. Garth, *The Internationalization of Palace Wars: Lawyers, Economists, and the Contest to Transform Latin American States* (University of Chicago Press, 2002), 228.

prosecuted.[31] Importantly, the Truth Commission would not upset Chile's landowning elites because it would not investigate the violence (such as extreme poverty) accentuated by the dictatorship's market-based economic model, which benefited and protected the interests of those elites.[32]

José Zalaquett – a renowned human rights activist, Aylwin's close adviser and later a member of the Truth Commission – was instrumental in the design of the Truth Commission process.[33] For Zalaquett, balance was essential for the success of the Chilean Transición. This was the case, according to Zalaquett, not only because it was legally impossible to prosecute Pinochet and his regime (and any attempt to override the current juridical and political system could lead to another coup),[34] but also because Chilean society was deeply divided about 'the truth' of the events that led to the 1973 coup d'état and subsequent seventeen years of military dictatorship.[35] In 1988 the Chilean situation, and different ideas on how to best proceed in such circumstances, were discussed at a conference funded by the Ford Foundation and organized by the Aspen Institute, a United States-based think tank.[36] The aim of the conference was to "develop an intellectual framework" to "clarify the political, moral, and the legal challenges" faced by states transitioning from

31 Patricio Aylwin, "El Desafío de Mirar al Futuro," in *Las Voces de la Reconciliación*, Joaquín Castillo Vial, Hernán Larraín, and Ricardo Nuñez (eds) (Instituto de Estudios de la Sociedad, 2013).

32 Tomás Moulian, "A Time of Forgetting: The Myths of the Chilean Transition," *NACLA Report on the Americas*, no 2 (1998).

33 Dezalay and Garth, *The Internationalization of Palace Wars*, 147.

34 The 1978 Amnesty Law impeded this. See Loveman and Lira, *Las Ardientes Cenizas del Olvido*, 451–469; Mansuy, *Nos Fuimos Quedando en Silencio*, 21–48.

35 Naomi Roht-Arriaza and José Zalaquett, "The Need for Moral Reconstruction in the Wake of Past Human Rights Violations: An Interview with José Zalaquett," in *Transitional Justice: Handbook for Latin America*, Félix Reátegui (ed) (Brazilian Amnesty Commission, Ministry of Justice; International Center for Transitional Justice, 2011), 162–163.

36 Alice H. Henkin, "Preface," in *State Crimes: Punishment or Pardon: Papers and Report of the Conference, The Aspen Institute* (The Aspen Institute, 1988), v. On the role in Latin America of United States-based foundations see Inderjeet Parmar, *Foundations of the American Century: The Ford, Carnegie, and Rockefeller Foundations in the Rise of American Power* (Columbia University Press, 2012).

dictatorships to democracy.[37] To do this, the Aspen Institute invited a select group of scholars, activists, and government advisers from all around the world, to specifically reflect on how to best address past human rights violations.[38]

Among the conference participants was Zalaquett and Jaime Malamud-Goti, one of the two Argentinean jurists who designed the 1983 Argentinian Truth Commission (as noted in Chapter 2).[39] One of the conference's common points of agreement was that "truth-telling efforts" in transitions from dictatorship to democracy were a normative "minimum requirement of justice."[40] On this matter Zalaquett emphasized that the authorized truth had to be disseminated to be widely known across society so that it would be indisputable.[41] This was, for Zalaquett, a more desirable programmatic position for a state to address past human rights violations than the radical decision of punishing (through criminal trials) the former regime.[42] At the Aspen conference, Zalaquett also argued that the fragility of the Chilean transitional moment required a non-straightforward institutional action to address the human rights violations of the previous regime, and at the same time to prevent the repetition of the violence.[43] The notion of 'violence' informing the Aspen conference participants' understanding of 'human rights violations' did not seem to consider the human suffering caused by exploitation, starvation, land displacement and poverty (to name a few), as forms of violence that had been enabled by the socioeconomic model consolidated by the Pinochet regime. That logic of decoupling the regime's "economic policies and sociopolitical setting" was

[37] Paige Arthur, "How 'Transitions' Reshaped Human Rights: A Conceptual History of Transitional Justice," *Human Rights Quarterly*, vol 31, no 2 (2009), 349.

[38] Ibid, 322; Henkin, "Preface," in *State Crimes*, 1–2.

[39] Arthur, "How 'Transitions' Reshaped Human Rights," 335–336; The Aspen Institute, *State Crimes*, 94–96.

[40] Arthur, "How 'Transitions' Reshaped Human Rights," 356.

[41] José Zalaquett, "Confronting Human Rights Violations Committed by Former Governments: Principles Applicable and Political Constraints," in *Transitional Justice: How Emerging Democracies Reckon with Former Regimes*, Neil J. Kritz (ed) (United States Institute of Peace Press, 1995), 3; 6.

[42] Arthur, "How 'Transitions' Reshaped Human Rights," 358. Zalaquett discusses this point in, Zalaquett, "Confronting Human Rights Violations," 3; 6–9.

[43] Arthur, "How 'Transitions' Reshaped Human Rights," 335–336.

exposed by Orlando Letelier, an influential former minister of Salvador Allende.[44] Letelier argued that such decoupling was a "particularly convenient concept of a social system in which 'economic freedom' and political terror coexist without touching each other" because it "allow[ed] ... financial spokesmen to support their concept of 'freedom' while exercising their verbal muscles in defense of human rights."[45] Although Letelier was presenting a fierce critique of the international financial institutions and professionals that supported the dictatorship's neoliberal economic policies, his argument went both ways. It was also illustrating how human rights law groups and experts in Chile and abroad were (and still tend to) also decoupling the dictatorship's economic violence from their human rights-informed understanding of state violence.[46] In the case of the Aspen conference, for example, "[e]stablishing the truth" was considered one of the "[m]inimum [o]bligations of [s]tates," but their notion of 'truth' was decoupled from any notion that economic policies could also be used to exercise state violence.[47]

Unsurprisingly, the Aspen understanding of state violence informed the view of Aylwin's government about the need to establish as 'truth' a collective and authoritative account of the dictatorship's state violence, and to take steps to ensure Chileans would know it and widely accept it.[48] For the Chilean government, given the legal, social, political, and economic circumstances mentioned before, it was essential to make clear that the Truth Commission was not a trial;[49] it was only a truth-seeking

44 Orlando Letelier, "Economic 'Freedom's' Awful Toll: The 'Chicago Boys' in Chile," *Review of Radical Political Economics*, vol 8, no 3 (1976), 44.

45 Ibid, 44. On the role of Ford Foundation's in funding the training of the Chicago Boys see generally, Valdés, *Pinochet's Economists*; Parmar, *Foundations of the American Century*; Klein, *The Shock Doctrine.*

46 On this see, Javier Couso, "The Limits of Law for Emancipation (in the South): Dealing with Prisoners' Rights in Post-authoritarian Chile," *Griffith Law Review*, vol 16, no 2 (2014); Jessica Whyte, *The Morals of the Market: Human Rights and the Rise of Neoliberalism* (Verso, 2019), 197.

47 Alice H. Henkin, "Conference Report," in *State Crimes: Punishment or Pardon: Papers and Report of the Conference, The Aspen Institute* (The Aspen Institute, 1988), 4.

48 Fernando Atria, "The Time of Law," 140–141.

49 Zalaquett sketches out here the mechanism that later took the form of the 1990 Chilean Truth Commission. See, Zalaquett, "Confronting Human Rights Violations," 7. See also, Comisión Nacional de Verdad y Reconciliación, *Informe de la*

process based on 'facts,' which were called 'human rights violations.'[50] The aim of the Truth Commission process was to offer Chilean society a "full, officially sanctioned" truth about the human rights violations committed by the Chilean state during Pinochet's dictatorship.[51] That was the Truth Commission's *raison d'être.*[52]

To fulfill its mission, the Truth Commission established that the Universal Declaration of Human Rights (UDHR) provided "the norms, concepts and criteria that served as the framework for its [the Truth Commission's] deliberations and conclusions."[53] In Chapter II of the Final Report, titled "Norms, Concepts and Criteria on which the Commission's conclusions have been based," it describes how international human rights law informs the "forms of human rights violations" used by the Truth Commission to categorize situations that occurred during dictatorship.[54] For example, the Final Report uses the phrase "extreme forms of human rights violations" to refer to the continuous disappearances and detention of persons committed by the Chileans state's security agents.[55] This official recognition of the situation of the detained-disappeared as a human rights violation is exemplary of how the Truth Commission gave specific legal form to one of the dictatorship's most significant (and traumatizing) sociopolitical situations.[56] In doing

Comisión Nacional de Verdad y Reconciliación (Corporación Nacional de Reparación y Reconciliación, 1991) xi–xiv; 4.

50 On this narrow framing of the Southern Cone dictatorships' practices as human rights violations, see Klein, *The Shock Doctrine.* On international human rights law as a genre of storytelling see, Joseph R. Slaughter, "Hijacking Human Rights: Neoliberalism, the New Historiography, and the End of the Third World," *Human Rights Quarterly*, vol 40, no 4 (2018), 741.

51 Zalaquett, "Confronting Human Rights Violations," 7.

52 Roht-Arriaza and Zalaquett, "The Need for Moral Reconstruction," 162.

53 Comisión Nacional de Verdad y Reconciliación, *Report*, 42; 51.

54 Ibid, 35–49. For 'categories' as technologies of jurisdiction, see Shaunnagh Dorsett and Shaun McVeigh, *Jurisdiction* (Routledge, 2012), 71–76. On how law frames testimonies in a Truth Commission, see Mark Sanders, *Ambiguities of Witnessing: Law and Literature in the Time of a Truth Commission* (Stanford University Press, 2007). For a full list of the Final Report's forms of human rights violations, see Comisión Nacional de Verdad y Reconciliación, *Report*, 51–56.

55 Ibid, 23.

56 In Chile, those who disappeared during the dictatorship are referred as the 'detained-disappeared' ('*detenidos-desaparecidos*'). In Chile happened what Slaughter calls

so, the Truth Commission constituted the 'detained-disappeared' and the actions of 'execution,' 'torture,' or 'abuse of power' as legal objects of international human rights law, thus into legal objects of the Truth Commission's investigation too.[57] This shows how the Truth Commission drew on the language of international human rights law to authorize its account of the dictatorship.

In the remainder of this chapter (Sections 3.3 and 3.4), I recreate my experience as a visitor of the Museo, to show how the Museo, as a sociocultural and educational institution, gives material form and temporal continuity to the Truth Commission's internationally authorized truth.

3.3 THE MUSEO FROM THE OUTSIDE

The Museo de la Memoria y los Derechos Humanos, situated in Santiago, capital city of Chile, was inaugurated in January 2010 under the presidency of Michelle Bachelet. The Museo is located across Quinta Normal Park in Barrio Yungay, one of Santiago's central and vibrant neighborhoods, home to important national museums and cultural centers.[58] The Museo's precinct is demarcated by a fence that visually delimits the physical space where the museum is located. However, the lines that give form to the building's minimalist style are not overshadowed by the fence of the precinct. The elegance of the building's architectural design, enhanced by its deep emerald green and rectangular form, makes the Museo visible and yet discrete.

Visibility and discretion characterize the Museo's main entrances too. While the museum is directly accessible from Matucana Avenue, from Catedral Street and from a side entrance on Chacabuco Street, as well as

a "rollback" or repossession of human rights, in Slaughter, "Hijacking Human Rights," 765. On how norms "operate through frames" to "govern" what is human and grievable, in Judith Butler, "Torture and the Ethics of Photography," *Environment and Planning D: Society and Space*, vol 25, no 6 (2007), 953.

57 On this imperial impetus of international law see, Peter Fitzpatrick, "Gods Would Be Needed: American Empire and the Rule of (International) Law," *Leiden Journal of International Law*, vol 16, no 3 (2003): 459–460. See also note 54 above on categorizing.

58 Mario Figueroa, Lucas Fehr, and Carlos Dias, "Espacios Para la Cultura," *ARQ (Santiago)*, no 81 (2012).

from the underground access in the subway station at Quinta Normal Park, the Museo has only two main street entrances.[59] One of these entrances is on Matucana Avenue (the 'Matucana entrance'), and the other is on the corner between Matucana Avenue and Catedral Street (the 'Catedral entrance'). Although equally important, there are slight differences between these two entrances. Catedral entrance is located opposite the street access to Quinta Normal Park's subway station, urban bus stops, and the entrance of Quinta Normal Park itself. This detail is significant because the location of the Catedral entrance gives it more visibility and facilitates access to the Museo's precinct, compared to the Matucana entrance, which from this perspective goes almost unnoticed. Another important detail is the colorful banners hanging next to the Catedral entrance, welcoming visitors to the museum and also advertising specific exhibitions.

Observing the structure of the Museo from the outside – that is, without entering into the museum's precinct – the viewer might have different interpretations of the activities that take place inside. Only if pedestrians or drivers pay close attention to the features previously described is it possible to imagine what the beautiful and captivating building is for.

Chile's Museo belongs to what museology and cultural studies refers to as 'new museums.'[60] New museums are considered those that "invite reflection"[61] through multiple curatorial techniques, beyond the traditional or 'old' museum practices of preservation and display of historical objects, images, or artistic pieces.[62] Aiming to be inclusive and responsive to contemporary social concerns, new museums "are not based on collections but focus on crucial historical events which are deemed essential for interpreting the present and envisaging the future."[63] Indeed, Chile's

59 Museo de la Memoria y los Derechos Humanos, "Visítanos." web.museodelamemoria.cl/visitanos/.

60 See generally, Silke Arnold-de Simine, *Mediating Memory in the Museum: Trauma, Empathy, Nostalgia* (Palgrave Macmillan, 2013).

61 Jens Andermann and Silke Arnold-de Simine, "Introduction: Memory, Community and the New Museum," *Theory, Culture & Society*, vol 29, no 1 (2012): 4.

62 On the transformation of museums, see generally, Peter Vergo (ed), *The New Museology* (Reaktion Books, 1989); Tony Bennett, *The Birth of the Museum: History, Theory, Politics* (Routledge, 1995).

63 Arnold-de Simine, *Mediating Memory*, 10; Andermann and Arnold-de Simine, "Introduction: Memory," 6.

Museo was created in order "to draw attention to human rights violations committed by the Chilean state between 1973 and 1990,"[64] a period corresponding to Pinochet's seventeen-year dictatorship. Whether the visitor has informed herself or not of the content of the Museo's displays prior to visiting, the Museo's name – the "Museum of Memory and Human Rights" – singles out the organizing themes of the exhibitions.

Even more specifically, the Museo is a 'memory museum.' As Arnold-de Simine explains, what makes memory museums distinct is that their "specific forms of narration and presentation and the display tactics" use 'memory' as the "framework" and "paradigm" to "relate to the past."[65] Chile's Museo follows that line by stating that its mission is to "stimulate reflection and debate and to promote respect and tolerance in order that these events never happen again."[66] Furthermore, the Museo is officially described as a place where:

> through objects, documents and archives in different supports and formats, as well as innovative visual and audio displays, it is possible to know part of this history: the coup d'état, the repression that took place in the following years, the resistance movement, exile, international solidarity and the defense of human rights.[67]

Both the description of its curatorial practices and its mission denote the Museo's intention to represent this period of Chile's history (Pinochet's dictatorship between 1973 and 1990) by articulating it 'as,' and 'through,' memory and human rights.[68]

This is reflected in the speech given by the then president of Chile, Michelle Bachelet, at the Museo's inaugural ceremony in January 2010. Bachelet's opening words were: "[t]his Museum is where Chilean society encounters and re-encounters itself. Where Chilean society confronts its

64 Museo de la Memoria, "About the Museum."

65 Arnold-de Simine, *Mediating Memory*, 10–11.

66 Museo de la Memoria, "About the Museum."

67 In the text in Spanish, the Museum adds to this paragraph: "and the defense of human rights" ("y la defensa de los derechos humanos"). Museo de la Memoria y Derechos Humanos, "Sobre el Museo." web.museodelamemoria.cl/sobre-el-museo/.

68 I am borrowing Huyssen's idea of "representation of the past" in order to "articulate memory." Andreas Huyssen, *Twilight Memories: Marking Time in a Culture of Amnesia* (Routledge, 1995), 2–3.

own history."[69] Bachelet, who along with her parents was detained and tortured during the dictatorship, stated that visiting the Museo's exhibition had been a difficult experience.[70] The building contained "images that I do not wish to remember," Bachelet confessed.[71] At the same time, Bachelet shared with the audience attending the event the realization that she had when visiting the Museo's exhibitions, that "we cannot change our past, but only learn from what was lived,"[72] and stressed that precisely because of that, the Museo is necessary.

For Bachelet, that necessity emerged from the "deep political crisis" that Chile went through between 1973 and 1990, which affected the "minimum grounds for coexistence that every society requires."[73] These "grounds for coexistence" were shattered, Bachelet stated, by the "grave and systematic violations of human rights."[74] Human rights, Bachelet emphasized, are universal because they are at the core of the grounds of coexistence of any democratic society; therefore human rights "must be and can be respected under any circumstance."[75] Bachelet concluded her speech by saying that the Museo represented the diversity of memories of Chile's painful past, and at the same time, the Museo was a public space to learn and make a "commitment that never again will something like that occur."[76]

This articulation of memory coupled with the continued references to human rights, both in the Museo's statements and in Bachelet's speech, denote the Museo's twofold educational objective: (1) to remember the specific events and actions that occurred during the Chilean dictatorship, considered 'the historical past' as human rights violations; and (2) to remind visitors to the Museo that abiding by international human

[69] ("este Museo donde se encuentra y se reencuentra la sociedad chilena"). Michelle Bachelet, "Inauguración Museo de la Memoria y los Derechos Humanos" (11 January 2010), 1.

[70] Ibid. [71] ("imágenes que yo no quisiera recordar"). Ibid.

[72] ("no podemos cambiar nuestro pasado); (sólo nos queda aprender de lo vivido"). Ibid.

[73] ("profunda crisis política"); ("afectaran las bases mínimas de convivencia que requiere toda sociedad"). Ibid, 2.

[74] ("graves y sistemáticas violaciones a los derechos humanos"). Ibid.

[75] ("derechos humanos deben y pueden ser respetados en cualquier circunstancia"). Ibid.

[76] ("compromiso de que algo así nunca más vuelva a suceder"). Ibid, 4.

rights law will ensure that the events of the past will "never happen again."[77] In this way, the Museo instructs visitors – and Chilean society in particular – to remember the history of the dictatorship as a past that shall not be repeated, and to understand the necessity of international human rights law as the universal grounds that every society needs to peacefully coexist.

However, the Museo's authority to educate about Chile's dictatorship and international human rights does not solely stem from its own cultural form – that is, from being a state-created museum – but also from the 1990 Truth Commission. What makes the Museo's account of the history of Chile's dictatorship a truthful one is, as previously discussed in this chapter, the way in which international human rights law authorizes this truth. In the following part, I take the reader inside the Museo, to show how the Truth Commission's truth is authorized by international human rights law. I do this by focusing on the arrangement of the Museo's space and the conceptualization of its architectural design.

3.4 THE MUSEO FROM THE INSIDE

Inside the Museo's precinct, the grounds surrounding the building were conceived as one big space known as the esplanade, or more formally, Memory Square. When the visitor enters the precinct, she does so through this esplanade. The visitor can access the museum directly from the street, through the two main entrances located on Matucana Avenue and Catedral Street, as well as a third side entrance on the less busy Chacabuco Street. Depending on the entrance the visitor chooses to access the museum, she will encounter different objects, installations, and artworks. Each piece addresses different themes, such as memory, conscience, forced exile, education and activism, or displacement, to name a few. Yet there is one theme that consistently accompanies the visitor, irrespective of her entrance of choice. That is: universal human rights.

As the visitor enters through Catedral entrance, she walks down the inclined surface of the wide space that the esplanade offers. The esplanade, or Memory Square, is surrounded to the left and right by two small

[77] Museo de la Memoria, "Sobre el Museo."

yet long walls, on which the Museo's green squared building rests. On the right side of the rough and grayish surface of the wall the visitor can see various writings. Getting closer, the visitor sees that these are a reproduction of the UDHR as seen in Figure 3.1.

The UDHR is cast in metal letters, which have been installed all along the right wall of the Memory Square. The installed UDHR begins by reproducing the Preamble on three iron plates. At the bottom of the third plate a paragraph explains that the UDHR "was approved and proclaimed" by the United Nations General Assembly on December 10, 1948, and that "one of the leading drafters was the Chilean jurist and diplomat Hernán Santa Cruz Barceló."[78] By emphasizing that fact, the Museo highlights that the Chilean state was an active participant in the emergence of contemporary international human rights law.[79] In a similar way, the Truth Commission's Final Report stressed that the "Universal Declaration of Human Rights and other

3.1 Esplanade or Memory Square at the Museum of Memory and Human Rights in Santiago (Chile). Photograph by Valeria Vázquez Guevara (2018).

[78] ("siendo uno de sus principales redactores, el jurista y diplomático chileno Hernán Santa Cruz"). Taken from plaque at Museo display. Image on file with author.

[79] On Santa Cruz see Daniel Ricardo Quiroga-Villamarín, "'An Atmosphere of Genuine Solidarity and Brotherhood': Hernán Santa-Cruz and a Forgotten Latin American Contribution to Social Rights," *Journal of the History of International Law*, vol 21, no 1 (2019).

relevant international documents proclaimed rights which in essence were already part of the legislation and the finest civic traditions in Chile."[80] The Final Report added that international human rights law shows the "shortcomings and inadequacies" of the Chilean national legislation not only during dictatorship but also before the 1973 coup d'état.[81] With this, although separated by a period of almost thirty years, both the Final Report (in 1991) and the Museo (since 2010) reassert and communicate the understanding that the violent events and situations during the dictatorship constituted an 'exception' in the historical conduct of the Chilean state.

By declaring the dictatorship a parenthesis in Chile's role as an international lawmaker, the Museo and the Final Report reaffirm the idea that international human rights law is 'universal' and the expression of 'global' values.[82] This is also apparent in how, to the left side of the Preamble, the Museo reproduces in separate metal pieces each of the thirty articles of the UDHR. The UDHR articles cover this entire wall, ending at what the Museo's architects call the "horizontal" part of the Memory Square, or what appears to the eye as the space's visible horizon, a horizon in which the UDHR stands out, and welcomes visitors by reminding them of a promise: with international human rights law "the creation of a world of the good," in this case a good Chilean state, is possible.[83]

80 Comisión Nacional de Verdad y Reconciliación, *Report*, 42.

81 ("carencias e insuficiencias"). Ibid.

82 Scholars who support this view include Kathryn Sikkink, *Evidence for Hope: Making Human Rights Work in the 21st Century* (Princeton University Press, 2017); Steven L. B. Jensen, *The Making of International Human Rights: The 1960s, Decolonization, and the Reconstruction of Global Values* (Cambridge University Press, 2016); Paolo G. Carozza, "From Conquest to Constitutions: Retrieving a Latin American Tradition of the Idea of Human Rights," *Human Rights Quarterly*, vol 25, no 2 (2003). For scholarship that considers the quality of the participation of states of the global South see, Slaughter, "Hijacking Human Rights," 741–744; Sundhya Pahuja, "Laws of Encounter: A Jurisdictional Account of International Law," *London Review of International Law*, vol 1, no 1 (2013); Luis Eslava, Michael Fakhri, and Vasuki Nesiah (eds), *Bandung, Global History, and International Law: Critical Pasts and Pending Futures* (Cambridge University Press, 2017).

83 Shane Chalmers, "The Beginning of Human Rights: The Ritual of the Preamble to Law," *Humanity*, vol 9, no 1 (2018): 111. Nesiah discusses how in political transitions, human rights were mobilized as the normative foundation for a state's "renewal and rebirth" in, Vasuki Nesiah, "Theories of Transitional Justice: Cashing in the Blue Chips," in *The Oxford Handbook of The Theory of International Law*, Anne Orford and Florian Hoffmann (eds) (Oxford University Press, 2016), 781.

Going back to the gate at Catedral entrance, the visitor can see on the left side of the esplanade a handrail and a ground-level rail running along the wall. These two rails create a narrow space similar to a pathway, which directs the visitor to move along the wall until it ends at the entrance of the Museo's building. On the wall a plaque has been installed (in 2017) with a summary in Braille of the articles of the UDHR. This joint project was part of a larger initiative led by the Museo and the University of Santiago.[84] The initiative sought to make the Museo's infrastructure a more inclusive space by facilitating the transmission of information through devices that enabled a first-hand experience of the museum (hence the pathway enables wheel-chair access, while the Braille enables blind visitors to read the exhibit).[85] Also, on this left wall but toward its middle point, the visitor encounters an engraving by the Uruguayan artist Luis Camnitzer. The artwork, titled "El Museo es una Escuela" ("The Museum is a School"), became part of the Museo's permanent collection in 2013,[86] and is part of Camnitzer's broader political work.[87] As seen in Figure 3.2, the engraving reads: "*El Museo es una Escuela: el artista aprende a comunicarse, el público aprende a hacer conexiones*" (The Museum is a School: the artist learns to communicate, the public learns to make connections).

With this artwork, Camnitzer asks visitors to consider the educational relationship between the museum and society. For Camnitzer, Chile's Museo, as a museum, should be a space where visitors can "question what is being shown [at the Museo],"[88] to be able to "understand how power is distributed, which interests the museum is serving with its display . . . and

[84] Museo de la Memoria y Derechos Humanos, "Museo de la Memoria se Transforma en un Espacio de Inclusión y Accesibilidad Universal" (5 December 2017). web.museodelamemoria.cl/museo-de-la-memoria-se-transforma-en-un-espacio-de-inclusion-y-accesibilidad-universal/.

[85] Ibid.

[86] Adriana Valdés, "La Geometría de la Conciencia" (Undated). web.museodelamemoria.cl/exposiciones/la-geometria-de-la-conciencia/.

[87] Ibid.

[88] ("a cuestionar lo que se está mostrando"). Tatiana Oliveros and Marco Fajardo, "Camnitzer en Chile: 'Un Museo Debe Enseñarle al Espectador a Cuestionar lo que Muestra'," *El Mostrador* (20 August 2018). www.elmostrador.cl/cultura/2018/08/20/camnitzer-en-chile-un-museo-debe-ensenarle-al-espectador-a-cuestionar-lo-que-muestra/.

3.2 UDHR in Braille (left) and Camnitzer's "The Museum is a School" (right) at the Museum of Memory and Human Rights in Santiago (Chile). Photograph by Valeria Vázquez Guevara (2018).

in what way those interests are useful or not for the people who go to the museum, if those interests are oppressive or mind-opening."[89] In this sense, for Camnitzer a museum should be a space where visitors are exposed to particular information through the museum's exhibitions, not for the purpose of "consuming" it as passive learners, but to ask critical questions about how such information or knowledge is being taught, and most importantly, for what.

Thus what the visitor encounters on the walls of Memory Square are two invitations for reflection. On the one hand, the Museo presents the installation and display of the UDHR on both walls of Memory Square as a "permanent invitation to defend and promote them [human rights] every day."[90] On the other hand, Camnitzer's invites the Museo's visitors

[89] ("entender cómo está distribuido el poder, a qué intereses le sirve lo que el museo está mostrando . . . y en qué medida esos intereses son útiles para la gente que va al museo o no, son oprimentes o abren la mente"). Ibid.

[90] ("una invitación permanente a defenderlos y promoverlos cada día"). Museo de la Memoria y Derechos Humanos, "Exposición Permanente – La Declaración Universal De Los Derechos Humanos." web.museodelamemoria.cl/talleres/declaracion-universal-derechos-humanos/.

to "make connections" and to ask critical questions about what is being shown at the museum.

However, Camnitzer's artwork as part of the Museo's permanent exhibition, struggles to achieve its mission of challenging the museum's narrative. It rather complements the educational aim of the Museo in its appeal to memorialize Chile's dictatorship through international human rights law. That is, the Museo, through the representations of international human rights located at Memory Square, educates the visitor in how Chile's dictatorship is an international human rights law story. The Museo's permanent installations, comprising representations of international human rights law (the complete UDHR and the UDHR in Braille) in a museological space of high-visibility, shows how human rights occupies a core place in the Museo's memorialization and presentation of Chile's dictatorship. This gives material continuity to the Truth Commission's Final Report, which also placed international human rights law at the heart of Chile's truth about the dictatorship.

Although Memory Square connects the museum's entrances to the building, access from Matucana Avenue and Chacabuco Street offer the visitor another way of encountering universal human rights. When accessing the museum through these entrances (which are opposite each other) the visitor walks less on the esplanade's grounds, because the entrances are closer to the Museo's building. Nonetheless, the two entrances lead to a small common space, which is also used for museum-organized open-air events. As the visitor approaches the Museo's building, the articles of the UDHR, cast in metal on the esplanade's wall, can be seen all the time.

If the visitor enters through Matucana Avenue's stairs, the UDHR is located in front and toward the far right. A few steps after stepping down the stairs, the visitor encounters an underground entrance to the Chilean artist Alfredo Jaar's installation art, titled "Geometría de la Conciencia" ("Geometry of Conscience").[91] Jaar's art installation invites the visitor to sense and experience in her own way the disappearances that occurred during the dictatorship.[92] Playing with light and darkness in a closed room of 500 portrait silhouettes and mirror-walls, Jaar, through the use of

91 Valdés, "La Geometría de la Conciencia." 92 Ibid.

metaphor, invites the visitor to consider the simultaneous presence and absence of the disappeared.

If the visitor enters the Museo from Chacabuco Street, to her right is the inclined surface of the esplanade. In this case, the UDHR is located immediately to the right of the visitor as she passes by the entrance of the museum's auditorium and an aircraft boarding staircase with the words "*Asilo-Exilio*" ("Asylum-Exile"), which symbolizes the situations of asylum and exile caused by the dictatorship.[93] At that point the visitor has the option to wander on the grounds of the esplanade or walk a few meters to enter the building.

However, if the visitor turns to the right, and decides to go over the UDHR articles, she will have to walk up the esplanade in order to start from the beginning of the UDHR. If not, the visitor on her way to the building encounters one last artwork on the grounds of the esplanade. This final artwork is Fernando Prat's 2017 piece, titled "Acción Medular: Memorial en Homenaje al General Carlos Prats González" ("Medullary Action: Memorial in Homage to General Carlos Prats González").[94] Prat's artwork reproduces excerpts of the memoirs of General Carlos Prats, who was murdered along with his wife Sofía by agents of the Chilean state in Argentina in 1974. The letters are written with neon lights and rest on several cylindrical rock core samples that "represent Chile's four cardinal points as a gesture that incorporates both a country's geography, as well as its memory."[95] Finally, after passing by Prat's piece, one arrives at the doors of the Museo's building.

Although the aircraft staircase with the words "Asylum-Exile" and the artworks of Jaar ("Geometría de la Conciencia") and Prat ("Acción Medular") are museological objects that specifically refer to events in the history of Chile's dictatorship, the Museo's architectural design facilitates the visual dominance of the UDHR over them. The Museo,

[93] Museo de la Memoria y Derechos Humanos, "Asilo/Exilio." web.museodelamemoria.cl/asiloexilio/.

[94] Museo de la Memoria y Derechos Humanos, "Acción Medular: Memorial en Homenaje al General Carlos Prats González." https://web.museodelamemoria.cl/exposiciones/accion-medular-en-homenaje-al-general-carlos-prats-gonzalez/.

[95] ("representan los cuatro puntos cardinales de Chile, como un gesto que incorpora tanto la geografía de un país, como su memoria"). Ibid.

like the Truth Commission's Final Report, places the UDHR, as the ultimate expression of international human rights law, at the heart of the truth of the Chilean dictatorship. At the Museo, as in the Truth Report, the Chilean dictatorship is represented and memorialized, and thus preserved or kept alive, as an account of human rights violations. This manifests materially in Memory Square, where the UDHR is not only visible at all times, but also physically reproduced and installed on both of the walls surrounding Memory Square.

While the two artworks and the aircraft staircase work as devices that facilitate the visitor's learning of, and immersion into, important events of the dictatorship – detained-disappeared (Jaar), forced exile (aircraft stairs), and murders committed by the Chilean state's security forces (Prat) – they are accommodated within the framework of international human rights law as seen in Figure 3.3. It is in Memory Square, as a space for reflection, where it becomes difficult for the Museo's visitor to 'hear' only the 'local' stories told by the artworks and the aircraft staircase because they are overshowed by the omnipresent UDHR.

That shows, once again, how the Museo gives continuity and reasserts the Truth Commission's gesture of drawing on international human rights law to authorize the 'local' Chilean truths. The Museo places

3.3 UDHR (right) and "Asylum-Exile" staircase (center) at Memory Square at the Museum of Memory and Human Rights in Santiago (Chile). Photograph by Valeria Vázquez Guevara (2018).

international human rights law, like the Final Report did, as the authority that supports and informs how Chile's dictatorial 'past' is officially articulated, by authorizing what the dictatorship was, and how it is and will be remembered. The authorizing of this truth through international human rights law gives the Truth Commission and the Museo's truth of the dictatorship a powerful international authority. In turn, this internationally authorized truth displaces the plurality of truths that emerge from the stories, from "the knowledges of the land and territory" that Memory Square is also meant to preserve and transmit.[96]

Thus, no matter which entrance the visitor walks through to enter the grounds of the Museo, she constantly encounters universal human rights as a dominant message in Memory Square. As a 'new museum,' the Museo aims, through "experiential learning," to "develop" in visitors "more personal and immediate forms of affective engagement" with the historical 'past' being represented there.[97] To achieve this, Memory Square is the museological space conceptualized and designed to prepare visitors to "connect with their state of mind" before entering into the Museo's main building.[98] The effect of Memory Square on visitors might be similar to that of a "front plaza – the entry into the temple," as a "preambular passage,"[99] which prepares visitors to enter into a sacred place to connect with her God/s. Memory Square works as an "active frame" that represents the social suffering caused by the dictatorship as a violation of international human rights law.[100]

As such, Memory Square – by preparing the visitor to enter into the Museo's building, where a detailed account of the lawful truth of Chile's dictatorship awaits her – "allocates the recognizability" of the Chilean

96 ("a la reflexión . . . a los conocimientos de la tierra y del territorio"). Figueroa, Fehr, and Dias, "Espacios Para la Cultura," 28.

97 Jens Andermann and Silke Arnold-de Simine, "Introduction: Museums and the Educational Turn: History, Memory, Inclusivity," *Journal of Educational Memory, Media, and Society*, vol 4, no 2 (2012): 2.

98 ("conectar con el estado de ánimo"). Museo de la Memoria y Derechos Humanos, "Arquitectura: Propuesta Ganadora." https://ww3.museodelamemoria.cl/wp-content/uploads/2016/02/Texto-arquitectos1.pdf.

99 Chalmers, "The Beginning of Human Rights," 108.

100 Butler, "Torture and the Ethics of Photography," 952.

dictatorship with the articles of UDHR and international human rights law, as the "broader norms" that determine what stories belong to such frame.[101] That is, it authorizes what accounts of the dictatorship fit into the scope of international human rights law and thus become true and worthy of memorialization at the Museo. The UDHR, physically and thematically embedded in Memory Square, gives narrative coherence to the plural accounts of the history of the dictatorship presented inside the Museo's building. International human rights law at the Museo, like in the Final Report, works as the authorized interpretative framework through which the violence of the dictatorship is represented as 'the' historical and truthful memory.

On entering the Museo's building the visitor is welcomed into a new museological space. This space, called the Access Hall, houses a permanent exhibition titled "Derechos Humanos, Desafío Universal" ("Human Rights, A Universal Challenge").[102] Thus, even if the visitor does not pay much attention to the physical manifestations of the UDHR at Memory Square, she will keep encountering universal human rights in the Access Hall's display. This display brings together four permanent collections that introduce the visitor to the Museo's articulation of 'memory as the truth' of Chile's dictatorship between 1973 and 1990.[103]

The Access Hall is presided over by a giant world map. Although this map is visually captivating, the intended pathway through the "Human Rights, A Universal Challenge" exhibition starts to the far right of the Access Hall. The visitor is guided to start with the display "Comisiones de Verdad en el Mundo" ("Truth Commissions in the World"). An emerald green glass plaque with blue tones displays a text under the title "Comisiones de Verdad" ("Truth Commissions"). This four-paragraph text starts by explaining that the legacy of violence across "America, Africa, Asia and Europe has left a wake of suffering and mourning in

101 Ibid, 951.

102 Museo de la Memoria y Derechos Humanos, "Exposición Permanente – Derechos Humanos, Desafío Universal." https://web.museodelamemoria.cl/exposicion-principal/.

103 Ibid.

the context of dictatorial regimes, civil wars or invasions."[104] The following paragraph states that, "in more than 30 countries Truth Commissions have been created. These are investigative organs, non-judicial, charged to inquire into the denunciated abuses."[105] The third paragraph gives examples of the general object of inquiry of Truth Commissions, and establishes that "victims . . . and their families have the right to know the truth and to a public acknowledgment of their suffering."[106] The last paragraph then provides a brief overview of the two Chilean Truth Commissions. Directly below the Truth Commissions plaque and the world map on the wall, there is a long red shelf with silver frames on it. Each frame contains a summary of one of the thirty truth commissions implemented all over the world.[107]

Continuing with the "Truth Commissions in the World" display, one is guided to the world map, which displays a 'global' contemporary account of violent conflict and presents Truth Commissions as the mechanism that helped societies to live together again. The photographs comprising the world map visualize how violent conflict has taken place in all states and societies, causing human rights violations across the globe. The world map thus represents violent conflict as a global problem, which affects all of 'us' because it violates 'our' human rights. To address human rights violations, the "Human Rights, A Universal Challenge" exhibition proposes the implementation of a Truth Commission. In the Truth Commissions' silver frames below the world map, the Museo revisits thirty violent conflicts that occurred between 1974 (in Uganda)

104 ("América, África, Asia y Europa, la violencia ha dejado una estela de sufrimiento y luto en el contexto de regímenes dictatoriales, guerras civiles o invasiones"). Taken from plaque at Museo display. Image on file with author.

105 ("En más de 30 países del mundo se han creado Comisiones de Verdad. Son organismos de investigación, no judiciales, encargados de indagar los abusos denunciados"). Ibid.

106 ("Las víctimas . . . y sus familias tiene derecho a saber la verdad y a que se reconozca públicamente su sufrimiento'." Ibid.

107 The Auschwitz Institute for the Prevention of Genocide and Mass Atrocities, "Truth Commissions and Their Contributions to Atrocity Prevention" (2020), 29–30. www.auschwitzinstitute.org/wp-content/uploads/2020/05/AIPG-TruthCommissionsReport.pdf.

and 2010 (in Honduras).[108] These conflicts ranged from civil wars, dictatorships, or forms of state repression, all involving human rights violations. According to this exhibition, the Truth Commission implemented in each of the thirty states was able to investigate and offer a public account of the truth of the human rights violations committed during violent conflict. The Museo represents Truth Commissions as 'the common' post-conflict institution that has helped those states to deal with the legacy of human rights violations by offering an official account of the truth.

Taking together the different elements comprising the first part of "Human Rights, A Universal Challenge" – the Truth Commission plaque, silver frames, and world map – the exhibition transmits a 'global' account of violence and proposes Truth Commissions as the normative post-conflict institution to deal with the past.[109] Furthermore, this part of the exhibition shows how, regardless of the particular context in which each of the thirty violent conflicts developed, it is a 'global' problem that concerns 'us' because it violates international human rights – 'rights' that are inherent to *all*.[110]

Once the 'global' context in which Truth Commissions and universal human rights operate is established, the Museo introduces the visitor to how they worked in the 'local' Chilean context. The collection that follows, within the "Human Rights, A Universal Challenge" exhibition, has two major parts: "Comisiones de Verdad en Chile" ("Truth Commissions in Chile") and "Memoriales" ("Memorials"). The visitor is guided to stand in front of a white robust table with a glass box protecting five documents on display. Inside the glass box are the reports of Chile's two Truth Commissions (1990 Comisión Nacional de Verdad y Reconciliación and 2004 Comisión de Prisión Política y Tortura) and two presidential commissions (1996 Corporación Nacional de Reparación y Reconciliación and

108 Information taken from plaque at Museo display. Image on file with author.

109 For a discussion and critique of Truth Commissions as 'ideal' mechanisms see generally, Vasuki Nesiah, "Discussion Lines on Gender and Transitional Justice: An Introductory Essay Reflecting on the ICTJ Bellagio Workshop on Gender and Transitional Justice," *Columbia Journal of Gender and Law*, vol 15, no 3 (2006); Anne Orford, "Commissioning the Truth," *Columbia Journal of Gender and Law*, vol 15, no 3 (2006).

110 For a critique see, Walter D. Mignolo, "Delinking," *Cultural Studies*, vol 21, no 2/3 (2007), 497.

2011 Comisión Presidencial Asesora para la Calificación de Detenidos Desaparecidos, Ejecutados Políticos y Víctimas de Prisión Política).[111] Above the white table, hanging from a narrow wall, a white glass plaque states: "The Museum ... is sustained by the Reports of the Truth Commissions, which are the essential reference of its permanent exhibition and its heritage."[112] With this, the Museo proclaims that the arrangement of the museum's space and practices are integrally related to the Final Reports of Chile's Truth Commissions and presidential commissions.

Across the white table with Chile's Truth Commissions' Final Reports on display is the "Memorials" collection. With this collection, the visitor can use an interactive screen to locate the memorial sites and monuments that have been built all around Chile to honor the disappeared.[113] This collection then offers a display of images with a brief description of the memorial sites and monuments. Each image stands on a thin metal rod that is placed on the geographical site where each memorial or monument is located. The metal rods stand on rocky pieces that have been molded to represent the geographical space of the Chilean state. Apart from the Access Hall's exhibition's name – "Human Rights, a Universal Challenge" – and the references that each Truth Commission silver frame might have to human rights, the exhibition does not display material objects that are explicitly about human rights (as in Memory Square). There is one exception: the bright red wall to the far end of the Access Hall, which also marks the end of the exhibition.

On the way to the red wall, the visitor comes across two objects: "Cruz Patio 29" ("Patio 29 Cross") and Pieza del Mes ("Monthly Piece"). "Cruz Patio 29" is an iron cross on loan to the Museo from Santiago's General Cemetery. This cross is one of the many created to mark a mass grave in the General Cemetery, where unidentified bodies were being buried during dictatorship. The other object that the visitor encounters is the "Monthly Piece," a piece that belongs to the Museo's collection. By showcasing this

[111] See note 1 above.

[112] ("El Museo ... se sustenta en los Informes de las Comisiones de Verdad, estos son el referente esencial de su muestra permanente y de su patrimonio"). Taken from plaque at Museo display. Image is on file with author.

[113] Museo de la Memoria y Derechos Humanos, "Memoriales (Interactive Database)." http://interactivos.museodelamemoria.cl/memoriales/.

object, the Museo highlights an historical event or moment during dictatorship.[114] Finally, after the visitor passes by these two objects on display, she stands in front of the red wall. Although the extract on the red wall does not indicate it, the text corresponds to the section "Marco Político" ("Political Context") of the 1991 Final Report of Chile's Truth Commission. This Final Report's section describes the coup d'état of September 11, 1973, that removed President Salvador Allende from government, thus marking the beginning of the 1973–1990 dictatorship. In this section, the Final Report affirms that it will not make a value judgment on the September 11 events. Nonetheless, it describes the Chilean state's institutional and social situation as an "acute crisis in our national life" leading "to the destruction or deterioration of numerous points of consensus among Chileans ... which served to safeguard respect for *human rights*."[115] With this description of the 1973 coup d'état as a breakdown of a way of living together with human rights in Chile, the "Human Rights, a Universal Challenge" exhibition concludes.

Importantly, although the second part of the exhibition specifically refers to the work of Chile's Truth Commission (and subsequent policies of memorialization), the arrangement of the exhibition situates the Chilean Truth Commission in a 'global' setting. That is, although the 1990 Truth Commission was Chile's ('local') way of dealing with the past, the exhibition shows how the implementation of the Truth Commission in 1990 guaranteed that the Chilean state was addressing the 'global' concern or problem of human rights violations in an internationally acceptable way, just like other states had done since 1974.[116] Indeed, at the Museo, even the regional is subsumed by the global. This can be seen in the way that the Museo highlights, using a large banner titled "Condena Mundial" (the "World Condemns"), the role of the UN from the early years of the dictatorship (in 1974) in denouncing the violence of the Pinochet regime. On display in that same space, among other

114 Museo de la Memoria y Derechos Humanos, "Pieza Del Mes." https://web.museodelamemoria.cl/sobre-las-colecciones/pieza-del-mes/.

115 Comisión Nacional de Verdad y Reconciliación, *Report*, 63. Italics mine.

116 Pahuja, "Laws of Encounter." On indigenous responses to violence measured against 'human rights standards' see Phil Clark, *The Gacaca Courts, Post-Genocide Justice and Reconciliation in Rwanda: Justice without Lawyers* (Cambridge University Press, 2010).

organizations' reports and documents, is a sample of the Inter-American Commission of Human Rights' "Third Report on the State of Human Rights in Chile."[117] This minor detail shows, once again, how the 'regional' is placed within, and subordinate to, the 'global' form of human rights.[118] With this museological arrangement, "Human Rights, a Universal Challenge" reasserts that, with the 1990 Truth Commission, the Chilean state was complying with international human rights law, the international law that the Chilean state violated from the coup d'état in 1973 until the end of the dictatorship in 1990.[119]

In doing so, with this exhibition the Museo represents (using different means, such as a map, fact-sheets, documents, images, or objects) and gives continuity to the Final Report's assertion that, before the coup d'état and the dictatorship (1973–1990), living together within the Chilean state had been according to international human rights law. In adhering with international human rights law since with the work of the Truth Commission in 1990, the Chilean state is represented as having redressed its own dictatorial conduct.[120] By supporting an investigation into its own state-led human rights violations, the Chilean state redeemed itself from its past. In doing so, international human rights law became ('again') the foundation on which Chileans would live together after dictatorship.

3.5 AUTHORIZING 'MINOR' TRUTHS: THE ACCOUNTS OF THE ARPILLERISTAS AND THE MAPUCHE

After visiting the "Human Rights, a Universal Challenge" exhibition, the visitor is guided to walk up the stairs to another museological space called

117 Inter-American Commission of Human Rights, Organization of the American States, "Third Report on the State of Human Rights in Chile" (25 October 1974).

118 See similar observations in Jens Andermann, "Showcasing Dictatorship: Memory and the Museum in Argentina and Chile," *Journal of Educational Media, Memory, and Society*, vol 4, no 2 (2012), 77.

119 On human rights as a tool for global governance see generally, David Kennedy, "The International Human Rights Regime: Still Part of the Problem?," in *Examining Critical Perspectives on Human Rights*, Rob Dickinson et al. (eds) (Cambridge University Press, 2012).

120 On how as the operation of international law 'actualizes' the state see generally Pahuja, "Laws of Encounter."

"Pre-Coup Situation." On the wall next to the stairs is a photographic mural, titled "A Society in Movement." The stairs and the mural were conceptualized to represent the social instability that Chilean society was going through before the 1973 coup.

The stairs take the visitor up to a more distinct museological and architectural space: the one accommodated in the emerald green structure of the Museum seen from outside. The emerald green structure was conceptualized by the architects to represent "a manifestation of [Chile's] history."[121] As such, this part of the building houses a detailed display, arranged in chronological order, of the events of Chile's dictatorship, which follows the official account produced in the 1991 Final Report.[122] The historical account in the emerald green structure begins with two exhibitions, titled "September 11" and "End of the Rule of Law," which recount how the 1973 coup unfolded and outline the subsequent institutional practices and laws established by the Junta to consolidate the dictatorship. This historical account ends with a permanent exhibition, called "Return to Hope, End of the Dictatorship," focusing on the events, such as the 1989 plebiscite and Patricio Aylwin's 1990 presidential inauguration, which are considered to mark the end of the dictatorship and the return to democracy.

The transition within this architectural space, from the ground floor or plinth to the emerald green structure, gives physical form to the idea that Chile's history rests,[123] physically and institutionally, *on* the museological spaces of Memory Square and the Access Hall. Physically, the exhibitions concerning 'the history' of the dictatorship are located above and rest upon what the Museo's architects call the "plinth." In architecture, a plinth is a structure designed to support or sustain a visible part of a building, in this case the emerald green structure of the Museo. Institutionally, the Museo declares in the Access Hall's "Human Rights, a Universal Challenge" exhibition that the museological script – that is, the narrative that the Museo develops and communicates through the

121 ("manifestación de la historia"). Figueroa, Fehr, and Dias, "Espacios Para la Cultura," 28.

122 For an analysis of these exhibitions, see Andermann, "Showcasing Dictatorship," 76–83.

123 In architecture, a 'plinth' is a structure designed to support or sustain a visible part of a building, in this case, the emerald green structure of the Museo.

aesthetic arrangements of its exhibitions – is sustained by, or based on, the Truth Commission's account.

At the same time, in creating this internationally authorized truth, both the Truth Commission and the Museo created 'minor' truths.[124] Although the official account produced in the 1991 Final Report and reproduced in the Museo draws on the testimonies of many of those who experienced or were affected by the violence that occurred during the dictatorship, it also subordinates and displaces truths that do not fit with the human rights story.[125] This can be observed in how the Museo places the accounts of the Arpilleristas and the Mapuche outside the dominant account.

The Arpilleristas were groups of women – mothers, wives, daughters, sisters – who were relatives of the detained-disappeared.[126] These women collectively created *arpilleras* (patchwork tapestries), displaying images of their everyday life during the dictatorship. Each *arpillera* "is an intimate memory, narrating the family history of a human being violated and left destitute,"[127] which at the same time "document[s] the social situation of the country."[128] The images of the everyday represented in the *arpillera* cover the multiple ways in which the dictatorship touched their lives: "[t]he struggles for the right to land, water, electricity and education."[129] The initial groups of Arpilleristas emerged out of "a vital and urgent necessity: hunger."[130] The disappearances of the families' breadwinners (then, mostly men), or the dictatorship's

[124] Thanks to Peter Rush for suggesting the word 'minor.' These 'minor' authorized truths could be understood, in Goodrich's words, as "minor jurisprudences or forms of legal knowledge that escape the phantom of a sovereign and unitary law": Peter Goodrich, *Law in the Courts of Love: Literature and Other Minor Jurisprudences* (Routledge, 1996), 2.

[125] Sundhya Pahuja, "Letters from Bandung: Encounters with Another International Law," in *Bandung, Global History, and International Law: Critical Pasts and Pending Futures,* Luis Eslava, Michael Fakhri, and Vasuki Nesiah (eds) (Cambridge University Press, 2017), 555; Mignolo, "Delinking," 460–470.

[126] Marjorie Agosín, *Tapestries of Hope, Threads of Love: The Arpillera Movement in Chile* (Rowman & Littlefield Publishers, 2008), 15.

[127] Ibid, 17. [128] Ibid, 30. [129] Ibid, 32.

[130] Marjorie Agosín, "Agujas Que Hablan: Las Arpilleristas Chilenas," *Revista Iberoamericana,* vol 51, no 132–133 (1985), 525.

economic policies, left many families in an increasingly precarious socioeconomic situation.[131]

Under the protection of the Catholic Church through the Vicaría de la Solidaridad,[132] the Arpilleristas began the tapestries.[133] The *arpilleras* express the everyday violence of the dictatorship suffered not only by Arpilleristas but also by many others. For this reason, the Museo considers the Arpilleristas' tapestries to be a "testimony" that helped to "build a wide social picture" of the years of dictatorship.[134] And yet, despite the apparent importance that the Museo gives to the Arpilleristas' truths in the crafting of a social 'collective memory,' the tapestries are not part of the narrative of the dictatorship that the Museo displays. The tapestries are rather located as a side, or 'minor,' truth – exhibited in the last room of the Museo, on the top floor of the emerald green structure. Furthermore, the *arpilleras* exhibition is located after a plaque titled "Gratitude to the International Community," in which the Museo thanks foreign artists, citizens, states and diplomats as well as international organizations and world forums for supporting the efforts to "bring back democracy" to Chile.[135] The location that the Museo gives to that plaque over the *arpilleras* display is telling of the sociopolitical recognition of the Arpilleristas' contribution to the struggle for democracy and socioeconomic justice in Chile. During the dictatorship the sales of the *arpilleras* not only provided a source of income for the Arpilleristas' families,[136] but also denounced and raised awareness of the regime's violence.[137] The power of the *arpillera* was such that the regime had to publicly deny the truths told by the tapestries.[138] However, since the

[131] Ibid, 526; Jacqueline Adams, *Art against Dictatorship: Making and Exporting Arpilleras under Pinochet* (University of Texas Press, 2013), 26–29.

[132] Adams, *Art against Dictatorship*, 39–45.

[133] Agosín, *Tapestries of Hope*, 47; 52–54; Adams, *Art against Dictatorship*, 244.

[134] ("testimonio"); ("construyendo un amplio retrato social"). Museo de la Memoria y Derechos Humanos, "Exposición Permanente – Arpilleras." web.museodelamemoria.cl/publicaciones/arpilleras/.

[135] ("retorno a la democracia"). Image on file with author. This also shows how in the Museo's script the 'international' form of human rights carries more weight than the 'local.'

[136] Adams, *Art against Dictatorship*, 207–215; 142–153.

[137] Ibid, 220–232; 150–153; Marjorie Agosín, "Patchwork of Memory," *NACLA Report on the Americas*, vol 27, no 6 (1994).

[138] Adams, *Art against Dictatorship*, 208–219; 243–244.

democratic period began in 1990, the Vicaría and international organizations considered the struggle against the dictatorship to be over. Consequently, those Chilean organizations (the Vicaría de la Solidaridad) and international organizations (notably, Amnesty International), withdrew crucial support to the Arpilleristas.[139] Now, many Arpilleristas "associate democracy with the image of a country molded from indifference and pain."[140] Although much changed in Chile, the transition to democracy not only retains the socioeconomic inequalities that dictatorship accentuated with its market-based economic policies, but also keeps displacing the Arpilleristas' personal and collective truths. The location of the tapestries reveals how there is what might be called a 'major' truth, which is given a predominant, visible, authoritative position, while reducing other truths, such as those of the Arpilleristas, to a 'minor' position.

Equally telling of how the Museo and the Truth Commission have created 'minor' accounts is the photographic exhibition, titled "Layelewün: Estar Sintiendo la Ausencia" ("Layelewün: To Be Feeling Absence"), by the Chilean artist Danilo Espinoza. The Museo housed the "Layelewün" (temporary) exhibition as part of the museum's Year of Indigenous Memories, which was the 2018 annual theme.[141] Through the Year of Indigenous Memories initiative, the Museo sought to "give visibility to the human rights violations" suffered by the Mapuche, one of the Indigenous peoples of South America. Within the Chilean state, the Mapuche inhabited, and continue to inhabit, the Auracanía region.

Espinoza's "Layelewün" exhibition is a collection of images from the family picture albums of some of the fifty Mapuche-origin detained-disappeared.[142] The images have been smoked using a Mapuche smoking technique, which is used in rituals as well as in everyday life, for cooking or

[139] Ibid, 265–267; Agosín, "Patchwork of Memory."

[140] Agosín, "Patchwork of Memory."

[141] Museo de la Memoria y Derechos Humanos, "Exposición Temporal – Exposición sobre Detenidos Desaparecidos Mapuche Llega al Museo de la Memoria." web.museodelamemoria.cl/Informate/exposicion-sobre-detenidos-desaparecidos-mapuche-llega-al-museo-de-la-memoria/.

[142] ("visibilizar las violaciones a los derechos humanos"). Ibid.

heating the house.[143] For Espinoza, using Mapuche smoke has a double aim: to denounce the violence of the dictatorship's objective to erase, and therefore forget, the presence of the Mapuche, and in doing so, to "reconstruct the biographic identity" of Mapuche detained-disappeared.[144] With "Layelewün" and the Year of Indigenous Memories initiative the Museo aims to conduct an "exercise of memory through art," because there is a "*deuda pendiente*" (a situation of owing something to someone, like a debt) to address the human rights violations suffered by the Mapuche peoples, since the Spanish colonization in the year 1540.[145] The Museo, through one sentence in the exhibition's description at the entrance of the gallery, also acknowledges that the dictatorship's violence against the Mapuche was motivated by historic landownership conflicts. Those conflicts are also mentioned in the Truth Commission's Final Report,[146] but as part of the broader "acute crisis" and "sharp polarization," leading up to the 1973 coup.[147] The Report portrays the Mapuche as victims "with no indigeneity,"[148] despite documenting the violence in Auracanía,[149] land of the Mapuche,[150] and recognizing that the violence in that region before and during the dictatorship was "rooted in land tenure … major social conflicts."[151] Against the homogenizing gesture of the Final Report, a different report, authored by Mapuche historian Hernán Curiñir (from the Asociación de Investigación y Desarrollo Mapuche), shows how the violence suffered by the Mapuche during the dictatorship was part of the Chilean

143 Joseph Gómez Villar, "Exposición "Layelewün: Estar Sintiendo La Ausencia," La Memoria Del Humo," *El Mostrador* (7 August 2018). www.elmostrador.cl/cultura/2018/08/07/exposicion-layelewun-estar-sintiendo-la-ausencia-la-memoria-del-humo/.

144 ("reconstruir la identidad biográfica"). Museo de la Memoria, "Exposición Sobre Detenidos Desaparecidos Mapuche."

145 Ibid. On root causes of human rights violations see Susan Marks, "Human Rights and Root Causes," *The Modern Law Review*, vol 74, no 1 (2011).

146 Comisión Nacional de Verdad y Reconciliación, *Report*, 67–68. 147 Ibid, 63; 64.

148 Daniela Jara, et al., "Tracing Mapuche Exclusion from Post-Dictatorial Truth Commissions in Chile: Official and Grassroots Initiatives," *International Journal of Transitional Justice*, vol 12, no 3 (2018), 489.

149 Ibid, 507–545; 552.

150 José Bengoa, *Historia del Pueblo Mapuche: Siglo XIX y XX* (Ediciones Sur, 1987). Pedro Cayuqueo, *Historia Secreta Mapuche* (Editorial Catalonia, 2018).

151 Comisión Nacional de Verdad y Reconciliación, *Report*, 507.

state's (and Spanish colonial) systematic conduct toward the Mapuche.[152] That is a form of violence that had, and still has, landownership at its heart.

Importantly, the truths of the Mapuche, represented in the "Layelewün" exhibition, are part of a temporary initiative, and are therefore not part of the Museo's (and Truth Commission's) permanent account of the dictatorship. This approach has not changed since I visited the Museo in 2018. For instance, in 2023 the Museo hosted another temporary guided tour to memorialize the violence that the Mapuche suffered during the dictatorship.[153] This reveals how, although the Museo recognizes the lack of official and public acknowledgment of, and redress for, the violence that the Mapuche suffered for nearly 500 years, and that continues in the present, the Museo places Mapuche's truths under the dominant – internationally authorized – truth. An example is the effect of the "Nueva Imperial Agreement," signed in 1989 between the Mapuche and other Indigenous peoples and Patricio Aylwin (then presidential candidate), which led to *Law 19.253*.[154] The "Nueva Imperial Agreement" was the outcome of mass mobilization and consultation among Indigenous peoples in Chile. It sought to communicate and open a dialogue with the Chilean state about their historical treatment. With *Law 19.253*, the Chilean state recognized Indigenous peoples rights, but as a Mapuche leader said, such recognition "reproduces the forms of discrimination the Mapuche have always experienced,"[155] by prioritizing the interests of national "progress," "development," and "modernization"

[152] Hernán Curiñir, "Informe Final Trabajo de Investigación, de Ejecutados y Desaparecidos, 1973-1990, Pertenecientes a la Nación Mapuche" (Asociación de Investigación y Desarrollo Mapuche, 2016).

[153] Diario UChile – Universidad de Chile, "Visitas 50 años 'Pueblo Mapuche y Dictadura: Cosmovisión de la Memoria'," *Diario UChile – Universidad de Chile* (6 April 2023). https://radio.uchile.cl/2023/04/06/visitas-50-anos-pueblo-mapuche-y-dictadura-cosmovision-de-la-memoria/.

[154] See, Organizaciones Indígenas Mapuche, Huilliches, Aymaras and Rapa Nui, and Patricio Aylwin, "Acta de Compromiso de Nueva Imperial" (1 December 1989); Congreso Nacional de Chile, *Ley 19.253 Crea Corporación Nacional de Reparación y Reconciliación, Establece Pensión de Reparación y Otorga otros Beneficios en favor de Personas que Señala* (8 February 1992). On this see, Rosa Isolde Reuque Paillalef and Florencia E. Mallon, *When a Flower Is Reborn: The Life and Times of a Mapuche Feminist* (Duke University Press, 2002), 180–203.

[155] Paillalef and Mallon, *When a Flower Is Reborn*, 202.

over Indigenous peoples understandings and experiences.[156] In another telling moment, during the Museo's inauguration, two Mapuche women interrupted President Bachelet's speech to "remind" her "that no institutional narrative of memory of human rights violations could ever be imposed" on the Mapuche.[157]

The Museo's staging of the truths of the Mapuche and the Arpilleristas outside the authorized truth is thus a telling instance of how international human rights law displaces other (rival) truths, and renders them 'minor,' in the process of trying to forge a new society after violent conflict.

3.6 CONCLUSION

Almost exactly a year after I left Chile, in October 2019, the streets of Santiago witnessed the *estallido social* (social outbreak). Thousands of Chileans turned to the streets to protest the rampant socioeconomic inequality and never-ending cost of living crisis.[158] The *estallido social* has been interpreted as an overt popular rejection of a legacy from Pinochet – the 1980 Constitution – which has continued to shape state-society relations in Chile long after the dictatorship was over. Chilean political scientist, Claudia Heiss, aptly described the 1980 Constitution "as a straitjacket, impeding the political process from leading to social transformations and deepening the neoliberal model."[159] The legal-political pressure of the *estallido social* was such that, between 2021 and 2022, it led to an ambitious nation-wide constitution-making process that aimed to offer Chileans a new, more socially oriented Constitution.[160] Importantly,

[156] Ibid, 202–204.

[157] Nelly Richard, *Eruptions of Memory: The Critique of Memory in Chile, 1990–2015*, trans by Julia Sanches (Polity Press, 2019), 130.

[158] Francisco Jiménez De La Fuente, "Protestas en Chile: 'Si tú no tienes plata en este país, te mueres,' La Dura Realidad de la Salud Pública del país Sudamericano," *BBC Mundo* (20 November 2019). www.bbc.com/mundo/noticias-america-latina-50405749.

[159] Claudia Heiss, "Chile: Entre el Estallido Social y la Pandemia," *Análisis Carolina*, vol 18 (2020), 1.

[160] Claudia Heiss and Julieta Suárez-Cao, "Constitution-Making in the 21st Century: Lessons from the Chilean Process," *PS, Political Science & Politics*, vol 57, no 2 (2024).

the process ensured that there was meaningful Indigenous participation and gender equality in producing a draft Constitution, which culminated in a national plebiscite in September 2022.[161] The draft Constitutional text was not approved by 61.86 percent of Chileans enrolled to vote.[162] A year later, a new Constitutional text was drafted through a process that was substantially less inclusive for Indigenous peoples (there was only one representative this time compared to seventeen in 2020–2021).[163] That second draft Constitutional text was also rejected, by 55.73 percent of Chileans, at a plebiscite in December 2023.[164]

A detailed discussion of the shortcomings and limitations of the *estallido social*, the failure of the constitutional plebiscites, and their implications for Chilean public life, is beyond the scope of this book. Nonetheless, it seems clear that the *estallido social* and its legacies are bound up with how authoritative accounts of 'past violence' are sustained over time. Indigenous peoples, for centuries – within the post-colonial Chilean state, during Pinochet's dictatorship, and since 1990 under many democratically elected governments – have been racialized, displaced, silenced, and excluded from meaningful participation in public life. The same can be said of many other Chileans, for whom the presidency of Salvador Allende was supposed to be the beginning of more lawful and equitable state-society relations. Neither the 1990 Truth Commission and the Museo, nor the language of international human rights law, are exceptions in the perpetuation of state violence against Indigenous peoples in Chile, and against the communities of people who continue to live under unbearable socioeconomic duress.

As I have shown in this chapter, the Chilean Truth Commission used the language of international human rights law to authorize the Final Report's account. From its conception Chile's Truth Commission

161 Ibid, 282.

162 Biblioteca del Congreso Nacional de Chile, "Con Histórica Participación Electoral Propuesta de Nueva Constitución fue Rechazada" (4 September 2022). www.bcn.cl/portal/noticias?id=historica-participacion-plebiscito-2022.

163 For a brief discussion of the process see, Heiss and Suárez-Cao, "Constitution-Making in the 21st Century."

164 Biblioteca del Congreso Nacional de Chile, "Resultados del Plebiscito Constitucional 2023" (18 December 2023). www.bcn.cl/portal/noticias?id=resultados-del-plebiscito-constitucional-2023.

worked with international human rights law to frame the object of investigation in terms of 'human rights violations,' a language that the Truth Commission used to give meaning to the violent events caused by the dictatorship. This is then given continuity through the Museo. Through its architectural spaces and museological practices, the Museo placed international human rights law at the heart of its narrative about the dictatorship's violence, reproducing, and further authorizing, the Truth Commission's account as the 'major' truth while hierarchically ordering coexisting truths as 'minor.' This can be seen in the way that the Truth Commission/Museo include the views of the Arpilleristas and the Mapuche as expressions of a 'minor' truth about the dictatorship, because their accounts do not accord with a narrative of human rights violations.

In the next chapter, I continue the analysis by focusing on El Salvador's UN 1992–1993 Truth Commission. In the post-Cold War geopolitical context, with the dissolution of the Soviet Union's power and influence in the Global South, the UN was gaining status as the 'ideal' international institution with the resources and power to bring about peace in post-conflict states such as El Salvador. The point of the next chapter is to show how the Salvadoran Truth Commission was able to authorize its account by linking it to the idea of making the country a model post-conflict state, drawing on the identity and status of the UN at that time.

CHAPTER 4

Linking the 'Local' to the 'International'

4.1 INTRODUCTION

WITH THE END OF THE COLD WAR, the relationship between Truth Commissions and international law and its institutions became more explicit. Until 1992, Truth Commissions – including the two analyzed in the preceding chapters – were established by a state to investigate a dictatorship's state violence, which was often asserted as being in violation of international law (especially human rights law).[1] That changed with the 1992–1993 United Nations Commission on the Truth for El Salvador (the 'UN Truth Commission'). The UN Truth Commission was created with the 1992 Chapultepec Peace Agreement (the 'Chapultepec Agreement' or 'peace agreements'),[2] which marked the end of the Salvadoran civil war (1980–1992).[3] The UN Truth

[1] See for instance the decrees establishing these two Truth Commission: Gobierno de la Argentina, *Decreto 187/83 Comisión Nacional sobre la Desaparición de Personas – Constitución – Integración y Funciones* (15 December 1983); Gobierno de Chile, *Decreto Supremo No. 355 Crea Comisión De Verdad y Reconciliación* (25 April 1990).

[2] The mandate of the Truth Commission was established in the agreement resulting from the Mexico City negotiation round in 1991. See, UN Doc A/46/553 – S/23130 (9 October 1991), *Letter dated 8 October 1991 from the Permanent Representative of El Salvador to the United Nations addressed to the Secretary-General* (*Mexico Agreements,* 27 April 1991), 16–18; and UN Doc A/46/664 – S/23501 (30 January 1992), *Letter dated 27 January 1992 from the Permanent Representative of El Salvador to the United Nations addressed to the Secretary-General* (*Chapultepec Peace Agreement,* 16 January 1992), 6; 8.

[3] The Chapultepec Agreement was a final document, which incorporated the set of agreements reached in six previous negotiation rounds: Geneva (1990), Caracas (1990), San José (1990), Mexico City (1991), and New York (1991 and 1992). See, UN Doc A/46/551 – S/23128 (9 October 1991), *Letter dated 8 October 1991 from the Permanent Representative of El Salvador to the United Nations addressed to the Secretary-General* (*Geneva Agreements,* 4 April 1991); UN Doc A/46/552 – S/23129 (9 October 1991),

Commission differed from previous Truth Commissions in two main aspects: in terms of who authorized its creation and how it was implemented; and in terms of the laws informing its investigation, or its "applicable law."[4]

Regarding the first aspect, the creation of the UN Truth Commission was authorized through the UN-mediated 1992 Chapultepec Agreement. Through the peace agreement the parties in conflict – the Salvadoran state and the guerrillas – agreed for the UN to establish a Truth Commission.[5] In doing so, as I explain in greater detail throughout this chapter, the UN Truth Commission would be designed and operated under the sole authority of the UN. As I have shown in previous chapters, before 1992 a Truth Commission was typically authorized through national legislation (for example, executive decrees in the cases of Argentina and Chile, and a legal notice in the case of Uganda),[6] and implemented by the commissioners, in an 'independent' fashion but on behalf of the state. Nevertheless, as I showed in the preceding chapters, a Truth Commission was a state's formal response to a subtle yet powerful

General Agenda and Timetable for the Comprehensive Negotiation Process (Caracas Agenda, 21 May 1990); UN Doc A/44/971 – S/21541 (16 August 1991), *Note Verbale dated 14 August 1990 from the Chargé d'affaires a.i of the Permanente Mission of El Salvador to the United Nations addressed to the Secretary-General (Agreement on Human Rights/San José Agreement, 26 July 1990)*; UN Doc A/46/553 – S/23130 (9 October 1991), *Mexico Agreements*; UN Doc A/46/502/Add.1 – S/23082/Add.1 (7 October 1991), *Letter dated 91/10/04 from the Permanent Representative of El Salvador to the United Nations addressed to the Secretary-General (The Compressed Negotiations signed at United Nations Headquarters by representatives of the Government of El Salvador and Frente Farabundo Martí para la Liberación Nacional-Frente Democrático Revolucionario, 25 September 1991)*; UN Doc A/46/863 – S/23504 (30 January 1992), *Letter dated 92/01/27 from the Permanent Representative of El Salvador to the United Nations addressed to the Secretary-General (New York Act I (1991) and New York Act II (1992) signed by the Government of El Salvador and the Frente Farabundo Martí para la Liberación Nacional-Frente Democrático Revolucionario, 31 December 1991 and 13 January 1992)*; UN Doc A/46/664 – S/23501 (30 January 1992), *Chapultepec Peace Agreement.*

4 UN Doc S/25500 (1 April 1993), *Letter dated 93/03/29 from the Secretary-General addressed to the President of the Security Council* (*From Madness to Hope: The 12-year war in El Salvador: Report of the Commission on the Truth for El Salvador*), 20–22.

5 See note 2 above.

6 See note 1 above for decrees of the Truth Commissions of Argentina and Chile. For Uganda, see Government of Uganda, *The Commission of Inquiry Act (Cap. 56), Legal Notice No 2 of 1974* (30 June 1974).

international expectation – especially from international organizations, advocacy groups, and powerful Global North states – to show that the state was abandoning dictatorship as a form of government, and embracing three institutions: international law, democracy, and the rule of law. El Salvador's UN Truth Commission was the first one of its kind created at the explicit proposal of an international organization,[7] the UN in this case. The UN Truth Commission was also exclusively comprised of non-Salvadoran commissioners (and staff), who were appointed by the UN Secretary-General.[8]

Concerning its "applicable law,"[9] the UN Truth Commission was tasked to inquire into "serious acts of violence" committed during the civil war.[10] These "serious acts of violence"[11] were categorized by the UN as a noninternational armed conflict under Article 3 Common to the 1949 Geneva Conventions.[12] For that reason, the commissioners determined that the "rules of international law," specifically international humanitarian law and international human rights law, were the legal "basis" for the UN Truth Commission's investigation of the civil war's violent events.[13] The inclusion of international humanitarian law in the UN Truth Commission's "applicable law" makes this Truth Commission stand out from preceding ones.[14] As I showed in Chapters 2 and 3 of this book, the Truth Commission of Chile used the language of international

7 I develop this point throughout this chapter, but specifically in Section 4.4. See also, Diana Villiers-Negroponte, *Seeking Peace in El Salvador: The Struggle to Reconstruct a Nation at the End of the Cold War* (Palgrave Macmillan, 2012), 45; 185 at note 191.

8 UN Doc A/46/553 – S/23130 (9 October 1991), *Mexico Agreements*, 16.

9 UN Doc S/25500 (1 April 1993), *From Madness to Hope*, 20–22.

10 See, UN Doc A/46/553 – S/23130 (9 October 1991), *Mexico Agreements*, 16; UN Doc S/25500 (1 April 1993), *From Madness to Hope*, 11.

11 Ibid.

12 Hellen Kinsella, *The Image before the Weapon: A Critical History of the Distinction between Combatant and Civilian* (Cornell University Press, 2011), 156. See also, *Protocol Additional to the Geneva Conventions of 12 August 1949, and Relating to the Protection of Victims of Non-International Armed Conflicts (Protocol II) of June 1977* (1977). For a recent historical analysis of the innovations in the application of international law through Article 3 see, Kathryn Greenman, "Common Article 3 at 70: Reappraising Revolution and Civil War in International Law," *Melbourne Journal of International Law*, vol 27, no 1 (2020).

13 UN Doc S/25500 (1 April 1993), *From Madness to Hope*, 20–22; 201 at note 4.

14 Ibid.

human rights law, and Argentina's invoked the post-conflict promises of international law.[15] And as I also show in Chapter 5, Uganda's 1974 Commission of Inquiry only became the 'inaugural' Truth Commission in the 1990s when it was redescribed as an institution that was advancing human rights.

El Salvador's UN Truth Commission was established on the premise, and promise, that "the complete truth" about the "serious acts of violence" committed during the 1980–1992 civil war,[16] would "contribute to reconciliation and to abolishing such patterns of behavior in the new society."[17] However, in 2018, during a UN-organized event in El Salvador to commemorate the twenty-fifth anniversary of the UN Truth Commission's Final Report, Douglass Cassel, who served as legal advisor to the UN Truth Commission,[18] admitted to the audience: "we couldn't tell all the truth that we knew."[19] The untold truth that Cassel refers to is concerned with how at least six members of some of the (still) wealthiest Salvadoran families provided financial assistance and supplied arms to the state's death squads during the civil war.[20] Cassel's confession reveals not only how the UN Truth Commission's account, while being presented to Salvadorans as "the complete truth," was inherently partial,[21] but it also raises questions about those 'other' truths left out from the UN's official account – 'other' truths that, in turn, were excluded from a peace process aimed at "democratizing," "restor[ing] peace, national

15 The Final Report explicitly compares this Truth Commission with the Truth Commissions of Argentina and Chile in, UN Doc S/25500 (1 April 1993), *From Madness to Hope*, 12.

16 UN Doc A/46/553 – S/23130 (9 October 1991), *Mexico Agreements*, 16.

17 UN Doc S/25500 (1 April 1993), *From Madness to Hope*, 11.

18 Ibid, 193; 196.

19 ("no pudimos contar toda la verdad que conocimos"). Office United Nations High Commissioner for Human Rights, "A 25 años del Informe de la Comisión de la Verdad de El Salvador" (18 March 2018). www.youtube.com/watch?v=RN9BnaTZE8Y.

20 United States Department of Justice, Federal Bureau of Investigation, "Secret Report: Unknown Subjects; Furnishing Funds and Weapons to Salvadoran Death Squads in El Salvador" (15 May 1984), (Digital National Security Archive's Collection: El Salvador: War, Peace, and Human Rights, 1980–1994).

21 UN Doc A/46/553 – S/23130 (9 October 1991), *Mexico Agreements*, 16. In the Truth Commission's Final Report the expression is "the whole truth" in, UN Doc S/25500 (1 April 1993), *From Madness to Hope*, 11.

reconciliation and the reunification of Salvador[a]n society."[22] Importantly, this peace process was claimed to be conducted "in accordance with the common will of the Salvador[an] people,"[23] and it is considered by the UN, to this day, as a success for El Salvador, for the UN, and a "gift to humanity."[24]

The argument that I develop through the chapter is that El Salvador's Truth Commission drew on the identity and status of the UN as an international institution to authorize its account of the unlawfulness of the violence of the 1980–1992 civil war. By 'identity and status' I mean the UN's position as the premier international institution created for, and committed to, the preservation of world peace.[25] On the one hand, the Truth Commission's own authority to speak the truth about the civil war was strengthened by its connection with the UN, which in turn was shaping the UN Truth Commission's account of the civil war in El Salvador. As I show through this chapter, the UN Truth Commission's account is one that fit within the UN's emerging vision for peacebuilding interventions in post-conflict states in the Global South after the Cold War.[26] One consequence of this, I argue, is that the UN Truth Commission's account has worked to deauthorize other coexisting accounts of the civil war which do not fit, or indeed rival, this international understanding of unlawful violence and post-conflict state-society relations. This includes truths about the socioeconomic circumstances that led to, and sustained, the civil war. As I show, these other Salvadoran truths have been denied by the UN

22 UN Doc A/46/551 – S/23128 (9 October 1991), *Geneva Agreements*, 2; UN Doc A/46/553 – S/23130 (9 October 1991), *Mexico Agreements*, 2.

23 UN Doc A/46/553 – S/23130 (9 October 1991), *Mexico Agreements*, 2.

24 UN Secretary-General Statement – Ban Ki-moon, "Secretary-General's Remarks at Ceremony for XXIII Anniversary of the Peace Agreements in El Salvador" (16 January 2015). www.un.org/sg/en/content/sg/speeches/2015-01-16/remarks-ceremony-xxiii-anniversary-peace-agreements-el-salvador.

25 See generally, *United Nations Charter* (24 October 1945); UN Doc A/47/277– S/24111 (17 June 1992), *An Agenda for Peace: Preventive Diplomacy, Peacemaking and Peace-keeping: Report of the Secretary-General pursuant to the statement adopted by the Summit Meeting of the Security Council on 31 January 1992.*

26 On the conceptual and political use of 'Third World' see, B. S. Chimni, "Third World Approaches to International Law: A Manifesto," *International Community Law Review*, vol 8, no 1 (2006): 4–7. See also, Alfred Sauvy, "Document: Trois Mondes, Une Planète," *Vingtième Siècle. Revue d'histoire*, no 12 (1986).

Truth Commission's framing of El Salvador as a model peacebuilding intervention for other post-conflict states.

To develop this argument, I analyze the account of the UN Truth Commission's Final Report alongside another account, which I encountered embroidered in a tapestry. The tapestry was handmade in the 1980s by a Salvadoran woman while she was living in the UN Office of the High Commissioner for Refugees (UNHCR) refugee camps, located in the neighboring country of Honduras.[27] It depicts the first reported massacre of the Salvadoran civil war, committed against peasants by the Salvadoran Armed Forces in 1980. This massacre, known as 'Masacre del Río Sumpul' ('Sumpul River Massacre'),[28] was investigated thirteen years later by the UN Truth Commission, and recorded in its Final Report.[29] And yet, while both the UN Truth Commission's Final Report and the tapestry record the same event, they do so in remarkably different ways, and with different aims. By juxtaposing the tapestry's account with that of the UN Truth Commission's, I show how the tapestry contests the official truth about the "democratic reunification of Salvador[a]n society" that had been promised and that eventually took place.[30]

I begin the analysis by redescribing the UN's account as expressed in the Final Report (Section 4.2), and by presenting the account of the Salvadoran woman as represented in the tapestry (Section 4.3). I approach these rival accounts as two 'points of view' about the Salvadoran civil war.[31] In organizing and presenting the analysis around these points of view, I seek to show how the UN (as a fundamental

[27] For an ethnographic account about life in the camps see, Beth Cagan and Steve Cagan, *This Promised Land, El Salvador: The Refugee Community and Their Return to Morazán* (Rutgers University Press, 1991). See also, UN Doc A/36/12 (28 August 1981), *Report of the United Nations High Commissioner for Refugees: Supplement No. 12.*

[28] Also called 'Masacre de Las Aradas.' See, Asociación de Sobrevivientes de la Masacre del Sumpul, *Memorias del Sumpul: Testimonios del Genocidio contra Población Campesina Organizada en Las Aradas, Chalatenango, Mayo de 1980* (Equipo Maíz, 2019), 7.

[29] UN Doc S/25500 (1 April 1993), *From Madness to Hope*, 121–124.

[30] UN Doc A/46/664 – S/23501 (30 January 1992), *Chapultepec Peace Agreement*, 31.

[31] This point is inspired by: John Berger, *Ways of Seeing* (Penguin Books, 2009); Edward Said and Raymond Williams, "Appendix. Media, Margins and Modernity," in Raymond Williams, *Politics of Modernism: Against the New Conformists* (Verso, 2007), 181.

institution of international law) and the Salvadoran woman (as a survivor of a peasant community targeted during the civil war) have particular, and rival, "way[s] of looking at the world," which are telling of "a certain relationship with" it.[32] In this sense, the activity of 'viewing' or 'seeing' is a way of engaging with something (e.g., events, objects, experiences, nature, institutions, or human conducts) *from* the viewer's particular position at a given time and place.

I analyze the two rival viewpoints using the technique of 'critical redescription,' which I borrow from Sundhya Pahuja. In Pahuja's approach, critical redescription is understood as "an attempt to redefine through narrative, a world we take for granted, inviting it to be seen differently as a mode of political engagement."[33] In this case, the UN Truth Commission's account of El Salvador's civil war is one that we are supposed to "take for granted."[34] It is an account that is actively promoted as representing *all* of the accounts about the civil war,[35] and authorized as such by international law as an objective, universal truth. In contrast, the tapestry is also "take[n] for granted," but as a cultural object that only offers a subjective and imprecise account of the massacre and the civil war.[36] As the analysis in this chapter shows, while the work of law and humanities scholars continues to inform my critical understanding of Truth Commissions and international law, my reading of the tapestry was also informed by the work of Colombian artist, Doris Salcedo. Analyzing the tapestry in conversation with Salcedo's artwork allowed for an analysis sensitive to the story about the 'past' being told, here and now, by the tapestry's own materiality.

Redescribing the accounts of the Final Report and the tapestry as viewpoints requires first approaching them as expressions of particular worldviews; thus, as representing potentially distinct ways of seeing and

[32] John Berger, *Landscapes: John Berger on Art* (Verso; Kindle edition, 2016), 145–146.

[33] Sundhya Pahuja, "Laws of Encounter: A Jurisdictional Account of International Law," *London Review of International Law*, vol 1, no 1 (2013), 65.

[34] Ibid. [35] UN Doc S/25500 (1 April 1993), *From Madness to Hope*, 11.

[36] For a critique of how modern law and institutions render cultural artifacts as subjective see, Jeffery G Hewitt, "Certain (mis)Conceptions: Westphalian Origins, Portraiture and Wampum," in Shane Chalmers and Sundhya Pahuja (eds), *Routledge Handbook of International Law and the Humanities* (Routledge, 2021).

experiencing the Salvadoran civil war. This approach allows for a more nuanced understanding of the rationalities underpinning the UN Truth Commission's account, as well as its claims and aims. In doing so, keeping the redescription of the Final Report and the tapestry separate (in Sections 4.2 and 4.3 respectively), affords an engagement – especially with the tapestry – on its own terms, and not through the Final Report's internationally authorized account of the civil war.

In Section 4.2, my redescription shows how the Final Report represents the civil war as an unlawful event in international law.[37] I show how the UN Truth Commission produced an account that fit the UN's post-Cold War peacebuilding vision for post-conflict states. This was a vision that was formalized after the UN's experience in El Salvador in the 1990s. Through it, the UN aimed to 'build peace' by establishing democracy, rule of (international) law, and human rights.[38] These were understood as fundamental pillars for 're-building' and 'developing' a successful 'new' post-conflict state.[39] Yet, my analysis of how the UN Truth Commission's Final Report represents the civil war in relation to international law's promises of peace, reconciliation, democracy, and economic prosperity, reveals that the Salvadoran state's protracted socioeconomic, legal, and political inequalities leading to the civil war, were addressed as problems of 'development.' I show how according to the UN Truth Commission, these problems would be 'solved' through international post-conflict peace/state-building institutions, development projects (often funded by the UN, development agencies, and international financial institutions), as well as through the privatization of public services and land, at the hands of a Salvadoran elite.

In Section 4.3, I focus on how the Salvadoran peasant woman represents the Sumpul Massacre in relation to the civil war. I begin the analysis by recounting my encounter with the tapestry while visiting the Museo de la Palabra y la Imagen (Museum of the Word and the Image, known as MUPI) in San Salvador in early 2020. I discuss how MUPI – a privately owned Salvadoran museum of memory – recovered the tapestry in 2019 to promote its historical storytelling value and its contribution to local

[37] UN Doc S/25500 (1 April 1993), *From Madness to Hope*, 154.
[38] UN Doc A/47/277– S/24111 (17 June 1992), *An Agenda for Peace*. [39] Ibid.

accounts of the social roots of the civil war. I then proceed to redescribe and analyze the circumstances in which the woman, as a survivor, in crafting the tapestry bears witness to the injustice of the destruction of her community's way of life. My analysis shows how the tapestry's truth, seen against the UN Truth Commission's account, reveals how the latter obscures and silences the inequalities that the former illuminates and represents. In doing so, the tapestry's account can be seen to "cu[t] across . . . time,"[40] contesting the UN Truth Commission's internationally authorized truth.

I conclude this chapter in Section 4.4 by showing how the post-conflict state represented in the UN Truth Commission's Report, and promoted and deployed through the Chapultepec Peace Agreements, worked to control and tame Salvadorans' post-conflict expectations of seeing many of the socioeconomic claims underpinning the civil war realized. I show how, through the Final Report's internationally authorized truth, the commissioners not only downplayed the jurisdictional force of the UN's post-conflict peacebuilding vision and state-building model. While claiming to be 'the truth' for *all* Salvadorans, ultimately the UN Truth Commission served to reconcile the interests of international law's post-Cold War institutions. In doing so, the UN Truth Commission has contributed to constraining the capacity of the Salvadoran state and its peoples to authorize their own visions for post-conflict state-society relations.

4.2 AUTHORIZING THE UN'S TRUTH FOR EL SALVADOR: THE FINAL REPORT OF THE UN'S COMMISSION ON THE TRUTH

4.2.1 INAUGURATING A "LASTING BOND". The UN's prominent mediating role in El Salvador's peace negotiations (1990–1992), and later, in monitoring the implementation of the agreements (1992–1995), is regarded as the beginning of a positive relationship between the UN and the Salvadoran state. During the twenty-third anniversary celebrations of the signature of the 1992 Chapultepec Agreement in San Salvador, Secretary-General Ban Ki-Moon referred to this relationship as

[40] Desmond Manderson, *Danse Macabre: Temporalities of Law in the Visual Arts* (Cambridge University Press, 2019), 5.

"a lasting bond."[41] In the UN's view, this bond worked as a relationship through which both El Salvador and the UN were positively transformed. The UN helped to "transform" the Salvadoran state by establishing a "solid foundation for a peaceful future,"[42] thereby "[bringing] a better future to the people."[43] For its part, El Salvador changed the UN by "becom[ing] a model for UN peacemaking efforts" around the world.[44] The impact was such that, in his 1992 *An Agenda for Peace,* in thinking explicitly about the UN's role in El Salvador,[45] Secretary-General Boutros-Ghali named "post-conflict peace-building" as the UN's novel model for post-Cold War interventions.[46]

Through the peace process (1990–1995), the UN-El Salvador relationship led to some meaningful changes, such as the suppression of the state's death squads; limiting (to some degree) the power of the armed forces in governance; and holding periodical democratic elections.[47] Yet, in contrast to the UN's enthusiastic, if unnuanced, view of the changes brought by this relationship, those with an intimate understanding of everyday life in the post-conflict Salvadoran state know that "El Salvador's hardest lesson" is that "the end of war [was] not necessarily the beginning of peace."[48]

41 UN Secretary-General Statement – Ban Ki-moon, "Secretary-General's Remarks at Ceremony for XXIII Anniversary of the Peace Agreements in El Salvador."

42 UN Doc [ST]/DPI/1475 (1995), *The United Nations and El Salvador, 1990–1995,* 3.

43 UN Doc SG/SM/10978 (7 May 2007), *Secretary-General Expresses 'Profound Gratitude' to Alvaro De Soto for 25 Years of Outstanding Service to United Nations.*

44 UN Doc SG/SM/10978 (7 May 2007), *Secretary-General Expresses 'Profound Gratitude.'* See also, UN Doc [ST]/DPI/1475 (1995), *The United Nations,* 3–4.

45 Peter Wallensteen, *Quality Peace: Strategic Peacebuilding and World Order* (Oxford University Press, 2015), 11–13.

46 UN Doc A/47/277– S/24111 (17 June 1992), *An Agenda for Peace,* 2; UN Doc A/RES/51/242 (26 September 1997), *Supplement to an Agenda for Peace: Resolution / adopted by the General Assembly.* See also, Álvaro de Soto and Graciana del Castillo, "Implementation of Comprehensive Peace Agreements: Staying the Course in El Salvador," *Global Governance,* vol 1, no 2 (1995): 190–191; Wallensteen, *Quality Peace,* 11–13.

47 See generally, Ellen Moodie, *El Salvador in the Aftermath of Peace: Crime, Uncertainty, and the Transition to Democracy* (University of Pennsylvania Press, 2012); Douglass Cassel, Verónica Hinestroza and Gino Costa, "Los Acuerdos de Paz de El Salvador y la Construcción de la Democracia: A 30 Años de su Firma" (Fundación para el Debido Proceso, 2022).

48 Óscar Martínez and Juan José Martínez, *The Hollywood Kid: The Violent Life and Death of an MS-13 Hitman* (Verso, 2019), 121.

Nearly thirty years after the signature of the peace agreements, there have been two intertwined major conflicts concerning post-conflict Salvadoran state-society relations. One is the gangs/*maras*, and the other is ongoing mass emigration.[49] From the point of view of international organizations (like the UN), international development agencies (e.g., UN Development Program (UNDP), World Bank, or USAID), and Global North states (especially the United States) these two Salvadoran conflicts are seen and treated as exclusively 'contemporary' phenomena or crises.[50] In contrast, there is strong evidence to suggest that both gangs and mass emigration are only contemporary in the sense that they are taking place 'now,' and are deeply rooted in enduring forms of inequality in the arrangement of state-society relations.[51] It is well-documented how the protracted historical conditions of socioeconomic, political and legal inequalities, in which the majority of the Salvadorans lived before the outbreak of the 1980–1992 civil war, were powerful drivers that led many to see war against the state as the only option to achieve meaningful change.[52] It is also well-documented that the peace

[49] On the *maras* see, José Miguel Cruz, "Criminal Violence and Democratization in Central America: The Survival of the Violent State," *Latin American Politics and Society*, vol 53, no 4 (2011). On mass emigration see, Leisy J. Abrego, "On Silences: Salvadoran Refugees Then and Now," *Latino Studies*, vol 15, no 1 (2017). See also, John Washington, *The Dispossessed: A Story of Asylum at the US-Mexican Border and Beyond* (Verso, 2020).

[50] See for example the descriptions in, Congressional Research Service, "Central American Migration: Root Causes and US Policy" (21 March 2022). https://sgp.fas.org/crs/row/IF11151.pdf; Amelia Cheatham and Diana Roy, "Central America's Turbulent Northern Triangle" (22 June 2022). www.cfr.org/backgrounder/central-americas-turbulent-northern-triangle#chapter-title-0-6.

[51] See, Óscar Martínez, *The Beast: Riding the Rails and Dodging Narcos on the Migrant Trail* (Icaria Editorial; Verso, 2010; 2013); José Miguel Cruz, "Central American Maras: From Youth Street Gangs to Transnational Protection Rackets," *Global Crime*, vol 11, no 4 (2010); Leisy J. Abrego, *Sacrificing Families: Navigating Laws, Labor, and Love Across Borders* (Stanford University Press, 2014); Martínez and Martínez, *The Hollywood Kid.*

[52] See generally, Rogelio Guillermo Velasco Ramírez, "Aspectos Jurídicos del Crédito Agrícola en El Salvador," (PhD Thesis, Universidad de El Salvador, 1975); Harald Jung, "Class Struggles in El Salvador," *New Left Review*, vol 122, no 1 (1980); Jeffrey M. Paige, *Coffee and Power: Revolution and the Rise of Democracy in Central America* (Harvard University Press, 1997), 230; Roque Dalton, *Las Historias Prohibidas del Pulgarcito* (Ocean Sur, 2014), 207–208; Erik Ching, *Stories of Civil War in El Salvador: A Battle over Memory* (The University of North Carolina Press, 2016), 24–40;

agreements, after a decade of civil war, were expected (even by the guerrillas) to somehow realize the desired change, which the war had been unable to achieve.[53]

During his speech at the 1992 peace agreement signing ceremony, Schafik Hándal, a high-ranking commander of the Frente Farabundo Martí para la Liberación Nacional (Farabundo Martí National Liberation Front, or FMLN for its acronym in Spanish) and its lead negotiator in the peace process, described the Chapultepec Agreement as "having within it the design of the new country that we Salvadorans desire; of the life that we Salvadorans want to live."[54] Hándal was right about one thing: that the Chapultepec Agreement held within it a "design" for post-conflict state-society relations.[55] Yet, the gangs and mass emigration conflicts reveal that the resulting Salvadoran post-conflict state did not become "the new country" in the sense that Hándal suggested.[56]

Héctor Lindo-Fuentes, *Weak Foundations: The Economy of El Salvador in the Nineteenth Century 1821–1898* (University of California Press, 1990).

53 See for example these three public opinion polls from 1992, Instituto Universitario de Opinión Pública, "Encuesta sobre la Firma de los Acuerdos de Paz" (1992). https://uca.edu.sv/iudop/encuestas-de-opinion/1992/. Particularly interesting is this poll, Instituto Universitario de Opinión Pública, "Encuesta sobre la Firma de los Acuerdos de Paz: Los Salvadoreños ante los Acuerdos Finales de Paz" (1992), 911. Available at: https://uca.edu.sv/iudop/wp-content/uploads/informe31.pdf. See also this 1989 essay by Villalobos, one of the most influential guerrilla leaders and strategist in, Joaquín Villalobos, "Popular Insurrection: Desire or Reality?," *Latin American Perspectives*, vol 16, no 3 (1989). See also, Carlos Henríquez Consalvi, "El Recorrido Clandestino de Carlos Henríquez Consalvi para Gritar la Paz," *ElSalvador.com* (3 January 2017). www.youtube.com/watch?v=aPd1xdvxzwo; Óscar Martínez Peñate, *El Salvador: Del Conflicto Armado a la Negociación, 1979–1989* (Editorial Nuevo Enfoque, 2013), 200–201. For contemporary analysis and reporting see, Marlon Carranza, "Los Acuerdos de Paz, 15 años Después: Una mirada desde la Opinión Pública," *Estudios Centroamericanos*, vol 62, no 701–702 (2007); Instituto Universitario de Opinión Pública, "Encuesta sobre la Firma de los Acuerdos De Paz: Las Salvadoreñas y Salvadoreños Evalúan los Acuerdos de Paz a 28 Años de su Firma y Opinan sobre la Democracia en el País" (2020). https://uca.edu.sv/iudop/wp-content/uploads/BOLETÍN_AA-1.pdf; Cassel, Hinestroza and Costa, "Los Acuerdos de Paz de El Salvador."

54 ("contienen el diseño del nuevo país que deseamos los salvadoreños, de la vida que queremos vivir los salvadoreños"). Schafik Hándal, "Discurso de Schafik Handal Durante la Ceremonia de la Firma del Acuerdo de Paz" (Centro de Documentación de los Movimientos Armados, 2006). https://cedema.org/digital_items/4261.

55 ("diseño"). Ibid. 56 ("del nuevo país"). Ibid.

As I explain in detail in this chapter, the design was presented as 'new' largely because it created, or reformed existing, institutions for the purpose of organizing lawful state-society relations. However, as I show, the design did not afford "the life" that those Salvadorans who had been historically marginalized "desire[d]" and deserved.[57] Instead, it reformed state-society relations according to the UN's vision of what a lawful post-conflict Global South state should look like. In doing so, it gave lawful continuity, albeit with additional complexities, to the socio-economic, political, and legal inequalities that led to the civil war. Taking this into account, the tension that can be seen by juxtaposing the UN's celebratory depiction of its relationship with the Salvadoran state, on the one hand, and on the other hand, the ongoing conflicts characterizing Salvadoran state-society relations, suggests that the UN-El Salvador "lasting bond"[58] had significant consequences.

The UN-El Salvador "bond" is one manifestation of a complex jurisdictional relationship between an international institution and a Global South state.[59] Through this relationship the UN asserts itself as the authority "giv[ing] legal form to life and life to law" within Global South states.[60] However, what counts as lawful state-society relations for international institutions like the UN (and others, including the World Bank and International Monetary Fund (IMF)) is largely informed by the developmental rationality structuring how international law re-arranges state-society relations in Global South states.[61] As others have shown, this developmental way of seeing Global South states and social life within them, was institutionalized and internationalized in the early Cold War years by the US, and specifically by President Truman during his 1949 inaugural address.[62] In its initial articulation, Truman put forward the view that Global South states

57 ("la vida"); ("deseamos"). Ibid. 58 See note 41 above.

59 For a full discussion of jurisprudence of jurisdiction see Chapter 1 of this book. Also, see generally, Shaunnagh Dorsett and Shaun McVeigh, *Jurisdiction* (Routledge, 2012); Peter Rush, "An Altered Jurisdiction: Corporeal Traces of Law," *Griffith Law Review*, vol 6 (1997).

60 Dorsett and McVeigh, *Jurisdiction*, 1.

61 On this see, Sundhya Pahuja, *Decolonising International Law: Development, Economic Growth, and the Politics of Universality* (Cambridge University Press, 2011), 10–43.

62 Harry S. Truman, "Inaugural Address, 20 January 1949" (Harry S. Truman Library and Museum, 1949). www.trumanlibrary.gov/library/public-papers/19/inaugural-

needed to "embark" on a process of 'evolving' into 'developed' states – which were, first and foremost, financially wealthy through a market-based economy, thus sociopolitically stable, and democratically governed by rule of law abiding institutions.[63] Later, this developmental view of Global South states was incorporated into the operation of the post-WWII "new international order" institutions: the UN (1945) and the Bretton Woods Institutions (1944) (the World Bank and the IMF).[64]

The end of the Cold War enabled the expansion of that old developmental rationality for organizing North-South relations, but disguised as the inauguration of 'new' international relations.[65] This expansion reached El Salvador through its 1992 Chapultepec Agreement. Importantly, the Salvadoran peace negotiations (1990–1992), and the implementation of the Chapultepec Agreements (1992–1995), coincided with the UN's "new founding moment" as the end of the Cold War unraveled.[66] The UN, through the Salvadoran peace process, seized the opportunity to expand this developmental rationality to the Global South's post-conflict situations. From the international perspective, the view was that the civil wars in Global South states were proxy wars of the Cold War's superpowers.[67] As such, war-torn Global South states like El Salvador had now the opportunity to achieve the social peace and economic development that had been promised by "international law and institutions in 1945" and 'frozen' by the Cold War.[68]

address. For a critical reading of Truman's speech see, Pahuja, *Decolonising International Law*, 59–69; Gilbert Rist, *The History of Development from Western Origins to Global Faith* (Zed Books, 2014), 69–79. On the concept of 'development' see Gustavo Esteva, "Development," in *The Development Dictionary: A Guide to Knowledge as Power*, Wolfgang Sachs (ed), (Zed Books, 2010), 1–22.

63 Esteva, "Development," 8.

64 Pahuja, *Decolonising International Law*, 13; 59–69. On the World Bank and the development project see generally, Guy Fiti Sinclair, *To Reform the World: The Legal Powers of International Organizations* (Oxford University Press, 2017), 202–235.

65 See generally, Pahuja, *Decolonising International Law*.

66 Mark Mazower, *No Enchanted Palace: The End of Empire and the Ideological Origins of the United Nations* (Princeton University Press, 2009), 2.

67 Álvaro de Soto and Graciana del Castillo, "Obstacles to Peacebuilding," *Foreign Policy*, no 94 (1994): 69.

68 Matthew Craven, Sundhya Pahuja, and Gerry Simpson (eds), *International Law and the Cold War* (Cambridge University Press, 2019), 1–2.

In El Salvador, the UN led that process according to its developmental way of seeing how lawful post-conflict state-society relations should be. In essence, this developmental perspective was (and still is) oriented by the Truman view that there are 'developed' (First World/Global North) and 'underdeveloped' (Third World/Global South) states.[69] In this reasoning, Global South states like El Salvador were 'underdeveloped,' but they could achieve 'development' through what Truman described in 1949 as "a bold new program," designed by the US and other 'developed' states, which possess "technical knowledge" about how to achieve a state of 'development.'[70] The aim of such a program was to share with "peace-loving peoples" that knowledge "in order to help them realize their aspirations for a better life."[71] The UN's assertion of itself as possessing 'the' expert knowledge to 'develop' the Salvadoran post-conflict state 'properly' can be seen in Secretary-General Boutros-Ghali's 1995 reflection on the organization's role in El Salvador.[72] Boutros-Ghali affirmed that, while there was still much work ahead, it was the "United Nations experts in human rights, civilian policing and economic development" who had "steered the country into far-reaching democratic, social and institutional reforms."[73]

Although the majority of Salvadorans saw in the Chapultepec Agreement the inauguration of what they hoped would be a better way to live together,[74] the institutions established by the peace process/agreement conditioned life in the post-conflict Salvadoran state according to a particular international lawfulness. The understanding of lawfulness embedded in the international law deployed by the new institutions in El Salvador, contributed to "constrain[ing]" the state's "structural" capacity to authorize lawful post-conflict state-society relations, until today.[75]

69 Esteva, "Development," 1–3.

70 Harry S. Truman, "Inaugural Address, 20 January 1949." See also note 62 above.

71 Ibid. 72 See, UN Doc [ST]/DPI/1475 (1995), *The United Nations.*

73 Ibid, 3. See also, Shane Chalmers, "The Mythology of International Rule-of-Law Promotion," *Law & Social Inquiry*, vol 44, no 4 (2019).

74 Instituto Universitario de Opinión Pública, "Encuesta sobre la firma de los Acuerdos de Paz: Visión del Cumplimiento de los Acuerdos de Paz y Valoraciones Políticas de los Salvadoreños" (1992), 3–5. https://uca.edu.sv/iudop/publicacion/encuesta-sobre-la-firma-de-los-acuerdos-de-paz-5/.

75 Chimni, "TWAIL: A Manifesto," 5.

As I outlined in the Introduction of this chapter, one of those institutions was the UN Truth Commission – officially named the Commission on the Truth for El Salvador.[76] Its task was "to seek, find and publicize the truth" about the civil war's violence against Salvadoran society.[77] In the following section, I show how the UN Truth Commission did that, by drawing on international law to authorize (through its Final Report) its account about the unlawfulness of the 1980–1992 civil war's violence as the truth.

4.2.2 THE FINAL REPORT OF THE UN'S COMMISSION ON THE TRUTH FOR EL SALVADOR. As part of the implementation of the Chapultepec Agreement, the UN Truth Commission began its eight-month investigation in 1992 in San Salvador, the capital of El Salvador, and concluded it at the UN's New York headquarters in 1993.[78] According to its mandate, the UN Truth Commission was the joint response of the Salvadoran state and the FMLN guerrillas to the "need to put an end to impunity" for "situations whose complexity warrants independent treatment."[79] To fulfill that need, the UN Truth Commission was created to "investigat[e] serious acts of violence that have occurred" during the Salvadoran civil war between 1980 and 1991 "and whose impact on society urgently demand[ed] that the public should know that truth."[80] The parties also agreed that the Secretary-General would appoint non-Salvadoran commissioners, so that they "could not be accused of having some domestic Salvadoran political stake or motive in reaching a particular decision."[81] Finally, in March 1993, a ceremony was held in New York to publicly present the findings, recorded in the Final Report titled *From Madness to Hope: The 12-year War in El Salvador.*[82]

76 UN Doc S/25500 (1 April 1993), *From Madness to Hope.* 77 Ibid, 11.

78 UN Doc [ST]/DPI/1475 (1995), *The United Nations,* 33; Thomas Buergenthal, "The United Nations Truth Commission for El Salvador," *Vanderbilt Journal of Transnational Law,* vol 27, no 3 (1994), 504–505.

79 UN Doc A/46/553 – S/23130 (9 October 1991), *Mexico Agreements,* 16. 80 Ibid.

81 Buergenthal, "United Nations Truth Commission," 541.

82 It was published on 1 April 1993. See, ibid, 498–499; UN Doc S/25500 (1 April 1993), *From Madness to Hope.*

The account of the civil war written in the Final Report begins with the following epigraph: "all these things happened among us."[83] This quotation is used just once more in the Final Report's Epilogue to re-state its preceding account of the civil war.[84] The location of the quotation, as the Final Report's opening and closing texts, is important because it subtlety guides the interpretation of the Final Report.[85] Yet, my focus here is on what choosing this particular quotation reveals about the rationalities underpinning the UN Truth Commission's account.

Beyond referring to the quotation as a "Mayan poem," the commissioners do not cite its source, contextualize it, or explain its relevance for the Final Report's subject matter.[86] Given that the UN Truth Commission's truth was presented as "the bright light ... that would contribute to reconciliation and to abolishing such patterns of" violence,[87] the location of the quotation suggests that the "Mayan poem" ("all these things happened among us") is meaningful for El Salvador, where there was a small Mayan presence.[88] Indeed, the implication of choosing the poem is that, at the very least, it was written by a Mayan poet who once lived in the country now called 'El Salvador.' And yet, that is not the case. The poem does not even belong to the Mayan people, but to their old rival, the Aztec, who lived on the land now known as 'Mexico.' The poem is an *icnocuícatl*, one of the Aztec's "songs in funeral rites."[89] *Icnocuícatl* in Spanish/English means a song expressing "sorrow and death" or "orphanhood."[90] Importantly, through an *icnocuícatl* Aztecs created a "sacred space-time" to communicate with their ancestors during mourning rites.[91] The quotation inserted in the Final Report is an *icnocuícatl* sung by the Aztec *tlatoani* (ruler) Moctezuma

[83] UN Doc S/25500 (1 April 1993), *From Madness to Hope*, 9; 187. [84] Ibid, 187.
[85] On this see generally, Gérard Genette, *Paratexts: Thresholds of Interpretation*, trans by Jane E. Lewin (Cambridge University Press, 1997).
[86] UN Doc S/25500 (1 April 1993), *From Madness to Hope*, 9. [87] Ibid, 11.
[88] Ministerio de Cultural de El Salvador, "Parque Arqueológico El Tazumal." www.cultura.gob.sv/parque-arqueologico-tazumal/.
[89] Patrick K. Johansson, "Miccacuicatl: Cantos Mortuorios Nahuas Prehispánicos. Textos y 'con-textos'," *Estudios de Cultura Náhuatl*, vol 48 (2014): 7.
[90] Ibid. See also, Online Nahuatl Dictionary, Stephanie Wood (ed), "Icnocuícatl." https://nahuatl.uoregon.edu/content/icnocuicatl.
[91] Johansson, "Miccacuicatl," 27.

II, to express his heartbreak at the unfolding tragedy of Castilian colonization.[92]

The issue is not so much that choosing Moctezuma's *icnocuícatl* shows the shallowness of the commissioners' knowledge of the histories of the peoples inhabiting North and Central America. Rather, opening and closing the Final Report with this quotation is telling of the 'place' from which the commissioner's viewed the Salvadoran civil war, as well as the sensitivities and rationalities informing the UN Truth Commission's resulting truth. 'Place' here is not necessarily a geographical location, but "where" we "*dwell*."[93] A 'dwelling place' – for example, events, experiences, or memories – is a place *from where* we "perceive the world," which informs how we think about and analyze it.[94] Even though the UN Truth Commission's investigation began *in* El Salvador, the epigraph's *icnocuícatl* suggests that the commissioners' dwelling place was elsewhere.[95]

The commissioners' dwelling place, from which they crafted and deployed their account of the truth, was informed by the convergence of two orientations. One is an Eurocentric/Anglo-American but mostly United States-centric triumphalist Cold War position. The second is the UN's developmental rationality toward Global South states, which I previously discussed. Although both orientations manifest throughout the Final Report, for the purposes of this chapter, I will focus on two instances: first, the Final Report's title; and second, sections of the Final Report's Introduction and Epilogue, where the commissioners analyze the nature of the civil war's violence. The convergence of both orientations shaped the UN Truth Commission's account of the civil war, as an account about an unlawful violent event that violated international law.

[92] Miguel León-Portilla, "El Ocaso de los Dioses. Moctezuma II," *Arqueología Mexicana*, no 98 (2009). The colonization of what is now 'Latin America' was done on behalf of the Kingdom of Castille, which is now a region of the state known as 'Spain.'

[93] Walter D. Mignolo, *The Darker Side of Western Modernity: Global Futures, Decolonial Options* (Duke University Press, 2011), xiii.

[94] Horacio Legrás, "The Rule of Impurity: Decolonial Theory and the Question of Literature" in, Juan G. Ramos and Tara Daly (eds), *Decolonial Approaches to Latin American Literature and Cultures* (Palgrave Macmillan, 2016), 20.

[95] Mignolo, *The Darker Side*, xiii; Berger, *Landscapes*, 147.

4.2.2.1 The Title of the Final Report

The commissioners titled the Final Report *From Madness to Hope: The 12-year War in El Salvador.*[96] It is often assumed that titles are just descriptive elements of a particular work. Understood in that way, the Final Report's title has a simple function, which is to tell its readers that the text they are about to read is an historical account of the civil war in El Salvador,[97] and that this can be understood to have unfolded in a developmental way, proceeding from "madness" to "hope."[98]

The first part of the Title (*From Madness to Hope*) is reproduced in the Final Report's opening paragraph, where the non-Salvadoran commissioners (indirectly) explain that the Title illustrates what the Chapultepec Agreement represented for Salvadorans. The commissioners state that it was not "until the day – 16 January 1992 – when the parties, reconciled, signed the Peace Agreement ... and brought back the light and the chance to *re-emerge from madness to hope.*"[99] In the sentences preceding the temporal preposition "until," the commissioners describe the civil war as a situation which "plunged Salvador[a]n society into violence."[100] In the commissioners' view, the Chapultepec Agreement and the institutions it established were the outcome of "the partie[s'] reconcil[iation]" and were also what enabled Salvadoran society to "re-emerge" from a "mad," violent war into a situation of "hope" and peace.[101] Although that opening paragraph is the only place in the Final Report where this part of the title is entirely reproduced and somewhat explained, it is clear that the title is doing more than just descriptive work.[102] In describing the war in this way, the title is also functioning as an "identifying device,"[103] which facilitates the "transmi[ssion]" and "circulat[ion]" of its historical account.[104] It does this by giving the account a particular gloss, which makes it easy to recognize and remember, regardless of whether the audience has meaningfully engaged with the actual account contained in the Report.

96 UN Doc S/25500 (1 April 1993), *From Madness to Hope*, 3. 97 Ibid. 98 Ibid.
99 UN Doc S/25500 (1 April 1993), *From Madness to Hope*, 10. Italics mine. 100 Ibid.
101 Ibid.
102 For a comprehensive analysis of the literary history, genre, and function of titles see, Genette, *Paratexts*, 55–103.
103 Ibid, 80. 104 Ibid, 75.

In this sense, the Final Report's title is transmitting the UN Truth Commission's account of the civil war and the 'new' post-conflict Salvadoran state, by representing the history as a linear movement from one emotional state or feeling to another, which represents its overcoming: "from madness to hope."[105] On the one hand, the title guides how readers should interpret and remember the civil war, as the outcome of the parties' (Salvadoran state/armed forces and FMLN guerrillas) state of "madness" or irrationality. On the other hand, the title presents the 'new' post-conflict Salvadoran state as the outcome of the parties' rational decision to "reconcile," which is conducive to a "hope[ful]" future.[106] That way of associating the UN Truth Commission's account of the civil war and the post-conflict state as a logical movement "from madness to hope" is telling of the developmental rationality orienting the commissioners' understanding of the Salvadoran civil war. It is also telling of how the international development project is advancing the very imperialism toward Global South states that Global North states, especially the US, claimed was 'over' by the 1990s.

As Luis Eslava argues, the "developmental state" that emerged with "the end of formal imperialism" and decolonization in the Global South "was the vehicle through which this imperial restructuring was executed" in the decades that followed.[107] The UN played an active role in this "imperial restructuring," which, as Eslava reminds us, was "never fully hegemonic, but never fully emancipatory either" for the Global South, including for the Latin American states that achieved independence earlier (in the late eighteenth century).[108] As I discussed above, in the case of El Salvador, the UN assumed the position of authority over the post-conflict Salvadoran state. The UN took up the role of the international organization that would administer the 'rebuilding' of a lawful

[105] UN Doc S/25500 (1 April 1993), *From Madness to Hope*. [106] Ibid, 10.

[107] Luis Eslava, "The Developmental State: Independence, Dependency, and the History of the South," in *The Battle for International Law: South-North Perspectives on the Decolonization Era*, Jochen von Bernstorff and Philipp Dann (eds), (Oxford University Press, 2019), 71–72.

[108] Ibid, 82. For general histories of Latin America see generally, Tulio Halperín Donghi, *The Contemporary History of Latin America*, trans by John Charles Chasteen (Duke University Press, 1993), 1–73; James Dunkerley, *Power in the Isthmus: A Political History of Modern Central America* (Verso, 1988).

post-conflict Salvadoran state, to 'undo' the unlawfulness of the civil war period.

While the Final Report's title works to identify the civil war as an internationally unlawful event, and to publicly justify the authority of the UN over the post-conflict Salvadoran state, the title does not do all the work. In what follows, I analyze sections of the Final Report's Introduction and Epilogue to show how, through them, the UN Truth Commission enables the UN to exercise its authority to administer, and thus control, the lawfulness of the post-conflict state.

4.2.2.2 The Introduction and Epilogue of the Final Report

As I discussed in this chapter's Introduction, the Final Report explicitly establishes international (humanitarian and human rights) law as the "applicable law" for the UN Truth Commission's investigation.[109] This is important not only because it formalizes the relationship between Truth Commissions and international law, but also for two additional reasons. First, it explicitly shows how the UN Truth Commission's investigation gives selected Salvadoran cases international legal form by categorizing them as violations of international law.[110] And second, it is telling of how the UN Truth Commission makes these cases into events of international law;[111] and, importantly, how in doing so, it expands and asserts the authority of the UN over the Salvadoran post-conflict state.[112] However, the way in which the UN Truth Commission does this cannot only be seen in the explicit legal categorization of events under "the applicable [international] law,"[113] but also through the more subtle but equally powerful Final Report's Introduction and Epilogue.

In an article reflecting on the UN Truth Commission's work, Thomas Buergenthal, chair of the UN Truth Commission, explained that the

109 UN Doc S/25500 (1 April 1993), *From Madness to Hope*, 20.

110 Ibid, 22. See generally also the conclusions of each case in the Final Report in, ibid, 43–174. On how legal categories are technologies of jurisdiction, see Dorsett and McVeigh, *Jurisdiction*, 71–76.

111 Fleur Johns, Richard Joyce, and Sundhya Pahuja (eds), *Events: The Force of International Law* (Routledge, 2010), 7.

112 Dorsett and McVeigh, *Jurisdiction*, 117.

113 UN Doc S/25500 (1 April 1993), *From Madness to Hope*, 20.

commissioners' "reflections on the violence chronicled in the [Final] Report" and their "hopes for national reconciliation" are set out in the Introduction and Epilogue.[114] Yet, in those framing sections of the Report, the commissioners are doing more than sharing their "reflections" on El Salvador's civil war and their "hopes" for lasting peace and "reconciliation."[115] The commissioners' writing in the Introduction and Epilogue cannot be understood as "reflections" entirely independent from the institution that they represent (the UN), and which authorizes their work.

The commissioners were professionals appointed to the office of the Truth Commission by the Secretary-General who commissioned them to conduct an investigation on behalf of the UN.[116] According to its mandate, the main purpose of the UN Truth Commission's investigation was to make "public" to Salvadoran "society" its account of the civil war's violence.[117] As such, in their capacity as commissioners, they are representing the UN before the Salvadoran state, the FMLN guerrillas and Salvadorans.[118] Ultimately, as the cover of the Final Report reminds its readers, the UN Truth Commission's account is "for El Salvador."[119] Indeed, the Introduction and Epilogue play a fundamental role in asserting the UN's power to authorize the lawfulness of the Salvadoran post-conflict state, and thus arrange state-society relations accordingly.

The commissioners do that by representing the UN Truth Commission's account of the civil war's violence against Salvadorans as the outcome of the Salvadoran state and the FMLN's violation of the (international) "rule of law."[120] This can be seen in the Introduction's opening paragraphs, in which the commissioners describe how "[v]iolence" moved across El Salvador – from the countryside to the cities – and "turned everything to death and destruction."[121] The Introduction then states that this "death and destruction" was the consequence of "the senselessness of that breach of the calm plenitude which accompanies the rule of law."[122] In this understanding, the "rule of law" is generative of

[114] Buergenthal, "United Nations Truth Commission," 525. [115] Ibid.
[116] UN Doc A/46/553 – S/23130 (9 October 1991), *Mexico Agreements*, 16. [117] Ibid.
[118] Ibid. [119] UN Doc S/25500 (1 April 1993), *From Madness to Hope.* [120] Ibid, 10.
[121] Ibid. [122] Ibid.

"sens[e]" as opposed to "senselessness"; of "calm plenitude" as opposed to violence; and of instilling "certainty ... in human beings" as opposed to uncertainty and unpredictable human behavior.[123]

This way of conceptualizing 'the rule of law' through binaries has the effect of representing the Salvadoran civil war as an event of "[l]awlessness," and of El Salvador as a geographical place "in which law is absent."[124] In that image, El Salvador's lawlessness, and its civil war's unlawfulness, have its origins in "the essential nature of [the] violence" that the parties in the war embraced and inflicted upon "Salvador[a]ns and foreigners of all backgrounds and all social and economic classes."[125] In this view, the civil war's violence led to the abandonment of "the normal mechanisms of the rule of law," which allow a society to pursue change in a predictable and measured way, as opposed to the war's "sudde[n]," forceful, violent attempt to change El Salvador.[126]

The commissioners' way of seeing El Salvador – as a lawless place – deploys a representation of it "as deficien[t] in the rule of law,"[127] and therefore of needing 'the rule of law' to make Salvadoran post-conflict state-society relations lawful. But importantly, as Cait Storr argues, "the international order one perceives is radically determined by the place in which one stands."[128] Indeed, the Introduction's representation of the Salvadoran post-conflict state as in need of rule of law not only shows the commissioners' developmental gaze toward El Salvador as an 'underdeveloped' and 'lawless' place; but it also "reveal[s] the imagery and vision of the world which has generated" it.[129] That post-Cold War "world" in which the UN Truth Commission operated, as I discussed above, although disguised as a 'new' international one, in which *all* states are 'equal' and 'free' to determine their 'own' "destiny,"[130] was still profoundly organizing North-South relations according to international law's imperial rationalities.

[123] Ibid. [124] Chalmers, "The Mythology," 6.
[125] UN Doc S/25500 (1 April 1993), *From Madness to Hope*, 10. [126] Ibid.
[127] Chalmers, "The Mythology," 11.
[128] Cait Storr, *International Status in the Shadow of Empire: Nauru and the Histories of International Law* (Cambridge University Press, 2020), 8.
[129] Desmond Manderson, "Beyond the Provincial: Space, Aesthetics, and Modernist Legal Theory," *Melbourne University Law Review*, vol 20 (1995–1996): 1050.
[130] Craven, Pahuja, and Simpson, *International Law and the Cold War*, 2.

In this post-Cold War international world, as I previously showed, that imperial relationship not only took the form of 'international development' (following the Truman rationality),[131] but married it to international rule of law promotion.[132] As Chalmers and Pahuja argue, since the late 1980s, international rule of law promotion has become "a multi-billion dollar industry that is centrally concerned with 'the rule of law' as instrument, end, and indicator of 'development,' positioned at the heart of state-making."[133] Although according to the 1990 Chapultepec Agreements, the UN Truth Commission was conceived as an institution that would help the post-conflict state to "put an end to any indication of impunity," especially in relation to the armed forces,[134] the Final Report's Introduction and Epilogue show how the UN Truth Commission sought to do more than that. In this post-Cold War context, the UN Truth Commission was crucial not only to advance the UN's peacebuilding vision and state-building model in El Salvador, but also to authorize, and thus control, the lawfulness of its post-conflict state-society relations.

One way in which the Introduction and Epilogue do that is by portraying Salvadorans as lacking agency and capacity to organize their own post-conflict, lawful state-society relations, and therefore in desperate need of the UN's intervention. This manifests in one of the Introduction's opening paragraphs. Here, Salvadorans are described using nouns denoting sentiments, rather than with the verbs used to describe the UN's active role. For example, the commissioners describe Salvadorans as peoples who, toward the end of the war, collectively "pause for thought" and "put their hands to their hearts and felt them pound with joy" at the realization that "[n]o one was winning the war."[135] In contrast, immediately after that, the then Secretary-General Pérez de Cuéllar is characterized as the hero. Pérez de Cuéllar is

131 See note 62 above.

132 See generally, Pahuja, *Decolonising International Law*, 172–253; Shane Chalmers, *Liberia and the Dialectic of Law: Critical Theory, Pluralism, and the Rule of Law* (Routledge, 2018), 70–100.

133 Shane Chalmers and Sundhya Pahuja, "(Economic) Development and the Rule of Law," in *The Cambridge Companion to the Rule of Law*, Martin Loughin and Jens Meierhenrich (eds), (Cambridge University Press, 2021), 377.

134 UN Doc A/46/664 – S/23501 (30 January 1992), *Chapultepec Peace Agreement*, 8.

135 UN Doc S/25500 (1 April 1993), *From Madness to Hope*, 10.

described as the "visionary" who "[h]eeded" and "answered" Salvadorans' "unanimous outcry" for peace.[136]

The Epilogue also reproduces such characterizations. There, Salvadorans are depicted as victims who were "pawn[s] in the East-West conflict" and "buffeted by a turbulent sea of waning ideologies and global contradictions."[137] In this context, the Salvadoran parties to the conflict are described as "embrac[ing] one another in a sign of reconciliation."[138] In contrast, once again it is the UN – this time through its UN Truth Commission – that is "contributing to restoring the institutional fabric of El Salvador."[139] Through those comparisons, the Final Report on the one hand frames the parties' agency as generative of violence against their own people,[140] and on the other hand, as an emotional people, who move from interpersonal enmity to reconciliation.[141] In this portrayal, the Salvadoran parties are characterized as capable of interpersonal reconciliation, and of reflecting on the wrongfulness of their violence. In contrast, it is the UN's expert knowledge[142] that has the intellectual and political capacity to realize the 'necessary' (internationally) lawful transformation of Salvadoran state-society relations.

Furthermore, there is another dimension to the commissioners' characterization of the Salvadoran parties' lack of agency. Toward the end of the Epilogue, the commissioners state that:

> it is for Salvador[a]ns themselves to take the fundamental decisions that will lead to a full-fledged peace. Salvador[a]n society must decide about accountability for past actions and new statutes of limitations. It has the power to grant pardons. It is also this society, steeped in the painful lessons of war, that will have to settle the dispute about new appointments to high office.[143]

In this the need for the UN's intervention has disappeared, and the commissioners now represent the Salvadoran parties and society as having the agency to shape peaceful and lawful state-society relations. Yet, on a closer reading, the paragraph reveals another aspect of the

136 Ibid. 137 Ibid, 188. 138 Ibid. 139 Ibid. 140 Ibid, 10. 141 Ibid, 10; 188.
142 UN Doc [ST]/DPI/1475 (1995), *The United Nations*.
143 UN Doc S/25500 (1 April 1993), *From Madness to Hope*, 188.

developmental rationality informing the UN Truth Commission's account: the responsibility of becoming either a 'successful' or 'failed' post-conflict state depends on Salvadorans' decision-making capacity.

Similarly, that way of placing the responsibility for the post-conflict state's 'future' on the Salvadoran parties and society also manifests in the Introduction's last paragraph. There, the commissioners state that the Salvadoran parties to the conflict are being "watch[ed]" by both "Salvador[a]n society" and "the international community."[144] Yet, in the commissioners' view, the activity of "watching" – as a way of formulating a value judgment – over the conduct of the Salvadoran parties in the post-conflict state has different aims and temporalities. For the UN Truth Commission, while Salvadorans are "watching them [the parties] from the vantage point of history" – that is from the 'future' – the international community is "watching ... in gladness" in the present (in 1993, the year that the Final Report is published).[145]

This distinction between 'when' the activity of "watching" happens, and 'who' is doing it, is important. Here, while the commissioners place on Salvadorans sole responsibility for their post-conflict 'future,' the international community is depicted as approving ("watching ... in gladness") the 'current' post-conflict state (in 1993). In this representation, the Salvadorans 'of 1993' are characterized as being "a society of sacrifice and hope," and as going through a process of becoming "[a] new people ... rising from the ashes of a war in which all were unjust."[146] For that reason, they are not yet equipped to 'watch over' the 1993 post-conflict state, but they will, and have to, in the 'future.'

The analysis in this section has shown how the UN Truth Commission drew on the identity and status of the UN as an international institution to authorize its truth about the unlawfulness of the 1980–1992 civil war's violence. My close reading of three key sections of the Final Report – Title, Introduction, and Epilogue – revealed the 'developmental' sensitivities and rationalities underpinning the UN Truth Commission's internationally authorized truth. A truth that fitted the UN's peacebuilding vision for post-conflict states in the Global South, in the aftermath of the

[144] Ibid. [145] Ibid, 17. [146] Ibid.

Cold War. In what follows (Section 4.3), I turn to the truth represented in the tapestry about the 1980 Sumpul River Massacre.

4.3 A PEASANT WOMAN'S TRUTH FOR EL SALVADOR: THE TAPESTRY ABOUT THE 1980 SUMPUL RIVER MASSACRE

Bodies on the ground; a river; people running; more bodies on the far side; mountains on fire; people drowning. That is what I first saw as I stood before a tapestry displayed at El Salvador's Museo de la Palabra y la Imagen (Museum of the Word and the Image, or MUPI), located in San Salvador. Then I noticed, as seen in Figure 4.1, the words stitched at the bottom of the tapestry: "THIS IS THE STORY THAT WE THE PEASANTS HAVE LIVED IN WHICH MANY BROTHERS DROWNED BECAUSE OF THE REPRESSION."[147] What civil war story, I wondered, is the tapestry representing?

As I stood before the tapestry, its image had a striking resemblance to contemporary images of Central American migrants crossing Río Bravo/ Grande River at the Mexico-US border.[148] At MUPI the tapestry is displayed as a cultural object telling a story not about 'the present,' but about 'the past': the civil war; and yet the story represented in the tapestry seemed so contemporary.

At MUPI, I learned that the tapestry accounts for the Sumpul River Massacre of May, 13–14, 1980.[149] The massacre took place at the Sumpul River and in the area surrounding the village of Las Aradas, located next to the river.[150] The river area runs along the

147 ("esta es la historia que los campesinos hemos vivido donde muchos hermanos se ahogaron por causa de la represi[ó]n"). Capitalization in original. In the dominant Spanish grammatical gender convention, plural nouns referring to a group of people, are expressed using a masculine gender-inflection. This is the case of the sentence in the tapestry. I translated "*hermanos*" into English as "brothers" to remain faithful to the tapestry's original text.

148 Mónica González, "La Foto del Último Abrazo de Óscar y Valeria: El Periodismo que Duele," *El Faro* (16 July 2019). https://elfaro.net/es/201907/defensoria/23500/La-foto-del-último-abrazo-de-Óscar-y-Valeria-el-periodismo-que-duele.htm; Nelson Rauda Zablah, "Lecciones Aprendidas del Río Suchiate" (3 November 2018). elfaro.net/es/201811/centroamerica/22663/Las-lecciones-aprendidas-del-r%C3%ADo-Suchiate.htm.

149 Asociación de Sobrevivientes de la Masacre del Sumpul, *Memorias del Sumpul*, 18–37.

150 Ibid.

4.1 Author Unknown. "Esta es la Historia." Undated – 1980s. Museo de la Palabra y la Imagen in San Salvador (El Salvador). Reproduced with permission of the museum.

border between El Salvador's northern province of Chalatenango and Honduras' southern province of Lempira.[151] The massacre was the result of the first major, planned military operation against

151 There is a history of conflict between El Salvador and Honduras, which unfolded along this border and its neighboring areas. The conflict led to a brief war called "Hundred Hours' War of 14–18 July 1969." On this see, Jorge Arieh Gerstein, "El Conflicto entre Honduras y El Salvador: Análisis de sus Causas," *Foro Internacional*, vol 11, no 4 (1971); Obdulio Nunfio, "Radiografía de la Guerra del Futbol o de las Cien Horas," *Revista Mexicana de Sociología*, vol 32, no 3 (1970). See also, United States Office of the Historian, "Nixon Presidential Materials, NSC Files, Box 786, Country Files, Latin America, Honduras–Salvador Dispute. 644. Memorandum from the President's Assistant for National Security Affairs (Kissinger) to President Nixon (1969)" (National Archives Collection: Foreign Relations of the United States, 1969–1976, Volume E–10, Documents on American Republics, 1969–1972: Soccer

peasants at the beginning of the civil war.[152] It was coordinated by the Salvadoran Armed Forces with the support of the Honduran military.[153] During the night of the massacre, while over 300 peasants were attempting to survive, at the Salvadoran Armed Forces' request Honduran soldiers blocked the peasants from crossing the Sumpul River into Honduras.[154] The Sumpul Massacre is telling of the rage of the state's violence against Salvadorans who represented a threat to the state and the elite's economic, sociopolitical, and legal power. Whenever the Salvadoran Armed Forces launched anti-guerrilla military operations in the countryside, they destroyed everything – people, houses, infrastructure, nature – to make sure peasants would not support the guerrillas in any way. This type of military operation was known as '*tierra arrasada*' (scorched earth).[155] That is what happened at the Sumpul River and its surroundings, and what forced the woman who crafted the tapestry and her community to flee El Salvador.

What makes the tapestry especially relevant is that, as I show in detail in this part, the tapestry's account powerfully "disrupts" the UN Truth Commission's internationally authorized account.[156] That disruptive force, I suggest, stems from the tapestry's material life, which allows it

War); James Dunkerley, *The Long War: Dictatorship and Revolution in El Salvador* (Verso, 1982), 83; Dalton, *Las Historias Prohibidas*. To settle this conflict, the Organization of American States intervened by creating a demilitarized zone under its control, see "El Salvador-Honduras: Agreement on Security Zone for Purposes of Pacification," *International Legal Materials* vol 9, no 6 (1970).

152 See Asociación de Sobrevivientes de la Masacre del Sumpul, *Memorias del Sumpul*; Christopher Dickey, "Salvadoran Refugees Caught Between 'Hammer and Anvil'," *The Washington Post* (6 July 1980); Hilary DeVries, "Massacre in El Salvador Reported by London Paper," *The Christian Science Monitor* (24 February 1981); Warren Hoge, "Slaughter in Salvador: 200 Lost in Border Massacre," *New York Times* (8 June 1981).

153 Asociación de Sobrevivientes de la Masacre del Sumpul, *Memorias del Sumpul*, 25.

154 Ibid, 25–28.

155 Annette Georgina Hernández Rivas, "Cartografía de la Memoria: Actores, Lugares y Prácticas en El Salvador de Posguerra (1992–2015)" (PhD Thesis, Universidad Autónoma de Madrid, 2015), 67–68; Ching, *Stories of Civil War*, 102; 122; Kinsella, *The Image before the Weapon*, 183.

156 Desmond Manderson, "Bodies in the Water: On Reading Images More Sensibly," *Law & Literature*, vol 27, no 2 (2013): 281.

not only to be a representation of a past event, but also to speak across time, to contemporary events.[157]

As I explain in the following section, I understand the tapestry's 'material life' as the convergence of three qualities. The first is the tapestry's physical existence over forty years; while the second is the nature and origin of the materials used to craft the visual representation of the massacre. At the same time, those two qualities (the temporal and the material) are inextricably connected to the third quality: the personal and communal history of the woman who handcrafted the tapestry while in exile, out of a need to bear witness to her community's suffering during the Sumpul Massacre. In the analysis below, I show how the synergy between those three qualities give material life, and thus disruptive force, to the tapestry.

4.3.1 ENCOUNTERING THE TAPESTRY. Carlos 'Santiago' Henríquez Consalvi, the director of MUPI, introduced me to the tapestry in early 2020. During the civil war, Carlos was an important member of the FMLN guerrillas. He was responsible for establishing, and was the leading voice of, Radio Venceremos (Radio We Will Win), the guerrillas' clandestine radio broadcast.[158] After the signature of the Chapultepec Agreement, a group of people led by Carlos founded MUPI.[159] The original idea was not to create a museum, but rather a "documentation center" to safeguard all the information – radio and audio-visual materials, personal accounts, photos, artwork – that the Radio Venceremos team gathered throughout the war.[160] In the words of Georgina

[157] See generally, ibid.; Shane Chalmers, "The Visual Force of Justice in the Making of Liberia," in *Law and the Visual: Representations, Technologies, and Critique*, Desmond Manderson (ed), (University of Toronto Press, 2018).

[158] For Carlos's experience with Radio Venceremos see, Carlos 'Santiago' Henríquez Consalvi, *La Terquedad del Izote: La Historia de Radio Venceremos* (Ediciones Museo de la Palabra y la Imagen, 2018). For its version in English see, Carlos 'Santiago' Henríquez Consalvi, *Broadcasting the Civil War in El Salvador: A Memoir of Guerrilla Radio; Introduction by Erik Ching*, trans by Charles Leo Nagle and A. L. (Bill) Prince (University of Texas Press, 2010).

[159] Hernández Rivas, "Cartografía de la Memoria," 230. See also MUPI, "Equipo MUPI." http://museo.com.sv/2017/05/equipo-mupi/.

[160] ("centro de documentación"). Hernández Rivas, "Cartografía de la Memoria," 244.

Hernández, one of MUPI's co-founders, the team "noticed that they [Radio Venceremos' materials] were a source of information to research the 'regime of truth' or, at least, to validate 'other truths'" about the war.[161]

Nearly thirty years later, MUPI works as a museum of memory and as an historical archive.[162] As archive MUPI is custodian of a rich collection of audio-visual materials, written documents, artworks, and other objects that record mostly the civil war, but also important historical events such as the 1932 Peasant Uprising and the subsequent state-led massacre,[163] and the archives of prominent Salvadoran artists and intellectuals, such as rebel-poet Roque Dalton, and feminist thinker Prudencia Ayala.[164] As museum of memory,[165] through its exhibitions, social outreach, and educational programs, MUPI seeks to counter "the chaos of *desmemoria* [forgetting]" left after the twelve-year civil war.[166] For that reason, a fundamental aspect of MUPI's work has been to showcase its collections all around El Salvador and internationally.

It was during an international exhibition (around 2019) that MUPI learned about the existence of embroidered tapestries, which had been crafted during the civil war by Salvadoran women at refugee camps in Honduras.[167] While some tapestries had floral motifs, others represented scenes of the refugees' everyday life at the camps and their experiences

161 ("y observamos su valor como fuente de información para la investigación del "régimen de verdad" o, al menos, para validar "otras verdades"). Ibid.

162 MUPI, "Museum Information." http://museo.com.sv/2017/05/museum-information/. For a brief institutional history of MUPI see Hernández Rivas, *Cartografía de la Memoria*, 244–253.

163 On the 1932 uprising and massacre see Héctor Lindo-Fuentes, Erik Ching, and Rafael Lara-Martínez, *Remembering a Massacre in El Salvador: The Insurrection of 1932, Roque Dalton, and the Politics of Historical Memory* (University of New Mexico Press, 2007).

164 MUPI, "Museum Information."

165 Hernández Rivas, "Cartografía de la Memoria," 254–255. See also, Silke Arnold-de Simine, *Mediating Memory in the Museum: Trauma, Empathy, Nostalgia* (Palgrave Macmillan, 2013), 10–11.

166 MUPI, "Museum Information." On MUPI see also, Robin Maria DeLugan, *Reimagining National Belonging: Post-Civil War El Salvador in a Global Context* (University of Arizona Press, 2012), 117–121.

167 This was shared with me during an informal conversation with MUPI's Director Carlos Henríquez Consalvi in San Salvador in 2020.

fleeing the civil war's violence.[168] Due to the precarious conditions at the camps, to access basic needs – such as food – the refugees sold many of the tapestries to international NGO workers, who either worked or visited the camps throughout the 1980s.[169] Given the tapestries' storytelling power, in 2019 MUPI launched a social media campaign appealing to those who bought the tapestries to support MUPI's "historical memory" efforts in repatriating the tapestries to El Salvador.[170] The success of MUPI's campaign allowed it to permanently display the tapestries in San Salvador and to organize temporary exhibitions in other towns and overseas.[171]

Having the tapestries back in El Salvador also afforded MUPI the opportunity to collaborate with former refugee women living in Ciudad Segundo Montes, the rural town where many refugees settled in the 1990s on their return to El Salvador.[172] The town is located in the north-eastern province of Morazán, about 30kms from the UNHCR

168 See the collection in, The University of Texas at Austin, "Colección Bordadoras de Memorias" (Latin American Digital Archives). https://ladi-prod.lib.utexas.edu/en/mupi03. For a recent study about the importance of the embroidered tapestries for El Salvador's historical memory see, Rolando E. Chicas Alfaro, Gabriela O. Montes Polanco, and José D. Rodríguez Morales, "Importancia de la Memoria Histórica a través de la Representación Visual de la Producción en Bordados Realizados por Salvadoreños Refugiados en Colomoncagua, Honduras entre 1981 a 1992, Contenidos en la Colección del Museo de la Palabra y la Imagen (MUPI)" (Honours Thesis, University of El Salvador, 2019).

169 Cagan and Cagan, *This Promised Land*, 80–81. Previously in Chapter 3, I discuss the *arpilleras*, which are patchwork tapestries from Chile that narrate the violence suffered by women and their loved ones during Pinochet's dictatorship. For more of the *arpilleras* see, Marjorie Agosín, *Tapestries of Hope, Threads of Love: The Arpillera Movement in Chile* (Rowman & Littlefield Publishers, 2008). Over the last decade, especially in the field of transitional justice, there is an increasing focus on tapestries which bear witness of the suffering caused by war and violent conflict, especially in Chile and most recently in Colombia. On this see for example, the initiative at the Ulster University, Conflict Textiles, "About." https://cain.ulster.ac.uk/conflicttextiles/. Yet, it is also important to try to understand tapestry-making in context, that is, within the material culture of each community.

170 ("memoria histórica"). MUPI, "Tienes Bordados Realizados en los Refugios Durante la Guerra?." museo.com.sv/2019/08/tienes-bordados-realizados-en-los-refugios-durante-la-guerra/.

171 MUPI, "Bordadoras de Memorias conmemoran 'El Retorno'." https://museo.com.sv/2017/11/bordadoras-de-memorias-conmemoran-el-retorno/.

172 Ibid.

Colomoncagua camp in Honduras, where most Salvadoran refugees lived during the war.[173] Founding a new town was necessary because, in most cases – such as the 1980 Sumpul Massacre, the 1981 El Mozote Massacre, and other systematic attacks against rural communities – refugees had nowhere to go back to.[174] That was the case not only because the war was ongoing (despite the 1990 peace negotiations), but also because the state's armed forces destroyed the refugees' hometowns and/or killed their families, friends, and neighbors.[175]

MUPI's collaboration with the women at Segundo Montes was important because the tradition of embroidering tapestries continues to be undervalued and in decline in Salvadoran culture. The goods crafted through this artisan tradition have been historically seen as "inferior" in part due to a socioeconomic model which for a long time prioritized "urban manufactured goods" and encouraged the "'Americanization' of cultural values" in El Salvador.[176] For that reason, MUPI's collaboration with the communities aims not only to acknowledge the significant historical and testimonial value of the 1980s tapestries, but also to encourage former refugee women to continue the Salvadoran artisan tradition of embroidery and to pass it on to future generations.[177] This is a tradition that those Salvadoran women kept alive during a long decade in exile as refugees (1980–1990).

Encountering the tapestry and the histories of Salvadoran refugees at MUPI allows visitors to learn about the impact of the civil war on people outside the UN Truth Commission's account. As I previously mentioned, MUPI's co-founders consider it a 'museum of memory,'[178] that is, as

[173] See note 27 above.

[174] Mark Danner, *The Massacre at El Mozote: A Parable of the Cold War* (Vintage Books, 1994).

[175] See survivor accounts of Sumpul and El Mozote in, Asociación de Sobrevivientes de la Masacre del Sumpul, *Memorias del Sumpul*; Rufina Amaya, with Carlos 'Santiago' Henríquez Consalvi and Mark Danner, *Luciérnagas en El Mozote* (Ediciones Museo de la Palabra y la Imagen, 1996); Danner, *The Massacre at El Mozote: A Parable of the Cold War.*

[176] Liisa North, *Bitter Grounds: Roots of Revolt in El Salvador* (Lawrence Hill & Co., 1985), 46.

[177] MUPI, "Bordadoras de Memorias conmemoran 'El Retorno'."

[178] See generally, Hernández Rivas, "Cartografía de la Memoria."

a museum specifically created to "relate to the past through the framework of 'memory'."[179] Interestingly, in MUPI's museological script, 'memory' seems to be understood in plural terms, as 'memories.' Those memories are of ordinary Salvadorans' experiences of the civil war, with a particular focus on those historically repressed and targeted by the state, such as Indigenous peoples and peasants.[180] Importantly, MUPI's plural and people-centered memorialization of the war does not overpower the particular stories of resistance, loss, and survival being told through the cultural objects on display. On the contrary, MUPI's plural approach to memorialization strikes a balance between allowing visitors to 'hear' the stories being 'told' by the cultural objects. And to do so without forgetting MUPI's focus on the war and its historical connection with state-repression and elite power.

As I previously highlighted, the woman who crafted the tapestry of the Sumpul Massacre wrote on it "THIS IS THE STORY." In what follows, I redescribe how her tapestry tells that story.

4.3.2 REPRESENTING THE 1980 SUMPUL RIVER MASSACRE. In the early days at the UNHCR refugee camp in Colomoncagua (Honduras), women used spare fabric or cloths to cover the food they prepared, in the communal kitchen, for the Salvadoran refugee community.[181] The cloth was a substitute for the traditional Salvadoran embroidered fabric, which was (and still is) used in almost every Salvadoran household to keep food warm and clean, especially maize *tortillas* (thin flatbread). With time, as refugees began to organize life in community at the camp, they established a school and several crafts and vocational-training workshops, such as one on sewing and embroidery as seen in Figure 4.2.[182]

[179] Arnold-de Simine, *Mediating Memory*, 10.

[180] MUPI, "Exposiciones." http://museo.com.sv/exposiciones/.

[181] Chicas Alfaro, Montes Polanco, and Rodríguez Morales, "Bordados Realizados por Salvadoreños," 92. On women's collective cooking, see, Cagan and Cagan, *This Promised Land*, 51–52; 89–90.

[182] See generally, Cagan and Cagan, *This Promised Land*. See also Cagan's photographic work in, Steve Cagan, "Salvadoran Refugee Camps in Honduras 1980s." http://stevecagan.com/salvadoran-refugee-camp-campamento-de-refugiados-salvadoreoscolomoncagua-hondurasnew-gallery-1.

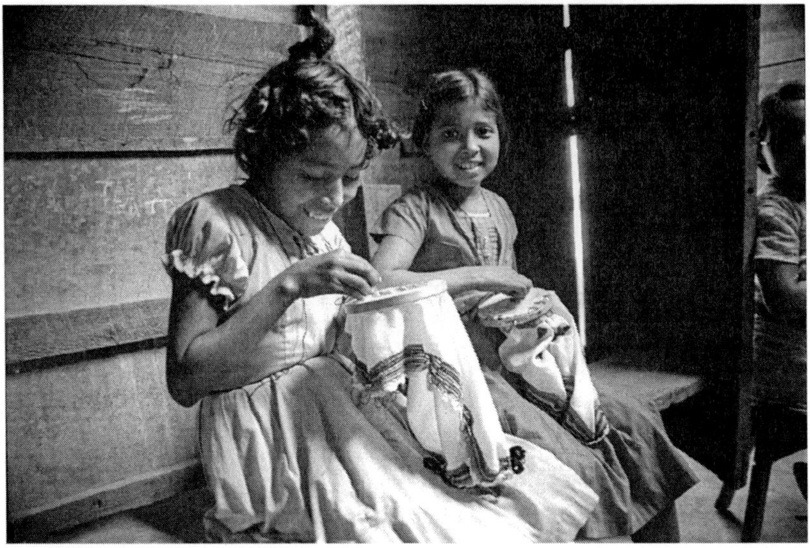

4.2 "Learning *manualidad* – embroidery" at the Colomoncagua Salvadoran refugee camp in Honduras. Photograph by Steve Cagan (www.stevecagan.com) (1988). Reproduced with permission of the photographer.

Unlike the traditional Salvadoran embroidered fabric, which is often made of a canvas-colored thin but resistant cotton fabric, the materials that the women used depended on what fabric was available. Women would use this spare material, such as flour sacks and rags, or fabric provided by the UNHCR and NGOs, to embroider floral motifs.[183] Applying the same embroidery technique, women also began to craft tapestries representing scenes of their everyday life at the camps.[184] Using needles and colorful threads, the scenes in these tapestries represented children attending school, men planting crops at the *milpa* (cornfield),[185] or women preparing food.[186] According to Irma Díaz, a woman who grew up at the camps, those tapestries were "an initiative coming from the people" because "people . . . needed to represent their

[183] Chicas Alfaro, Montes Polanco, and Rodríguez Morales, "Bordados Realizados por Salvadoreños," 91–95.

[184] Ibid. [185] Cagan and Cagan, *This Promised Land*, 197. [186] See note 168 above.

reality,"[187] a reality at the camps that was inextricably conditioned by the causes that led to a life in exile.

The refugees' tapestries continued the Salvadoran embroidery tradition of representing everyday life in rural towns. Yet, after some time, the women began to depict not only life at the camps, but also the circumstances that forced them to their life in exile. The tapestry examined in this chapter represents one of those circumstances: the Sumpul Massacre.

4.3.2.1 The Tapestry: "This Is the Story"

The tapestry is a Salvadoran woman's response to the Sumpul River Massacre. The tapestry is made of a white square cotton-like fabric with an embroidered edge. The texture of the fabric is smooth, soft, thin, and lightweight, which makes it almost translucent. On a closer look, the white fabric has slight rusty-yellow stains, similar to those that emerge on old fabrics. Coupled with the fabric's translucency, it looks fragile, vulnerable to be torn apart. The tapestry's fragile appearance, given by the qualities of the fabric on which it is crafted, is telling not only of the nature of the materials, but also of the passage of time. After all, this and the other tapestries in MUPI's collection were handmade almost forty years ago, in the 1980s.

As a finished object, the tapestry displays a representation of the Salvadoran war. In this, it is an "image of history,"[188] which represents one of the many tragic events in which the Salvadoran Armed Forces targeted, repressed, and destroyed peasant communities.[189] By "making history visible," the tapestry allows its viewers to learn about the Sumpul Massacre and the war. And yet, while the tapestry is an image of an historical, collective 'past,' it is doing more than just deploying an image *of* the past.[190] By giving visual form to an historical event, the

[187] ("esta fue iniciativa de la propia gente; acá la gente tenía la necesidad de retratar su realidad"). Chicas Alfaro, Montes Polanco, and Rodríguez Morales, "Bordados Realizados por Salvadoreños," 93; 106; 201.

[188] Chalmers, "The Visual Force," 142.

[189] See generally, note 152 above; Lindo-Fuentes, Ching, and Lara-Martínez, *Remembering a Massacre*; Dalton, *Las Historias Prohibidas*.

[190] Chalmers, "The Visual Force," 142.

woman who handcrafted this tapestry is also "providing a way of seeing and revealing" the massacre.[191] That is, through the activity of handcrafting the tapestry, the woman is not only representing the event of the massacre/war, but she is also "making meaning" of it as a survivor-witness.[192]

Seen in that way, the tapestry is a response to the woman's intimate experience of surviving and witnessing the murder of loved ones; to life in a refugee camp in a foreign, hostile country; and to a long history of state-repression, and peasant resistance to it. In this sense, the tapestry is also a representation of the woman's "lived memory,"[193] a memory that, as Andreas Huyssen writes, "is always located in individual bodies, their experience and their pain, even when it involves collective, political, or generational memory."[194] Approached in this way, the tapestry's physical existence has an inextricable relationship with the life and lived memory of its creator – a survivor-witness of the massacre.[195] The tapestry is the material means through which the woman turned her intimate memories of a traumatic experience into a publicly visible representation. She did so by using discarded materials – rags, spare fabric, and thread scarcely available at the refugee camp – to sketch, stitch, needle, embroider over and over again, her memories of what happened at the Sumpul River.

In the background of the tapestry, the woman depicts a hilly countryside. The mountains are on fire. In the sky, the woman embroidered two light planes using olive-green thread. At the bottom of the mountains, the woman depicted eleven people. As they walk, an olive-green helicopter flies over the area. While the adults and children are walking and carrying stuffed sacks on their backs or heads, one woman is carrying a baby and a man is sitting against a rock with a child hiding behind it. All of them are barefoot, except for two children and a man, who only wears one shoe. The man is the only person holding what seems to be an empty and upside-down brown sack. The people are depicted carrying heavy bags. This heaviness can be inferred not only from the rounded shape of

191 Ibid. 192 Ibid.

193 Andreas Huyssen, *Present Pasts: Urban Palimpsests and the Politics of Memory* (Stanford University Press, 2003), 110.

194 Ibid. 195 Ibid, 111.

the sacks, suggesting they are completely full, but also by how bent the people's backs and necks are. The subtle contrast between the stuffed sacks and the empty one is interesting because it is telling of the circumstances in which the man's sack was emptied.

What happened at the river is represented in the foreground of the tapestry. The woman wove two parallel, thin wavy lines to represent the contours of a turbulent river. In the river, there are fifteen people. But unlike those represented along the shore, the people in the river are only represented through certain parts of their uncovered bodies. While some of the people, whose torsos are visible, hold on to sacks or other big objects to stay afloat, others try to swim carrying children on their backs. The viewer can tell that the people are drowning.

Along the shore the woman represents a second group of people. Like the group on the other side of the river, the people in this group are barefoot. The woman represents all of the people in this group in some sort of movement, except for one man, who is lying on the ground, seemingly lifeless. Near him, a woman and a boy are represented walking at a fast pace while carrying on their shoulders or head heavy and full sacks. The distance between the man on the ground and the rest of the group suggests that they are moving away from where the man lies. To the right, the tapestry represents another man walking and supporting himself with a stick, while carrying on his bent back a heavy sack.

At the bottom-left of the tapestry the artisan wrote, in capitalized letters, "MG." While it could be the woman's initials, it could also indicate that the tapestry was made at Mesa Grande. Although the collection of tapestries held by MUPI were started in the Colomoncagua camp workshops, some of these tapestries, like this one, were made at the Mesa Grande refugee camp, which was established later and which replicated Colomoncagua's community organization.[196] At the bottom of the tapestry, the woman wrote, using the same thread, and in capitalized letters: "THIS IS THE STORY THAT WE THE PEASANTS HAVE LIVED IN WHICH MANY BROTHERS DROWNED BECAUSE OF THE REPRESSION"[197] With this sentence, the woman explains, to whoever is viewing the tapestry, that her representation of the drowning of her

[196] See generally, Cagan and Cagan, *This Promised Land.* [197] See note 147 above.

fellow "*hermanos*" [sisters and brothers] "is the story" [*la historia*] about the repression that Salvadoran peasants "lived" through.[198] It is a story in which, the woman tells us, some peasants survived – like her – and many others died.

Although the woman's representation does not explicitly identify who was responsible for the "repression" of her community, or how it was carried out, after reading her words details of the life-stories informing the tapestry emerge. Her words begin to give meaning to why the helicopter and two light planes are flying over the area of the Sumpul River as people walked, ran, swam, and drowned. To begin with, through the words on the tapestry, the woman attributes direct responsibility for the drowning of her fellow *hermanos* to "the repression." The tapestry suggests that the repression was done by the military, which is represented by the olive-green color used to depict the helicopter and planes. But the tapestry does not represent in detail how the repression operated. Furthermore, there are no symbols to help the viewer identify who the military served, and why the repression was directed against those peasants. Indeed, the tapestry does not provide answers about the massacre and the broader state-repression against peasant communities.

However, the tapestry does not seek to give those answers. The tapestry's representation deploys an image that "does not try to" be, and cannot be, "accurate" about the "event" of the massacre and the repression.[199] Colombian artist Doris Salcedo reminds us that the role of artwork in societies experiencing violent conflict "has nothing to do with . . . accurate statements."[200] Salcedo's own artwork, and her understanding of the role of art in contexts of violent conflict,[201] is helpful for understanding the tapestry's contemporary relevance and disruptive force.

198 In Spanish the noun '*historia*' is used to refer to both 'history' and 'story.' The meaning depends on the context of how '*historia*' is being used. In the tapestry's case, I translated '*historia*' as 'story' because it refers to a personal account about a lived experience.

199 Manderson, "Bodies in the Water," 218.

200 Doris Salcedo, "Doris Salcedo en el Guggenheim: "Treinta Años en el Duelo," *HINT* (11 September 2015). www.youtube.com/watch?v=Zae-MKJXiz8.

201 On this see generally, Mieke Bal, *Of What One Cannot Speak: Doris Salcedo's Political Art* (University of Chicago Press, 2010).

Salcedo collaborates with, and focuses on the suffering of, "victims of political violence and social marginalisation," primarily in, but not limited to, Colombia.[202] Her artwork – sculptures and installations – is characterized by the use of "domestic materials charged with significance and suffused with meanings accumulated over years of use in everyday life."[203] For example, she works with domestic or everyday life objects, such as shoes, clothes, wardrobes, and tables, as well as with organic matter (e.g., flowers, grass, animal skin) and inorganic matter (e.g., cement, metals, water).[204] Each of the objects and in/organic matter belonged to, or had a deep connection with, the victims and the violent circumstances that have caused their suffering.[205]

There are resonances between Salcedo's artwork and the Salvadoran woman's tapestry. Like in Salcedo's artistic process, the tapestry's materials would often be used to create a typical Salvadoran domestic object – an embroidered cloth used to keep food warm and clean. Embroidered fabrics are not only common domestic objects for everyday use in Salvadoran households, but they are also culturally representative of, and meaningful for, peasant communities. As I previously discussed, the tradition of embroidery has been an important means to record, represent, and transmit aspects of life in Salvadoran rural communities or villages.

However, at the refugee camps during the war, many of the embroidered fabrics that the women handcrafted at the workshops ceased to be crafted for domestic use in the communal kitchens. At some point, the embroidered cloths became tapestries – that is, textile fabrics representing an account of an event by giving it visual form. In particular, the refugees' tapestries became visual representations of the women's "lived memory" of the experience of surviving and resisting state-repression, and mourning the loss of loved ones.[206]

202 Helen Stoilas, "Salcedo: Silent Witness," *The Art Newspaper* (1 July 2015). www.theartnewspaper.com/feature/doris-salcedo-silent-witness.

203 White Cube Gallery, "Doris Salcedo." https://whitecube.com/artists/artist/doris_salcedo.

204 On Salcedo's work see for example, Julie Rodrigues Widholm and Madeleine Grynsztejn (eds), *Doris Salcedo* (University of Chicago Press, 2015).

205 Ibid. 206 Huyssen, *Present Pasts*, 110.

Similarly, Doris Salcedo, in the process of creating a sculpture or installation, transforms domestic objects and in/organic matter.[207] Curator Carlos Basualdo described that transformation as one in which the ordinary objects and in/organic matter acquire a "troubled materiality."[208] For Basualdo, it is that "troubled materiality" that "forces" the ordinary objects and in/organic matter "to *be at once witnesses and proof* of the procedures that made them what they are."[209] In that process of transformation, as Laura García Moreno explains, "[o]bjects meant for human use in Salcedo's work have been emptied of use, deprived of all possibility of exchange, and yet they acquire the function/use of exposing workings of violence."[210] The refugee woman's handcrafting of the tapestry shares a similar sensibility with Salcedo's artistic process. The way in which Salcedo works with, and on, materials that have a close relationship with victims gives visual form to how violent conflict intimately "assaults,"[211] and forever transforms, humans, and thus life in community.

It was not only embroidering a representation of the Sumpul River Massacre that transformed the fabric, or "emptied [it] of" domestic use;[212] it was also its materiality, the fact that its physical existence was fundamentally determined and shaped by how the Salvadoran state's "workings of violence" affected the life of peasants.[213] The tapestry's own material history and the woman's lived memory of the massacre come together in, and through, the material life of the tapestry. That makes the tapestry an object that is "at once witnesses and proof" of the historical circumstances in which it was created and, importantly, of the authority that enabled them.[214]

Indeed, the UN Truth Commission's Final Report attempts to, but cannot, contain the tapestry's representation of the truths about

207 Rodrigues Widholm and Grynsztejn, *Doris Salcedo.*

208 Carlos Basualdo, "A Model of Pain," in *Doris Salcedo: Neither,* Carlos Basualdo, Rod Mengham and Doris Salcedo (Jay Jopling/White Cube, 2004), 31–32.

209 Ibid, 32. Italics mine.

210 Laura García Moreno, "'Troubled Materiality': The Installations of Doris Salcedo," *Mosaic: An Interdisciplinary Critical Journal,* vol 43, no 2 (2010), 107.

211 Doris Salcedo, "A Work in Mourning," in *Doris Salcedo,* Julie Rodrigues Widholm and Madeleine Grynsztejn (eds), (Museum of Contemporary Art Chicago, 2015), 215.

212 García Moreno, "Troubled Materiality," 107. 213 Ibid.

214 Basualdo, "A Model of Pain," 32.

massacres in the context of the civil war and the broader Cold War international context. As I showed in Section 4.2 of this chapter, unlike the tapestry, the UN Truth Commission's Final Report deploys an internationally authorized account of the unlawfulness of the civil war's violence, which is deeply shaped by a developmental rationality. Through its Final Report, the UN Truth Commission drew on the identity and status of the UN as an international institution to authorize definitive answers and normative solutions to 'fix' the 'problem' of Salvadoran post-conflict lawfulness. In the resulting 'truth,' only the rule of (international) law could prevent the Salvadoran state from remaining lawless, and thus 'develop' and 'transform' Salvadoran state-society relations into modern, lawful, peaceful, and just ones.

In contrast, the material life of the tapestry compels viewers to question the ways in which the UN Truth Commission mobilized international law and its institutions to shape post-conflict state-society relations. The tapestry, unlike the UN Truth Commission's Final Report, does not represent the violence of the massacre and the civil war as the outcome of the state's lawlessness. Rather, the tapestry shows how Salvadoran state-society relations, both at the time of the massacre/war (1980–1992) and after the signature of 1992 Chapultepec Peace Agreements, were not lawless or unlawful, but were authorized according to a particular international lawfulness. The tapestry's representation shows that in two ways. On the one hand, it shows how the lawfulness of state-society relations before and during the civil war could not be separated from the Spanish empire's colonial rationality,[215] which racialized, exploited, and marginalized Salvadoran peasants and Indigenous peoples to the benefit of a European-origin minority.[216] On the other hand, engaging with the tapestry in the present compels viewers to question the ways in which that international lawfulness, mobilized by

215 On the central role of international law in the European colonial projects see generally, Antony Anghie, *Imperialism, Sovereignty and the Making of International Law* (Cambridge University Press, 2005).

216 See generally, Jung, "Class Struggles in El Salvador"; Dalton, *Las Historias Prohibidas*; Paige, *Coffee and Power*; Lindo-Fuentes, Ching, and Lara-Martínez, *Remembering a Massacre*.

UN Truth Commission, 'resolved,' 'fixed,' or 'improved' Salvadoran post-conflict state-society relations.

While the Sumpul Massacre was organized and perpetrated against specific peasant communities, the tapestry bears witness to, and is the result of, state-society relations characterized by deeply rooted socioeconomic and political marginalization. In the years prior to the war and the 1980 Sumpul Massacre, about 70 percent of the approximately 300,000 Salvadorans living in Honduras (by 1969) were peasants who migrated in search for land to cultivate.[217] This mass migration of peasants to Honduras was the outcome of the Salvadoran state's historical focus on protecting the political, economic, and social interests of the country's elite.[218] After El Salvador was established as an independent state in 1840,[219] the inheritance of the Spanish empire's colonial administration left to Salvadoran leadership the challenge of running their own institutions, to organize state-society relations within the new state.[220]

The leadership of the new state, in order "to assert its authority," not only relied on the rural police and the National Guard, but increasingly "also had to be backed by a stronger army."[221] Furthermore, as Salvadoran historian Héctor Lindo-Fuentes puts it, from the very beginning the priority for the leadership was "to profit from the new opportunities" that "the international economy," especially agricultural exports, seemed to offer to independent states.[222] That, Lindo-Fuentes argues, led to "the emergence of a powerful oligarchy,"[223] and to disregard any "serious discussion at the highest levels of government"[224] about how "to enable the majority of the population to take advantage of the opportunities created by international trade."[225] Tired of that situation, which worsened with the 1929 Great Depression's impact on coffee

217 Jenny Pearce, *Promised Land: Peasant Rebellion in Chalatenango, El Salvador* (Latin America Bureau, 1986), 31–32; North, *Bitter Grounds*, 61.

218 On this see, Héctor Lindo-Fuentes, *Weak Foundations*; Paige, *Coffee and Power*.

219 The state's official Independence Day is 15 September 1821. However, that date marks the independence of the Central American Provinces from the Spanish Empire. It was until after the dissolution of the Federal Republic of Central America, that in 1840 El Salvador became the Republic of El Salvador.

220 Lindo-Fuentes, *Weak Foundations*, 62–63. 221 Ibid, 64. 222 Ibid, 2. 223 Ibid, 4.

224 Ibid, 1. 225 Ibid, 5.

prices (on which El Salvador's economy depended), between 1930 and 1932 peasants organized to demand better working conditions.[226]

In 1932, the inevitable happened: the Peasant Uprising of 22–23 January.[227] Groups of organized peasants launched unexpected and simultaneous attacks against "sites of local power, such as municipal offices and homes of the elite,"[228] around El Salvador's Western provinces – the region where the majority of coffee plantations were located. The Martínez regime responded to the uprising with brutal large-scale repression, known as 'La Matanza' ('The Killing') in reference to the state's assassination of nearly 30,000 peasants.[229] It was only after Martínez quashed the uprising that the US and other Global North states decided to recognize his government as a legitimate one.[230]

With the fundamental support of the elite, a succession of military juntas kept governing El Salvador until the 1984 elections.[231] During those forty years, the elite continued to fiercely oppose (with the support of an influential section of the military) any attempts by the military-controlled governments to undertake meaningful "agrarian reform," to "control the financial sector," or to regulate the "benefits of export trade."[232] State-repression continued against forms of social organizing, and any attempt to advocate for better socioeconomic conditions, particularly in the countryside.

In 1966, Junta president Colonel Rivera[233] created the state-armed group Organización Democrática Nacionalista (Democratic Nationalist

226 Everett Alan Wilson, *La Crisis de la Integración Nacional en El Salvador, 1919–1935* (Consejo Nacional para la Cultura y el Arte, CONCULTURA, 2004), 26; Paige, *Coffee and Power*, 99–102; 187–188; Erik Ching, *Authoritarian El Salvador: Politics and the Origins of the Military Regimes, 1880–1940* (University of Notre Dame Press, 2014), 248–249.

227 See generally, Lindo-Fuentes, Ching, and Lara-Martínez, *Remembering a Massacre*. See also, Pearce, *Promised Land*, 82–83.

228 Lindo-Fuentes, Ching, and Lara-Martínez, *Remembering a Massacre*, 1.

229 Ibid, 2; 28–43.

230 Wilson, *La Crisis de la Integración*, 224–225.

231 Paige, *Coffee and Power*, 189; 210–211; Raymond Bonner, *Weakness and Deceit: US Policy and El Salvador* (Hamish Hamilton, 1985), 24–27. There were elections in 1964, but they were controlled by the military. On this see, North, *Bitter Grounds*, 43.

232 Enrique Baloyra, *El Salvador in Transition* (The University of North Carolina Press, 1982), 2.

233 Before 1961 the name of his party was Partido Revolucionario de Unificación Democrática. See in, Dunkerley, *Power in the Isthmus*, 121.

Organization), known as ORDEN.[234] ORDEN, which in Spanish means 'order,' was originally created as "an information-gathering network,"[235] which aimed "to counteract the efforts of the popular organizations, and especially of the peasant organizations."[236] But, by the 1970s, ORDEN was part of the Salvadoran state's security institutions, which included the National Guard (created in 1912 to control peasants and protect plantations and its owners), the National Police, and the Salvadoran National Security Agency (the intelligence agency).[237] Importantly, the United States through its intelligence agency, military and international aid program, played a crucial role in the consolidation of ORDEN.[238]

In parallel, the vulnerable position of peasant families and small farm-owners in El Salvador remained unchanged. Landless peasant families and small farm-owners were at the mercy of the rapidly changing demands of the international export market. As a response, the 1970s saw the formation of five guerrilla organizations, which by October 1980 were grouped as the FMLN.[239] During this decade numerous social groups and labor unions began to organize, and to successfully challenge the social, economic, political, and legal forms that conditioned life within the Salvadoran state.[240]

In January 1980, months before the outbreak of the civil war, social organizations, labor unions, professional associations and universities mobilized in San Salvador and called for peaceful demonstrations to demand the Salvadoran state dismantle ORDEN, to limit the intervention of the United States in Salvadoran affairs, to control the economic and political power of the elite, and to offer meaningful democratic

234 Baloyra, *El Salvador in Transition*, 64. 235 Pearce, *Promised Land*, 90.

236 Baloyra, *El Salvador in Transition*, 64.

237 Pearce, *Promised Land*, 88–91.

238 Ibid.

239 FPL (Fuerzas Populares de Liberación), ERP (Ejército Revolucionario del Pueblo), RN (Resistencia Nacional), PRTC (Partido Revolucionario de los Trabajadores Centroamericanos), and PCS (Partido Comunista Salvadoreño). See generally, Martínez Peñate, *El Salvador: Del Conflicto*, 62–63; Dunkerley, *The Long War*, 87–102.

240 On this see generally, Jeffrey L. Gould, *Solidarity Under Siege: The Salvadoran Labor Movement, 1970–1990* (Cambridge University Press, 2019); Ching, *Stories of Civil War in El Salvador*, Lindo-Fuentes, *Weak Foundations*.

participation for all Salvadorans.[241] In response, the government sent the Salvadoran Armed Forces to repress the demonstration, which resulted in the death of about 300 people.[242] At the same time, in the countryside state-repression against organized peasants intensified, and was inflicted not only by the Salvadoran Armed Forces, especially the paramilitary ORDEN and its affiliated (clandestine) death squads, but also by privately owned death squads of certain elite families.[243] The latter was the crucial information that Cassel revealed in 2018 was missing from the Truth Commission's account.[244]

Among the ordinary Salvadorans at the receiving end of state violence were peasant and Indigenous communities. The UN Truth Commission's Final Report records three selected cases in which the Salvadoran Armed Forces repressed and massacred peasant communities during the war.[245] Specifically, the Final Report frames the El Mozote, Sumpul River and El Calabozo massacres as "serious violation[s] of international humanitarian law and international human rights law."[246] However, those communities have a long history of resistance to the exploitation of the Salvadoran state and its elites.[247] That is what the tapestry shows us. It displays a powerful account that bears witness to the Sumpul Massacre, and to Salvadoran peasants' history of resistance to state and elite repression and exploitation. Yet, being before the tapestry brings the woman's lived memory of the massacre/repression to the present, a lived memory which, by being made visible, refuses to be 'of the past.' The tapestry's truth allows us to have an understanding of the violence suffered by peasants communities before and during the war. In doing so, the tapestry disrupts the UN Truth Commission's truth. The tapestry compels its contemporary viewers to ask whose truth was authorized in the UN Truth Commission's Final Report?

241 Martínez Peñate, *El Salvador: Del Conflicto*, 19–21; 64. 242 Ibid, 64.

243 Elizabeth Jean Wood, *Insurgent Collective Action and Civil War in El Salvador* (Cambridge University Press, 2003), 87–88.

244 See note 19 above.

245 UN Doc S/25500 (1 April 1993), *From Madness to Hope*, 114–126.

246 Ibid, 121; 124; 126.

247 See generally, Wood, *Insurgent Collective Action and Civil War in El Salvador*; Gould, *Solidarity Under Siege*; Héctor Lindo-Fuentes, *El Alborotador de Centroamérica: El Salvador frente al Imperio* (UCA Editores; El Colegio de Michoacán, AC, 2019).

4.4 THE UN'S "NEGOTIATED REVOLUTION" FOR EL SALVADOR

To fully understand the legacies of the UN Truth Commission's account for the Salvadoran post-conflict state, we also need to analyze the Truth Commission in light of the authority that established it: the Chapultepec Peace Agreements. Although the Chapultepec Agreements deserves greater attention and analysis, for the purposes of this chapter I focus on the pivotal role of the UN in the peace process and how it authorized the resulting Salvadoran post-conflict state. In turn, the Salvadoran post-conflict state was shaped to fit an emerging international order, which became more aligned with the interests of the West, primarily the United States. In what follows, I discuss how the Peace Agreements privileged legal and political reforms at the expense of addressing El Salvador's historical socioeconomic inequality. I also show how the UN Truth Commission's Final Report, in placing responsibility only on Salvadorans for the post-conflict state, was "conceal-[ing] the world-making – via state-making – work of international law and institutions."[248] As I show here, through the Final Report's internationally authorized truth, the commissioners downplayed the jurisdictional force of the UN's post-conflict peacebuilding vision (later, 'model') which was being advanced by the Chapultepec Agreements at the end of the Cold War.

4.4.1 THE UN IN EL SALVADOR. By 1989, with the end of the Cold War on the horizon, the prospects for political and military success that the FMLN had envisioned throughout the 1980s were not good. Throughout the war, the FMLN's international financial and military support mostly depended on Nicaragua's Sandinistas and the USSR. But things were changing. In the United States, the Bush Administration was supportive of a UN peacemaking role in El Salvador to bring an end to the war. The United States' position opened a space for the UN Observer Group in Central America (ONUCA), which was working with the Nicaraguan Sandinistas and the Contras, in collaboration with the Organization of the American States (OAS), toward democratic elections.[249] For the

[248] Luis Eslava and Sundhya Pahuja, "The State and International Law: A Reading from the Global South," *Humanity*, vol 11, no 1 (2020), 118.

[249] Javier Pérez de Cuéllar, *Pilgrimage for Peace: A Secretary-General's Memoirs* (Palgrave Macmillan,1997), 406.

FMLN, the immediate consequence was that the Sandinistas, which provided the FMLN with arms and political support, were now more constrained in their ability to provide assistance. At the same time, the USSR's geopolitical influence continued to recede. For its part, the Salvadoran government interpreted those changes as the beginning of the end for the FMLN. Aware of that, in May 1989 the FMLN proposed to the Salvadoran government to commence peace talks.[250]

The Salvadoran government, now under the presidency of Alfredo Cristiani, seemed more open to engage in peace talks. Cristiani's presidency had also renewed the image of his party, Alianza Republicana Nacionalista (ARENA for its acronym in Spanish). The right-wing political party was founded by the death squads' mastermind, Roberto D'Aubuisson, who was trained at the United States' counter-communist military program, the School of the Americas.[251] The bond between ARENA and D'Aubuisson compromised the United States' image. It was not a coincidence that the *New York Times* described ARENA under Cristiani's leadership as "a symbol of a two-year effort to transform" it "into a real political party acceptable to Washington and American taxpayers."[252] Thanks to Cristiani's credentials – wealthy, United States-educated at Georgetown University, and openly in favor of economic privatization – the United States interests were secured.[253] In supporting the UN and Cristiani's ARENA, the United States portrayed its renewed image of post-Cold War foreign policy toward El Salvador: a powerful, peaceful ally. When in 1989 the FMLN officially proposed peace talks, the Salvadoran government had the 'blessing' of the United States. That meant one problem less on the negotiation table – and one problem less for the UN.

The official negotiation process began in 1990 in Geneva, where the UN and the parties to the process (the 'Parties') – the Salvadoran government and FMLN – met "to agree on the format, mechanism and

250 UN Doc ST/DPI Oral History (02)/M385 (23 June 1998), *Interview with Ana Guadalupe Martínez by Jean Krasno, trans by Michael Lanchin*, 14–15.

251 Lesley Gill, *The School of the Americas: Military Training and Political Violence in the Americas* (2004), 84.

252 Lindsey Gruson, "The New Face of the Right: Alfredo Cristiani," *New York Times* (21 March 1989).

253 Ibid.

pace of a process aimed at bringing about as speedily as possible … a definitive end to the armed conflict in that country."[254] The Parties agreed to four negotiation objectives: (1) "to end the armed conflict by political means"; (2) "promote the democratization of the country"; (3) "guarantee unrestricted respect for human rights"; and (4) "reunify Salvador[a]n society."[255] An important outcome of the Geneva Agreement was to give the UN a more prominent and ongoing role. Until that point, the UN had been involved as an observer, at the request of the FMLN. The FMLN mistrusted the politics of the OAS, the premier regional organization,[256] and so, in 1989, the FMLN requested the UN to act as observer in possible peace talks with a reluctant Salvadoran government.[257] Ultimately, the Parties accepted the UN's role as mediator. This was not only a consequence of the Cold War shifting toward the United States, and decreasing support from East and West for both Parties. It was also because the UN was in a stronger international position to facilitate a negotiated solution. In Geneva, the Parties agreed that the process would "be conducted under the auspices of the Secretary-General, on a continuous and uninterrupted basis"; and "to ensure the success of the negotiating process," they agreed to "the active participation of the Secretary-General or his Representative, and an intermediary role." The Parties also accepted the UN's authority to decide what "public information on its progress shall be" shared.[258]

While the peace process was facilitated and largely funded by the UN, several countries were also essential for the success of the process. Canada, Costa Rica, Mexico, Sweden and Venezuela provided expert advice as well as financial and logistical assistance to host pre-negotiation meetings, brainstorming sessions, or formal negotiation rounds. Colombia, Mexico, Spain and Venezuela became known as the 'Friends of the Secretary-General,' a group created at the request of Pérez de Cuéllar to formalize those countries' support for the peace

[254] UN Doc A/46/551 – S/23128 (9 October 1991), *Geneva Agreement*, 2. [255] Ibid, 2.

[256] Óscar Martínez Peñate, *El Salvador: Las Negociaciones de los Acuerdos de Paz* (Editorial Nuevo Enfoque, 2011), 105.

[257] UN Doc ST/DPI Oral History (02)/M385, 22.

[258] UN Doc A/46/551 – S/23128 (9 October 1991), *Geneva Agreement*, 3.

process.[259] The aim of the 'Friends of the Secretary-General' was to provide diplomatic assistance on behalf of the Secretary-General to facilitate constructive diplomatic solutions to move the process forward.[260]

Of the countries directly involved in the peace process, Mexico was uniquely positioned to help both Parties work toward an agreement. Mexico was geographically close and had important trade and financial agreements with El Salvador.[261] From the FMLN's perspective, Mexico was a strategic and safe location to engage with the Salvadoran government. Mexico had not only been historically an anti-imperialist ally for the Global South,[262] but had also been welcoming to left-wing Salvadoran exiles and a base for the FMLN's 'Political and Diplomatic Commission.'[263] Importantly for the Salvadoran government, the socioeconomic politics of the Mexican leadership at that time could be trusted. Mexico's president was Carlos Salinas de Gortari, whose politics were very much in line with Cristiani and his government. Both governments were right-wing oriented and firm promoters of privatization of public services and limited governance. It is unsurprisingly, then, that Mexico hosted some of the peace process's most important meetings: the first pre-peace talks in 1989; eleven negotiation meetings between 1990 and 1991; and the signing of the Peace Agreements at Mexico's historically significant Chapultepec Castle, in 1992.[264] As the name of each agreement suggests,[265] the negotiations also took place in Costa Rica, Switzerland, the US, and Venezuela.

In what follows I discuss how international human rights came to be prioritized in the peace negotiations agenda over the country's socioeconomic challenges, and the consequences of the decision.

4.4.1.1 Defining an Agenda: Human Rights, First

A few months after the Geneva pre-talks, the Parties met in Venezuela's capital city Caracas, where they set an official agenda and timetable to

259 Martínez Peñate, *El Salvador: Las Negociaciones*, 97–103. 260 Ibid.
261 Ibid., 96–97.
262 See generally, Christy Thornton, *Revolution in Development: Mexico and the Governance of the Global Economy* (University of California Press, 2021).
263 Martínez Peñate, *El Salvador: Las Negociaciones*, 96.
264 Martínez Peñate, *El Salvador: Del Conflicto*, 201–204. 265 See note 3 above.

guide the negotiations.[266] The 1990 Caracas Agenda is important to understand Salvadorans' dissatisfaction toward the legacies of the Peace Agreements. The Parties' and the UN's treatment of the country's socioeconomic inequalities (a main root cause of the war) as a minor issue began in Caracas.[267] For instance, it is especially revealing that the Caracas Agenda prioritized human rights,[268] while the "economic and social issues" were at the bottom of the agreed negotiation items (something I discuss further in the following section).[269] As Salvadoran historian Martínez Peñate points out, after waging a war in the name of socioeconomic justice, the FMLN did not press hard to prioritize socioeconomic issues, and focused instead on ending the armed conflict and achieving political reforms.[270] This directly favored the Salvadoran government's interests. Led by Cristiani, who was himself a businessman and member of one of the country's most prominent land-owning families,[271] the main goal of the government's Economic and Social Development Plan was to strengthen the country's market economy, "reduc[e] the role of the State," and privatize public services.[272] While the Caracas Agenda clarified that "the sequence of the items . . . does not imply a strict order of consideration and may be changed by mutual consent,"[273] the order of the items coincided with UN interests.

Although 'human rights' was the second item in the Caracas Agenda, they were a UN priority. Accordingly, in July 1990, two months after meeting in Caracas, Sweden funded and hosted a secret human rights meeting, in which the UN and human rights experts discussed the establishment of human rights standards for the Salvadoran peace process.[274] This meeting had two major outcomes: first, to give the UN

266 UN Doc A/46/552 – S/23129 (9 October 1991), *Caracas Agenda.*

267 Martínez Peñate, *El Salvador: Las Negociaciones*, 153.

268 UN Doc A/46/552 – S/23129 (9 October 1991), *Caracas Agenda*, 2.

269 Ibid.

270 Martínez Peñate, *El Salvador: Las Negociaciones*, 153.

271 Paige, *Coffee and Power*, 23.

272 See generally, Gobierno de El Salvador, Ministerio de Planificación y Coordinación del Desarrollo Económico y Social, "Plan de Desarrollo Económico y Social 1989–1994" (1989).

273 UN Doc A/46/552 – S/23129 (9 October 1991), *Caracas Agenda*, 3.

274 Agneta Gunnarsson et al., "Cooperación Sueca en El Salvador: Una Relación un Poco más Allá" (Departamento Regional para América Latina de ASDI, 2004), 88.

the role of monitoring the Parties' human rights compliance, which later took the form of an innovative peacekeeping mission (ONUSAL); and second, to establish a Truth Commission. Ten days later, the first agreement that the Parties signed was the Agreement on Human Rights.[275] Joaquín Villalobos, a highly influential FMLN leader and signatory of the Chapultepec Agreements, was initially opposed to the agreement.[276] Villalobos believed that with the agreement "the FMLN was losing its revolutionary character," because, by leveling each Parties' violence around human rights, the agreement gave the impression that "the military was winning" too.[277] This was no minor objection, given that the formation of the FMLN, and the outbreak of the war, was in response to the historical violence of the Salvadoran Armed Forces against civilians and peasants who demanded better living and working conditions. Villalobos later changed his mind when fellow FMLN members and negotiators stressed that the UN, through its peacekeeping mission, would at least ensure that the Salvadoran army complied with the ceasefire and agreements reached at each negotiation round.[278]

4.4.1.2 Salvadoran Institutions

After the Human Rights Agreement, the negotiations followed the order established in the 1990 Caracas Agenda. Between July 1990 and April 1991, the negotiations continued in Costa Rica and Mexico. They resulted in the most substantive agreement, the Mexico Agreement.[279] In this document the Parties agreed to amend the Constitution, and to implement reforms that included overhauling the armed forces, the judicial system, the electoral system, and ensuring protection of human rights and establishing a UN Truth Commission.[280]

275 UN Doc A/44/971 – S/21541 (16 August 1991) *Agreement on Human Rights/San José Agreement.*

276 Martínez Peñate, *El Salvador: Las Negociaciones,*161–162.

277 ("los militares ganaban con ese acuerdo y el FMLN perdía su carácter revolucionario"). Ibid. El Mundo, "¿Qué recomendó Geovanni Galeas a los Diputados en la Ley de Justicia Transicional?", *El Mundo* (27 September 2021). https://diario.elmundo.sv/Política/que-recomendo-geovanni-galeas-a-los-diputados-en-la-ley-de-justicia-transicional.

278 Martínez Peñate, *El Salvador: Las Negociaciones,* 162–163.

279 UN Doc A/46/553 – S/23130 (9 October 1991), *Mexico Agreements.*

280 Ibid.

Achieving agreement on those reforms was no easy task. President Cristiani was caught between his ideological position, the business interests of his and other elite families, and the interests of the military. That became a major issue between Cristiani and the Secretary-General.[281] In a letter addressed to Cristiani, Pérez de Cuéllar said: "[y]ou are certainly the one who fixes the position of your Negotiating Commission, and you know to what extent you are prepared to make concessions."[282] Cristiani replied by warning that "any attitude of the intermediary [the UN] which could be interpreted as an inclination in favor of one of the parties, particularly if it was transferred to the [G]roup of [F]riends of the Secretary-General, would be an obstacle to progress toward the peace agreements we desire."[283] Cristiani was not concerned with international interference and protecting El Salvador's national interests. His concern was to not upset the country's business elite and the military. The pressure was enormous, to the point that the United States, now eager to showcase its renewed neighbor-friendly foreign policy, sent to El Salvador the highest-ranking officer in the United States Army, Collin Powell, and the Assistant Secretary of State, Bernard Aronson.[284] This was an effort to strengthen Cristiani's leadership which was also threaten by the risk of a military coup. Powell's task was "to speak to the military leaders of El Salvador, and suggest to them that now that the conflict was over they needed to move on so that democracy can get imbedded in the country."[285] That, and in particular a proposed constitutional reform, also generated public debate, and led to mass protests either supporting a more ambitious constitutional reform or a limited one.[286] According to some Salvadoran commentators, Cristiani finally changed his position when the country's business association (traditionally close with

[281] See letters between the Secretary-General and Cristiani in, UN Doc [ST]/DPI/1475 (1995), *The United Nations*, 133–141.

[282] Ibid, 134. [283] Ibid.

[284] Ricardo Ribera, "El Salvador: La Negociación del Acuerdo de Paz: ¿Un Modelo para el Mundo?", *Realidad: Revista de Ciencias Sociales y Humanidades* (1994), no 37, 107.

[285] The White House – President George W. Bush, "Press Briefing by Secretary of State Colin Powell and Press Secretary Ari Fleischer Aboard Air Force One" (24 March 2002). https://georgewbush-whitehouse.archives.gov/news/releases/2002/03/20020324.html.

[286] Ribera, "El Salvador," 107–108.

Cristiani's right-ring party, ARENA) publicly supported the constitutional reforms necessary for the success of the peace process.[287] Eliseo Ortíz, a prominent Salvadoran judge and constitutional law professor, argued that "the reform was "ad-hoc," done under the tutelage of the United Nations" and "with the explicit aim of giving visibility and formalizing the agreements."[288] Justice Ortíz also argued that, while "the reform ... was relatively deep because it democratized the rules of the game,"[289] it "did not affect the socio-economic model ... there was no substantive constitutional commitment that demanded a constitutional reform" to address the country's protracted socioeconomic problems.[290]

As I discuss in the following section, the remaining negotiation items set in the Caracas Agenda, including the country's socioeconomic issues, were addressed in two final short negotiation rounds in New York.

4.4.2 ADDRESSING THE CIVIL WAR'S SOCIOECONOMIC QUESTIONS

In a 2016 article, Álvaro de Soto (the Secretary-General's Special Representative and lead mediator in the peace process) and Graciana del Castillo (Boutros-Ghali's economic adviser, 1991–1995) argued that they were unaware that there was an agreement on "peace-related expenditure" between the Salvadoran government and the IMF.[291] What is relevant here is that, despite de Soto and del Castillo's high-level of involvement and responsibility in the peace negotiations and its aftermath, they placed exclusive responsibility on the Salvadoran state for the unsuccessful implementation of the peace agreements. De Soto and del Castillo stated that "neither" they nor "the UN nor the FMLN

[287] Ibid, 108–109; El Mundo, "¿Qué recomendó Geovanni Galeas ...?".

[288] ("puede decirse que se trató de una reforma 'ad-hoc,' tutelada por las Naciones Unidas, es decir, con el propósito expreso de viabilizar y formalizar los acuerdos de la negociación"). Francisco E. Ortíz Ruíz, "El Salvador 1991–1992: Acuerdo de Paz y Reforma Constitucional," *Perspectivas* (2017) no 4, 6.

[289] ("la reforma ... fue relativamente profunda, pues democratize las reglas de juego"). Ibid.

[290] ("no afectó el modelo económico ... no hubo algún compromiso sustancial al respecto que exigiera a una reforma constitucional"). Ibid.

[291] Álvaro de Soto and Graciana del Castillo, "Obstacles to Peacebuilding Revisited," *Global Governance* (2016) vol 22, no 2, 210.

knew" about the IMF agreement, which "effectively prevented the government from complying with the financial requirements of the peace accord."[292] Putting aside the intricacies of why, in the UN's view, the IMF-El Salvador agreement came as a surprise, the Chapultepec Agreements is enlightening on this issue.

According to Salvadoran historian Martínez Peñate, treating the socioeconomic inequalities as minor issues began early on in the peace negotiations.[293] It was not until the final stretch of the negotiations in New York (late 1991 and early 1992) that the Parties addressed the remaining issues.[294] The last item on the New York agenda was titled "economic and social questions."[295] This item was not only narrowly approached as a problem of land ownership, but it was also addressed briefly in comparison to the other items.[296] Tellingly, the in-depth negotiations of the "economic and social questions" was deferred to the "compressed negotiations," which took place just days before the Chapultepec Agreements signing ceremony.[297] That light and quick treatment manifests in the Chapultepec Agreements' Chapter V, titled "Economic and Social Questions."[298] Chapter V denotes the way in which the UN and the parties understood the socioeconomic roots of the civil war's outbreak.

In Chapter V, the Chapultepec Agreements sought to address the socioeconomic "causes of the war."[299] However, they were framed and addressed as problems of development and private property. This can be seen, to begin with, in Chapter V's "Preamble," which affirms that:

> One of the prerequisites for the democratic reunification of Salvador[a]n society is the sustained economic and social *development* of the country. At the same time, reunification of Salvador[a]n society and a growing degree of social cohesion are indispensable for fostering *development*. Hence, the

[292] Ibid. [293] Martínez Peñate, *El Salvador: Las Negociaciones*, 153.

[294] UN Doc A/46/863 – S/23504 (30 January 1992), *New York Act I and New York Act II.*

[295] UN Doc A/46/502 – S/23082 (7 October 1991), *Compressed Negotiations*, 6–7.

[296] Ibid.

[297] UN Doc A/46/863 – S/23504 (30 January 1992), *New York Act I and New York Act II.*

[298] UN Doc A/46/664 – S/23501 (30 January 1992), *Chapultepec Peace Agreement*, 31–38.

[299] Ibid.

set of agreements ... must include certain minimum commitments to *promote development* for the benefit of all sectors of the population.[300]

To achieve post-conflict "sustained economic and social development," Chapter V establishes the necessity of different types of "international cooperation," including "seeking external financial resources."[301] This can be seen in Chapter V's subsection six: "Measures to Alleviate the Social Cost of Structural Adjustment Programmes."[302] This subsection establishes three measures: "Consumer Protection," "Privatization," and "Social Welfare Programmes."[303] The agreements state that "Consumer Protection" and "Privatization" will be implemented by national legislation and the creation of public institutions.[304]

In contrast, the Chapultepec Agreements did not commit to create laws or public institutions to protect "Social Welfare Programmes," but favored procurement of "[a]dditional external resources."[305] The following subsection, titled "Procedures for Direct External Cooperation for Community Development and Assistance Projects," went further in encouraging agreements with international development/financial institutions.[306] Here the agreements explicitly state that "[t]he government of El Salvador shall facilitate private direct external cooperation ... provided that assistance is channeled in accordance with foreign exchange and lending regulations."[307] Following the same rationality to protect consumers and private property, this subsection also establishes that the government has to "grant legal and institutional facilities" to external cooperation as long as they are supporting "integrated development projects."[308]

Given the UN's highly influential role before and during the peace process, it is telling that its experts only placed responsibility on the Salvadoran state for the problems fulfilling the agreements. First, this shows how the UN's intervention in El Salvador was informed by a rationality like the one in its 1960 Congo intervention, which, as Guy Fiti Sinclair reminds us, "proved" to be "a powerful and persistent justification for further interventions ... in the decolonized world," and since

[300] Ibid., 31. Italics mine. [301] Ibid., 35. [302] Ibid., 35–36. [303] Ibid. [304] Ibid.
[305] Ibid., 36. [306] Ibid. [307] Ibid. [308] Ibid.

the 1990s in post-conflict states too.[309] Second, the UN's approach also reveals an incipient "new developmental" rationality, as Eslava and Pahuja call it,[310] informing the UN's emerging peacebuilding vision for the Salvadoran post-conflict state. In that new developmental rationality, the post-conflict state must "move away from state-based development," espousing "a constrained view of the state and strong support for market-based solutions,"[311] which required "governmental reforms and constitutional amendments" while "trade liberalization, privatization, and strong support for private property were enshrined alongside national commitments to protect human rights and foster democracy."[312] Third, we can see that when in 1995, three years after the signature of the Chapultepec Agreements, de Soto and del Castillo argued that the Chapultepec Agreements' institutions were reforms which could be understood as part of a "negotiated revolution."[313] De Soto and del Castillo borrowed this expression from T. L. Karl, who in 1989 was the chair of the pre-peace talks, and in the 1990s became adviser to de Soto's UN negotiating team. Karl's view of the "negotiated revolution" can be found in her 1992 *Foreign Affairs* article, "El Salvador's Negotiated Revolution."[314] There, Karl gives an account of what the Salvadoran peace process achieved and how it should continue. Specifically, Karl acknowledges that after signing the agreement, "[w]hat matter[ed]" was "the process of compromise."[315] For Karl, the Chapultepec Agreements was a "genuine compromise" in which "the left [FMLN] renounce[ed] its aspiration to seize the state by force and impose radical economic reforms," and "the right [Salvadoran government and elite] relinquish-[ed] its historical control and violent opposition to change."[316] In

[309] Sinclair, *To Reform the World*, 190; Vasuki Nesiah, "Theories of Transitional Justice: Cashing in the Blue Chips," in *The Oxford Handbook of The Theory of International Law*, Anne Orford and Florian Hoffmann (eds) (Oxford University Press, 2016) 779.

[310] Luis Eslava and Sundhya Pahuja, "The State and International Law: A Reading from the Global South," *Humanity*, vol 11, no 1 (2020), 118.

[311] Ibid., 128; 123. [312] Ibid., 126.

[313] de Soto and del Castillo, "Implementation of Comprehensive Peace Agreements," 189.

[314] Terry Lynn Karl, "El Salvador's Negotiated Revolution," *Foreign Affairs*, vol 71, no 2 (1992).

[315] Ibid., 148. [316] Ibid.

adopting Karl's view ("negotiated revolution"), de Soto and del Castillo advanced the position that "genuine compromise" would positively shape Salvadoran post-conflict state-society relations,[317] and those of many other states later.[318]

4.4.3 THE UN TRUTH COMMISSION'S COMPROMISE FOR EL SALVADOR

As I have shown throughout this chapter, the UN and its post-conflict state-building institutions were crucial in realizing a "compromise" to bring about rule of law, peace, and democracy.[319] They did so through a set of peace agreements and post-conflict institutions geared toward 'rebuilding' and 'developing' El Salvador into a peaceful and lawful post-conflict state. One of those institutions, as I have shown, was the UN Truth Commission. The Final Report's Introduction and Epilogue show how, through the UN Truth Commission's truth about the civil war, the UN was deploying a particular, normative international lawfulness in El Salvador.

Indeed, there is striking resemblance in the way the UN Truth Commission's Final Report replicates the views of de Soto, del Castillo and Karl about the need to "compromise" for the sake of post-conflict international lawfulness. That can be seen in, for example, how the Final Report portrays the creation of the UN Truth Commission as an outcome of that compromise. The Final Report states: "On the long road of the peace negotiations, the need to reach agreement on a Commission on the Truth arose from the Parties' recognition that the communism which had encouraged one side had collapsed, and perhaps also from the disillusionment of the Power which had encouraged the other."[320]

The Final Report portrays the UN Truth Commission as resulting from a 'new' post-Cold War international order, in which all states are 'free' from the geopolitical tensions between East and West. Yet there are two very important details that the Report's paragraph obscures about

[317] Ibid.

[318] See as examples the special UN publications documenting its contributions to international peace and security. Access them with search term "United Nations Blue Book Series." https://digitallibrary.un.org.

[319] Ibid. [320] UN Doc S/25500 (1 April 1993), *From Madness to Hope*, 10.

the role of the UN Truth Commission in authorizing the lawfulness organizing state-society relations in the aftermath of the civil war.

The first one is that, as I have shown, the post-conflict (developmental) state model that was institutionalized after the UN's intervention in El Salvador re-asserted the authority of international organizations and Global North states over Global South states. And second, the initiative to create the UN-Truth Commission did not come from the Salvadoran parties, but from Álvaro de Soto.[321] In an interview with researcher Diana Villiers-Negroponte, de Soto confirmed that he sketched out the UN-Truth Commission. He said that that happened in July 1990 during the secret human rights meeting in Switzerland (funded by Sweden), just days before the peace process officially began.[322]

The fact that it was de Soto who conceived idea of the UN-Truth Commission as part of the UN's human rights agenda for El Salvador says more about how the peace negotiations unfolded than how the Final Report describes them. For example, the commissioners openly praised Alfredo Cristiani, the then Salvadoran president. In the Final Report, Cristiani is called "the peace president" "who on many counts deserves widespread recognition as the driving force behind the peace agreements."[323] But historian Martínez Peñate records something that is *vox populi* in El Salvador: on the day of the peace agreements' signing ceremony in Mexico, the presidents of Mexico and Spain nearly had to force Cristiani to sign.[324] At present, thanks to the legal and political efforts of Salvadoran groups, there are strong indications that Cristiani was aware of the collaborations between the armed forces and the death squads, and that they were under his authority (and knowledge) when certain massacres were perpetrated.[325] In November 2024, their efforts resulted in

321 Villiers-Negroponte, *Seeking Peace*, 45 at note 91; 185 at note 138; Gunnarsson et al., "Cooperación Sueca en El Salvador," 88; Martínez Peñate, *El Salvador: Las Negociaciones*, 160–161.

322 Villiers-Negroponte, *Seeking Peace*, 45 at note 91; 185 at note 138.

323 UN Doc S/25500 (1 April 1993), *From Madness to Hope*, 17; 14.

324 Martínez Peñate, *El Salvador: Las Negociaciones*, 230–232; 226–227.

325 Marcos Alemán, "Detención para Expresidente Cristiani por Muerte de Jesuitas," *Los Angeles Times* (11 March 2022). www.latimes.com/espanol/internacional/articulo/2022-03-11/detencion-para-expresidente-cristiani-por-muerte-de-jesuitas; Christian Guevara, "Entrevista con José María Tojeira: 'Cristiani Encubrió a los Hechores del

Cristiani and other high-ranking military officers being charged for their involvement (in different ways) in the murder in November 1989 of the six Spanish Jesuit priests before a Salvadoran court.[326]

The FMLN did, initially, take seriously the UN Truth Commission's investigation. Unlike Cristiani's government, representatives of the FMLN were present when the UN released the Final Report's findings in New York.[327] In a 1997 interview for the "Yale-UN Oral History Project: Central American Peace Process," Ana Guadalupe Martínez, a member of the FMLN negotiation team, said that the UN Truth Commission could have had "a fundamental role in the process of reconciliation" and "democratization."[328] She then added that, instead, the UN Truth Commission only focused on "confirming facts and events of which there was already a lot of information recorded," and that the commissioners "were unwilling to investigate" how civilians were involved in supporting the death squads.[329] As a result, Martínez argues, members of the Salvadoran elite involved in financing and supporting the violence against ordinary Salvadorans "emerged clean" from the UN Truth Commission's investigation.[330] Indeed, the way in which the Final Report represents the civil war's unlawfulness obscures very important details about the post-conflict Salvadoran state.

The visible outcomes in El Salvador – a peace agreement, institutional reforms, democratic elections, human rights institutions, a Truth

Crimen'," *El Faro* (Undated). http://archivo.elfaro.net/dlgalp/ofensivafinal/jmt.html; Contra Punto, "IDHUCA Denuncia Crímenes Cometidos durante la Guerra," *Contra Punto* (17 October 2016). www.contrapunto.com.sv/idhuca-denuncia-crimenes-cometidos-durante-la-guerra/.

326 The Guardian Staff and Agencies in San Salvador, "El Salvador Ex-president among 11 to Face Trial for 1989 Murder of Jesuits," *The Guardian* (20 November 2024). www.theguardian.com/world/2024/nov/19/alfredo-cristiani-el-salvador-trial.

327 UN Doc [ST/DPI/PRESS/]SG/SM/4942 [ST/DPI/PRESS/]CA/76 (15 March 1993), *Secretary-General calls Report of Commission on Truth "watershed" in Process of Recovery, Indeed Rebirth which Salvadoran Society must Undergo: Remarks, 15 Mar. 1993, at a Ceremony for the Presentation of the Report of the Commission on the Truth concerning El Salvador.*

328 ("tenía un papel fundamental en el proceso de reconciliación y democratizador"). UN Doc ST/DPI Oral History (02)/M385 (23 June 1998), *Interview with Ana Guadalupe*, 24.

329 ("confirmar hechos y eventos que ya tenían bastante información recogida"); ("no la quiso investigar"). Ibid, 23.

330 ("salieron limpios"). Ibid, 24.

Commission – powerfully demonstrated the UN's capacity to successfully engage the institutions of the international order, to transform a country into a peaceful, rule of law-abiding, democratic post-conflict state. In particular, the Final Report's title, Introduction, and Epilogue show once more how the UN Truth Commission's internationally authorized truth about the civil war contributed to make El Salvador a post-conflict state model. Indeed, to an extent the UN's experience in El Salvador inspired the organization's ambitious new approach to international peace and security.[331] This was encapsulated in Secretary-General Boutros-Ghali's 1992 *An Agenda for Peace*,[332] which sought to respond to UN member-states' "conviction ... that an opportunity ha[d] been regained to achieve the great objectives of the Charter."[333] In turn, this invites the question: whose truth, and for whose post-conflict state was, and is, El Salvador for?

4.5 CONCLUSION

In this chapter, I examined El Salvador's UN-run 1992–1993 Truth Commission and the role of international law and its institutions. The analysis shows how the UN Truth Commission drew on the identity and status of the UN as an international institution to authorize its account of the unlawfulness of the violence of the civil war as the 'truth.' In doing so, the UN Truth Commission's account displaced 'other' coexisting truths that rivaled international law's authorized understanding of the civil war's violence. The consequence is that, in excluding local truths about the socioeconomic circumstances that led to, and sustained, the civil war, the UN Truth Commission contributed to making El Salvador a model of a 'post-conflict state.' The redescription that I have offered in this chapter shows how the Final Report represents the civil war as an unlawful event according to international law. My close reading of three key sections of the Final Report – the title, Introduction, and Epilogue – reveals the 'developmental' sensitivities and rationalities underpinning

[331] Wallensteen, *Quality Peace*, 11–13.

[332] UN Doc A/47/277–S/24111 (17 June 1992), *An Agenda for Peace*.

[333] Ibid, 2.

the UN Truth Commission's authorized truth. These 'developmental' sensitivities and rationalities were informed by the convergence of two orientations. One was a Eurocentric/Anglo-American but mostly United States-centric triumphalist Cold War position. The second was the UN's developmental rationality toward Global South states. The consequence was that the UN Truth Commission authorized an account that fitted the UN's peacebuilding vision for Global South post-conflict states after the Cold War. I then showed how the Salvadoran peasant woman represents the Sumpul Massacre in relation to the civil war. My analysis shows how the tapestry's truth, seen against the UN Truth Commission's truth, unsettles that internationally authorized account. In doing so, the tapestry compels its contemporary viewers to ask whose truth was authorized in the UN Truth Commission's Final Report.

The answer that I offer in this chapter is that, through the Final Report, the commissioners not only downplayed the jurisdictional force of the UN's peacebuilding vision for post-conflict states, but in turn, they also contributed to constrain the Salvadoran state and its peoples' capacity to organize their own lawful post-conflict state-society relations. This shows how the respective truths of the UN Truth Commission and the Salvadoran woman were oriented by rival viewpoints, resulting in fundamentally different representations of the violence of the civil war. In drawing on the identity and status of the UN as an international institution, the UN Truth Commission's truth displaced these 'other' rival truths, and in the process of excluding them, the UN Truth Commission authorized an account that has contributed to making El Salvador a model post-conflict state.

In the next and final substantive chapter of this book, I show how the international success of the three Truth Commissions studied in this book so far – Argentina (1983), Chile (1990), and El Salvador (1992) – was decisive in strengthening the authority of the international legal order after the Cold War in the 1990s, and the work of Truth Commissions in it. To show that, in the following chapter I discuss how, after the international success of the Argentinian, Chilean, and Salvadoran Truth Commissions, this institution was given an 'origins' story. This occurred when, between 1990 and 1994, international human rights and transitional justice experts redescribed Uganda's 1974 Commission of Inquiry as the 'inaugural' Truth Commission. The chapter shows how that redescription strengthened the vital relationship between Truth Commissions and international law, which in turn shaped how Truth Commissions have been, and continue to be, received.

CHAPTER 5

Receiving Truth Commissions through International Law

5.1 INTRODUCTION

IN THIS FINAL CHAPTER I TURN my attention to an understudied Truth Commission. Established in Uganda in 1974, this Truth Commission is generally considered to be the first.[1] It is officially called "The Commission of Inquiry into the Disappearances of People in Uganda since the 25th of January 1971" (the '1974 Commission of Inquiry').[2] Chronologically the 1974 Commission of Inquiry predates the Truth Commissions examined in the previous chapters of the book – Argentina (1983) in Chapter 2, Chile (1990) in

[1] The following sources identify Uganda's 1974 Commission of Inquiry as the 'inaugural' Truth Commission: Priscilla B. Hayner, *Unspeakable Truths: Transitional Justice and the Challenge of Truth Commissions* (Routledge, 2011); Amnesty International, "Commissioning Justice: Truth Commissions and Criminal Justice" (2010); Joanna R. Quinn, *The Politics of Acknowledgement: Truth Commissions in Uganda and Haiti* (UBC Press, 2010), 40; Alicia C. Decker, "'Sometime you may leave your husband in Karuma Falls or in the forest there': A Gendered History of Disappearance in Idi Amin's Uganda, 1971–79," *Journal of Eastern African Studies*, vol 7, no 1 (2013); The Auschwitz Institute for the Prevention of Genocide and Mass Atrocities, "Truth Commissions and Their Contributions to Atrocity Prevention" (2020). Available at: www.auschwitzinstitute.org/wp-content/uploads/2020/05/AIPG-TruthCommissionsReport.pdf; Carla Winston, "Truth Commissions as Tactical Concessions: The Curious Case of Idi Amin," *The International Journal of Human Rights*, vol 25, no 2 (2021). However, Eric Weibelhaus-Brahm argues that there is no general agreement as to whether Uganda's 1974 Commission of Inquiry "qualifies as a truth commission." Weibelhaus-Brahm notes that while Priscilla Hayner lists Uganda as the 'first' Truth Commission, Mark Freeman explicitly critiques Hayner's decision. See, Eric Wiebelhaus-Brahm, *Truth Commissions and Transitional Societies: The Impact on Human Rights and Democracy* (Routledge, 2010), 188 at 1; Mark Freeman, *Truth Commissions and Procedural Fairness* (Cambridge University Press, 2006), 21.

[2] Government of Uganda, *The Commission of Inquiry Act (Cap. 56), Legal Notice No 2 of 1974* (30 June 1974).

Chapter 3, and El Salvador (1992) in Chapter 4. That might give the impression that this chapter is out of synchrony, with the book's analysis ending in the 1970s, where it all began, with the inaugural Truth Commission.

However, the point of this chapter is that the 1974 Commission of Inquiry only gained meaningful international attention as a 'Truth Commission' in the mid-1990s, in the wake of the Cold War. At that time, the United Nations' (UN) expanding role in El Salvador and in Central America was helping to renew faith in the promises and potential of the international order to do good. This renewed faith was also channeling the geopolitical changes brought by the Cold War in the late 1980s and early 1990s. As the power of the United States strengthened, and Cold War geopolitics shifted in favor of Western interests, international actors developed new, and expanded existing, institutions and programs. For example, this period witnessed the authorization of numerous innovative peacekeeping operations;[3] the rise of a strong activist global human rights movement;[4] and the deployment of development, rule of law promotion, and democracy-building programs alongside IMF and World Bank economic interventions.[5] It was in this context that in 1990 Richard Carver, who at the time worked for Africa Watch (a predecessor of Human Rights Watch),[6] published an article describing the 1974 Commission of Inquiry as an imperfect but valuable attempt at

[3] UN Peacekeeping, "List of Peacekeeping Operations 1948–2020." Available at: https://peacekeeping.un.org/sites/default/files/un_peacekeeping_operation_list_3_2.pdf; Jerome Koops et al., "Introduction: Post-Cold War Peacekeeping: 1988–1998," in *The Oxford Handbook of United Nations Peacekeeping Operations*, Jerome Koops et al. (eds), (Oxford University Press, 2014), 315.

[4] Margaret E. Keck and Kathryn Sikkink, *Activists Beyond Borders: Advocacy Networks in International Politics* (Cornell University Press, 1998); Nicolas Guilhot, *The Democracy Makers: Human Rights and International Order* (Columbia University Press, 2005).

[5] Anne Orford, "Locating the International: Military and Monetary Interventions after the Cold War," *Harvard International Law Journal*, vol 38, no 2 (1997); Sundhya Pahuja, *Decolonising International Law: Development, Economic Growth, and the Politics of Universality* (Cambridge University Press, 2011) 13; 59–69; Guy Fiti Sinclair, *To Reform the World: The Legal Powers of International Organizations* (Oxford University Press, 2017), 202–235.

[6] Human Rights Watch, "History." Available at: www.hrw.org/about/about-us/history. On the institutional history of Human Rights Watch, including a discussion of the advocacy methods of Africa Watch see generally, Aryeh Neier, *The International Human Rights Movement: A History* (Princeton University Press, 2012), 204–232.

advancing respect for international human rights law.[7] Four years later, in 1994, Priscilla Hayner (who wrote the first set of comprehensive studies on Truth Commissions) listed the Ugandan 1974 Commission of Inquiry as the inaugural Truth Commission,[8] drawing on Carver's 1990 analysis.[9] Since then, others, including Amnesty International and the United States Institute of Peace, have continued to describe the 1974 Commission of Inquiry as the first Truth Commission.[10] The extent to which this description has been accepted as part of Truth Commission orthodoxy was also highlighted in Chapter 3 (Chile's Museum of Memory and Human Rights also identified Uganda's Commission of Inquiry as the first Truth Commission in its "Truth Commissions in the World" display).

When I began the research for this book, I wanted to understand what makes a Truth Commission uniquely capable of offering an authoritative account of past violent events. Put differently, I was puzzled about what makes this institution a 'Commission of Truth.' To answer that question, I turned to where the scholarly literature indicates that the story of Truth Commissions began: Uganda, and its 1974 Commission of Inquiry. In researching this origin story, I discovered that it was Uganda's military

7 Richard Carver, "Called to Account: How African Governments Investigate Human Rights Violations," *African Affairs*, vol 89, no 356 (1990). On the subtle but increasingly powerful importance of human rights in the 1970s, see Moyn, *The Last Utopia.* For a brief critical overview about the rise of human rights organizations in the 1970s and their goals see, Jessica Whyte, *The Morals of the Market: Human Rights and the Rise of Neoliberalism* (Verso, 2019), 26–31.

8 Priscilla B. Hayner, "Fifteen Truth Commissions – 1974 to 1994: A Comparative Study," *Human Rights Quarterly*, vol 16, no 4 (1994): 611–613; Hayner, *Unspeakable Truths: Transitional Justice*, xi–xii; 256–262.

9 Carver's article is the only source on which Hayner draws on for her analysis of the 1974 Commission of Inquiry. See, Hayner, "Fifteen Truth Commissions," 612–613. Jessica Whyte's excellent historical analysis about the marriage of human rights and the neoliberal project is helpful to understand the legal-political worldviews embedded in the mobilization of human rights across Third World states from the 1990s onwards. See generally, Whyte, *The Morals of the Market.*

10 Amnesty International, "Commissioning Justice: Truth Commissions and Criminal Justice" (2010), 8. The Trump administration dismantled USIP in 2025. Between 2017 and early 2025, I was able to access USIP database through: United States Institute of Peace Truth Commission Digital Collection (2011). Available at: www.usip.org/publications/2011/03/truth-commission-digital-collection.

president Idi Amin Dada who established the 1974 Commission of Inquiry during a tumultuous time. The Commission of Inquiry was part of Idi Amin's calculated response to growing international pressure from human rights groups,[11] particularly a report by the International Commission of Jurists about mass disappearances in Uganda during his term of government.[12] This discovery contrasted sharply with the description of Truth Commissions as drawing their authority to establish an official account of the truth from the reputation of their establishing body. As discussed in Chapter 1, the usual story is that all those involved in establishing or running a Truth Commission should be trustworthy themselves, with an unimpeachable moral and political reputation. The governments that were involved in establishing the three most acclaimed Truth Commissions (in South Africa, Argentina, and Chile) were led by politicians with a national and international reputation for being principled and committed to meaningful transformation of state-society relations: Nelson Mandela, Raúl Alfonsín, and Patricio Aylwin. In sharp contrast, Uganda's Idi Amin was regarded internationally as the opposite. That raised the question: what authorized the truthfulness of the 1974 Commission of Inquiry's account?

In turning to the 1974 Commission of Inquiry's Final Report to find an answer, I made a second discovery: the Commission avoided using human rights language and instead used its own legal language to give an account of the unlawfulness of the mass disappearances in Uganda.[13]

[11] See generally, Winston, "Truth Commissions as Tactical Concessions"; Thomas Lowman, "Amin Reframed: The UK, Uganda, and the Human Rights 'breakthrough' of the 1970s," *Cambridge Review of International Affairs* (online first, June 2022). For an excellent collection of essays on the histories and politics of human rights around the 1970s see, Samuel Moyn and Jon Eckel (eds), *The Breakthrough: Human Rights in the 1970s* (University of Pennsylvania Press, 2014). See also, Samuel Moyn, *The Last Utopia: Human Rights in History* (Harvard University Press, 2010).

[12] Michael Posner and International Commission of Jurists, "Violations of Human Rights and the Rule of Law in Uganda" (1974). Available at: www.icj.org/wp-content/uploads/2013/06/Uganda-violations-of-human-rights-thematic-report-1974-eng.pdf.

[13] See generally, Commission of Inquiry into the Disappearances of People in Uganda since the 25th of January 1971, *Final Report of the Commission of Inquiry into the Disappearances of People in Uganda since the 25th of January 1971* (1974). Available at: www.usip.org/publications/1974/06/truth-commission-uganda-74.

This was a 'discovery' for me because it seemed to contradict the analysis that I had read in Carver's 1990 article, in which he argued that the 1974 Commission of Inquiry was advancing international human rights. And yet, this suggested an answer to the question of what authorized the truthfulness of the 1974 Commission of Inquiry's account, and enabled the Commission of Inquiry to become the inaugural Truth Commission: its connection with the international legal form that was gaining strength throughout the 1990s, international human rights law. My focus in this chapter is on how this connection was made, retrospectively.

To do that, I undertake a close reading of three 'telling moments' in the institutional life of Uganda's 1974 Commission of Inquiry: (1) its establishment in 1974 by Idi Amin; (2) its redescription in 1990 as a human rights institution by Richard Carver; and (3) its redescription in 1994 as the inaugural Truth Commission by Priscilla Hayner. My argument is that, together, these three telling moments show how the 1974 Commission of Inquiry only became known as 'the inaugural' Truth Commission in the 1990s through its retrospective connection with international human rights. To be clear, I am not suggesting that the Truth Commissions of Argentina, Chile, and El Salvador were modeled after the 1974 Commission of Inquiry. Rather, the argument is that the international success of those three Truth Commissions contributed to the redescription of the 1974 Commission of Inquiry in the 1990s, as a Truth Commission that had been advancing international human rights (even if modestly). And in turn, the redescription of the 1974 Commission of Inquiry helped to give coherency to the institution of the Truth Commission in the 1990s, by providing an origin story, which drew on the authority of international law and its institutions in the form of human rights. As I briefly discuss in Section 5.3, this is also part of the origins of the field of transitional justice.

The chapter is divided into three parts, each corresponding to one of the 'telling moments.' Section 5.2 begins with a brief overview and analysis of the context in which Idi Amin established Uganda's 1974 Commission of Inquiry, and its Final Report, published in 1975. Section 5.3 analyzes how the 1974 Commission of Inquiry was redescribed as a human rights institution at the end of the Cold War. The focus here is on Richard Carver's influential article, published in 1990,

"Called to Account: How African Governments Investigate Human Rights Violations."[14] I read Carver's article alongside the 1974 Commission of Inquiry's Final Report to show how Carver framed the Commission of Inquiry as an institution that had advanced international human rights in Uganda. This is important because it effectively redescribes how the Commission of Inquiry was framed in the 1970s by the Commissioners, as an institution authorized by, and advancing, domestic law. Not only did the Commissioners seek to establish a clear hierarchy between domestic law and international law, but they also sought to give meaning to the concept of 'the rule of law' through Ugandans own experiences of state violence. This is reflected in the Final Report's finding that the mass disappearances in Uganda were the outcome of an "unlawful" exercise of power by state security agents, which was never described in terms of a violation of international human rights law.[15]

In the final part of the chapter (Section 5.4) I turn to the third telling moment that contributed to the redescription of the Commission of Inquiry as the inaugural Truth Commission. This focuses on Priscilla Hayner's highly influential 1994 article, "Fifteen Truth Commissions – 1974 to 1994: A Comparative Study,"[16] in which Hayner categorized Uganda's 1974 Commission of Inquiry as the first Truth Commission.[17] This section also analyzes how the two editions of Hayner's book, in 2001 and 2011, continued the redescription of the 1974 Commission of Inquiry. As I discuss, Hayner's retrospective redescription was influential for two main reasons.[18] For one, Hayner's 1994 article was the first dedicated "survey" of Truth Commissions, and the first to "generically" rename different investigatory institutions as Truth Commissions.[19] And

[14] Carver, "Called to Account." [15] 1974 Commission of Inquiry, *Final Report*, 781.

[16] Hayner, "Fifteen Truth Commissions"; Hayner, *Unspeakable Truths: Transitional Justice.*

[17] Hayner, "Fifteen Truth Commissions," 601; 608; 611–613.

[18] There are other interesting reasons, which are beyond the scope of this book, concerning the broader history and politics of human rights, that are helpful to understand why Hayner's redescription was well-received by the human rights movement and democracy promotion advocates at that time. On this see generally, Paige Arthur, "How 'Transitions' Reshaped Human Rights: A Conceptual History of Transitional Justice," *Human Rights Quarterly*, vol 31, no 2 (2009); Guilhot, *The Democracy Makers.*

[19] Hayner, "Fifteen Truth Commissions," 599; 599 at 2.

two, the article carried Hayner's growing professional authority. By 1994 Hayner was emerging as the leading international expert on Truth Commissions.[20] However, my argument here is that Hayner's success in renaming, or reauthoring, these disparate institutions as Truth Commissions depended not only on her personal authority, or on her being the first to undertake this work. Crucial to the re-author(iz)ing of these institutions as Truth Commissions was the connection that Hayner also drew between them and international law, especially international human rights law.

As I conclude, in Section 5.5, these three telling moments show how, from the 1990s onwards, Uganda's 1974 Commission of Inquiry was brought within a global story of Truth Commissions tied to international law and its institutions.

5.2 IDI AMIN'S 1974 COMMISSION OF INQUIRY

During the Cold War, the March 1977 cover of *TIME* magazine featured Idi Amin Dada, then president of Uganda, performing a military salute while looking to an unknown horizon.[21] The cover story was titled: "Uganda's Idi Amin: The Wild Man of Africa."[22] The issue not only gave an account of Idi Amin's violent treatment of the Ugandan people, but also discussed United States President Carter's decision to support Great Britain's request to the UN Commission on Human Rights to send a mission "into Uganda to assess the horrible murders that apparently are taking place in that country."[23] It was not the first time that the UN had

[20] Jamie Rowen, *Searching for Truth in the Transitional Justice Movement* (Cambridge University Press, 2017), 23; 28; 32–33; Sara Dezalay, "The Role of International NGOs in the Emergence of Transitional Justice: A Case Study of the International Center for Transitional Justice," in *Research Handbook on Transitional Justice*, Cheryl Lawther, Luke Moffett, and Dov Jacobs (eds), (Edward Elgar Publishing, 2017), 203 at note 7.

[21] Alain Nogues-Sygma, "Cover Story: Uganda's Idi Amin: The Wild Man of Africa," *TIME* (7 March 1977).

[22] Ibid.

[23] Ibid. See also, Jimmy Carter, "The President's News Conference" (23 February 1977), (Gerhard Peters and John T. Woolley, The American Presidency Project); Lowman, "Amin Reframed." See generally, David F. Schmitz and Vanessa Walker, "Jimmy

been requested to take action regarding the situation in Uganda,[24] which according to President Carter, "disgusted the entire civilized world."[25] By that point in the Cold War, Idi Amin had become one of the Western Bloc's *enfants terribles.*[26]

A few years earlier, in 1971, Idi Amin had the international community's – and especially its former colonizer, Great Britain's – support to lead a coup d'état against Uganda's President, Milton Obote.[27] However, once in power, Idi Amin turned his back on well-established economic, political, and military relations with Great Britain,[28] the United States, and even Israel, and instead allied his government with Muammar Gaddafi in Libya, and USSR.[29] The first of Idi Amin's decisions to attract the attention of the

Carter and the Foreign Policy of Human Rights: The Development of a Post-Cold War Foreign Policy," *Diplomatic History*, vol 28, no 1 (2003).

24 The International Commission of Jurist played a crucial role in this. See, Howard B. Tolley Jr., *The International Commission of Jurists: Global Advocates for Human Rights* (University of Pennsylvania Press, 1994), 204; 207–208. See also, International Commission of Jurists, "Uganda and Human Rights: Reports of the International Commission of Jurists to the United Nations" (1977).

25 Carter, "The President's News Conference." On Carter's key role in promoting human rights as part of the US's foreign policy see, Schmitz and Walker, "Jimmy Carter and the Foreign Policy of Human Rights"; Steven L.B. Jensen, *The Making of International Human Rights: The 1960s, Decolonization, and the Reconstruction of Global Values* (Cambridge University Press, 2016), 260–261.

26 See generally, Oliver Furley, "Britain from Uganda to Musevini: Blind Eye Diplomacy," in *Conflict Resolution in Uganda*, Kumar Rupesinghe (ed), (International Peace Research Institute; James Currey Ltd; Ohio University Press, 1989); Colin Legum, "Uganda Coup could lead to New Congo or Biafra," *The Observer* (31 January 1971). Legum's reference to Biafra in relation to Uganda is particularly telling of how human rights were being mobilized in the 1970s. On this see, Lesse Heerten, "The Dystopia of Postcolonial Catastrophe: Self-Determination, the Biafran War of Secession, and the 1970s Human Rights Moment," in *The Breakthrough: Human Rights in the 1970s*, Samuel Moyn and Jon Eckel (eds) (University of Pennsylvania Press, 2014).

27 Chibuike Uche, "The British Government, Idi Amin and the Expulsion of British Asians from Uganda," *Interventions: International Journal of Postcolonial Studies*, vol 19, no 6 (2017): 819; 828.

28 Lowman, "Amin Reframed," 7–10.

29 See Akiki Bomera Mujaju, "Internal Conflict and its International Context," in *Conflict Resolution in Uganda*, Kumar Rupesinghe (ed) (International Peace Research Institute; Ohio University Press, 1989). Colin Legum, "How Russia found a Friend in Amin," *The Observer* (29 June 1972); Christopher Munnion, "If Idi Amin of Uganda Is a Madman, He's a Ruthless and Cunning One," *New York Times* (12 November 1972).

Western Bloc was the expulsion of Uganda's Asian-origin population.[30] Idi Amin explained his decision by arguing that he wanted to protect the people of Uganda, that he wanted them to own and enjoy economic success, and that he wanted to make Uganda independent from Britain.[31] One of the leading voices against Idi Amin was the International Commission of Jurists, a prominent Geneva-based international organization.[32] The International Commission of Jurists was created in the early Cold War years, in 1952, as an "offshoot" of the United States' 'containment policy' during the Cold War.[33] The 'containment policy,' led by the United States' elite think tank, the Council on Foreign Relations, was aimed at countering the advancement of communist ideas and the expansion of the Soviet Bloc.[34] In support of this policy, the Central Intelligence Agency (CIA) secretly financed the 1952 West Berlin Congress, in which the International Commission of Jurists was founded, as well as its operations later.[35] The idea to create this organization came from jurists who felt an urgency to 'save' those who lived in 'slavery' as a result of the Soviet Bloc's 'laws' – laws that were considered unlawful because they lacked the moral content of human rights.[36] In other words, the International Commission of Jurists saw itself as an agent of the 'free world' tasked with saving the enslaved world during the Cold War.

The International Commission of Jurists responded to Idi Amin's expulsion of Uganda's Asian-origin population with a doctrinal-legal analysis of whether Idi Amin had authority under international law – as

30 BBC, "1972: Asians Given 90 Days to Leave Uganda," *BBC* (1972). On the role of journalists (especially, Colin Legum from *The Observer*) in drawing international attention see, Lowman, "Amin Reframed," 10. For Colin's reporting see for example, notes 26 and 29 above.

31 On this see generally, Uche, "The British Government, Idi Amin and the Expulsion of British Asians from Uganda."

32 See, International Commission of Jurists, "Uganda and Human Rights: Reports."

33 Tolley Jr., *The International Commission of Jurists: Global*, 25.

34 Ibid, 25–26. On the Council on Foreign Relations organizational history, see, Laurence H. Shoup and William Minter, *Imperial Brain Trust: The Council on Foreign Relations and United States Foreign Policy* (Monthly Review Press, 1977).

35 Howard B. Tolley Jr., "International Commission of Jurists," in *Encyclopedia of Human Rights*, David P. Forsythe (ed) (Oxford University Press, 2009), 84.

36 See generally, International Congress of Jurists, "International Congress of Jurists – West Berlin 1952 – Complete Report, Discourses and Protocols" (1952).

head of a recognized sovereign state – to expel foreigners *en masse.*[37] The author of the report, Richard Plender, concluded that Idi Amin was violating basic human rights because the expulsions were based on race, which specifically contravened the responsibilities that Uganda assumed by becoming a party to the UN Convention Relating to the Status of Stateless Persons of 1954.[38]

In response, on June 30, 1974, Idi Amin authorized the creation of the 1974 Commission of Inquiry.[39] The 1974 Commission of Inquiry was established to clarify the disappearances, killings, and displacement of people in Uganda since the coup d'état that brought him to power in 1971. Through *Legal Notice No 2,* the legal instrument authorizing the Commission of Inquiry, Idi Amin established the aims and scope of the investigation, which he framed as "instructions."[40] *Legal Notice No 2* also appointed four commissioners and one secretary to carry out the public investigation,[41] ordered them to start working on July 1, 1974, and required them to present a final report by September 30, 1974.[42] Idi Amin emphasized that the commissioners should follow the "instructions" given in order to "ascertain the truth of the matter."[43]

Idi Amin also explained, in *Legal Notice No 2,* that the main reason for establishing the Commission of Inquiry was that "it was alleged that some people have disappeared from Uganda since the Military take-over on 25th January 1971."[44] Although the document does not name who made the allegations, the Commission of Inquiry was Idi Amin's direct response to the International Commission of Jurists' 1974 investigation and its resulting report, titled "Violations of Human Rights and the Rule of Law in Uganda."[45]

[37] See Richard Plender, "The Ugandan Crisis and the Right of Expulsion under International Law," in *The Review,* Naill MacDermont (ed) (International Commission of Jurists, 1972).

[38] See, ibid, 29.

[39] Government of Uganda, *The Commission of Inquiry Act (Cap. 56), Legal Notice No 2.*

[40] Ibid.

[41] Ibid. See also a brief description of Judge Said, in Peter Allen, *Days of Judgment: A Judge in Idi Amin's Uganda* (William Kimber, 1987), 156.

[42] Government of Uganda, *The Commission of Inquiry Act (Cap. 56), Legal Notice No 2.*

[43] Ibid. [44] Ibid.

[45] Michael Posner and International Commission of Jurists, "Violations of Human Rights"; Winston, "Truth Commissions as Tactical Concessions," 10; Lowman,

On the same day that *Legal Notice No 2* was published, Idi Amin's presidential office released a four-page statement titled "Disappearances."[46] In this statement, there were appeals to Ugandans to collaborate with the Commission of Inquiry by "tell[ing] the truth."[47] The statement also included Idi Amin's explanation of the decision to expel "non-citizen Asians" from Uganda as part of his plan to fight back in the "Economic War" that was being waged against Uganda by the "imperialists."[48] The statement reminded Ugandans that the country had been "attacked by external forces" but the courageous army of Uganda "beat off the invasion and thus once again saved lives of civilians of Ugandans and consolidated her independence and sovereignty."[49] The statement concluded by emphasizing that it was in this context that many Ugandans disappeared, causing the "concern of everybody" and "untold misery."[50] And "[b]ecause of all this and more," Idi Amin, as president of Uganda, "decided that [it was] in the interest of justice, fairness, security and social tranquillity" to establish the Commission of Inquiry.[51]

With those instructions, as recorded in *Legal Notice No 2*, the Commission of Inquiry commenced its work in July 1974.[52] The commissioners began to meet in Kampala at Uganda's Parliamentary Buildings, as Idi Amin ordered in the "Disappearances" statement.[53] The commissioners wrote an 800-page Final Report,[54] and presented it to Idi Amin on June 13, 1975, in Kampala, Uganda's capital city.[55] However, Idi Amin did not authorize making the Final Report public in Uganda. The few sources that have focused on the 1974 Commission of Inquiry's Final Report do not provide further information about how the original

"Amin Reframed," 10–11. See also, Heerten, "The Dystopia of Postcolonial Catastrophe."

46 Government of Uganda, Office of the President, "Statement: Disappearances" (30 June 1974). The title of Idi Amin's statement is telling of the increasing international focus on this particular issue. For an historical overview specifically on that see Jensen, *The Making of International Human Rights*, 237–274.

47 Government of Uganda, Office of the President, "Statement: Disappearances," 3.

48 Ibid, 2. 49 Ibid, 4. 50 Ibid, 3. 51 Ibid.

52 Government of Uganda, *The Commission of Inquiry Act (Cap. 56), Legal Notice No 2.*

53 Government of Uganda, Office of the President, "Statement: Disappearances," 4.

54 The Final Report has 819 pages plus Appendices.

55 This date was an approved deadline extension, different to the initial due date established in *Legal Notice 2.* See also, 1974 Commission of Inquiry, *Final Report*, 819.

document or its copies were preserved. What is known is that eighteen years later, in 1993, a copy of the Final Report was microfilmed by the international human rights organization Amnesty International, with the copy kept in its London offices.[56] In 2017, I accessed the Final Report as well as other key documents of the 1974 Commission of Inquiry, through the United States Institute of Peace's Truth Commissions Digital Collection.[57] This digital collection makes available the Final Reports and other important documents of over thirty Truth Commissions.[58]

Unfortunately, the quality of this copy of the Commission of Inquiry's Final Report is poor and major parts are illegible.[59] Nonetheless, there are parts that can be read, and they offer relevant information on four important aspects: (1) how the Commissioners conducted the inquiry within the terms of reference set by Idi Ami; (2) the process of evidence gathering through witness hearings; (3) the final recommendations; and (4) the legal language and some legal sources used to narrate how and why disappearances, murders, and forced displacements occurred in the wake of the 1971 coup. In the following parts of the chapter, I read these aspects of the Final Report and its account of the truth about the mass disappearances. I do this in the next section alongside Carver's redescription of the Commission of Inquiry's work as a matter of human rights. This is followed, in Section 5.4, by analysis of Hayner's redescription of the institution as the 'inaugural' Truth Commission.

5.3 REDESCRIBING 1974 COMMISSION OF INQUIRY AS A HUMAN RIGHTS INSTITUTION

The late 1980s, and especially the 1990s, were crucial years for the global politics of human rights, particularly concerning their expansion and strengthening as a political (and economic) project across the Global

[56] Trudy Huskamp Peterson, *Final Acts: A Guide to Preserving the Records of Truth Commissions* (Woodrow Wilson Center Press; Johns Hopkins University Press, 2005), 79; Hayner, *Unspeakable Truths: Transitional Justice*, 240; 335 at 243.

[57] On the United States Institute of Peace see note 10 above. [58] Ibid.

[59] Decker also refers to this in, Decker, "Sometime You May Leave," 140 at 121.

South.[60] As others have shown, the expansion of human rights in the 1990s was also a direct response to the events driving the end of the Cold War.[61] One of those events was the dissolution of the USSR, which carried with it the weakening of communism as an alternative politico-economic project to liberal democracy and capitalism.[62] Other intimately related events included the "transitions to democracy" or "transition to more democratic regimes" occurring in Latin American states and in the newly established, post-soviet, Eastern European states.[63] In particular, the transition to democracy in Argentina in the 1980s, and in Chile in the early 1990s, seemed to back up the "evidence for hope"[64] offered by international human rights law and its advocates. It was also during this time that NGOs, experts, philanthropic foundations,[65] and international institutions began to explore a novel 'approach' to questions of post-

[60] On this see generally, Orlando Letelier, "Economic 'Freedom's' Awful Toll: The 'Chicago Boys' in Chile," *Review of Radical Political Economics*, vol 8, no 3 (1976); Naomi Klein, *The Shock Doctrine* (Penguin Books, 2008); Joseph R. Slaughter, "Hijacking Human Rights: Neoliberalism, the New Historiography, and the End of the Third World," *Human Rights Quarterly*, vol 40, no 4 (2018).

[61] Alice H. Henkin, "Conference Report," in *State Crimes: Punishment or Pardon: Papers and Report of the Conference*, The Aspen Institute (The Aspen Institute, 1988), 3; Neil J. Kritz (ed), *Transitional Justice: How Emerging Democracies Reckon with Former Regimes. Volume II: Country Studies* (United States Institute of Peace, 1995), 1–153; Ruti G. Teitel, *Globalizing Transitional Justice: Contemporary Essays* (Oxford University Press, 2014) 3; Marcos Zunino, *Justice Framed: A Genealogy of Transitional Justice* (Cambridge University Press, 2019), 11.

[62] Odd Arne Westad, *The Global Cold War: Third World Interventions and the Making of Our Times* (Cambridge University Press, 2007), 378–395.

[63] Teitel, *Globalizing Transitional Justice*, 3; Henkin, "Conference Report," 8.

[64] Kathryn Sikkink, *Evidence for Hope: Making Human Rights Work in the 21st Century* (Princeton University Press, 2017).

[65] See Arthur, "How 'Transitions' Reshaped Human Rights," 324. For example, the Aspen Institute organized in 1988 an influential workshop. The Ford Foundation funded the event, and the list of participants is particularly interesting as they were already, or would become, leading experts in this field of practice and research. See The Aspen Institute, *State Crimes: Punishment or Pardon: Papers and Report of the Conference* (The Aspen Institute, 1988). This edited volume was also influential see Neil J. Kritz (ed), *Transitional Justice: How Emerging Democracies Reckon with Former Regimes. Volume I: General Considerations* (United States Institute of Peace, 1995); Ruti G. Teitel, *Transitional Justice* (Oxford University Press, 2000).

conflict law, politics, and justice around the world.[66] As Paige Arthur has observed, between the late 1980s and early 1990s, this was far from being a coherent approach, or even a promising emerging field. It was, as Paige Arthur describes it, more like "an international web of individuals" whose "internal coherence [was] held together by common concepts, aims, and distinctive claims for legitimacy."[67] Furthermore, what brought them "directly" together was their "shared concerned with human rights and of 'transitions to democracy.'"[68] By the mid-1990s this new approach would be known as the field of 'transitional justice.'[69] Over the next years, Truth Commissions would begin to be increasingly associated with this field.[70] Yet before that, as Aryeh Neier (cofounder of Human Rights Watch) observed, the origins of Truth Commissions are also historically linked to the broader aims of international human rights.[71]

In this context, in July 1990, Richard Carver – then Research Director of Africa Watch, a predecessor of Human Rights Watch[72] – published an academic article descriptively titled "Called to Account: How African Governments Investigate Human Rights Violations."[73] In that article,

[66] Periodization of its 'origins' slightly varies. For detailed studies tracing how the international contexts of the 1980s and 1990s informed the historical development of transitional justice as a field of practice and research, see as examples, Arthur, "How 'Transitions' Reshaped Human Rights"; Zunino, *Justice Framed*; Neha Jain and Sarah M. H. Nouwen, "North-South Skirmishes over Transitional Justice: 1975–2000," in *The Battle for International Law II*, Jochen von Bernstorff, Philipp Dann and Surabhi Ranganathan (eds) (Oxford University Press, forthcoming). Elster, on the other hand, traces instances of transitional justice as far back as to Ancient Greece in, Jon Elster, *Closing the Books: Transitional Justice in Historical Perspective* (Cambridge University Press, 2004).

[67] Arthur, "How 'Transitions' Reshaped Human Rights," 324. [68] Ibid.

[69] Teitel coined the term in 1991, see in Teitel, *Globalizing Transitional Justice*, 3. But by 1995 according to Arthur, Jain and Nouwen 'transitional justice' became well-known after the success of Kritz's 1995 edited collection. Arthur, "How 'Transitions' Reshaped Human Rights," 330–331; Jain and Nouwen, "North-South Skirmishes over Transitional Justice," 8.

[70] As Hayer notes in the first edition of her book (which also has a different title as I discuss in Section 5.4). Priscilla B. Hayner, *Unspeakable Truths: Confronting State Terror and Atrocity* (Routledge, 2001).

[71] See discussion in, Neier, *The International Human Rights Movement*, 258–264.

[72] Human Rights Watch, "History"; Neier, *The International Human Rights Movement*, 215–217.

[73] Carver, "Called to Account."

Carver offered an overview of how, since the 1986 African Charter on Human and Peoples' Rights, "international law ha[d] been strengthened by the addition of a specifically African human rights treaty to which some 40 states are party."[74] Carver highlights that one of the most important aspects of the 1986 Charter is that, with Article 26, it "encourages governments to set up national institutions to protect human rights."[75] For Carver this is important because it creates the possibility to "hold governments accountable for their actions," and in doing so, it paves the way for "prosecuting those alleged to be responsible" as per the investigatory institution's findings.[76] In Carver's view, that would deter governments from committing "human rights abuses."[77] Carver acknowledges that some governments might establish institutions to investigate human rights violations "to divert public criticism."[78] Nonetheless, Carver argues that, "if certain procedural safeguards and standards are adopted when the investigation is set up," then those human rights institutions might not be used to advance a particular government's interests.[79]

Before I briefly outline what Carver means by "procedural safeguards and standards,"[80] there are two important points to highlight. The first is that, throughout the article, Carver not only begins to call this type of investigation "a human rights inquiry" or "human rights investigation,"[81] but also describes the different investigatory institutions created by "several African countries" as "cases of government human rights investigations."[82] This is important because it begins to show how these investigatory institutions, including Uganda's 1974 Commission of Inquiry, were already being redescribed as institutions advancing international law within a particular state.[83] The second relevant point is that, when Carver outlines the "procedural safeguards and standards" of human rights inquiries,[84] he places special importance on clarifying the

[74] Ibid, 392. [75] Ibid. [76] Ibid, 393. [77] Ibid. [78] Ibid. [79] Ibid.

[80] Carver outlines and briefly describes them in, ibid, 393–397.

[81] See for example the article's headings, ibid, 393; 397; 403; 411. [82] Ibid, 393.

[83] In relation to this point, see for example how Aryeh Neier (cofounder of Human Rights Watch) saw the role of Truth Commissions, see note 9 above.

[84] Carver, "Called to Account," 393.

relationship between those 'national' human rights investigations and questions of (international) law and justice.[85]

Carver outlined five "procedural safeguards and standards."[86] Four focused on issues concerning institutional independence, publicity of findings, timeliness, and accessibility; while one addresses questions of law and justice.[87] Regarding the latter, Carver argued that the "aim of a human rights inquiry" is not to adjudicate criminal responsibility, but rather "to establish whether ... human rights violations were committed by agents of the state."[88] While Carver recognizes that there "is clearly some overlap" between human rights inquiries and judicial institutions, he framed this relationship as one of "complementar[ity]."[89] For Carver, the "complementary" nature of the relationship emerges from a fundamental role that he attributes to human rights inquiries, which is to "monitor the adherence to the law,"[90] by which he means international human rights law.

With this general human rights framing in place, Carver then turns to Uganda's 1974 Commission of Inquiry, which he approaches as an example of an "African governmen[t]" institution created to "investigate specific human rights abuses."[91] Carver's analysis begins by highlighting how the commissioners were advised by Joseph Mulenga, who was the legal counsel to the Commission of Inquiry, on the relationship between the institution and questions of law, particularly on the adjudication of criminal responsibility.[92] With this, Carver aligns the Commission of Inquiry, as an investigatory institution tasked to "establish" and "monitor" the government's "adherence to the law,"[93] with his "procedural safeguards and standards" for human rights inquiries.[94]

As Carver notes in his article, the commissioners sought Mulenga's counsel to determine whether they were able to address one of the Commission of Inquiry's terms of reference. *Legal Notice No 2* (the legal instrument authorizing the Commission of Inquiry) required the commissioners to identify those "criminally responsible for disappearances or deaths of the missing persons" and to offer recommendations to the government on what to do with those found "criminally

85 Ibid, 393; 397; 403; 411. 86 Ibid, 393–397. 87 Ibid. 88 Ibid, 395–396.
89 Ibid, 397. 90 Ibid. 91 Ibid. 92 Ibid, 398–399. 93 Ibid, 397.
94 Ibid, 393–397.

responsible."[95] In this sense, Idi Amin explicitly authorized the Commission of Inquiry to determine criminal responsibility. Yet the commissioners "agreed with" Mulenga that "they were not vested with criminal jurisdiction of trying cases and establishing guilt,"[96] and argued that they did not have sufficient "evidence" (according to the rules of evidence) to undertake that task.[97]

Instead, as Carver notes, in his legal advice Mulenga argued that since the Commission of Inquiry "was not a criminal investigation," it was "prefer[able]" to use "the phrase 'unlawful responsibility,'" instead of 'criminal responsibility.'[98] As Carver points out, the commissioners, in following Mulenga's advice,[99] framed the scope of the Commission's investigation as "pin-pointing individuals or government establishment ... who were implicated in the unlawful disappearances or deaths" of Ugandans.[100] The commissioners explicitly stated that "the use of the word 'unlawful' ... was deliberate."[101] This is reflected in how the findings in the Final Report were presented, not as an account of "criminal responsibility," which could only be determined by "a court of law after a full trial,"[102] but as account of "unlawful responsibility" or "unlawful disappearances or deaths of people."[103]

What is important here is that, in order to give authority to the Commission's findings, the commissioners developed an understanding of 'unlawfulness' that was informed by local experiences of 'the rule of law.' In the Cold War context, in which Idi Amin established the Commission of Inquiry in response to the powerful pressure of international human rights advocates,[104] it is remarkable that the

95 See this in term of reference 'e' of *Legal Notice No 2*, in Government of Uganda, *The Commission of Inquiry Act (Cap. 56), Legal Notice No 2*, 2.

96 1974 Commission of Inquiry, *Final Report*, 781. 97 Ibid, 782–783.

98 Carver, "Called to Account," 398. See also, 1974 Commission of Inquiry, *Final Report*, 782–783.

99 Ibid. 100 1974 Commission of Inquiry, *Final Report*, 783. 101 Ibid. 102 Ibid.

103 Ibid, 781. In the Final Report's recommendations, the commissioners argued that the Director of Public Prosecutions, whose office had criminal jurisdiction, would be the appropriate official to determine the legal consequences for the persons listed by the commission as being involved in the disappearances. See, ibid, 787.

104 See notes 11 and 45 above. On Cold War politics in the Third World see generally, Odd Arne Westad, *The Global Cold War.*

Commissioners found a way to give local legal meaning and authority to their findings. The Commissioners did that in two ways: (a) by establishing a hierarchy between local law and international law; and (b) by giving meaning to the concept of 'rule of law' through Ugandans local experiences of state violence.

As the Final Report records in its first pages, the commissioners explicitly established a hierarchy between Ugandan law and international law. This can be seen in how the International Commission of Jurists' 1974 Uganda Report[105] is placed 'below' the Commission of Inquiry's own Final Report. Although the commissioners acknowledged that there were similarities and "obvious" differences in the experiences told by their witnesses and those of the International Commission of Jurists,[106] they established a clear legal hierarchy between both accounts. Tellingly, the commissioners not only included the International Commission of Jurists' Report as an annex to the Final Report,[107] but also stated in their Report:

> All we would like to say is that before anybody, who is interested in what happened, comes to any final conclusions, he should read the [International Commission of] Jurists' Report in the light of our Report, and as our Report is based on sworn testimony of witnesses, it should be preferred to the ICJ [International Commission of Jurists] Report wherever there is conflict and divergence between them.[108]

This explicit hierarchy between the reports was a clear attempt by the Commission to place Ugandan law and Ugandan accounts above international human rights law and the International Commission of Jurists' account.

In sum, while the International Commission of Jurists' Report established that the Ugandan disappearances were "violations of human rights and the rule of law,"[109] the Commission of Inquiry's Final Report

[105] 1974 Commission of Inquiry, *Final Report*, 703. [106] Ibid.

[107] The Final Report states that the International Commission of Jurists' Report was submitted to the Commission by its counsel after witness hearings were over. The Final Report does not specify whether this counsel is Joseph Mulenga or someone else who also advised the Commission. See, ibid, 7–8; 703.

[108] Ibid, 703.

[109] Posner and International Commission of Jurists, "Violations of Human Rights," 1.

established that they were the outcome of certain public servants' breach of the rule of law through an "unlawful" exercise of public "responsibility."[110] Therefore, the commissioners argued, the disappearances were 'unlawful' because they were the outcome of individuals' conduct that breached Ugandan laws.

At the same time, the commissioners' gave meaning to the concept of 'the rule of law' by connecting it to Ugandans' experiences of state violence. The commissioners did this by using the testimonies of witnesses, victims, and survivors to show the consequences of the disappearances for Ugandans. In the Final Report, the commissioners refer to these testimonies to describe how soldiers, immediately after the 1972 coup, "over-step[ped]" their authority without considering if their conduct was "justified or unjustified" by the decrees that regulated their public service as army officers.[111] In doing so, the commissioners framed the actions of the soldiers as a matter of "the supremacy of the Rule of Law."[112] The commissioners concluded that the decrees regulating the soldiers' conduct did not contravene the rule of law. Rather, the practices of the soldiers were not "in the spirit of the law as promulgated."[113] If the soldiers had acted lawfully, then "the Rule of Law would have reigned supreme and the citizens would have nothing to fear."[114] The Final Report also discussed the activities of the Military Police not only against Ugandans but also in conducting unjustified detentions of fellow police officers.[115] The commissioners concluded that the evidence showed that the Military Police's practices contravened the "Rule of Law," as set out in the decrees regulating their public service.[116] The investigation of the activities of the Intelligence Officers of the Army also showed that they did not comply with relevant legal provisions.[117]

As this shows, while the commissioners considered that the Commission of Inquiry was not authorized to determine criminal responsibility, it was authorized to investigate 'unlawfulness,' and the extent to which state officials had acted in violation of the rule of law. In other

[110] 1974 Commission of Inquiry, *Final Report*, 781. [111] Ibid, 712–722.
[112] Ibid, 714–715. [113] Ibid, 715. [114] Ibid. [115] Ibid, 722–723; 728.
[116] Ibid, 724; 728. [117] Ibid, 728–732.

words, in this account, the disappearances were 'unlawful' because they were the outcome of conduct by individuals that breached Ugandan laws.

In his 1990 article, Richard Carver gives a different account. For Carver the 1974 Commission of Inquiry contributed to "alleviating human rights abuse," and it did so in three ways. First, "for as long as" the Commission of Inquiry "was sitting," the "'disappearances' were reduced significantly."[118] Second, the account established by the Commission of Inquiry could be used as "evidence to refute" the "revisionist views of the 1970s in Uganda, attempting a partial rehabilitation of Amin."[119] And third, although no evidence is provided to support this claim, it was Mulenga's experience as counsel to the 1974 Commission of Inquiry which "presumably" informed the 1986 "new Commission of Inquiry into Human Rights Violations," which operated when Mulenga was Attorney General of Uganda in 1986.[120]

Carver briefly discusses the relationship between the 1974 Commission of Inquiry and the 1986 Human Rights Inquiry. In Carver's view, the "mandate" of the 1986 Human Rights Inquiry made "a clear and correct distinction between human rights abuse and maladministration."[121] Moreover, "a strength" of the 1986 Human Rights Inquiry was that it was "able to investigate reports by other bodies, such as non-governmental human rights organizations."[122] This goes to the point made earlier, that the 1974 Commission of Inquiry had established a hierarchical order between its account and the International Commission of Jurists' account, and between domestic law and international law. Under this hierarchy, international human rights law was not included in the 1974 Commission of Inquiry (as it "should" have been, according to Carver).[123] As discussed above, the Final Report of the 1974 Commission of Inquiry did not work with the language of human rights, nor did it turn to international human rights law for authority.[124] This is what makes the 1986 Commission of Inquiry into Human Rights Violations especially important for Carver – its contribution to "hold[ing]" an African government "accountable" to international human rights law.[125] It was also, however, the promise, and

[118] Carver, "Called to Account," 400. [119] Ibid. [120] Ibid, 399. [121] Ibid, 412.
[122] Ibid. [123] Ibid. [124] See generally, 1974 Commission of Inquiry, *Final Report*.
[125] Carver, "Called to Account," 394.

indeed contribution, in Carver's account, of the 1974 Commission of Inquiry, even if that earlier institution had fallen short.

5.4 REDESCRIBING 1974 COMMISSION OF INQUIRY AS THE 'INAUGURAL' TRUTH COMMISSION

In 1994 Priscilla Hayner published her influential article, "Fifteen Truth Commissions – 1974 to 1994: A Comparative Study,"[126] in which she identified Uganda's 1974 Commission of Inquiry as the world's first yet "forgotten" Truth Commission.[127] As the title suggests,[128] the aim of Hayner's article is to "describ[e]" and "compar[e]" investigatory institutions that are "examples of truth commissions," from 1974 to 1994.[129] The year 1974 of course corresponds to Uganda's 1974 Commission of Inquiry, which Hayner names the "first truth commission."[130] The year 1994 corresponds to the year of the article's publication, which, as Hayner notes, coincided with the announcement of the establishment of South Africa's Truth and Reconciliation Commission, as well as Guatemala's UN Truth Commission.[131]

The influence of Priscilla Hayner's 1994 article cannot be reduced to the fact that it was the first comprehensive survey of Truth Commissions. At the time Hayner also had considerable professional authority based on her first-hand experience in some of the most important Truth Commissions of the twentieth century, including the first UN-run Truth Commission – El Salvador's 1992 UN Truth Commission.[132] By

126 Hayner, "Fifteen Truth Commissions." 127 Ibid, 601; 608; 611–613. 128 Ibid.
129 Ibid, 599. 130 Ibid, 608. 131 Ibid, 598.
132 Hayner, *Unspeakable Truths: Transitional Justice*, xvi at 2. For a fascinating analysis of the involvement and influence of international experts, including Priscilla Hayner, non-profit international organizations (e.g., International Center for Transitional Justice), and wealthy philanthropic foundations (e.g., Ford Foundation) in mobilizing Truth Commissions and other transitional justice institutions around the world to "realize their goals," see Rowen, *Searching for Truth*, 4; 28–29; 32–56. For an informative (and celebratory) overview of Truth Commissions' 'insiders' experiences in the Truth Commission of South Africa and Guatemala, including Hayner's involvement and contribution to promoting Truth Commissions globally, see generally, Joanna R. Quinn and Mark Freeman, "Lessons Learned: Practical Lessons Gleaned from inside the Truth Commissions of Guatemala and South Africa," *Human Rights Quarterly*, vol 25, no 4 (2003).

1994, Hayner was already gaining international prominence as the leading expert on this novel post-conflict institution,[133] to which she gave the name "Truth Commission."[134]

In her 1994 article, while Hayner describes Truth Commissions as "*national* human rights commissions," or as "*national* truth commissions," she does not examine them in isolation from one another.[135] Hayner views these investigatory institutions from a global perspective, which draws them into a particular relation.[136] To achieve this coherence, Hayner's survey identifies, arranges and describes in chronological order the fifteen 'Truth Commissions' that have operated between 1974 and 1994.[137]

Hayner begins the discussion of each of the "Fifteen Truth Commissions" with "Uganda 1974." In this subsection, Hayner devotes roughly three pages to the 1974 Commission of Inquiry.[138] Here Hayner first briefly repeats background facts. She focuses, for example, on Idi Amin's role, the legal instruments he used to authorize the Commission, and the hurdles that the Commissioners faced from the government.[139] Until this point, the 1974 Commission of Inquiry is only referred to as "the commission."[140] Hayner then refers to the 1974 Commission of Inquiry as a Truth Commission by linking it to the growing family of Truth Commissions ("[a]s with most truth commissions, this commission clearly perceived its role as one of investigating disappearances, but not as serving a judicial criminal function").[141] Importantly, the link between the 1974 Commission of Inquiry with other existing Truth Commissions seems to arise from two shared features. These two features can be found in the broad "defining parameters" of Truth Commissions that Hayner puts forward in the 1994 article: (1) as "bodies set up to investigate a past history of violations of human rights in a particular country,"[142] and (2)

[133] UN Doc S/25500 (1 April 1993), *Letter dated 93/03/29 from the Secretary-General addressed to the President of the Security Council* (*From Madness to Hope: The 12-year war in El Salvador: Report of the Commission on the Truth for El Salvador*), 194; Hayner, *Unspeakable Truths: Transitional Justice*, xviii–xix.

[134] Hayner, "Fifteen Truth Commissions," 598. On Hayner coining the name 'Truth Commission,' see also Rowen, *Searching for Truth*, 28 at 16.

[135] Hayner, "Fifteen Truth Commissions," 598; 600. [136] Ibid, 598–599.

[137] Ibid, 611–635. [138] Ibid, 611–613. [139] Ibid, 611–612. [140] Ibid, 598–611.

[141] Ibid, 612. [142] Ibid, 600.

that "must be distinguished from the formal legal accountability achieved through the prosecution of individuals responsible for abuses."[143] While, the 1974 Commission of Inquiry fits within those two general parameters for a Truth Commission, it was at odds with a third fundamental element of Hayner's definition: its authority.

Hayner's argument here is that "a truth commission is always vested with some sort of authority, by way of its sponsor, that allows it greater access to information, greater security or protection to dig into sensitive issues, and a greater impact with its report."[144] For Hayner, 'authority' is drawn from the Truth Commission's "sponso[r]," which is "the executive branch of the legislative branch" or "[i]n the alternative a truth commission can be sponsored internationally, by the United Nations or by nongovernmental organizations."[145] In other words, 'authority' for Hayner seems to be what I call in Chapter 1 of this book the 'legal-institutional authority' that authorizes the establishment and operation of a Truth Commission. Indeed, as discussed in Section 5.2 of this chapter, the 1974 Commission of Inquiry was established through a legal instrument (*Legal Notice No 2*) authorized by Idi Amin. Based also on that understanding of legal-institutional authority, Hayner categorized the 1974 Commission of Inquiry as a Truth Commission while excluding other inquiries, "because they [were] not authorized in some way by the government or other official body."[146] Yet, the source of legal-institutional authority of the 1974 Commission of Inquiry was also deeply linked to Idi Amin's own personal-reputational authority. In Chapter 1, I explained that this latter source of authority of Truth Commissions relies on the moral and political standing of those fundamentally involved in lending authority to a Truth Commission. In the 1974 Commission of Inquiry this manifests in, as Hayner states, the fact that "Idi Amin set up a commission party in response to pressure from international human rights organizations. But Amin disregarded the commission's report, and continued his brutal rule."[147] We see here how – as is the case in any other Truth Commission – ultimately, without Idi Amin's "political will" the 1974 Commission of Inquiry would not have been established.[148] Indeed, that is a part of the story of the 1974

[143] Ibid, 604 [144] Ibid, 604. [145] Ibid, 603–604. [146] Ibid, 651. [147] Ibid, 608.
[148] Ibid, 608.

Commission of Inquiry that is hard to ignore. We can see this too in Hayner's lament that "[t]he commission was set up without any political will or commitment to real change in human rights policy or practice."[149] What is telling is that, in spite of that, the 1974 Commission of Inquiry is still considered a Truth Commission. Why, or rather, how?

Part of the answer can be found in a subtle gesture to toward cutting or separating the 1974 Commission of Inquiry's institutional life from Idi Amin's lack of personal-reputational authority. This gesture can be seen in how Hayner draws on Carver's "silver lining around a very dark cloud" to argue that "the importance of" the 1974 Commission of Inquiry rests on its role "of establishing historical record alone" which "should not be underrated."[150] Hayner then speculates that because the "commission worked under, and made recommendations to, the same government that it was investigating . . . its first priority *was probably* to try to prevent future abuses by government forces."[151] This seems to be for Hayner a goal linked with the broader goals of international human rights because achieving the institutional change proposed by the Commission "*could potentially* have been done by influencing the government's willingness (through public denunciation of the abuses) or its ability (through recommended reforms) to continue the same abuses."[152] And indeed, those were practices associated with the practices of the international human rights movements at that time – notably in this case, of the International Commission of Jurists. Nevertheless, Hayner acknowledges that while the 1974 Commission of Inquiry and its "report had little impact,"[153] its importance should be remembered.

What is especially important about Hayner's 1994 redescription of the 1974 Commission of Inquiry is the international legal standpoint from which she speaks, or authors her account. It is this international legal position, I argue, that authorizes the categorization of Uganda's 1974 Commission of Inquiry as "the first Truth Commission."[154] Her account appears to draw exclusively on Carver's description in his 1990 article. This can be seen in Hayner's reference to Carver's article for the details

[149] Ibid, 613. [150] Ibid, 613. [151] Ibid, 613. Italics mine.
[152] Ibid, 613. Italics mine. [153] Ibid, 612. [154] Ibid, 601; 608; 611–613.

of the 1974 Commission of Inquiry,[155] as well as the fact that, out of the six footnotes that substantiate Hayner's account, Carver's 1990 article is the sole source in five of them.[156] But it is also important to pay attention to how Hayner frames her account of Uganda's 1974 Commission of Inquiry (as well as her account of the subsequent fourteen Truth Commissions).

For Hayner, part of the significance of her article was its timeliness. The early 1990s was a time when investigatory institutions were "being considered in a number of other countries . . . in the midst of political transitions."[157] In this context, Hayner's task was to reflect back on the disparate national or state-authorized investigatory institutions that had been used over the past two decades, and give them a shared identity that would help her contemporary institution-builders. In Hayner's account, that shared identity is the institutions' relation to international law and its institutions. From Hayner's standpoint, Truth Commissions are part of an international legal order whose institutions and actors support and promote compliance with international law.[158] Throughout Hayner's article, this international law comprises above all international human rights law, international humanitarian law, the principles of the rule of law, as well as a novel 'right to truth' (based on Article 19 of the Universal Declaration of Human Rights (UDHR)).[159]

This international legal standpoint, from which Hayner authors her account of Truth Commissions, can be seen for example in the definition of Truth Commissions that Hayner uses to open her article. Truth Commissions, she writes, are "bodies set up to investigate a past period of *human rights* abuses or violations of *international humanitarian law*."[160] Tellingly, this general definition of Truth Commissions is informed above all by El Salvador's 1992–1993 UN-run Truth Commission, which was at that time the most recent Truth Commission and one on which Hayner had worked closely.[161] There is a striking similarity, and even

155 Ibid, 612 at 20. 156 Ibid, 611–613 at 20–24. 157 Ibid, 598.

158 See note 136 above. See also, Neier, *The International Human Rights Movement*, 254–264.

159 See for example in, Hayner, "Fifteen Truth Commissions," 600; 604; 608–609; 611. See also, Arthur, "How 'Transitions' Reshaped Human Rights."

160 Hayner, "Fifteen Truth Commissions," 598; 600; 604. Italics mine.

161 Ibid, 598–599.

symmetry, between Hayner's general definition of Truth Commissions, and her description of El Salvador's UN Truth Commission, which she understood as having a direct connection to international law (international human rights law and international humanitarian law). This can be seen in how, following her general definition of Truth Commissions, Hayner uses the same words to describe El Salvador's UN Truth Commission. For Hayner, El Salvador's UN Truth Commission was: "in many ways *a classic truth commission*: the commission, established as part of the peace agreement between the government and armed opposition in El Salvador, was given eight months to write a report *outlining the extent of human rights abuses* and *international humanitarian law* over twelve years of civil war."[162]

In this account, the relationship between Truth Commissions and international law is not incidental or minor – it is what makes the investigatory institution a Truth Commission.

It is also interesting to note how Hayner connects the Salvadoran UN Truth Commission with the Truth Commissions of Argentina (1983–1984) and Chile (1990–1991),[163] in a way that brings these three investigatory institutions together as part of a shared international legal order.[164] Hayner explains that the "idea for [El Salvador's] truth commission was based on the experiences of Chile and Argentina,"[165] which, in Hayner's account, were "the most well-known previous cases of national human rights commissions set up to investigate the past."[166] In this, international law – especially human rights – is the link that holds together three institutions which had been created, not only in different times and places, but also by three different legal authorities (two states, and the UN through a peace agreement between a state and a guerrilla group).[167]

Hayner makes international law integral to Truth Commissions through another framing move. Before proceeding to describe each of the fifteen Truth Commissions,[168] Hayner aligns the purpose for the

[162] Ibid, 599. Italics mine. [163] Ibid. [164] Ibid. [165] Ibid. [166] Ibid.

[167] Hayner discusses in detail the "defining parameters" of Truth Commissions in, ibid, 600–611. Note that this is Hayner's original articulation, which is also in the 2001 book. As I also show in this chapter, in response to Mark Freeman's critique, in 2011 Hayner updates the original 1994 and 2001 definitions of Truth Commissions.

[168] Ibid, 599.

existence of Truth Commissions with the normative 'universal' aims of international law. Hayner does this by addressing the "right to truth."[169] Hayner explains that "[h]uman rights advocates have recently begun to focus on an inherent right to truth in existing human rights law," and that "[i]nternational human rights law obliges states to investigate and punish violations of human rights."[170] Hayner then sharpens this by adding that a country's "citizenry" has an "inherent right" to "know the results of such investigations."[171] At this point Hayner's article explicitly draws on Richard Carver's human rights advocacy work through an organization called ARTICLE 19.[172] This organization, as its name suggests, focused on promoting the implementation of Article 19 of the UDHR, on the right to freedom of information and expression.[173] As Hayner highlights, Carver, in his work with ARTICLE 19, interpreted the UDHR's Article 19 as protecting "a 'right to know the truth' which is contained within the right to 'seek, receive and impart information.'"[174]

Hayner notes that "other human rights advocates" had suggested a similar interpretation in the context of the 1988 case *Velásquez Rodríguez v Honduras* before the Inter-American Court of Human Rights,[175] "which concluded that the state has a duty to investigate the fate of the disappeared and disclose the information to relatives."[176]

[169] Ibid, 611. For an analysis of the 'right to truth,' including its relationship with Truth Commissions, see generally Melanie Klinkner and Howard Davis, *The Right to the Truth in International Law: Victims' Rights in Human Rights and International Criminal Law* (Routledge, 2020).

[170] Hayner, "Fifteen Truth Commissions," 611. [171] Ibid.

[172] Ibid. Hayner also cites Frank LaRue, but only quotes Carver's work in ibid, 611 at 19. The name of the organization is stylized in capital letters.

[173] Ibid. See also, ARTICLE 19's website. www.article19.org. [174] Ibid, 611.

[175] Inter-American Court of Human Rights, *Case of Velásquez Rodríguez v Honduras, Velásquez Rodríguez v Honduras*, Merits, IACHR Series C No 4, [1988] IACHR 1, (1989) 28 ILM 291, (1988) 9 HRLJ 212, IHRL 1385 (IACHR 1988) (29 July 1988). As Klinkner and Davis note, the Inter-American Court has been fundamental in the development of the 'right to truth.' See in Klinkner and Davis, *The Right to the Truth in International Law*, 102–122.

[176] Hayner, "Fifteen Truth Commissions," 611. See also, Inter-American Court of Human Rights, *Case of Velásquez Rodríguez v Honduras*. Interestingly, Mark Freeman also draws on this decision (and other international norms and resolutions) to connect a 'right to truth or to know' with Truth Commissions in, Freeman, *Truth Commissions*, 7–10.

Although Hayner does not say who those "human rights advocates" were,[177] Carver mentions this case in his 1990 "Called to Account" article.[178] Interestingly, two Inter-American Court judges in the case went on to have prominent roles in El Salvador's UN-run Truth Commission (1992–1993).[179]

Following the success of her 1994 article, in 1996 Hayner published another article to provide an update on recent developments. While the focus of the 1996 article is more general, Hayner devotes a short paragraph of six sentences to the 1974 Commission of Inquiry. Here too, Hayner redescribes the 1974 Commission of Inquiry as a Truth Commission. But this time, compared to the 1994 article the analysis draws a more explicit conclusion about the 1974 Commission of Inquiry. Hayner concludes that from the 1974 Commission of Inquiry "we learn that a truth commission can sometimes be set up as a whitewash, projecting the image of a concern for rights, satisfying the donors who provide aid, but representing no will to change."[180] In this we can see how, while Idi Amin's lack of personal-reputation authority did compromise the success of the 1974 Commission of Inquiry for Hayner, it could still be considered a Truth Commission – a point that became the subject of debate a few years later.

In 2001 Hayner published the first edition of her path-breaking book, originally titled *Unspeakable Truths: Confronting State Terror and Atrocity.*[181] The book expands, revisits, and updates many of the ideas initially explored and presented in the 1994 and 1996 articles.[182] One of those

[177] Hayner, "Fifteen Truth Commissions," 611. [178] Carver, "Called to Account," 414.

[179] The UN Secretary-General appointed Thomas Buergenthal (from the US) as one of the three commissioners of El Salvador's UN Truth Commission. Buergenthal was also the chair of the Truth Commission. Pedro Nikken (from Venezuela) assisted the Truth Commission with "extensive" "knowledge of Central America." See in, UN Doc S/25500 (1 April 1993), *From Madness to Hope,* 5; 17. Nikken's legal expertise on human rights gave him sufficient credentials at the UN to be asked later in 1995 to go to Burundi to assess the possibilities of establishing a Truth Commission there. See, UN Doc S/1995/631 (28 July 1995), *Letter dated 95/07/28 from the Secretary-General addressed to the President of the Security Council.*

[180] Priscilla B. Hayner, "Commissioning the Truth: Further Research Questions," *Third World Quarterly,* vol 17, no 1 (1996), 24.

[181] Hayner, *Unspeakable Truths: Confronting.*

[182] See generally, Hayner, *Unspeakable Truths: Transitional Justice.* Hayner explains some of the conceptual changes between the 2001 and 2011 editions in, ibid, xv–xvi; 10–13.

ideas is the reassertion of Uganda's 1974 Commission of Inquiry as the 'inaugural' Truth Commission.[183] Before specifically discussing the 1974 Commission of Inquiry in the book, Hayner mentions it alongside the Truth Commissions in Uruguay and Zimbabwe. She describes them as Truth Commissions that "provide good examples of how not to put together a truth commission."[184] The main discussion of the 1974 Commission of Inquiry is included under the subheading "Uganda 1974" in Chapter five, titled "Sixteen Less-Prominent Truth Commissions."[185] Yet, before discussing each Truth Commission in this chapter, Hayner provides a short introduction in which she describes those Truth Commissions as being "more modest" (while "not all were successful" they nonetheless "offer[ed] important lessons").[186] The dedicated discussion of the 1974 Commission of Inquiry reproduces a shorter version of the 1996 article's analysis. But in the chapter's introduction, Hayner provides readers with important insights into the 1974 Commission of Inquiry: "set up with the primary purpose of heading off international criticism ... while that commission made every attempt to carry out a serious investigation, it became clear that the president's interests were not based in advancing human rights."[187] We see here how, once again, there was an expectation (perhaps even a hope) of advancing human rights through the operation of the 1974 Commission of Inquiry – even if it was authorized by Idi Amin who could not lend his personal-reputational authority to its resulting account. Rather, despite that, it could have been international human rights that would give the 1974 Commission of Inquiry authority to deliver a lawful account.

In the book's second edition (2011), the discussion of the 1974 Commission of Inquiry, along with other "[l]ess-[p]rominent" Truth Commissions, is moved to Appendix 1, under the title "Other Truth Commissions Described." There, Hayner reproduces what used to be chapter five of the 2001 book. In Appendix I, as in the 2001 edition, we once again find reproduced a short version of the 1996 article's analysis of the 1974 Commission of Inquiry. The decision to move this discussion to the book's appendix might suggest that, given its shortcomings, the

[183] Ibid, xi; 239–241; 335 at 5. [184] Hayner, *Unspeakable Truths: Confronting*, 15.
[185] Ibid, 50–71. [186] Ibid, 50. [187] Ibid, 51.

importance of the 1974 Commission of Inquiry is being downplayed. Yet, unlike the 2001 edition, the 2011 edition does include at the beginning of the book a timeline of Truth Commissions, in which the 1974 Commission of Inquiry features as the first of forty Truth Commissions. That became a point of contention for the prominent Canadian human rights lawyer, Mark Freeman, in his 2006 book *Truth Commissions and Procedural Fairness.*[188] Without entering into an extensive discussion of Freeman's book, what is relevant for the purposes of this chapter is that one of Freeman's main critiques of Hayner's definition, and her list of Truth Commissions, is that Hayner includes Uganda's 1974 Commission of Inquiry.[189] For Freeman, Truth Commissions are in essence "one form of human rights investigation," which necessarily excludes Uganda's 1974 Commission of Inquiry from the definition of Truth Commissions.[190] According to Freeman, Uganda's 1974 Commission of Inquiry was a case of institutional "displacement or reversal."[191] By that he means that, sometimes there can be an investigatory institution that has all the "virtues" of a Truth Commission,[192] and for that reason "some might have previously considered [it] to be" one. However, when another investigatory institution is established, which not only "conforms with the technical definition" of Truth Commission,[193] but also has "broad domestic and international consensus that it is a truth commission,"[194] then that "proper" Truth Commission "displaces" the earlier institution.[195] In Freeman's view, Uganda's 1974 Commission of Inquiry was the earlier institution, which was "displaced" by the 1986 Commission of Inquiry into Violations of Human Rights,[196] which was explicitly established to investigate human rights violations.[197] For Freeman, Uganda's 1986 Commission of Inquiry is "the only truth commission" that has operated in Uganda.[198]

188 Freeman, *Truth Commissions.*

189 Freeman dedicates several pages at the beginning of his book to explicitly challenge Hayner's definition of Truth Commissions (and does it again in other sections). Freeman does that by challenging each sentence of Hayner's definition. See in ibid, 12–22.

190 Ibid, 3. 191 Ibid, 20–21. 192 Ibid, 21. 193 Ibid. 194 Ibid, 21–22.

195 Ibid, 20. 196 Ibid, 20–21.

197 Government of Uganda, *The Commission of Inquiry Act (Cap. 56), Legal Notice No 5* (26 May 1986).

198 Freeman, *Truth Commissions*, 21.

The point here is that the debate between Freeman and Hayner over whether Uganda's 1974 Commission of Inquiry is a Truth Commission turns on its connection to international human rights. As I have shown, for Hayner it is a Truth Commission *because of* its role in advancing international human rights (as Carver had initially argued in his 1990 article).[199] And for Freeman, Uganda's 1974 Commission of Inquiry is not a Truth Commission because it was institutionally "displaced" by another Commission of Inquiry that was *itself* explicitly connected to international human rights.[200] Either way, what would or would not make Uganda's 1974 Commission of Inquiry the 'inaugural' Truth Commission is its connection to human rights – a connection that is found lacking in Freeman's account but sufficiently present in Hayner's. And in doing so, we can see how fundamental international law has been to authorizing even the very 'beginning' of Truth Commissions.

5.5 CONCLUSION

When I began the research for this book, in 2017, I was intrigued by what made Uganda's 1974 Commission of Inquiry the inaugural Truth Commission. What was it that connected its institutional history to that of the internationally successful Truth Commissions in Argentina, Chile, and El Salvador? My argument in this chapter is that the three telling moments in the institutional life of the 1974 Commission of Inquiry help to trace and understand how international law came to provide the foundation of a shared 'origins story' for what would otherwise be unrelated institutions. Truth Commissions did not have an institutional origin story until Hayner's article in 1994, which joined the 1974 Commission of Inquiry to an (international) family of Truth Commissions, with the link provided by international law, and human rights in particular. From the 'beginning,' then, it is international law that has enabled Truth Commissions to be an indispensable post-conflict institution, which transcends time, place, histories, and peoples at the same time as they are

[199] Carver, "Called to Account."

[200] Freeman, *Truth Commissions*, 21–22; Wiebelhaus-Brahm, *Truth Commissions and Transitional Societies*, 188 at 1.

presented in research and in practice as national institutions that are established as a result of locally led, public initiatives to address conflicts with their own specific backgrounds. If we are to celebrate, establish, and promote Truth Commissions, then we need to take seriously their tendency to draw, for better and for worse, on international law to authorize their accounts as truth.

CHAPTER 6

Conclusion: Truth Commissions and the Authority of International Law

THIS BOOK HAS OFFERED READERS an invitation to reconsider the relationship between Truth Commissions and international law. Through a close study of three of the most influential Truth Commissions of the twentieth century – Argentina's (1983–1984), Chile's (1990–1991), and El Salvador's (1992–1993) – as well as the putatively 'inaugural' Truth Commission, Uganda's 1974 Commission of Inquiry, it has offered a way of understanding Truth Commissions as post-conflict institutions that both harness and strengthen the authority of international law. The analysis has shown how these Truth Commissions drew on international law in different ways in 'authoring' their work, and how in each case the relationship worked to authorize the Truth Commissions' accounts of the causes and nature of past violence, and the Truth Commissions' visions for post-conflict state-society relations. In the case of Argentina, the Truth Commission invoked international law's post-conflict promises (Chapter 2); in Chile, it used international law's human rights language (Chapter 3); and in El Salvador, it authorized its account as the truth by linking its existence and operation to the identity and status of the United Nations (Chapter 4). The final substantive chapter (Chapter 5) contributes to this argument by showing how, in the 1990s, Truth Commissions were given an authoritative 'origins story' through the retrospective redescription of Uganda's 1974 Commission of Inquiry as an institution that advanced international human rights.

Taken together, these chapters show how, in the complex post-conflict contexts in which the Truth Commissions were established and operated, it became fundamental to connect their *raison d'être* to a 'higher' legal-institutional authority that transcended the conflicted state. This was necessary to give the Truth Commissions public credibility, and to generate sociopolitical trust in their findings, and by extension, to ensure credibility and trust in the post-conflict states and their new institutions. At the same time, the analysis shows how the authority of international law was also strengthened in the process. By drawing on international law's post-conflict promises, language, and the identity and status of its institutions, the Truth Commissions were 'authorizing' international law as the normative framework for peaceful coexistence within the post-conflict state.

In itself this is an important finding. But it becomes even more significant when one considers the consequences for the quality of state-society relations. At the heart of this 'authorizing' project is the need to ensure that the Truth Commissions' accounts are accepted as the truth – a project that has involved deauthorizing 'other' context-specific accounts. As I showed through the studies of Argentina, Chile, and El Salvador, the ways in which the Truth Commissions drew on international law to authorize their accounts as 'the truth' tended to re-narrate context-specific histories and experiences of violent events as stories of international law. Not only were the violent events represented in terms of international law (for example, as violations of universal human rights), but so too was the overcoming of violent conflict represented in terms of the global-historical triumph of international law. To the extent that local actors, including the respective post-conflict governments, were narrated as having played a part in this 'global' history, their roles and their triumphs were tied to their engagement with international law. This is significant because it has contributed to an ongoing displacement and silencing in public life of truths that rival or complicate the international legal narrative. This can be seen throughout the chapters in the ways in which the accounts of Indigenous peoples, women, peasants, and social justice activists have been, and continue to be, silenced or displaced from public life by the Truth Commissions. In short, if the overarching contribution of the book is to draw attention to a relationship of authority between Truth Commissions and international law, then the underlying contribution is to draw attention to how that relationship of authority can work to deauthorize 'other' truths, with harmful consequences for the shape and quality of state-society relations.

As a matter of methodology, the book also contributes to the study of Truth Commissions as an institution with an ongoing presence in public life. As the three core chapters show, the fact that Truth Commissions cease to have an official physical presence in public life once their work has concluded does not constrain their potential transformative power. On the contrary, these temporal and material qualities of Truth Commissions are integral to their transformative power. Put simply, the work of the Truth Commissions examined in this book did not end with the delivery of their Final Report, but has continued through a broad range of public cultural institutions and objects. In the language of 'jurisdiction,' it is through the jurisdictional technique of representation that the Truth Commissions have been able to continue to author and authorize their accounts, in ways that continue to shape how the past should be remembered and the future envisioned. This can be seen through the studies of the literary prologue in Argentina and the museum of memory in Chile, while the tapestry in El Salvador can be seen to contest the account of the truth established by the United Nations Truth Commission. By focusing the analysis on these representations of truth and authority, the book has been able to show how the Truth Commissions' accounts were given a prominent and privileged place in the post-conflict states' public life, and how this has displaced or silenced 'other' accounts.

It is increasingly common in the research on, and practices of, transitional justice and international law to include 'local' or contextual representations of violent events in the processes and operations of post-conflict institutions. My analysis of the textual, spatial, and visual representations of truth and authority in the Argentinian literary prologue, the Chilean museum of memory, and the Salvadoran tapestry, is an invitation to reconsider what work this is doing. In particular, it shows the importance of paying attention to who is authorizing the inclusion of cultural expressions of violent conflict; who benefits from it; and what ends it serves. In paying attention to these questions, this book offers a way of examining – textually, visually, and spatially – how context-specific truths account for violent events, and how they can be deauthorized by their inclusion in the processes and operations of international post-conflict institutions.

Select Bibliography

Abrego, Leisy J., "On Silences: Salvadoran Refugees Then and Now," *Latino Studies*, vol 15, no 1 (2017).

Sacrificing Families: Navigating Laws, Labor, and Love across Borders (Stanford University Press, 2014).

Adams, Jacqueline, *Art against Dictatorship: Making and Exporting Arpilleras under Pinochet* (University of Texas Press, 2013).

Agosín, Marjorie, "Agujas Que Hablan: Las Arpilleristas Chilenas," *Revista Iberoamericana*, vol 51, no 132–133 (1985).

"Patchwork of Memory," *NACLA Report on the Americas*, vol 27, no 6 (1994).

Tapestries of Hope, Threads of Love: The Arpillera Movement in Chile (Rowman & Littlefield Publishers, 2008).

Aguiló, Ignacio, *The Darkening Nation: Race, Neoliberalism and Crisis in Argentina* (University of Wales Press, 2018).

Aksenova, Marina, Tanja Aalberts, Karima Bennoune, Emiliano J. Buis, Mark A. Drumbl, Maria Elander, Rachel Kerr, and Sofia Stolk, "AJIL Unbound by Symposium: Art, Aesthetics, and International Justice," *AJIL Unbound*, vol 114 (2020).

Alfonsín, Raúl, *Memoria Política: Transición a la Democracia y Derechos Humanos; con prólogo de Juan Carlos Portantiero* (Fondo de Cultura Económica, 2009).

"Prólogo," in *Juicio Al Mal Absoluto: ¿Hasta Dónde Debe Llegar la Justicia Retroactiva en Casos de Violaciones Masivas de los Derechos Humanos?*, Carlos Santiago Nino, trans by Martín Böhmer (Siglo Veintiuno Editores, 1996; 2015).

Allen, Peter, *Days of Judgment: A Judge in Idi Amin's Uganda* (William Kimber, 1987).

Amaya, Rufina, with Carlos 'Santiago' Henríquez Consalvi and Mark Danner, *Luciérnagas en El Mozote* (Ediciones Museo de la Palabra y la Imagen, 1996).

Andermann, Jens, "Showcasing Dictatorship: Memory and the Museum in Argentina and Chile," *Journal of Educational Media, Memory, and Society*, vol 4, no 2 (2012).

Andermann, Jens, and Silke Arnold-de Simine, "Introduction: Memory, Community and the New Museum," *Theory, Culture & Society*, vol 29, no 1 (2012).

"Introduction: Museums and the Educational Turn: History, Memory, Inclusivity," *Journal of Educational Memory, Media, and Society*, vol 4, no 2 (2012).

Anghie, Antony, *Imperialism, Sovereignty and the Making of International Law* (Cambridge University Press, 2005).

Anghie, Antony, and B. S. Chimni, "Third World Approaches to International Law and Individual Responsibility in Internal Conflicts," *Chinese Journal of International Law*, vol 2, no 1 (2003).

Anker, Elizabeth S., *Fictions of Dignity: Embodying Human Rights in World Literature* (Cornell University Press, 2012).

Anker, Elizabeth S. and Bernadette Meyler (eds), *New Directions in Law and Literature* (Oxford University Press, 2012).

Apter, David E., *The Politics of Modernization* (University of Chicago Press, 1965).

Aristodemou, Maria, *Law and Literature: Journeys from Her to Eternity* (Oxford University Press, 2000).

Arnold-de Simine, Silke, *Mediating Memory in the Museum: Trauma, Empathy, Nostalgia* (Palgrave Macmillan, 2013).

Arthur, Paige, "How 'Transitions' Reshaped Human Rights: A Conceptual History of Transitional Justice," *Human Rights Quarterly*, vol 31, no 2 (2009).

Atria, Fernando, "The Time of Law: Human Rights between Law and Politics," *Law & Critique*, vol 16, no 2 (2005).

Aylwin, Patricio, "El Desafío De Mirar Al Futuro," in *Las Voces De La Reconciliación*, Joaquín Castillo Vial, Hernán Larraín, and Ricardo Nuñez (eds) (Instituto de Estudios de la Sociedad, 2013).

Bak McKenna, Miriam, "Designing for International Law: The Architecture of International Organizations 1922–1952," *Leiden Journal of International Law*, vol 34, no 1 (2020).

Bakiner, Onur, "One Truth among Others? Truth Commissions' Struggle for Truth and Memory," *Memory Studies*, vol 8, no 3 (2015).

"Truth Commission Impact: An Assessment of How Commissions Influence Politics and Society," *International Journal of Transitional Justice*, vol 8, no 1 (2014).

Truth Commissions: Memory, Power, and Legitimacy (University of Pennsylvania Press, 2015).

Bal, Mieke, *Of What One Cannot Speak: Doris Salcedo's Political Art* (University of Chicago Press, 2010).

Balardini, Lorena, "Argentina: Regional Protagonist of Transitional Justice," in *Transitional Justice in Latin America: The Uneven Road from Impunity Towards Accountability*, Cath Collins, Jemima Garcia-Godos, and Elin Skaar (eds) (Routledge, 2016).

Balint, Jennifer, Julie Evans, and Nesam McMillan, "Justice Claims in Colonial Contexts: Commissions of Inquiry in Historical Perspective," *Australian Feminist Law Journal*, vol 42, no 1 (2016).

Baloyra, Enrique, *El Salvador in Transition* (The University of North Carolina Press, 1982).

Barr, Olivia, *A Jurisprudence of Movement: Common Law, Walking, Unsettling Place* (Routledge, 2016).

Basualdo, Carlos, "A Model of Pain," in *Doris Salcedo: Neither*, Rod Mengham and Doris Salcedo (eds) (Jay Jopling/White Cube, 2004).

Beard, Jennifer, *The Political Economy of Desire: International Law, Development and the Nation State* (Routledge, 2007).

Becker Lorca, Arnulf, *Mestizo International Law: A Global Intellectual History 1842–1933* (Cambridge University Press, 2014).

Bedjaoui, Mohammed, *Towards a New International Economic Order* (Holmes & Meier, 1979).

Bell, Vikki, *The Art of Post-Dictatorship: Ethics and Aesthetics in Transitional Argentina* (Routledge, 2014).

Bengoa, José, *Historia Del Pueblo Mapuche: Siglo XIX y XX* (Ediciones Sur, 1987).

Bennett, Tony, *The Birth of the Museum: History, Theory, Politics* (Routledge, 1995).

Berger, John, *Landscapes: John Berger on Art* (Verso; Kindle edition, 2016).

Ways of Seeing (Penguin Books, 2009).

Besson, Samantha, "The Authority of International Law: Lifting the State Veil," *Sydney Law Review*, vol 31, no 3 (2009).

Besson, Samantha, and Jean d'Aspremont (eds), *The Oxford Handbook of the Sources of International Law* (Oxford University Press, 2017).

Bevernage, Berber, *History, Memory, and State-Sponsored Violence: Time and Justice* (Routledge, 2011).

Bhandar, Brenna, *Colonial Lives of Property: Law, Land, and Racial Regimes of Ownership* (Duke University Press, 2018).

Biekart, Kees, "Guillermo O'Donnell's 'Thoughtful Wishing' about Democracy and Regime Change," *Development & Change*, vol 46, no 4 (2015).

Birrell, Kathleen, *Indigeneity: Before and Beyond the Law* (Routledge, 2016).

Bisset, Alison, *Truth Commissions and Criminal Courts* (Cambridge University Press, 2012).

Blum, William, *Killing Hope: US Military and CIA Interventions since World War II* (Common Courage Press, 1995).

Bonner, Raymond, *Weakness and Deceit: US Policy and El Salvador* (Hamish Hamilton, 1985).

Boraine, Alex, *A Country Unmasked: Inside South Africa's Truth and Reconciliation Commission* (Oxford University Press, 2000).

Bowden, Brett, Hilary Charlesworth, and Jeremy Matam Farrall (eds), *The Role of International Law in Rebuilding Societies after Conflict: Great Expectations* (Cambridge University Press, 2009).

Brysk, Alison, *The Politics of Human Rights in Argentina: Protest, Change, and Democratization* (Stanford University Press, 1994).

Buergenthal, Thomas, "The United Nations Truth Commission for El Salvador," *Vanderbilt Journal of Transnational Law*, vol 27, no 3 (1994).

Butler, Judith, "Torture and the Ethics of Photography," *Environment and Planning D: Society and Space*, vol 25, no 6 (2007).

Cagan, Beth, and Steve Cagan, *This Promised Land, El Salvador: The Refugee Community and Their Return to Morazán* (Rutgers University Press, 1991).

Cali, Başak, *The Authority of International Law: Obedience, Respect, and Rebuttal* (Oxford University Press, 2015).

Cantillon, Alain, and Nigel Saint, "Louis Marin: An Introduction," *Early Modern French Studies*, vol 38, no 1 (2016).

Carmody, Michelle Frances, *Human Rights, Transitional Justice, and the Reconstruction of Political Order in Latin America* (Palgrave Macmillan, 2018).

Carothers, Thomas, "The Rule-of-Law Revival," in *In Promoting the Rule of Law Abroad: In Search of Knowledge*, Thomas Carothers (ed) (Carnegie Endowment for International Peace, 2006).

Carozza, Paolo G., "From Conquest to Constitutions: Retrieving a Latin American Tradition of the Idea of Human Rights," *Human Rights Quarterly*, vol 25, no 2 (2003).

Carranza, Marlon, "Los Acuerdos De Paz,15 Años Después: Una Mirada Desde La Opinión Pública," *Estudios Centroamericanos*, vol 62, no 701–702 (2007).

Carver, Richard, "Called to Account: How African Governments Investigate Human Rights Violations," *African Affairs*, vol 89, no 356 (1990).

Cayuqueo, Pedro, *Historia Secreta Mapuche* (Editorial Catalonia, 2018).

Chalmers, Shane, "The Beginning of Human Rights: The Ritual of the Preamble to Law," *Humanity*, vol 9, no 1 (2018).

Liberia and the Dialectic of Law: Critical Theory, Pluralism, and the Rule of Law (Routledge, 2018).

"The Visual Force of Justice in the Making of Liberia," in *Law and the Visual: Representations, Technologies, and Critique*, Desmond Manderson (ed) (University of Toronto Press, 2018).

"The Mythology of International Rule-of-Law Promotion," *Law & Social Inquiry*, vol 44, no 4 (2019).

"The Festival as Constitutional Event and as Jurisdictional Encounter: Colonial Victoria and the Independent Order of Black Fellows," *Griffith Law Review*, vol 30, no 4 (2021).

Chalmers, Shane, and Desmond Manderson, "Vortext," *Law & Literature*, vol 36, no 2 (2024).

Chalmers, Shane, and Sundhya Pahuja (eds), *Routledge Handbook of International Law and the Humanities* (Routledge, 2021).

Chalmers, Shane, and Sundhya Pahuja, "(Economic) Development and the Rule of Law," in *The Cambridge Companion to the Rule of Law*, Martin Loughin and Jens Meierhenrich (eds) (Cambridge University Press, 2021).

Chapman, Audrey R., and Patrick Ball, "The Truth of Truth Commissions: Comparative Lessons from Haiti, South Africa, and Guatemala," *Human Rights Quarterly*, vol 23, no 1 (2001).

Chehtman, Alejandro, "Latin America as a Laboratory of Transitional Justice," in *Latin American International Law in the Twenty-First Century*, Alejandro Chehtman, Alexandra Huneeus, and Sergio Puig (eds) (Oxford University Press, 2025).

Chicas Alfaro, Rolando E., Gabriela O. Montes Polanco, and José D. Rodríguez Morales, "Importancia de la Memoria Histórica a Través de la Representación Visual de la Producción en Bordados Realizados por Salvadoreños Refugiados en Colomoncagua, Honduras entre 1981 a 1992, contenidos en la Colección del Museo de la Palabra y la Imagen (MUPI)" (Honours Thesis, University of El Salvador, 2019).

Chimni, B. S., "Third World Approaches to International Law: A Manifesto," *International Community Law Review*, vol 8, no 1 (2006).

"A Just World under Law: A View from the South," *American University International Law Review*, vol 22, no 2 (2007).

Ching, Erik, *Authoritarian El Salvador: Politics and the Origins of the Military Regimes, 1880–1940* (University of Notre Dame Press, 2014).

Stories of Civil War in El Salvador: A Battle over Memory (The University of North Carolina Press, 2016).

Clark, Phil, *The Gacaca Courts, Post-Genocide Justice and Reconciliation in Rwanda: Justice without Lawyers* (Cambridge University Press, 2010).

Clarke, Kamari Maxine, *Affective Justice: The International Criminal Court and the Pan-Africanist Pushback* (Duke University Press, 2019).

Clarkson, Carrol, *Drawing the Line: Toward an Aesthetics of Transitional Justice* (Fordham University Press, 2013).

Cohen, Cynthia E., et al., "Special Issue: Creative Approaches to Transitional Justice: Contributions of Arts and Culture," *International Journal of Transitional Justice*, vol 14, no 1 (2020).

Collins, Cath, Jemima Garcia-Godos, and Elin Skaar, *Transitional Justice in Latin America: The Uneven Road from Impunity Towards Accountability* (Routledge, 2016).

Couso, Javier, "The Limits of Law for Emancipation (in the South): Dealing with Prisoners' Rights in Post-authoritarian Chile," *Griffith Law Review*, vol 16, no 2 (2014).

Craven, Matthew, "Between Law and History: The Berlin Conference of 1884–1885 and the Logic of Free Trade," *London Review of International Law*, vol 3, no 1 (2015).

Craven, Matthew, Sundhya Pahuja, and Gerry Simpson (eds), *International Law and the Cold War* (Cambridge University Press, 2019).

Crenzel, Emilio A., "Dos Prólogos Para Un Mismo Informe. El Nunca Más Y La Memoria De Las Desapariciones," *Prohistoria*, vol 9, no 11 (2007).

"Argentina's National Commission on the Disappearance of Persons: Contributions to Transitional Justice," *International Journal of Transitional Justice*, vol 2, no 2 (2008).

The Memory of the Argentina Disappearances: The Political History of Nunca Más, trans by Laura Pérez Carrara (Routledge, 2012).

"El Prólogo Del Nunca Más y La Teoría de los Dos Demonios. Reflexiones sobre una Representación de la Violencia Política en la Argentina," *Contenciosa*, vol 1, no 1 (2013).

Cruz, José Miguel, "Central American Maras: From Youth Street Gangs to Transnational Protection Rackets," *Global Crime*, vol 11, no 4 (2010).

"Criminal Violence and Democratization in Central America: The Survival of the Violent State," *Latin American Politics and Society*, vol 53, no 4 (2011).

Cusato, Eliana, "International Law, the Paradox of Plenty and the Making of Resource-Driven Conflict," *Leiden Journal of International Law*, vol 33, no 3 (2020).

Dalton, Roque, *Las Historias Prohibidas del Pulgarcito* (Ocean Sur, 2014).

Daly, Erin, "Truth Skepticism: An Inquiry into the Value of Truth in Times of Transition," *International Journal of Transitional Justice*, vol 2, no 1 (2008).

Danner, Mark, *The Massacre at El Mozote: A Parable of the Cold War* (Vintage Books, 1994).

De Soto, Álvaro, and Graciana del Castillo, "Obstacles to Peacebuilding," *Foreign Policy*, no 94 (1994).

"Implementation of Comprehensive Peace Agreements: Staying the Course in El Salvador," *Global Governance*, vol 1, no 2 (1995).

"Obstacles to Peacebuilding Revisited," *Global Governance*, vol 22, no 2 (2016).

De Ycaza, Carla, "A Search for Truth: A Critical Analysis of the Liberian Truth and Reconciliation Commission," *Human Rights Review*, vol 14, no 3 (2013).

Dearnley, Elizabeth, *Translators and Their Prologues in Medieval England* (Boydell and Brewer, D. S. Brewer, 2016).

Decker, Alicia C., "'Sometime You May Leave Your Husband in Karuma Falls or in the Forest There': A Gendered History of Disappearance in Idi Amin's Uganda, 1971–79," *Journal of Eastern African Studies*, vol 7, no 1 (2013).

DeLugan, Robin Maria, *Reimagining National Belonging: Post-Civil War El Salvador in a Global Context* (University of Arizona Press, 2012).

Dezalay, Sara, "The Role of International NGOs in the Emergence of Transitional Justice: A Case Study of the International Center for Transitional Justice," in *Research Handbook on Transitional Justice*, Cheryl Lawther, Luke Moffett and Dov Jacobs (eds) (Edward Elgar Publishing, 2017).

Dezalay, Yves, and Bryant G. Garth, *Dealing in Virtue: International Commercial Arbitration and the Construction of a Transnational Legal Order* (University of Chicago Press, 1996).

The Internationalization of Palace Wars: Lawyers, Economists, and the Contest to Transform Latin American States (University of Chicago Press, 2002).

Dorsett, Shaunnagh, and Shaun McVeigh, "Questions of Jurisdiction," in *Jurisprudence of Jurisdiction*, Shaun McVeigh (ed) (Routledge, 2007).

Dorsett, Shaunnagh, and Shaun McVeigh, *Jurisdiction* (Routledge, 2012).

Douglas, Stacy, *Curating Community: Museums, Constitutionalism, and the Taming of the Political* (University of Michigan Press, 2017).

Dulitzky, Ariel E, "Argentina, Desapariciones Forzadas Y El Sistema Interamericano De Derechos Humanos: A Propósito Del Caso Julien-Grisonas," *Revista de Pensamiento Penal* (2020).

Dunkerley, James, *Power in the Isthmus: A Political History of Modern Central America* (Verso, 1988).

The Long War: Dictatorship and Revolution in El Salvador (Verso, 1982).

Elander, Maria, "Education and Photography at Tuol Sleng Genocide Museum," in *The Arts of Transitional Justice: Culture, Activism, and Memory after Atrocity*, Peter Rush and Olivera Simić (eds) (Springer, 2014).

Figuring Victims in International Criminal Justice: The Case of the Khmer Rouge Tribunal (Routledge, 2018).

"Images of Victims: The ECCC and the Cambodian Genocide Museum," in *Law and the Visual: Representations, Technologies, and Critique*, Desmond Manderson (ed) (University of Toronto Press, 2018).

Elster, Jon, *Closing the Books: Transitional Justice in Historical Perspective* (Cambridge University Press, 2004).

Ensalaco, Mark, "Truth Commissions for Chile and El Salvador: A Report and Assessment," *Human Rights Quarterly*, vol 16, no 4 (1994).

Escobar, Arturo, *Encountering Development: The Making and Unmaking of the Third World* (Princeton University Press, 2012).

Eslava, Luis, *Local Space, Global Life: The Everyday Operation of International Law and Development* (Cambridge University Press, 2015).

"The Moving Location of Empire: Indirect Rule, International Law, and the Bantu Educational Kinema Experiment," *Leiden Journal of International Law*, vol 31, no 3 (2018).

"The Developmental State: Independence, Dependency, and the History of the South," in *The Battle for International Law: South-North Perspectives on the Decolonization Era*, Jochen von Bernstorff and Philipp Dann (eds) (Oxford University Press, 2019).

"Trigueño International Law: On (Most of the World) Being (Always, Somehow) out of Place," in *Out of Place: Power, Person and Difference in Socio-Legal Research*, Lynett Chua and Mark Massoud (eds) (Cambridge University Press, 2024).

Eslava, Luis, Michael Fakhri, and Vasuki Nesiah (eds), *Bandung, Global History, and International Law: Critical Pasts and Pending Futures* (Cambridge University Press, 2017).

Eslava, Luis, and Sundhya Pahuja, "The State and International Law: A Reading from the Global South," *Humanity*, vol 11, no 1 (2020).

Esteva, Gustavo, "Development," in *The Development Dictionary: A Guide to Knowledge as Power*, Wolfgang Sachs (ed) (Zed Books, 2010).

Fakhri, Michael, *Sugar and the Making of International Trade Law* (Cambridge University Press, 2014).

Feitlowitz, Margarite, *A Lexicon of Terror: Argentina and the Legacies of Torture* (Oxford University Press, 1998).

Ferrara, Anita, "Assessing the Long-Term Impact and Legacy of Truth Commissions," in *The Global Impact and Legacy of Truth Commissions*, Jeremy Sarkin (ed) (Intersentia, 2019).

Assessing the Long-Term Impact of Truth Commissions: The Chilean Truth and Reconciliation Commission in Historical Perspective (Routledge, 2015).

Figari Layus, Rosario, *The Reparative Effects of Human Rights Trials: Lessons from Argentina* (Routledge, 2017).

Figueroa, Mario, Lucas Fehr, and Carlos Dias, "Espacios Para La Cultura," *ARQ (Santiago)*, no 81 (2012).

Fitzpatrick, Peter, *The Mythology of Modern Law* (Routledge, 1992).

"Gods Would Be Needed: American Empire and the Rule of (International) Law," *Leiden Journal of International Law*, vol 16, no 3 (2003).

Fögen, Marie Theres, "The Legislator's Monologue: Notes on the History of Preambles," *Chicago-Kent Law Review*, vol 70 (1995).

Franco, Marina, "La 'Teoría de los Dos Demonios': Un Símbolo de la Posdictadura en la Argentina," *A Contra Corriente: A Journal on Social History and Literature in Latin American*, vol 11, no 2 (2014).

"El 'Documento Final' y las Demandas en torno a los Desaparecidos en la Última Etapa de la Dictadura Militar Argentina," *Antítesis*, vol 11, no 11 (2018).

Freeman, Mark, *Truth Commissions and Procedural Fairness* (Cambridge University Press, 2006).

Furley, Oliver, "Britain from Uganda to Musevini: Blind Eye Diplomacy," in *Conflict Resolution in Uganda*, Kumar Rupesinghe (ed) (International Peace Research Institute; James Currey Ltd; Ohio University Press, 1989).

Galante, Diego, *El Juicio a Las Juntas: Discursos Entre Política Y Justicia En La Transición Argentina* (Universidad Nacional de General Sarmiento; Universidad Nacional de La Plata; Universidad Nacional de Misiones, 2019).

García Moreno, Laura, "'Troubled Materiality': The Installations of Doris Salcedo," *Mosaic: An Interdisciplinary Critical Journal*, vol 43, no 2 (2010).

Garnsey, Eliza, *The Justice of Visual Art: Creative State-Building in Times of Political Transition* (Cambridge University Press, 2019).

Gearey, Adam, *Law and Aesthetics* (Hart Publishing, 2001).

Genette, Gérard, *Paratexts: Thresholds of Interpretation*, trans by Jane E. Lewin (Cambridge University Press, 1997).

Genovese, Ann, Shaun McVeigh, and Peter Rush, "Lives Lived with Law: An Introduction," *Law Text Culture*, vol 20, no 1 (2016).

Gerstein, Jorge Arieh, "El Conflicto entre Honduras y El Salvador: Análisis de sus Causas," *Foro Internacional*, vol 11, no 4 (1971).

Gevers, Christopher, "International Law, Literature and Worldmaking," in *Routledge Handbook of International Law and the Humanities*, Shane Chalmers and Sundhya Pahuja (eds) (Routledge, 2021).

Gill, Lesley, *The School of the Americas: Military Training and Political Violence in the Americas* (Duke University Press, 2004).

Goh, Benjamin, "Planetary Gifts of Law and Literature," *Law & Literature* (online first, March 2024).

Goodrich, Peter, *Law in the Courts of Love: Literature and Other Minor Jurisprudences* (Routledge, 1996).

Gould, Jeffrey L., *Solidarity under Siege: The Salvadoran Labor Movement, 1970–1990* (Cambridge University Press, 2019).

Grady, Kate, "For Whom the Bell Tolls: London's Iraq and Afghanistan Memorial 1990–2015," *London Review of International Law*, vol 7, no 3 (2019).

Grandin, Greg, "The Instruction of Great Catastrophe: Truth Commissions, National History, and State Formation in Argentina, Chile, and Guatemala," *The American Historical Review*, vol 110, no 1 (2005).

"Living in Revolutionary Time: Coming to Terms with the Violence of Latin America's Long Cold War," in *A Century of Revolution: Insurgent and Counterinsurgent Violence During Latin America's Long Cold War*, Greg Grandin and Gilbert M. Joseph (eds) (Duke University Press, 2010).

The Last Colonial Massacre: Latin America in the Cold War (University of Chicago Press, 2011).

Greenman, Kathryn, "Common Article 3 at 70: Reappraising Revolution and Civil War in International Law," *Melbourne Journal of International Law*, vol 27, no 1 (2020).

Grenfell, Laura, *Promoting the Rule of Law in Post-Conflict States* (Cambridge University Press, 2013).

Grover, Leena, "Transitional Justice, International Law and the United Nations," *Nordic Journal of International Law*, vol 88, no 3 (2019).

Guilhot, Nicolas, *The Democracy Makers: Human Rights and International Order* (Columbia University Press, 2005).

Guzmán Bouvard, Marguerite, *Revolutionizing Motherhood: The Mothers of the Plaza de Mayo* (Scholarly Resources Inc., 1994).

Halperín Donghi, Tulio, *The Contemporary History of Latin America*, trans by John Charles Chasteen (Duke University Press, 1993).

Harvey, David, *A Brief History of Neoliberalism* (Oxford University Press, 2005).

Hayner, Priscilla B., "Fifteen Truth Commissions – 1974 to 1994: A Comparative Study," *Human Rights Quarterly*, vol 16, no 4 (1994).

"Commissioning the Truth: Further Research Questions," *Third World Quarterly*, vol 17, no 1 (1996).

Unspeakable Truths: Confronting State Terror and Atrocity (Routledge, 2001).

"International Center for Transitional Justice (ICTJ)," in *Encyclopedia of Human Rights*, David P. Forsythe (ed) (Oxford University Press, 2009).

Unspeakable Truths: Transitional Justice and the Challenge of Truth Commissions (Routledge, 2011).

Heerten, Lesse, "The Dystopia of Postcolonial Catastrophe: Self-Determination, the Biafran War of Secession, and the 1970s Human Rights Moment," in *The Breakthrough: Human Rights in the 1970s*, Samuel Moyn and Jon Eckel (eds) (University of Pennsylvania Press, 2014).

Heiss, Claudia "Chile: Entre el Estallido Social y la Pandemia," *Análisis Carolina*, vol 18 (2020).

Heiss, Claudia, and Julieta Suárez-Cao, "Constitution-Making in the 21st Century: Lessons from the Chilean Process," *PS, Political Science & Politics*, vol 57, no 2 (2024).

Henkin, Alice H., "Preface," in *State Crimes: Punishment or Pardon: Papers and Report of the Conference, The Aspen Institute* (The Aspen Institute, 1988).

"Conference Report," in *State Crimes: Punishment or Pardon: Papers and Report of the Conference, The Aspen Institute* (The Aspen Institute, 1988).

Henríquez Consalvi, Carlos 'Santiago', *La Terquedad del Izote: La Historia de Radio Venceremos* (Ediciones Museo de la Palabra y la Imagen, 2018).

Broadcasting the Civil War in El Salvador: A Memoir of Guerrilla Radio; Introduction by Erik Ching, trans by Charles Leo Nagle V wand A. L. (Bill) Prince (University of Texas Press, 2010).

Hernández Rivas, Annette Georgina, "Cartografía de la Memoria: Actores, Lugares y Prácticas en El Salvador de Posguerra (1992–2015)" (PhD Thesis, Universidad Autónoma de Madrid, 2015).

Hodge, Joseph Morgan, "Writing the History of Development (Part 1: The First Wave)," *Humanity: An International Journal of Human Rights, Humanitarianism, and Development*, vol 6, no 3 (2016).

"Writing the History of Development (Part 2: Longer, Deeper, Wider)," *Humanity: An International Journal of Human Rights, Humanitarianism and Development*, vol 7, no 1 (2017).

Hohmann, Jessie, and Daniel Joyce (eds), *International Law's Objects* (Oxford University Press, 2018).

Humphreys, Stephen, *Theatre of the Rule of Law: Transnational Legal Intervention in Theory and Practice* (Cambridge University Press, 2012).

Huyssen, Andreas, *Present Pasts: Urban Palimpsests and the Politics of Memory* (Stanford University Press, 2003).

Twilight Memories: Marking Time in a Culture of Amnesia (Routledge, 1995).

Jara, Daniela, Manuela Badilla, Ana Figueiredo, Marcela Cornejo, and Victoria Riveros, "Tracing Mapuche Exclusion from Post-Dictatorial Truth Commissions in Chile: Official and Grassroots Initiatives," *International Journal of Transitional Justice*, vol 12, no 3 (2018).

Jeffrey, Renee, "Truth Commissions and Democratic Transitions: Neither Truth and Reconciliation nor Democratization in Nepal," *Journal of Human Rights*, vol 20, no 3 (2021).

Jensen, Steven L. B., *The Making of International Human Rights: The 1960s, Decolonization, and the Reconstruction of Global Values* (Cambridge University Press, 2016).

Jain, Neha, and Sarah M. H. Nouwen, "North-South Skirmishes over Transitional Justice: 1975–2000," in *The Battle for International Law II*, Jochen von Bernstorff, Philipp Dann and Surabhi Ranganathan (eds) (Oxford University Press, forthcoming).

Johansson, Patrick K., "Miccacuicatl: Cantos Mortuorios Nahuas Prehispánicos. Textos y 'Con-Textos'," *Estudios de Cultura Náhuatl*, vol 48 (2014).

Johns, Fleur, Richard Joyce, and Sundhya Pahuja (eds), *Events: The Force of International Law* (Routledge, 2010).

Jolles, André, *Simple Forms: Legend, Saga, Myth, Riddle, Saying, Case, Memorabile, Fairytale, Joke*, trans by Peter J. Schwartz (Verso, 2017).

Joyce, Daniel, and Gabrielle Simm, "Zero Dark Thirty: International Law, Film and Representation," *London Review of International Law*, vol 3, no 2 (2015).

Joyce, Richard, "Westphalia: Event, Memory, Myth," in *Events: The Force of International Law*, Fleur Johns, Richard Joyce and Sundhya Pahuja (eds) (Routledge, 2010).

Jung, Harald, "Class Struggles in El Salvador," *New Left Review*, vol 122, no 1 (1980).

Kalter, Christoph, *The Discovery of the Third World: Decolonization and the Rise of the New Left in France, c. 1950–1976* (Cambridge University Press, 2016).

Karl, Terry Lynn, "El Salvador's Negotiated Revolution," *Foreign Affairs*, vol 71, no 2 (1992).

Kazan, Helene, "The Architecture of Slow, Structural, and Spectacular Violence and the Poetic Testimony of War," *Australian Feminist Law Journal*, vol 44, no 1 (2018).

Keck, Margaret E, and Kathryn Sikkink, *Activists Beyond Borders: Advocacy Networks in International Politics* (Cornell University Press, 1998).

Kedar, Claudia, "The Beginning of a Controversial Relationship: The IMF, the World Bank, and Argentina, 1943–1946," *Canadian Journal of Latin American & Caribbean Studies*, vol 35, no 69 (2010).

The International Monetary Fund and Latin America: The Argentine Puzzle in Context (Temple University Press, 2013).

Kendall, Sara, "New Histories of the Present: Revisiting Post-WWII Juridical Forms (Review Essay of Heller and Tanaka, et al.)," *Melbourne Journal of International Law*, vol 12, no 1 (2012).

Kennedy, David, "The International Human Rights Regime: Still Part of the Problem?," in *Examining Critical Perspectives on Human Rights*, Rob Dickinson, Elena Katselli, Colin Murray and Ole W. Pedersen (eds) (Cambridge University Press, 2012).

Kinsella, Hellen, *The Image before the Weapon: A Critical History of the Distinction between Combatant and Civilian* (Cornell University Press, 2011).

Klein, Naomi, *The Shock Doctrine* (Penguin Books, 2008).

Klinkner, Melanie, and Howard Davis, *The Right to the Truth in International Law: Victims' Rights in Human Rights and International Criminal Law* (Routledge, 2020).

Koops, Jerome, et al., "Introduction: Post-Cold War Peacekeeping: 1988–1998," in *The Oxford Handbook of United Nations Peacekeeping Operations*, Jerome Koops et al. (eds) (Oxford University Press, 2014).

Krever, Tor, "Ending Impunity? Eliding Political Economy in International Criminal Law," in *Research Handbook on Political Economy and Law*, John D. Haskell and Ugo Mattei (eds) (Edward Elgar, 2015).

Krisch, Nico, "Symposium: Liquid Authority in Global Governance," *International Theory*, vol 9, no 2 (2017).

Kritz, Neil J. (ed), *Transitional Justice: How Emerging Democracies Reckon with Former Regimes. Volume I: General Considerations* (United States Institute of Peace Press, 1995).

Transitional Justice: How Emerging Democracies Reckon with Former Regimes. Volume II: Country Studies (United States Institute of Peace, 1995).

"Where We Are and How We Got Here: An Overview of Developments in the Search for Justice and Reconciliation," in *The Legacy of Abuse: Confronting the Past, Facing the Future*, Alice H. Henkin (ed) (The Aspen Institute, 2002).

Kurze, Arnaud K., and Christopher Lamont (eds), *New Critical Spaces in Transitional Justice: Gender, Art, and Memory* (Indiana University Press, 2019).

Laidlaw, Zoë, "Investigating Empire: Humanitarians, Reform and the Commission of Eastern Inquiry," *Journal of Imperial & Commonwealth History*, vol 40, no 5 (2012).

Lawther, Cheryl, "Transitional Justice and Truth Commissions," in *Research Handbook on Transitional Justice*, Cheryl Lawther, Luke Moffett and Dov Jacobs (eds) (Edward Elgar Publishing, 2017).

Legrás, Horacio, "The Rule of Impurity: Decolonial Theory and the Question of Literature," *Decolonial Approaches to Latin American Literature and Cultures*, Juan G. Ramos and Tara Daly (eds) (Palgrave Macmillan, 2016).

León-Portilla, Miguel, "El Ocaso De Los Dioses. Moctezuma II," *Arqueología Mexicana*, vol 98 (2009).

Lessa, Francesca, *The Condor Trials: Transnational Repression and Human Rights in South America* (Yale University Press, 2022).

Letelier, Orlando, "Economic 'Freedom's' Awful Toll: The 'Chicago Boys' in Chile," *Review of Radical Political Economics*, vol 8, no 3 (1976).

Levine, Caroline, *Forms: Whole, Rhythm, Hierarchy, Network* (Princeton University Press, 2015).

Lindo-Fuentes, Héctor, *Weak Foundations: The Economy of El Salvador in the Nineteenth Century 1821–1898* (University of California Press, 1990).

El Alborotador De Centroamérica: El Salvador Frente al Imperio (UCA Editores; El Colegio de Michoacán, AC, 2019).

Lindo-Fuentes, Héctor, Erik Ching, and Rafael Lara-Martínez, *Remembering a Massacre in El Salvador: The Insurrection of 1932, Roque Dalton, and the Politics of Historical Memory* (University of New Mexico Press, 2007).

Lira, Elizabeth, Historia, *Política y Ética de la Verdad en Chile, 1891–2001: Reflexiones Sobre la Paz Social y la Impunidad* (LOM Ediciones; Universidad Alberto Hurtado, 2001).

Littlemore, Jeannette, *Metonymy: Hidden Shortcuts in Language, Thought and Communication* (Cambridge University Press, 2015).

Lixinski, Lucas, *Legalized Identities: Cultural Heritage Law and the Shaping of Transitional Justice* (Cambridge University Press, 2021).

López, Fernando, "The Feathers of Cóndor: Transnational State Terrorism, Exiles and Civilian Anticommunism in South America" (PhD Thesis, University of New South Wales, 2014).

Loveman, Brian, and Elizabeth Lira, *Las Ardientes Cenizas Del Olvido: Vía Chilena De Reconciliación Política 1932–1994* (LOM Ediciones; DIBAM, 2000).

Lowman, Thomas, "Amin Reframed: The UK, Uganda, and the Human Rights 'Breakthrough' of the 1970s," *Cambridge Review of International Affairs*, vol 36, no 4 (2022).

Madlingozi, Tshepo, "On Transitional Justice Entrepreneurs and the Production of Victims," *Journal of Human Rights Practice*, vol 2, no 2 (2010).

Malamud-Goti, Jaime, *Game without End: State Terror and the Politics of Justice* (University of Oklahoma Press, 1996).

Manderson, Desmond, "Beyond the Provincial: Space, Aesthetics, and Modernist Legal Theory," *Melbourne University Law Review*, vol 20 (1995–1996).

"Indigenous People and the Law," *Australian Financial Review* (2008).

Kangaroo Courts and the Rule of Law: The Legacy of Modernism (Routledge, 2012).

"Bodies in the Water: On Reading Images More Sensibly," *Law & Literature*, vol 27, no 2 (2013).

(ed), *Law and the Visual: Representations, Technologies, and Critique* (University of Toronto Press, 2018).

Danse Macabre: Temporalities of Law in the Visual Arts (Cambridge University Press, 2019).

Mansuy, Daniel, *Nos Fuimos Quedando En Silencio: La Agonía del Chile de la Transición* (Instituto de Estudios de la Sociedad, 2016).

Marin, Louis, *Portrait of the King* (Springer, 1988).

Martínez Peñate, Óscar, *El Salvador: Las Negociaciones de los Acuerdos de Paz, 1990–1992* (Editorial Nuevo Enfoque, 2011).

El Salvador: Del Conflicto Armado a la Negociación, 1979–1989 (Editorial Nuevo Enfoque, 2013).

Martínez, Óscar, *The Beast: Riding the Rails and Dodging Narcos on the Migrant Trail* (Icaria Editorial; Verso, 2010; 2013).

Martínez, Óscar, and Juan José Martínez, *The Hollywood Kid: The Violent Life and Death of an MS-13 Hitman* (Verso, 2019).

Mazower, Mark, *No Enchanted Palace: The End of Empire and the Ideological Origins of the United Nations* (Princeton University Press, 2009).

Mbengue, Makane Moïse, "Preamble," in *Max Planck Encyclopedia of Public International Law*, Rüdiger Wolfrum (ed) (Oxford University Press, 2006).

McEvoy, Kieran, "Beyond Legalism: Towards a Thicker Understanding of Transitional Justice," *Journal of Law and Society*, vol 34, no 4 (2007).

McEvoy, Kieran, and Lorna McGregor (eds), *Transitional Justice from Below: Grassroots Activism and the Struggle for Change* (Hart Publishing, 2008).

McSherry, J. Patrice, *Predatory States: Operation Condor and Covert War in Latin America* (Rowman & Littlefield Publishers, 2005).

McVeigh, Shaun (ed), *Jurisprudence of Jurisdiction* (Routledge, 2007).
"Critical Approaches to Jurisdiction and International Law," in *The Oxford Handbook of Jurisdiction in International Law*, Stephen Allen, Daniel Costelloe, Malgosia Fitzmaurice, Paul Gragl, and Edward Guntrip (eds) (Oxford University Press, 2019).
McVeigh, Shaun, and Sundhya Pahuja, "Rival Jurisdictions: The Promise and Loss of Sovereignty," in *After Sovereignty: On the Question of Political Beginnings*, Charles Barbour and George Pavlich (eds) (Routledge, 2010).
Meiksins Wood, Ellen, "The Separation of the Economic and the Political in Capitalism," *New Left Review*, vol 127, no 1 (1981).
Mignolo, Walter D., "Delinking," *Cultural Studies*, vol 21, no 2/3 (2007).
The Darker Side of Western Modernity: Global Futures, Decolonial Options (Duke University Press, 2011).
Mignone, Emilio, *Derechos Humanos y Sociedad: El Caso Argentino* (Centro de Estudios Legales y Sociales; Ediciones del Pensamiento Social, 1991).
Miles, Kate, "Visuality of a Treaty: Reflection on Versailles," *London Review of International Law*, vol 8, no 1 (2020).
Miller, Zinaida, "Settling With History: A Hybrid Commission of Inquiry for Israel/Palestine," *Harvard Human Rights Journal*, vol 20 (2007).
Moodie, Ellen, *El Salvador in the Aftermath of Peace: Crime, Uncertainty, and the Transition to Democracy* (University of Pennsylvania Press, 2012).
Moon, Claire, "Narrating Political Reconciliation: Truth and Reconciliation in South Africa," *Social and Legal Studies*, vol 15, no 2 (2006).
Moulian, Tomás, "A Time of Forgetting: The Myths of the Chilean Transition," *NACLA Report on the Americas*, no 2 (1998).
Moyn, Samuel, *The Last Utopia: Human Rights in History* (Harvard University Press, 2010).
Moyn, Samuel, and Jon Eckel (eds), *The Breakthrough: Human Rights in the 1970s* (University of Pennsylvania Press, 2014).
Mujaju, Akiki Bomera "Internal Conflict and Its International Context," in *Conflict Resolution in Uganda*, Kumar Rupesinghe (ed) (International Peace Research Institute; Ohio University Press, 1989).
Natarajan, Usha, "Creating and Recreating Iraq: Legacies of the Mandate System in Contemporary Understandings of Third World Sovereignty," *Leiden Journal of International Law*, vol 24, no 4 (2011).
Neier, Aryeh, *The International Human Rights Movement: A History* (Princeton University Press, 2012).
Nesiah, Vasuki, "Placing International Law: White Spaces on a Map," *Leiden Journal of International Law*, vol 16, no 1 (2003).
"Discussion Lines on Gender and Transitional Justice: An Introductory Essay Reflecting on the ICTJ Bellagio Workshop on Gender and Transitional Justice," *Columbia Journal of Gender and Law*, vol 15, no 3 (2006).
"The Specter of Violence That Haunts the UDHR: The Turn to Ethics and Expertise," *Maryland Journal of International Law*, vol 24, no 1 (2009).
"The Trials of History: Losing Justice in the Monstrous and the Banal," in *Law in Transition: Human Rights, Development and Transitional Justice*, Ruth Buchanan and Peer Zumbansen (eds) (Bloomsbury, 2014).

"Theories of Transitional Justice: Cashing in the Blue Chips," in *The Oxford Handbook of the Theory of International Law*, Anne Orford and Florian Hoffmann (eds) (Oxford University Press, 2016).

"Freedom at Sea," *London Review of International Law*, vol 7, no 2 (2019).

"The Ambitions and Traumas of Transitional Governance: Expelling Colonialism, Replicating Colonialism," in *International Law and Transitional Governance: Critical Perspectives*, Emmanuel H. D. De Groof and Micha Wiebusch (eds) (Routledge, 2020).

Nino, Carlos Santiago, "The Duty to Punish Past Abuses of Human Rights Put into Context: The Case of Argentina," *The Yale Law Journal*, vol 100, no 8 (1991).

Radical Evil on Trial (Yale University Press, 1996).

Juicio Al Mal Absoluto: ¿Hasta Dónde Debe Llegar la Justicia Retroactiva en Casos de Violaciones Masivas de los Derechos Humanos?, trans by Martín Böhmer (Siglo Veintiuno Editores, 2015).

North, Liisa, *Bitter Grounds: Roots of Revolt in El Salvador* (Lawrence Hill & Co., 1985).

Nunfio, Obdulio, "Radiografía De La Guerra del Fútbol o de Las Cien Horas," *Revista Mexicana de Sociología*, vol 32, no 3 (1970).

O'Donnell, Guillermo, *Modernization and Bureaucratic-Authoritarianism: Studies in South American Politics* (University of California Press, 1979).

O'Donnell, Guillermo, Philippe C. Schmitter, and Laurence Whitehead (eds), *Transitions from Authoritarian Rule* (Johns Hopkins University Press, 1986).

Obregón, Liliana, "The Civilized and the Uncivilized," in *The Oxford Handbook of the History of International Law*, Bardo Fassbender and Anne Peters (eds) (Oxford University Press, 2012).

Olson, Greta, "De-Americanizing Law and Literature Narratives: Opening up the Story," *Law & Literature*, vol 22, no 2 (2010).

Orentlicher, Diane F., "Settling Accounts: The Duty to Prosecute Human Rights Violations of a Prior Regime," *The Yale Law Journal*, vol 100, no 8 (1991).

"A Reply to Professor Nino," *The Yale Law Journal*, vol 100, no 8 (1991).

Orford, Anne, "Locating the International: Military and Monetary Interventions after the Cold War," *Harvard International Law Journal*, vol 38, no 2 (1997).

Reading Humanitarian Intervention: Human Rights and the Use of Force in International Law (Cambridge University Press, 2003).

"Commissioning the Truth," *Columbia Journal of Gender and Law*, vol 15, no 3 (2006).

International Authority and the Responsibility to Protect (Cambridge University Press, 2011).

Ortíz Ruíz, Francisco E., "El Salvador 1991–1992: Acuerdo de Paz y Reforma Constitucional," *Perspectivas* (2017) no 4.

Pahuja, Sundhya, *Decolonising International Law: Development, Economic Growth, and the Politics of Universality* (Cambridge University Press, 2011).

"Laws of Encounter: A Jurisdictional Account of International Law," *London Review of International Law*, vol 1, no 1 (2013).

"Letters from Bandung: Encounters with Another International Law," in *Bandung, Global History, and International Law: Critical Pasts and Pending Futures*, Luis Eslava, Michael Fakhri, and Vasuki Nesiah (eds) (Cambridge University Press, 2017).

Paige, Jeffrey M., *Coffee and Power: Revolution and the Rise of Democracy in Central America* (Harvard University Press, 1997).

Pal, Maïa, *Jurisdictional Accumulation: An Early Modern History of Law, Empires, and Capital* (Cambridge University Press, 2020).

Parfitt, Rose, *The Process of International Legal Reproduction: Inequality, Historiography, Resistance* (Cambridge University Press, 2019).

Parker, James E. K., *Acoustic Jurisprudence: Listening to the Trial of Simon Bikindi* (Oxford University Press, 2015).

Parmar, Inderjeet, *Foundations of the American Century: The Ford, Carnegie, and Rockefeller Foundations in the Rise of American Power* (Columbia University Press, 2012).

Pearce, Jenny, *Promised Land: Peasant Rebellion in Chalatenango, El Salvador* (Latin America Bureau, 1986).

Pérez de Cuéllar, Javier, *Pilgrimage for Peace: A Secretary-General's Memoirs* (Palgrave Macmillan, 1997).

Peters, Timothy D., and Karen Crawley (eds), *Envisioning Legality: Law, Culture and Representation* (Routledge, 2017).

Peterson, Trudy Huskamp, *Final Acts: A Guide to Preserving the Records of Truth Commissions* (Woodrow Wilson Center Press; Johns Hopkins University Press, 2005).

Petras, James F., Fernando Ignacio Leiva, and Henry Veltmeyer, *Democracy and Poverty in Chile: The Limits to Electoral Politics* (Westview Press, 1994).

Popkin, Margaret, and Naomi Roht-Arriaza, "Truth as Justice: Investigatory Commissions in Latin America," *Law & Social Inquiry*, vol 20, no 1 (1995).

Porqueras Mayo, Alberto, *El Prólogo como Género Literario: Su Estudio en el Siglo de Oro Español* (Consejo Superior de Investigaciones Científicas, 1957).

Quinn, Joanna R., *The Politics of Acknowledgement: Truth Commissions in Uganda and Haiti* (UBC Press, 2010).

Quinn, Joanna R., and Mark Freeman, "Lessons Learned: Practical Lessons Gleaned from inside the Truth Commissions of Guatemala and South Africa," *Human Rights Quarterly*, vol 25, no 4 (2003).

Quiroga-Villamarín, Daniel Ricardo, "'An Atmosphere of Genuine Solidarity and Brotherhood': Hernán Santa-Cruz and a Forgotten Latin American Contribution to Social Rights," *Journal of the History of International Law*, vol 21, no 1 (2019).

Raimundo, Filipa, and Joana Rebelo Morais, "Is Anyone Listening? A Review of the Research on Attitudes Towards Truth Commissions," in *The Global Impact and Legacy of Truth Commissions*, Jeremy Sarkin (ed) (Intersentia, 2019).

Rajagopal, Balakrishnan, *International Law from Below: Development, Social Movements and Third World Resistance* (Cambridge University Press, 2003).

Ramshaw, Sara, *Justice as Improvisation: The Law of the Extempore* (Routledge, 2013).

"Law and Humanities: A Field without a Canon," *Law, Culture and the Humanities* (online first, November 2019).

Ramshaw, Sara, and Paul Stapleton, "From Prepeace to Postconflict: The Ethics of (Non)Listening and Cocreation in a Divided Society," in *Playing for Keeps: Improvisation in the Aftermath*, Daniel Fischlin and Eric Porter (eds) (Duke University Press, 2021).

Reátegui, Félix, "The Victims Remember. Notes on the Social Practice of Memory," in *Transitional Justice: Handbook for Latin America*, Félix Reátegui (ed) (Brazilian Amnesty Commission, Ministry of Justice; International Center for Transitional Justice, 2011).

Reuque Paillalef, Rosa Isolde, and Florencia E. Mallon, *When a Flower Is Reborn: The Life and Times of a Mapuche Feminist* (Duke University Press, 2002).

Ribera, Ricardo, "El Salvador: La Negociación del Acuerdo de Paz: ¿Un Modelo para el Mundo?," *Realidad: Revista de Ciencias Sociales y Humanidades*, vol 37 (1994).

Richard, Nelly, *Eruptions of Memory: The Critique of Memory in Chile, 1990–2015*, trans by Julia Sanches (Polity Press, 2019).

Rist, Gilbert, *The History of Development from Western Origins to Global Faith* (Zed Books, 2014).

Rodrigues Widholm, Julie, and Madeleine Grynsztejn (eds), *Doris Salcedo* (University of Chicago Press, 2015).

Roht-Arriaza, Naomi, and José Zalaquett, "The Need for Moral Reconstruction in the Wake of Past Human Rights Violations: An Interview with José Zalaquett," in *Transitional Justice: Handbook for Latin America*, Félix Reátegui (ed) (Brazilian Amnesty Commission, Ministry of Justice; International Center for Transitional Justice, 2011).

Roos, Jerome E., *Why Not Default? The Political Economy of Sovereign Debt* (Princeton University Press, 2019).

Rotberg, Robert I., "Truth Commissions and the Provision of Truth, Justice, and Reconciliation," in *Truth V. Justice: The Morality of Truth Commissions*, Robert I. Rotberg and Dennis F. Thompson (eds) (Princeton University Press, 2000).

Roughan, Nicole, *Authorities: Conflicts, Cooperation, and Transnational Legal Theory* (Oxford University Press, 2013).

Rowen, Jamie, *Searching for Truth in the Transitional Justice Movement* (Cambridge University Press, 2017).

Rush, Peter, "An Altered Jurisdiction: Corporeal Traces of Law," *Griffith Law Review*, vol 6 (1997).

"Dirty War Crimes: Jurisdictions of Memory and International Criminal Law," in *The Hidden Histories of War Crimes Trials*, Gerry Simpson and Kevin John Heller (eds) (Oxford University Press, 2013).

Rush, Peter, and Olivera Simić, *The Arts of Transitional Justice: Culture, Activism, and Memory after Atrocity* (Springer, 2014).

Rush, Peter, and Maria Elander, "Working through the Cinematography of International Criminal Justice: Procedures of Law and Images of Atrocity," *London Review of International Law*, vol 6, no 1 (2018).

Said, Edward, and Raymond Williams, "Appendix: Media, Margins and Modernity," in Raymond Williams, *Politics of Modernism: Against the New Conformists* (Verso, 2007).

Salcedo, Doris, "A Work in Mourning," in *Doris Salcedo*, Julie Rodrigues Widholm and Madeleine Grynsztejn (eds) (Museum of Contemporary Art Chicago, 2015).

Sanders, Mark, *Ambiguities of Witnessing: Law and Literature in the Time of a Truth Commission* (Stanford University Press, 2007).

Sarkin, Jeremy, "Redesigning the Definition a Truth Commission, but Also Designing a Forward-Looking Non-Prescriptive Definition to Make Them Potentially More Successful," *Human Rights Review*, vol 19, no 3 (2018).

"Introduction," in *The Global Impact and Legacy of Truth Commissions*, Jeremy Sarkin (ed) (Intersentia, 2019).

Sauvy, Alfred, "Document: Trois Mondes, Une Planète," *Vingtième Siècle. Revue d'Histoire*, no 12 (1986).

Scarfi, Juan Pablo, *El Imperio de la Ley: James Brown Scott y la Construcción de un Orden Jurídico Interamericano* (Fondo de Cultura Económica, 2014).

The Hidden History of International Law in the Americas: Empire and Legal Networks (Oxford University Press, 2017).

"Francisco De Vitoria and the (Geo)Politics of Canonization in Spain/America," *Leiden Journal of International Law*, vol 35, no 3 (2022).

Schabas, William A., "The Relationship between Truth Commissions and International Courts: The Case of Sierra Leone," *Human Rights Quarterly*, vol 25, no 4 (2003).

Schmitz, David F., and Vanessa Walker, "Jimmy Carter and the Foreign Policy of Human Rights: The Development of a Post-Cold War Foreign Policy," *Diplomatic History*, vol 28, no 1 (2003).

Schneider, Brian W., *The Framing Text in Early Modern English Drama: 'Whining' Prologues and 'Armed' Epilogues* (Ashgate, 2011).

Schwöbel-Patel, Christine, "Spectacle in International Criminal Law: The Fundraising Image of Victimhood," *London Review of International Law*, vol 4, no 2 (2016).

Shaw, Malcolm N., *International Law*, 9th ed. (Cambridge University Press, 2021).

Shefik, Sherin, "Reimagining Transitional Justice through Participatory Art," *International Journal of Transitional Justice*, vol 12, no 2 (2018).

Shoup, Laurence H., and William Minter, *Imperial Brain Trust: The Council on Foreign Relations and United States Foreign Policy* (Monthly Review Press, 1977).

Sikkink, Kathryn, *The Justice Cascade: How Human Rights Prosecutions Are Changing World Politics* (W. W. Norton & Company, 2011).

Evidence for Hope: Making Human Rights Work in the 21st Century (Princeton University Press, 2017).

Sikkink, Kathryn, and Carrie Walling Booth, "Argentina's Contribution to Global Trends in Transitional Justice," in *Transitional Justice in the Twenty-First Century: Beyond Truth Versus Justice*, Naomi Roht-Arriaza and Javier Mariezcurrena (eds) (Cambridge University Press, 2006).

Silva, Eduardo, *The State and Capital in Chile: Business Elites, Technocrats, and Market Economics* (Westview Press, 1996).

Simpson, Gerry, *Law, War and Crime: War Crimes Trials and the Reinvention of International Law* (Polity, 2007).

Sinclair, Guy Fiti, *To Reform the World: The Legal Powers of International Organizations* (Oxford University Press, 2017).

Sitze, Adam, *The Impossible Machine: A Genealogy of South Africa's Truth and Reconciliation Commission* (University of Michigan Press, 2013).

Skaar, Elin, "Transitional Justice for Human Rights: The Legacy and Future of Truth and Reconciliation Commissions," in *International Human Rights Institutions, Tribunals, and Courts*, Gerd Oberleitner (ed) (Springer, 2018).

Slaughter, Joseph R., "Enabling Fictions and Novel Subjects: The 'Bildungsroman' and International Human Rights Law," *PMLA*, vol 121, no 4 (2006).

Human Rights, Inc.: The World Novel, Narrative Form, and International Law (Fordham University Press, 2007).

"Hijacking Human Rights: Neoliberalism, the New Historiography, and the End of the Third World," *Human Rights Quarterly*, vol 40, no 4 (2018).

Stone Peters, Julie, "Law, Literature, and the Vanishing Real: On the Future of an Interdisciplinary Illusion," *PMLA*, vol 120, no 2 (2005).

Storr, Cait, *International Status in the Shadow of Empire: Nauru and the Histories of International Law* (Cambridge University Press, 2020).

Stromseth, Jane, David Wippman, and Rosa Brooks, *Can Might Make Rights? Building the Rule of Law after Military Interventions* (Cambridge University Press, 2006).

Susan, Marks, "Human Rights and Root Causes," *The Modern Law Review*, vol 74, no 1 (2011).

Tadjo, Véronique (ed), *The Culture of Dissenting Memory: Truth Commissions in the Global South* (Routledge, 2019).

Teitel, Ruti G., *Transitional Justice* (Oxford University Press, 2000).

Globalizing Transitional Justice: Contemporary Essays (Oxford University Press, 2014).

Thornton, Christy, *Revolution in Development: Mexico and the Governance of the Global Economy* (University of California Press, 2021).

Tolley Jr., Howard B., *The International Commission of Jurists: Global Advocates for Human Rights* (University of Pennsylvania Press, 1994).

"International Commission of Jurists," in *Encyclopedia of Human Rights*, David P. Forsythe (ed) (Oxford University Press, 2009).

Trejo, Guillermo, Juan Albarracín, and Lucía Tiscornia, "Breaking State Impunity in Post-Authoritarian Regimes: Why Transitional Justice Processes Deter Criminal Violence in New Democracies," *Journal of Peace Research*, vol 55, no 6 (2018).

Tzouvala, Ntina, *Capitalism as Civilisation: A History of International Law* (Cambridge University Press, 2020).

Uche, Chibuike, "The British Government, Idi Amin and the Expulsion of British Asians from Uganda," *Interventions: International Journal of Postcolonial Studies*, vol 19, no 6 (2017).

Valdés, Juan Gabriel, *Pinochet's Economists: The Chicago School in Chile* (Cambridge University Press, 1995).

van Zyl, Paul, and Mark Freeman, "The Legacy of Abuse: Conference Report," in *The Legacy of Abuse: Confronting the Past, Facing the Future*, Alice H. Henkin (ed) (The Aspen Institute, 2002).

Vázquez Guevara, Valeria, "Crafting the Lawful Truth: Chile's 1990 Truth Commission, International Human Rights and the Museum of Memory," *London Review of International Law*, vol 7, no 2 (2019).

"Prologue to Truth: Argentina's National Commission on the Disappeared and the Authority of International Law," *Leiden Journal of International Law*, vol 35, no 1 (2022).

Velasco Ramírez, Rogelio Guillermo, "Aspectos Jurídicos del Crédito Agrícola en El Salvador" (PhD Thesis, Universidad de El Salvador, 1975).

Verbitsky, Horacio, Malvinas: *La Última Batalla de la Tercera Guerra Mundial* (Editorial Sudamericana, 2002).

Vergo, Peter (ed), *The New Museology* (Reaktion Books, 1989).

Villalobos, Joaquín, "Popular Insurrection: Desire or Reality?," *Latin American Perspectives*, vol 16, no 3 (1989).

Villiers Negroponte, Diana, *Seeking Peace in El Salvador: The Struggle to Reconstruct a Nation at the End of the Cold War* (Palgrave Macmillan, 2012).

Voermans, Wim, Maarten Stremler, and Paul Cliteur, *Constitutional Preambles: A Comparative Analysis* (Edward Elgar, 2017).

von Bernstorff, Jochen, and Philipp Dann (eds), *The Battle for International Law: South-North Perspectives on the Decolonization Era* (Oxford University Press, 2019).

von Bogdandy, Armin, Rüdiger Wolfrum, Jochen von Bernstorff, Philipp Dann, and Matthias Goldmann, "Special Issue: The Exercise of Public Authority by International Institutions," *German Law Journal*, vol 9, no 11 (2008).

(eds), *The Exercise of Public Authority by International Institutions: Advancing International Institutional Law* (Springer, 2010).

von Bogdandy, Armin, Matthias Goldmann, and Ingo Venzke, "From Public International to International Public Law: Translating World Public Opinion into International Public Authority," *European Journal of International Law*, vol 28, no 1 (2017).

Wallensteen, Peter, *Quality Peace: Strategic Peacebuilding and World Order* (Oxford University Press, 2015).

Wan, Marco, *Masculinity and the Trials of Modern Fiction* (Routledge, 2017).

Wandita, Galuh, et al., *Chega! Book 1: What Happened and How to Stop It Happening Again*, trans Mayra Walsh (AJAR, STP-CAVR, INSISTPress, 2010; 2015).

Washington, John, *The Dispossessed: A Story of Asylum at the US-Mexican Border and Beyond* (Verso, 2020).

Westad, Odd Arne, *The Global Cold War: Third World Interventions and the Making of Our Times* (Cambridge University Press, 2007).

Whyte, Jessica, *The Morals of the Market: Human Rights and the Rise of Neoliberalism* (Verso, 2019).

Wiebelhaus-Brahm, Eric, *Truth Commissions and Transitional Societies: The Impact on Human Rights and Democracy* (Routledge, 2010).

Wilson, Everett Alan, *La Crisis de la Integración Nacional en El Salvador, 1919–1935* (Consejo Nacional para la Cultura y el Arte, CONCULTURA, 2004).

Wing, Adrien Katherine, "A Truth and Reconciliation Commission for Palestine/Israel: Healing Spirit Injuries?," *Transnational Law & Contemporary Problems*, vol 17, no 1 (2008).

Winston, Carla, "Truth Commissions as Tactical Concessions: The Curious Case of Idi Amin," *The International Journal of Human Rights*, vol 25, no 2 (2021).

Wood, Elizabeth Jean, *Insurgent Collective Action and Civil War in El Salvador* (Cambridge University Press, 2003).

Xavier, Sujith, "Locating and Situating Justice Pal: TWAIL, International Criminal Tribunals, and Judicial Powers," *Asian Journal of International Law* (2022).

Zalaquett, José, "Confronting Human Rights Violations Committed by Former Governments: Principles Applicable and Political Constraints," in *Transitional Justice: How Emerging Democracies Reckon with Former Regimes. Volume I: General Considerations*, Neil J. Kritz (ed) (United States Institute of Peace Press, 1995).

Zunino, Marcos, *Justice Framed: A Genealogy of Transitional Justice* (Cambridge University Press, 2019).

Index

Abuelas de Plaza de Mayo, 51
Africa Watch, 192, 204
African Charter on Human and Peoples' Rights, 205
al-Assad, Bashar, xvi
Alfonsín, Raúl, 50, 64, 65, 69, 70, 84, 194
  amnesty laws, 80, 83
  ceremony of Final Report CONADEP, 53, 54
  creation of CONADEP, 70
  critique of international law and institutions, 75, 81, 83
  inaugural address, 53, 69, 73
  prosecute military/Junta, 52, 69
  rewriting of Prologue, 79
  subject to authority of international law, 84
Algeria, xv
Alianza Republicana Nacionalista (ARENA), 175, 181
Allende, Salvador, 33, 98, 117, 126
  memorial at General Cemetery in Santiago (Chile), 33
al-Sharaa, Ahmed, xvi
Amin, Idi, 40, 194, 195, 197, 198
Amnesty International, xvii, 71, 122, 193, 202
Anghie, Antony, 11, 23, 24
archive, 28, 32, 34, 35, 43, 81
Argentina, 195, 203, 223
  Documento Final, 51
  Junta (Argentina), 51, 65, 76, 77
  Junta Trials, 64, 68, 69, 70
  Kirchner governments, 50, 61, 77, 80, 81
  negacionistas, 45, 85
  new Junta Trials, 80
  post-dictatorial public life, 64
  Secretary of Human Rights, 78, 79
  self-amnesty law, 52
  theory of two demons, 61, 62, 85, *See* teoría de los dos demonios
  transition to democracy of, 44, 62, 64
armed conflict, xv
arpilleras, 120, 121
Arpilleristas, 38, 39, 91, 120, 121, 122, 125, 127
  minor of, 121
Arthur, Paige, 204
Aspen Institute, The, 96, 97
  Aspen conference, 97, 98
Australia, xv, xviii, xxi, 42
authority, 5, 7, 8, 10, 11, 12, 13, 35, 195, 213
  as authoring, 223, 225
  as authorizing, 12, 13, 194, 224, 225, *See* to authorize
  as jurisdiction, 12, 16
  as reauthorizing, 197
  authoritative account, 8
  authorize, 223
  authorizing, 225
  in international law, 10, 11
  lack of personal-reputational authority, 214
  legal-institutional authority, 6, 7, 20, 200, 212, 224
  of Idi Amin, 199
  of international law, 223, 224
  personal-reputational authority, 6, 7, 197, 213
  professional authority, 197
  sources of, 5, 6
Aylwin, Patricio, 92, 94, 95, 96, 98, 119, 124, 194
  inaugural presidential address, 95

Bachelet, Michelle, 100, 102, 103, 125
Ban, Ki-Moon, 136
Bangladesh, xvi
Bonafini, Hebe de, 61
Boutros-Ghali, Boutros, 137, 142
Bretton Woods Institutions, 141
Buergenthal, Thomas, 148

Camnitzer, Luis, 107, 108, 109
  El Museo es una Escuela (artwork), 107
Canada
  in Salvadoran peace process, 176
Canadian Truth and Reconciliation Commission, xix
capitalism, 203
Carter, Jimmy, 197, 198
Carver, Richard, 40, 195, 202, 204, 205, 206, 210
  ARTICLE 19 (organization), 217
Cassel, Douglass, 131, 173
categories, 38, 68, 73, 196
Central Intelligence Agency (CIA), 76
Chapultepec Peace Agreement, 128, 136, 169, 174, 184
  anniversary, 136
  compromise in, 184
  development projects in, 183
  international development/financial institutions, 183
  legacies of, 178
  signing ceremony of, 186
  signing of, xxi, 139, 177, 179, 182
  socioeconomic issues in, 182, 183
Chicago Boys, 94
Chile, 195, 203, 223
  estallido social, 125, 126
  Junta (Pinochet), 119
  Transición, La, 94, 95, 96
Ciudad Segundo Montes (El Salvador), 159, 160
civilize, 26, 66, 67, 68
Cold War, 63, 74, 141, 189, 195
  containment policy, 199
  end of, 141, 174
  free world, 199
  geopolitics of, 36
  ideological paradigms of, 63, 65
  in Latin America, xxi, 62, 63, 64
  in Uganda, 197
  late-Cold War, 85
  post-Cold War international order, 185
  shifts, 176
  West Berlin Congress (1952), 199
Colombia
  Colombian Truth Commission, 18
  in Salvadoran peace process, 176
  Special Jurisdiction for Peace, 18
Colomoncagua (Honduras), 160, 161, 165
  community at the camp, 161
  workshops at, 161, 165, 167
Colonel Julio A. Rivera, 171
Comisión Nacional sobre la Desaparición de Personas (CONADEP), 42, 43, 45
  accessible truth of, 59
  achievements of, 43, 84
  as model, 44
  commissioners of, 49, 50
  creation of, 53
  Final Report/*Nunca Más*, 43
  international law embedded in, 70
  legacies of, 44
  mandate of, 46
  records of meetings, 49, 50
Commission of Inquiry into the Disappearances of People in Uganda since the 25th of January 1971 (1974 Commission of Inquiry), 9, 25, 191, 193
  aims and scope of, 200
  as human rights institution, 195, 223
  as inaugural Truth Commission, 40, 131, 190, 192, 193, 195, 196, 202
  creation of, 200
  Final Report of, 194, 195, 196, 201, 202
  institutional life of, 195
  truthfulness of, 195
commissioners, 55, 129, 152, 208, 209
  non-Salvadoran commissioners, 130
communism, 63, 203
  communist ideas, 199
compromise, 185
Concertación de Partidos por la Democracia, 92, 93, 94, *See* Concertación
  Chile, la Alegría Ya Viene (jingle), 93
Congo
  UN intervention 1960, 183
context-specific truths, 225
Costa Rica
  in Salvadoran peace process, 176, 179
credibility, 224
  public credibility, 224
Cristiani, Alfredo, 175, 177, 178, 180, 186, 187
critical redescription, 134

cultural artefacts, 89
cultural objects, 13, 14, 15, 28, 32, 34, 36, 161, 225

Dalton, Roque, 158
Davis, Megan, xix, xx
De Greiff, Pablo, 6
De Soto, Álvaro, 181, 184, 185, 186
death-squads, 131, 173, 186, 187
deauthorize, 14, 37, 132, 225
 deauthorizing, 31, 224
del Castillo, Graciana, 181, 184, 185
democracy, 58, 63, 130, 203, 204
 as peaceful coexistence, 65, 84
 as political model, 66
 democratization, 73, 176
 promises of, 9, 66, 84
desaparecidos, 42, 49, 51, 52, 68, 70, 71, 72, 74, 76, 85
 relatives of, 41, 51, 61, 69, 84
development, 26
 developmental gaze, 140, 142, 150
 developmental rationality, 140, 141, 145, 147, 153, 169, 184, 189
 developmental sensitivities, 153, 188, 189
 developmental state, 147
 economic development, 141
 problems of, 182
 Truman rationality, 151
dictatorship, 62
 socioeconomic violence in, 10
 state-violence in, xv
disappearances, 45, 51, 54, 77, 84, 85, 95, 99, 120
 detained-disappeared, 91, 99, 100, 111, 120
 in Uganda, 194, 200, 201, 202
 portraits of, 35, 42
displacement, 39, 97
 displace, 10, 126, 188, 189, 224, 225
 displaced, 31
 displacing, 27, 122
Duterte, Rodrigo, xvi

El Mozote Massacre (1981), 160, 173
El Salvador, xxi, 195, 223
 border with Honduras, 39, 155
 civil war, 172
 coffee in, 171
 Junta (El Salvador), 171
 privatization of public services, 178, 183
 tradition of embroidery, 160, 161, 163
empire, 169, 170
Espinoza, Danilo, 122, 123
 Layelewün (exhibition), 122, 123
ethics
 as judgement, 54
 ethically lawful 'future', 58
Ex-ESMA, 34, 35, 41, 42, 43

Férnandez de Kirchner, Cristina, 80
Final Report/*Nunca Más* of CONADEP, 43, 44
 authority in, 48
 in public life, 45, 46
 re-edition, 50
 re-edition of, 45
 state-violence, 50
 structure of, 49, 57
Ford Foundation, 96
Ford Motor Company, 76, 77
 Ford Falcon cars, 76
forensic truth, 8
France
 French-Algerian War, xv
Freeman, Mark, 220
 debate on 1974 Commission of Inquiry, 221
 debate on human rights, 221
Frente Farabundo Martí para la Liberación Nacional (FMLN), 139, 143, 147, 149, 157, 175, 176, 178, 187, *See* FMLN guerrillas
 foreign support for, 174
 history of, 172, 179
From Madness to Hope, 143, 146

Global North, 130
 promise of prosperity, 63
Great Britain, 197, 198, 199
Guatemalan UN Truth Commission, 211
Guzmán, Jaime, 93

habeas corpus, 51
Hándal, Schafik, 139
Hasina, Sheikh, xvi
Hayner, Priscilla, 17, 193, 195, 196, 197, 202, 211, 215
 "Fifteen Truth Commissions – 1974 to 1994: A Comparative Study", 196, 211
 international law in Truth Commissions, 216
 Salvadoran UN-run Truth Commission, 215

Salvadoran UN-Truth Commission, 216
Unspeakable Truths: Confronting State Terror and Atrocity, 218
Honduras, 133
military, 156
Salvadorans peasants in, 170
Truth Commission, 115
human rights, 90, 95, 111
as authority, 88, 90, 112
as literature, 38
experts and activists of, 14
framework of, 111
language, 9, 10, 33, 87, 223
legal object of, 100
human rights organizations, xvii, 52, 69, 70
Human Rights Watch, xvii, xviii, 192, 204
Huyssen, Andreas, 164

icnocuícatl, 144, 145
identity, 9, 12, 223
imagination, 14, 27, 44, 57, 85
as social imaginary, 58, 59
Indigenous peoples/communities, 39
in Chile, 10, 38, 124
indigeneity, 123
truth-telling process of, xix
Inter-American Court of Human Rights, 217
judges of, 218
International Center for Transitional Justice (ICTJ), xvii, xviii, xx
International Commission of Jurists, 194, 199, 208, 214
international community, 50, 54, 64, 85, 95, 121, 153, 198
International Criminal Court (ICC), xvi, 18
international humanitarian law, 130
international law, 36, 130
'global' history of, 37, 224
as language, 12, 38, 49
as normative framework, 224
legal narrative of, 224
post-conflict promises of, 131, 223, 224
promises of, 12, 37, 38, 48, 64
promises of democracy, 37
promises of peace, 20, 37
stories of, 224
triumph of, 224
violation of, 72
weaponizing critiques of, 86
world-making power of, 36, 85
International Monetary Fund (IMF), 74, 75, 81, 140, 141, 181, 182, 192
internationally authorized truth, 10, 13, 31, 50, 78, 136, 153, 174, 188, 189
creates minor truths, 90
displaces plurality, 112
Israel, xvi

Jaar, Alfredo, 109
Geometría de la Conciencia (installation), 109, 110
Jesuits
killing of, 33
trial for the killing of, 187
jurisdiction, 12, 15, 16, 21, 174, 225
thinking jurisdictionally, 14, 16, 19, 25, 37
jurisdictional questions, 19, 21, 31
jurisdictional thought, 12, 14, 15, 16, 21
justice, 42, 64, 66, 70, 201, 204
socioeconomic justice, 65, 121, 178

Karl, T.K., 184, 185
Kirchner, Néstor, 78, 80

Latin America, 203
law and humanities, 37
law and literature, 38, 48
lawfulness, 26, 68, 142, 150, 151, 152, 186, 189
authorized conception of, 84
post-conflict international lawfulness, 185
lawless, 150
lawmakers, 56, 57, 106
legal, 70
legal form, 16, 57, 67, 71, 72, 99, 140, 172
international legal forms, 20, 24, 66, 148, 195
Letelier, Orlando, 98
Lindo-Fuentes, Héctor, 170
López, Jorge Julio, 80

Macri, Mauricio, 45, 50, 79, 80, 81
Macron, Emmanuel, xv
Madres de Plaza de Mayo, 33, 51, 61, 81
Malamud-Goti, Jaime, 77, 97
Manderson, Desmond, 27
Mapuche people, 38, 122
at museum of memory, 122, 125
colonial violence against, 124
detained-disappeared, 91, 122, 123
erasure, 123

Mapuche people (cont.)
  human rights of, 122, 123, 125
  in Final Report, 123
  landownership, 123, 124
  minor truth of, 122
  minor truths of, 124, 125
  smoking technique, 122
  systematic violence against, 124
Martínez, Ana Guadalupe, 175, 187
Mary Hoch Centre for Reconciliation, xx
material continuity, 32
material life, 156, 157
materiality, 28, 134
  material continuity, 109, 111
  material form, 25, 39, 90, 100, 157
memorialization, 18, 28, 31, 88, 109, 111
  policies of, 28, 80, 83
  public policies of, 80
  sites of, 33, 34, 35, 80, 81, 116
  spaces of, 28
memorials, 33, 89
memory museums, 13, 28, 89, 102, 225, *See* museums of memory
Memory Space and Human Rights, 34, 35
metonymy, 89
  metonymic relationship, 89, 90
Mexico, 176
  in Salvadoran peace process, 176, 177, 179
  Mexico-US border, 154
Milei, Javier, 45, 85
model, 63
  El Salvador as, 189
  of development, 63
  of peacebuilding, 39
  of state-building, 63
  of Truth Commissions, xx, 195
  post-conflict (developmental) state of, 186
Monument for the Disappeared at General Cemetery in Santiago (Chile), 33
Mulenga, Joseph, 206, 207, 210
MUPI (Museo de la Palabra y la Imagen), 135, 154, 157, 158, 159, 160, 161, 163, 165
  as historical archive, 158
  as museum of memory, 158
museological space, 90, 91, 109, 112, 113, 118, 119
Museum of Memory and Human Rights, 39, 88, 89, 90, 91, 92, 100, 102, 193, *See* Museo
  Chilean Truth Commissions in, 115, 116
  Memory Square at, 104, 105, 106, 108, 109, 111, 112, 113, 116, 119
  precinct of, 100
  reproduction of UDHR at, 105, 106, 108, 109, 110, 111, 113
  Truth Commissions in, 113, 114, 115
  UDHR in Braille at, 107, 109

National Archive of Memory, 33, 34, 43, 49
Netanyahu, Benjamin, xvii
never again (expression), 66, 103
new museums, 101
Nino, Carlos Santiago, 64, 65, 77
Nuremberg Trials, 65, 67, 71

O'Donnell, Guillermo, 72, 73
Operation Cóndor, 76
ORDEN (Organización Democrática Nacionalista), 172, 173
Organization of the American States (OAS), 174, 176

Pahuja, Sundhya, 74, 134, 151, 184
Palestine, xvi
peace, 9, 66, 93
  as human rights, 104
  in post-conflict states, 74, 127
  peace talks, 175
  peaceful, 4, 26
peacebuilding, 63, 184
peasants, 39, 166, 167, 168, 169, 170, 171, 172, 224
  in Honduras, 170
  landless, 172
  Peasant Uprising (1932), 171
  working conditions of, 171
Pérez de Cuéllar, Javier, 151, 176, 180
philanthropic foundations, 203
Philippines, xv
Pinochet, Augusto, 20, 33, 38, 93, 94, 102, 117, 125, 126
  economy under, 94
  prosecution of, 95, 96
plurality, 7, 8, 26, 27
post-conflict institutions, 10, 225
post-conflict law, 205
post-conflict state, xxi, 3, 22, 174, 184
  development in, 183
  organize state-society relations in, 151, 170, 189
  peaceful coexistence in, 224

post-conflict law, 204
post-conflict state-building in, 185
public life of, 225
state-society relations in, 4, 7, 10, 14, 16, 17, 21, 40, 85, 88, 139, 169, 170, 185, 223, 225
Prat, Fernando
Acción Medular (artwork), 110
preamble
as law, 56
as literary device, 56
in constitutions, 56
in international law, 57
prologue, 13, 225
Prologue to the Final Report/Nunca Más of CONADEP, 45
as literature, 37, 50, 55
as prologue, 49, 79
rewriting of, 45, 50, 79
use of international law, 48, 49
public life, 8, 10, 13, 26, 28, 32, 50, 72, 126, 224
ongoing presence in, 225

race
racialized, 126, 169
Radio Venceremos, 157, 158
reconciliation, 95, 131, 132, 152, 187
redescription, 10, 131, 135, 188, 190, 195, 196
retrospective redescription, 196
refugees, 160, 161
refugee camps, 39, 133, 158, 161, 164, 165, 167
tapestries of, 167
representations, 12, 13, 26, 27, 30, 32, 38, 68, 164, 165, 166, 225
as practice, 27
as technique, 12, 13, 225
by commissioners, 152, 153
of everyday life, 162
of post-conflict state, 150
of repression, 166
of state-violence, 77
of truth and authority, 14, 35, 225
of violent events, 225
rival representations, 35, 36
repression, 166, 171, 173
responsibility, 11, 22, 50, 57, 61, 72, 73, 77, 153, 166, 174, 181, 183
public responsibility, 58
revolution, 61, 63, 179, 184
Romero, Óscar Arnulfo. *See* Monsignor Romero
crypt at Metropolitan Cathedral of San Salvador (El Salvador), 33
rule of law, 63, 65, 130, 151, 192, 208, 209
as pillar, 84
in Uganda, 207
international promotion of, 151

Sábato, Ernesto, 54, 55, 58, 59, 79
Salinas de Gortari, Carlos, 177
Santa Cruz Barceló, Hernán, 105
School of the Americas, 76, 175
silence, 10, 37, 38, 41, 74, 75
silenced, 10, 31, 224, 225
silencing, 27, 49
Slaughter, Joseph, 37, 48, 56
South Africa Truth and Reconciliation Commission, 211
South African Truth and Reconciliation Commission, xix
Spain, xxi
colonial administration, 170
colonial rationality, 169
colonization, 123
in Salvadoran peace process, 176
spatial and experiential form, 39, 88, 90
spatial representations, 13, 31, 32, 35, 88, 225
state-society relations, 2, 4, 57, 58, 72, 74
as hell, 77
status, 9
Sumpul River Massacre (1980), 160, 163, 173
memory of, 168
witness to, 170
Sweden
in Salvadoran peace process, 176, 178
Syria, xvi, xviii

tapestry, 13, 157, 160, 164, 165, 173, 225
activity of handcrafting, 164
as response, 164
as witnessing, 164
disruptive force of, 156, 157, 166
telling moments, 195, 197
temporal continuity, 32, 39, 90, 100, 157
textual representations, 13, 31, 32, 225
Tokyo Trials, 67
transitional justice, xvii, 29, 30, 36, 37, 45, 190, 195, 204, 225
transmission, 90, 107

Truman, Harry, 140, 142
  international development, 151
truth, 64, 78
  context-specific truths, 39, 224
truth as justice, xvii, 95
Truth Commissions
  as national human rights commissions, 212
  as part of the international legal order, 215
  as post-conflict institutions, 221, 223
  database of, 202
  family of, 221
  legal work of, 16, 36, 46
  named by Priscilla Hayner, 212
  other Chilean Truth Commissions, 114
  physical presence in public life of, 225
  truth-telling process, 70

Uganda, 9, 114, 191, 223
  Attorney General of, 210
  Commission of Inquiry into Human Rights Violations in, 210
  expulsion of Asian-origin population, 199, 201
  laws of, 210
  military police of, 209
  state-violence in, 196
UN Commission on Human Rights, 197
UN Convention on the Non-Applicability of Statutory Limitations to War Crimes and Crimes Against Humanity, 83
UN Convention Relating to the Status of Stateless Persons, 200
UN Development Program (UNDP), 33, 138
UN Observer Group in Central America (ONUCA), 174
UN Office of the High Commissioner for Refugees (UNHCR), 39, 133, 159, 161, 162
UN Secretary-General (UNSG), 130
  Friends of the Secretary-General, 177
UN Security Council, 18
UN Special Rapporteur on the Promotion of Truth, Justice, Reparation and Guarantees of Non-Recurrence, 7, 30, 31
UN Working Group on Enforced or Involuntary Disappearances, 71
underdeveloped, 72, 142, 150
United Nations (UN), xviii, 213, 223, 225
  role in Central America, 174, 192
United Soviet Socialist Republic (USSR), 62, 174, 175, 203
United States (US), xv, 32, 36, 94, 138, 145, 198
United States Agency for International Development (USAID), 138
United States Institute of Peace (USIP), 193, 202
Universal Declaration of Human Rights (UDHR), 105, 109, 215
  Article 19 of, 217
unlawfulness, 39, 46, 48, 59, 60, 66, 150, 169, 187, 188, 194, 196, 207
  as Eurocentric meaning, 78
  as worldview, 49
  in civil war, 132, 143, 148, 153
US Central Intelligence Agency (CIA), 76, 199

values
  Christian, 65
  Western, 65
Venezuela
  in Salvadoran peace process, 176, 177, 178
Vicaría de la Solidaridad, 121, 122
Villalobos, Joaquín, 179
Viola, Roberto, 76
violence
  against society, xv
visual representations, 13, 31, 32, 225

World Bank, 74, 138, 141, 192
World War II (WWII), 68, 71, 72, 74, 141

Yoorrook Justice Commission, xv, xviii, xix, xx
  commissioners of, xx

Printed in the United Kingdom by TJ Clays Ltd.